HORACE GREELEY'S
NEW-YORK TRIBUNE

HORACE GREELEY'S
NEW-YORK TRIBUNE

CIVIL WAR–ERA SOCIALISM
AND THE CRISIS OF FREE LABOR

ADAM TUCHINSKY

CORNELL UNIVERSITY PRESS
Ithaca and New York

Copyright © 2009 by Cornell University

First published 2009 by Cornell University Press

Printed in the United States of America

Library of Congress Cataloging-in-Publication Data

Tuchinsky, Adam-Max.
 Horace Greeley's New-York tribune : Civil War-era socialism and the crisis of free labor / Adam Tuchinsky.
  p. cm.
 Includes bibliographical references and index.
 ISBN 978-0-8014-4667-2 (cloth : alk. paper)
  1. Greeley, Horace, 1811–1872.   2. New York tribune.
3. Socialism—United States—History—19th century.
4. United States—Politics and government—1783–1865.
I. Title.

  E415.9.G8T83 2009
  973.7—dc22   2009019267

Cornell University Press strives to use environmentally responsible suppliers and materials to the fullest extent possible in the publishing of its books. Such materials include vegetable-based, low-VOC inks and acid-free papers that are recycled, totally chlorine-free, or partly composed of nonwood fibers. For further information, visit our website at www.cornellpress.cornell.edu.

Figure 5—Southworth and Hawes, American, 19th century; after: John Plumbe, American (born in Wales), 1809–1857; *Margaret Fuller,* 1850–55; photograph, daguerreotype; plate: 10.8 x 8.3 cm (4 1/4 x 3 1/4 in.); Museum of Fine Arts, Boston; gift of Edward Southworth Hawes in memory of his father Josiah Johnson Hawes, 43.1412.

Cloth printing   10 9 8 7 6 5 4 3 2 1

For Jennifer and my two little Whigs, Sophia and Eli

Contents

PREFACE

    This book is an intellectual history of the *New-York Tribune* during the Civil War era. The *Tribune* of that period was in many ways a unique institution. It had a mass audience, with the largest national circulation of any newspaper in the mid-nineteenth-century United States. But it was also an institution that published many of the leading minds of the age. It was part of a surge of penny papers that made an extensive variety of printed material available to ordinary readers, but like later opinion magazines it distilled for a general public many of the more progressive reform ideas of the time. With a relatively consistent ideology, it contained within its pages rigorous debate on most of the important social and political questions of the day. Its reach was also international, reflecting the way in which nineteenth-century social reform was a transatlantic venture. Forging important connections to reform communities abroad, the *Tribune*'s domestic politics were shaped, in part, by international events. But the *Tribune* was also a mainstream newspaper, a leading organ of both the Whig and Republican parties, so it bridged the worlds of politics, literature, and social reform.

  Over the years, there have been a handful of works on Greeley and the *Tribune,* but few of them address the central thematic question of this study: How was it that the leading ideologue of the Whig and Republican parties was also, throughout nearly his entire public life, a socialist?[1] In answering this question, most previous work on the subject has followed the lead of James Parton who remarked in his 1872 biography of Greeley that his paper's socialism was not to be taken seriously. Its columns on socialist theory, he wrote, were regarded as "articles to be skipped."[2] To the populist biographer William Harlan Hale, nineteenth-century socialism was little more than a utopian humbug, bohemian "nonsense" that was out of step with the concerns of ordinary workers. Later, writing at greater length on Karl Marx's decadelong tenure as the *Tribune*'s European correspondent, he implied that socialism was simply alien to the American experience. "Few episodes in journalism seem more singular and unlikely," Hale concluded, "than this association of the frowning ideologist [Marx] of Soho on the one hand and, on the other the moonfaced, owlish Vermont Yankee known affectionately to legions of readers in North and West as 'Uncle Horace.'"[3] This study, in contrast, views socialism as central not only to Greeley and the *Tribune's* circle of intellectuals and reformers but to the emerging American reform tradition. The core contribution of this book is to present the Greeley-era *Tribune* as a journal that was at the center of a profound reexamination of conventional political economy in a moment of rapid social and economic change.

Greeley launched the *Tribune* in a period marked by transportation, market, and communication revolutions. The end of the paper's Greeley era coincided with industrialization and the emergence of a modern industrial working class. Apart from the final year or two of his life, he and his paper wrestled with the significance of these changes in a distinctly progressive way. Their discomfort with the prospect of a permanent wage-earning class inspired a sense of engagement with political economy and the labor question that resulted in one of the first popular discussions of socially democratic liberal principles in the history of the United States. In its pages, the *Tribune* put forward a series of reforms designed to protect independent producers from proletarianization. Though never explicitly anticapitalist, the *Tribune* also recognized the way that markets aggregate wealth, capital, power, and freedom in the hands of the few. In this basic sense, it set forth the idea of social equality as a critical element of American democracy.

My effort to identify and contextualize the *Tribune's* social democratic ethos takes part in a number of important and ongoing scholarly conversations. In a chronological and empirical sense, it contributes to the large literature on party ideology in nineteenth-century America. Most previous work on the history of party ideology has understated progressive elements in the cultures of the Whig and Republican parties and has failed to focus on the connections between the second and third American party systems. One of the major books on the subject tries to unite the two eras, but posits an unlikely political tradition that links Abraham Lincoln to Andrew Jackson.[4] The institutional focus of this book enables it to connect the two eras, but in a different way. This study maintains that the search for cohesive party ideologies is fundamentally flawed; ideological differences within parties were nearly as stark as the differences between them. There was also incredible diversity among state party organizations.[5] Parties were, instead, institutional vehicles within which ideologically coherent factions wrestled for power. The *Tribune,* for its part, became the representative voice first of the "reform Whigs" and then the Radical Republicans, and I maintain that the intellectual origin of both factions' commitment to antislavery and various kinds of labor reform was rooted in liberal socialism.

From the beginning of his public career, Greeley was steeped in the larger Whig ideal of social harmony and individual self-realization. Like many Whigs, Greeley recoiled from market culture's rampant individualism and disorder, but unlike more conservative party brethren he turned in the aftermath of the 1837 Panic to quasi-radical reform. Not long after launching the *Tribune,* Greeley opened the paper to American disciples of the French communitarian socialist Charles Fourier. Over the course of the early 1840s, American socialists distilled Fourier's works into a practical program of reform and a larger ideology. The *Tribune* thus not only played a decisive role in making American Fourierism into a large-scale social movement but also propagated a larger indictment of the various side effects of market culture: deadening specialization, social stratification, unemployment, frequent economic dislocations, hardened class boundaries, and the failure to reward workers with the fruits of their own labors. By the late 1840s, though, most of the Fourierist communities had failed; abroad, Fourierism was eclipsed by social revolution. During the 1850s, the building crisis over slavery, at least on the surface, also diminished the urgency of the labor question. Fourierism, though, was hardly a temporary diversion, fad, or sideshow. In the long run, stripped of its communitarian elements, Fourierism presented a general liberal socialist critique of contemporary political economy—that individual liberty, self-reliance, and democracy are threatened by the untrammeled operations of the market—and these remained a vital part of the *Tribune*'s worldview into the 1850s and 1860s and of the American reform tradition more generally.

Communitarian socialism was, in short, an original social democratic program in embryo form, and one with important near- and long-term consequences. In an immediate sense, liberal socialist reform ideas meshed with the traditional republican producerist emphasis on the widespread distribution of property to advance a "people's" free labor ideology. The importance of free labor ideology cannot be overstated: it was the linchpin of the North's political argument with the South, and thus a foundation of the Civil War. Free labor ideology was what stitched together the Republican Party and steeled it against efforts to expand slavery beyond the states where it had already been established. Some historians have concluded, though, that beneath Northern denunciations of Southern slavery was an implicit defense of a bourgeois social order based in freely contracting individuals. During the 1840s, like many labor reformers, Greeley shared this concern, remarking, "if I am less troubled concerning Slavery in Charleston and New Orleans, it is because I see so much slavery in New-York."[6] But by the 1850s there was little tension in the pages of the *Tribune* between antislavery and labor reform, precisely because the very idea of free labor had became a universal platform, and one that to some had little to do with modern corporate capitalism.

Although the free labor ideal rallied the North politically, there was little consensus in the antebellum period or after about what it actually was. To some, the idea of a free labor society was synonymous with the free operation of a market whose outcomes rationally measured character and talent. For others, a free labor society depended on the widespread ownership of property and social mobility. The *Tribune* and most of its contributors were in this latter camp, and even pushed it one step further. The socialist character of the most important venue for Republican thought and reform suggests that the idea of free labor contained quasi-radical potential within it. In diverse ways, the various reformers who wrote for the *Tribune* argued that the market itself threatened the basic foundations of free labor—self-ownership and propertied independence—and insisted that the main goal of political and nonstatist reform should be to protect those values from external threats such as slavery and global competition. The roots of the Republican Party's ideology lay at least in part in the socialism of the 1840s, which voiced the fears of independent producers threatened by the rise of the market and economic consolidation. Few works on the history of the idea of free labor have acknowledged its diverse intellectual sources. This is curious given the fact that so much of the work on Reconstruction focuses on free labor's contradictions and limits when, after the war, it confronted social inequality in the South and the emergence of industrial capitalism in the North.

The character and nature of free labor ideology is also a subject that transcends the Civil War era. The basic issues raised by mid-nineteenth-century social democrats about freedom, liberty, property, and the organization of labor were those that preoccupied most liberal societies as they approached industrial modernity. In a broad sense, this book is part of a recent revival of interest in the history of liberalism, provoked by the end of the cold war. Despite rather nuanced and self-conscious retrospective assessments by such varied "liberals" as John Dewey and F. A. Hayek, the liberal tradition that conventionally operated in the minds of historians has been rather monolithic and ahistorical. During the 1950s and 1960s, consensus historians either celebrated or lamented Americans' uncomplicated notions of rights, property, liberty, markets, and the limited state. When colonial historians in particular began excavating alternative ideological traditions such as republicanism, their understanding of liberalism itself remained locked in its older consensus-era conception, a kind of historical straw man. Only recently have scholars such as James Kloppenberg, Dorothy Ross, Ruth Bloch, Richard

Schneirov, and Nancy Cohen begun teasing out liberalism's assorted sources and emphasizing tensions within it.

In modern liberalism, there is a rather basic division between its classical and social democratic wings. Most of the historians interested in the latter, especially Elizabeth Sanders, Richard Schneirov, and Martin Sklar, maintain that the roots of New Deal–style state activism and suspicion of untrammeled capitalism lie in turn-of-the-century social movements. These accounts, though, understate the importance of earlier confrontations with the social question. Although antebellum socialists hardly laid the foundation of the modern administrative welfare state, their efforts did help undermine the authority and legitimacy of the market. Early socialists questioned the justice and efficiency of market outcomes, and thus provided a basis for later efforts to address them. Among those antebellum socialists, the *Tribune* took the lead.

Despite its daily and popular character, the *Tribune* was a newspaper in which intellectuals and reformers debated one of the most basic problems of liberal political economy in the nineteenth century: How should labor be organized? It was the question that preoccupied the North as it made the rapid transition to an individualistic society based on contract and consent. It was the question that preoccupied the South as it became a lonely outpost, defending what most increasingly regarded as an archaic social system. It was the key question that divided the North from the South during the Civil War, and it became the central question during Reconstruction when the North itself was revolutionized by industrial capitalism. The *Tribune* absorbed much of this debate, and itself became a locus of, and important point of origin for, a new sort of socially democratic political economy that forces us to reassess the way we think about the contours of American thought and reform.

Though Greeley was a socialist and enmeshed in his era's various labor movements, he was also a Whig; he believed that debts should be repaid, and so do I. When this project began, my intention had been to write a history of New York's 1850s counterculture. A year of research on one element of the *Tribune* led to a timely intervention by Charlie Capper, then of the University of North Carolina. His work models the sort of contextual intellectual history to which this book aspires. The University of North Carolina was a stimulating environment to begin a project of this sort. John Kasson, Philip Gura, and William Barney introduced me to diverse aspects of nineteenth-century culture. And Peter Coclanis was a friend and mentor after the fashion of a Chicago precinct captain, always anticipating ways he could help.

The intellectual origin of key elements of this project was the Sawyer Seminar on liberalism. Convened by Charlie Capper, Malachi Hacohen, Tony LaVopa, Steven Vincent, and others at the National Humanities Center, the seminar brought scholars such as Gerald Izenberg, James Kloppenberg, and Martha Nussbaum, whose work helped me understand the *Tribune*'s broader significance.

I would like to thank Cornell University Press, particularly my two editors, Alison Kalett and Michael McGandy. Both were attentive, professional, and, most important, insightful in suggesting ways to distill the essence of the book's contribution. Their advice, along with that of the manuscript's anonymous readers, made this a better book. I would also like to acknowledge the *Journal of American History* and *American Nineteenth Century History* for graciously allowing me to reprint portions of articles that appeared earlier.[7] I am grateful for the chance, too, to acknowledge the help of archivists at the New York Public Library and the Library of Congress, and the librarians at the University of North Carolina and the University of Southern Maine. All libraries are strapped for resources, but even at the latter it never felt impossible to complete a book of this sort. Overall, the History Department at the University of Southern Maine has been incredibly supportive and collegial. I appreciate all of my colleagues' encouragement and good cheer. I would like to thank Pat Finn in particular for introducing me to the university, to Portland, and most of all to many fantastic students.

Thanks also to friends, Spencer Downing, Steve Keadey, Brian Steele, Leah Potter, Blain Roberts, Tom Baker, Seth Rogoff, David Carey, Mike and Ashley Ross, Stacy Braukman and Beth Mauldin, Leigh and Chris Fisher, Susan Pearson and Michael Kramer, Bill Wright, Natalie Fousekis, Rodney Reyes, Joel Revill, David Sartorious, and Eve Duffy. Some are fellow historians who read portions of the manuscript and some not; all helped me enjoy life while avoiding my book. I am especially indebted to Matthew Brown and Ethan Kytle who, at critical moments, suspended their own work (and pleasures) to help me with mine.

Lastly, I would like to thank my family. This book has a chapter on marriage, family, and divorce. For me, divorce brought with it a wonderful extended family. My stepparents, Ivan Kayser and Terry Philips, have always loved me like one of their own, and given both of my parents happiness. It also meant three brothers and their families, Adam, Sherry, and Gracie Kayser, Chet and Ava Wallenstein, Chris Diamonti, and Billy Wallenstein. My sister Jessica taught me how to tie my shoes and has watched out for me ever since. Love to her and her family, Jason, Charlie, and Nic Hoffs. My own marriage has brought with it another supportive extended family that, somehow, never expressed any doubts about a decade devoted to Horace Greeley. Thanks to Carol and Terry Sanford, Katy Sanford, and Nicole, Terry, Maddie, and Abby Sanford. The debt that I owe my parents, Gretchen Raab and Spencer Tuchinsky, is equaled only by the one they owe theirs, Sylvia and David Tuchinsky and Margaret and Charles Raab. They are my closest friends, too. I treasure the time I have with them. This book is dedicated to my wife, Jennifer, and to our children, Sophia and Eli. They will never know how much I love them, and neither will I. It grows.

HORACE GREELEY'S
NEW-YORK TRIBUNE

A People's Newspaper

> On every side we are confronted by evidences of movement, progress, advance, and all in the Associative direction. Trades Unions, Protective Unions, Sons of Temperance, Odd-Fellowship, Mutual Insurance, Life Insurance, Building and Mutual Benefit Societies of all shapes and sizes, attest the existence of a principle, an instinct, a perception, which is everywhere impelling the members of civilized communities to form closer and more intimate relationships and alliances for mutual assistance and protection.
>
> Horace Greeley, *Hints Toward Reforms*

In *The Souls of Black Folk*, W. E. B. DuBois wrote that the "problem of the twentieth century is the problem of the color-line."[1] The problem of the nineteenth century was the "labor question," what nineteenth-century socialists referred to as the "organization of labor," and it was at the heart of the seemingly disparate histories of race and class, of North and South, of rural and urban life, and of gender and the family. Broadly considered, the central question of the Civil War era was "how shall labor be organized." The wealthy regions of the South clung to a slave-based system rooted in coercion and violence. In the North, the convulsive changes of the nineteenth century brought forth a radically new "free labor" system that removed individuals from traditional familial bonds and constraints and restructured social and economic life on the basis of self-interest, social mobility, and individual initiative. The free-labor system eventually became central to the way the North understood itself culturally and politically. The ideal of free labor rallied the North in its increasingly heated conflicts with the slave South. Even so, Northerners were conflicted about what exactly the freedom of labor actually meant. It is often tempting to equate the rise of free labor with the triumph of a capitalist or market ethos, but careful attention to the varied character of Northern politics and reform cultures should make such an assumption impossible to sustain.

The *New-York Tribune,* the subject of this study, was at the heart of this reform culture, and it manifested many of its contradictions. Explicitly attached to both the Whig and Republican parties, it proudly pressed Northern faith in individual self-improvement and national economic development. Explicitly socialist, it advanced a distinctly progressive version of free labor, becoming arguably the first popular forum where opposition to market values was vented in a developed way. Not exactly anticapitalist, the paper instead set forth a variety of programs designed to defend the prerogatives and status of independent producers against competition from enslaved and foreign pauper labor; more generally, it identified and condemned the structural tendency of national and international markets to concentrate wealth and capital and to reduce workers to a state of permanent dependence on wages. The *Tribune* was among the North's most strident antislavery voices, but when it called for the freedom of labor it meant something quite distinct from the wage-based order that emerged over the course of the nineteenth century. Rather, it articulated a socialist variant of free-labor ideology, which would become the intellectual basis of modern liberal efforts to defend working people from the vagaries and consolidated power of markets and capital. Its story is a testament to the complexity of nineteenth-century political and reform culture.

Greeley, the *Tribune,* and Its World

Horace Greeley's *New-York Tribune* was the most important newspaper in antebellum America. George Fitzhugh called it "the most . . . influential paper in the world": "Other great papers, such as the London Times, are quick to perceive and to follow each new direction of public opinion. . . . The Tribune alone does actually form, direct, and control it." E. L. Godkin, whose *Nation* magazine was patterned on the *Tribune's* example of unsparing social and cultural criticism, recalled that the paper gave writers a "patent of literary nobility," that it "welcomed talent, male and female, from any quarter and in every field." In the *Atlantic Monthly,* James Ford Rhodes remembered the *Tribune* as a "political bible." As Rhodes wrote, "If you want to penetrate into the thoughts, feelings, and ground of decision of the 1,866,000 men who voted for Lincoln in 1860, you should study with care the New York weekly *Tribune.*"[2] By 1856, nearly 280,000 readers subscribed to one of the daily, weekly, or semiweekly editions of *Tribune.* Countless more read it, either sharing others' subscriptions or reading its articles and opinions after they were reprinted in other newspapers. In 1841, the circulation of the large metropolitan dailies was skyrocketing, but thousands of rural paper remained, often reprinting news from their urban counterparts. By the 1850s, New York became the center of the newspaper universe with the creation of what came to be called the Associated Press. In the city, the *Tribune's* New England moralism was inimical to the city's financial and immigrant character, and its circulation lagged behind James Gordon Bennett's *Herald*. Its national weekly edition, though, resonated with readers throughout New England and areas of New England migration. The *Tribune's* appeal to both independent farmers and the artisanal working class gave it the largest national circulation of any newspaper in the United States. Its importance, moreover, went beyond its natural audience. Even though the *Tribune's* circulation was limited in the South and undoubtedly among Democrats, nativists, religious conservatives, and other groups unsympathetic to its politics, Greeley quickly became a stock character and a popular foil against which other journalists, intellectuals, and politicians carved out their antireform cultural politics, and through this sort of public dialogue, it acquired a kind of shadow readership. The *Tribune* became a key conceptual map, shaping the way its readers and shadow readers, to echo one print culture historian, "construed events and found some meaning in the blooming, buzzing confusion of the world around them."[3]

Little in Greeley's family history, on either his mother's or his father's side, suggested that he was destined to become an arbiter of public opinion, a pioneer American socialist, and part of the national mythology of self-made men, a nineteenth-century Ben Franklin. Born in meager economic circumstances on a farm near Amherst, New Hampshire, on February 3, 1811, Horace was the eldest child of Zaccheus and Mary Woodburn Greeley. Though his parents were literate and Mary Greeley regularly read to her children, the Greeleys were traditional rural people. Horace's father loved to drink, dance, and play the fiddle. His mother smoked a corncob pipe, told homespun stories, and sang ballads in the evening. Without any formal schooling, Horace had begun to read by the age of three. At four, he started school, but even then he could already read virtually as well as any adult in his community. By the age of thirteen, a local schoolmaster sent Horace home, admitting that given his own limited education there was nothing left he could teach the boy. In the end, Horace's formal schooling amounted to only forty-five months, scattered over a ten-year period.

Greeley's prodigious, if undirected, reading drew him to the world of print, but as with Franklin and Walt Whitman, Greeley's humble upbringing forced him to take a distinctively traditional route. Before he could become an intellectual or even a journalist, Greeley became a printer, first in minor print shops scattered in the outer reaches of New England, western Pennsylvania, and New York, and then, in the summer of 1831, New York City. During his first year and a half in the great metropolis, Greeley worked whenever he could as a journeyman printer, and by 1833 he was able to go into business on his own, opening a small printing shop, the bulk of his business coming from lotteries. But Greeley was restless for more. Although he wrote occasional paragraphs for various newspapers, including one self-serving defense of lotteries, Greeley was ambitious and the success of his printing business, moderate as it was, convinced him that the time was ripe for more audacious ventures.[4]

The first was the *New-Yorker.* Started in the spring of 1834, it was like other contemporary literary periodicals, such as the *North American Review* or the *Knickerbocker,* but one third the price and aimed at a more common audience. It published jokes and popular songs, and descended into such sordid matters as politics and reform. In the pages of the *New-Yorker,* Greeley protested such injustices as slavery, the conquest of Native Americans, and imprisonment for debt.[5] Greeley's *New-Yorker* series, "What Shall Be Done for the Laborer," attracted the attention of the city's reform community.[6] While he was editing the *New-Yorker,* the 1837 financial panic struck. It hit New York City especially hard. When the price of cotton fell, prominent Southern financial houses defaulted on their New York notes, which in turn moved some city banks to call in their loans in a cash-poor economy and still others to fold entirely in the face of European pressure to settle outstanding accounts. Real estate prices collapsed, stocks and most consumer goods could not be unloaded at any price, and some of the city's wealthiest merchants found themselves, within the space of months, completely bankrupt.[7] Many New Yorkers "talk[ed] ominously about rebellions" and conservatives, such as George Templeton Strong, worried that "we shall have a revolution here."[8] The sense of desperation aroused Greeley's reform instincts.

As a Henry Clay Whig, Greeley pressed for internal improvements, a national bank, and a publicly regulated currency. Like most in his party, he blamed President Andrew Jackson's war on the United States Bank for bringing about financial anarchy, but Greeley also looked for measures, public and private, that would relieve the distress of labor. Greeley served on a relief committee in the city's Sixth Ward and was shocked by the extent of the poverty, especially the number of ambitious and "worthy poor." In New York State, he advocated a safety-fund system that would protect the economy from bank failures. In 1837, Greeley called upon the federal government to distribute seventy-five million dollars to the states to inflate the currency and, more radically, he proposed five million dollars for public works.[9] Greeley also hoped that a determined effort on behalf of labor would make a political point by exposing the insolvency of the free-market ideology that dominated the Democratic Party.

One of the other casualties of the 1837 panic was Greeley's *New-Yorker.* Though its circulation had reached nine thousand by 1837, which then was a sizable number, it was not managed well and struggled to turn a profit. Greeley, however, managed to move forward. Though the panic of 1837 eventually killed the *New-Yorker,* it was a boon for his party. The depression discredited the Democrats' economic vision and gave the loosely allied Whigs a political opportunity to win power. Greeley soon met Thurlow Weed, editor of the *Albany Evening Journal* and the political boss who was one of the principals organizing the Whig Party in the state. It was a relationship that would change the course of Greeley's life.[10] Weed was often a cynical party operative, but he also represented a faction of the Whig Party that had not been born out of the conservative Federalist tradition. A democrat, he pioneered a political style that would eventually make inroads against the Jacksonians' populist monopoly. Greeley became a key ally in this endeavor when Weed anointed him editor of the state's Whig campaign newspaper. Reflecting the Weed faction's aversion to Federalist conservatism, Greeley and the Albany boss titled their paper the *Jeffersonian.* The first issue was published on February 17, 1838, and it was an instant success. Almost overnight, its circulation reached fifteen thousand, and by that fall its populism helped elect the young and relatively unknown William Henry Seward as governor of New York.

The *Jeffersonian* signaled a new style of politics and its success in New York augured well nationally for the approaching presidential election in 1840. The populism of 1838 would be the order of the day. In April 1840, Greeley and prominent New York Whig politicians agreed, in effect, to revive the *Jeffersonian* to promote the political fortunes of Whig presidential candidate William Henry Harrison, a popular general with virtually no political record. The *Log Cabin,* which the paper was renamed in honor of the candidate, was an overnight success. Within two months, its circulation had reached fifty-six thousand. The populist assumptions of the *Jeffersonian* were magnified in the *Log Cabin.* Greeley framed the election as a contest between Harrison, a simple farmer, and Van Buren, a corrupt, aristocratic, political dandy whose White House, with its wasteful luxury and hints of infidelity, reflected the excesses of European courts. By the end of the campaign, the *Log Cabin's* circulation had risen to over eighty thousand and Greeley's thoughts naturally turned toward establishing a permanent, inexpensive Whig daily in New York City. That paper was the *Tribune.*

The *Tribune,* launched in April 1841, fused the *New-Yorker's* literary and reform ambitions to the political aims of Greeley's campaign newspapers. At

FIGURE 1. Daguerreotype of Horace Greeley, taken at Matthew Brady's studio, ca. 1844–60. Courtesy of the Library of Congress, Prints and Photographs Division, LC-USZ62-8776.

bottom, it was Greeley's hope that the *Tribune* could be a journal of Whig democracy that would elicit the sympathy of labor and, in turn, transform the Whig Party into a legitimate political alternative to the Democrats. On the eve of the *Tribune*'s launch, he wrote a politically cautious Thurlow Weed that "hitherto all devotees of social reform of any kind—all the advocates of higher destiny for labor—all the combatants against unjust and false social principles—in short, all the social discontent of the country has been regularly repelled from the Whig Party and attracted to its opposite.... This forms a heavy dead-weight against us, unless we are ambitious to be considered the enemies of improvement and the bulwarks of an outgrown aristocracy in the country."[11]

The *Tribune*'s founding came in the midst of a communications revolution, a transformation that was itself part of a larger maturation of transportation and market networks that by midcentury crisscrossed the continent and facilitated the flow of commodities, people, and ideas. This sweeping and dizzyingly swift reconfiguration of economic life for most Americans revolutionized the most basic facets of existence: family, work, community, and the self. In most industries and crafts, the spread of the market did not initially mean industrialization; rather it was a more subtle and, to some contemporaries, invisible evolution that slowly reordered social relationships. During the early decades of the nineteenth century, few farmers produced goods for distant national or international markets, and most artisans owned their own tools and could reasonably expect to one day work for themselves. By 1850, that balance had tipped, and farmers who had moved to the more fertile lands of the modern Midwest concentrated production on farm staples, which, mediated through the new transportation networks and the cash economy, they exchanged for manufactured goods. Manufacturing centers, in turn, now relied on a labor force that through the division of labor had been deskilled; in most industries, workers now had a less than one in two chance of becoming self-employed. Capital and labor, once wedded to one another in an intimate and nearly familial condition, were now linked by the indifference and anonymity of cash, contract, and commodity. The *Tribune*'s own institutional history mimicked this vast transformation of social and economic relationships even as it labored to document them. The fate of labor and social relations in a society and economy becoming ever more impersonal and complex became its central intellectual preoccupation.[12]

The newspaper was among the most visible and important components of this new America and was among the first commodities whose production was reshaped by the spread of the market.[13] It was one of the first industries to mechanize, starting in the 1830s, which dramatically reduced costs. The United States, particularly in the Northeastern and upper Midwestern markets where most of the *Tribune*'s subscribers lived, had unusually high literacy, and mechanical reproduction brought a plethora of reading matter—periodicals, novels, religious tracts, and especially newspapers— before ordinary readers for the first time. The steam engine, the railroad, and eventually the telegraph meant that information and "news" could circulate with near instantaneous speed, creating a newly robust national conversation about politics and culture, an "imagined national community."[14] For the first time, there was both a national and a democratic market for news and other reading matter. It would be some two decades, however, before mechanization resulted in the sort of corporate consolidation that transformed other industries even later, after the Civil War.

When the *Tribune* was founded, the first phase of this modern print revolution was coming to a close. Starting in the early 1830s, ambitious printers in New York City and elsewhere experimented with cheap dailies that became known as penny papers. Although there were quite a few failures, the successes, Benjamin Day's *Sun* and James Gordon Bennett's *Herald,* quickly dwarfed their six-penny rivals, attracting circulations in the tens of thousands. Unlike the traditional sheets' dry political and commercial reporting, the penny papers appealed to a new class of readers by publishing racy matter—police reports, reports of scandals and trials, and society news—that became synonymous with the urban experience. Though unprecedented in size and scale, the pennies were identified closely with their proprietors whose distinctive voices made them a symbolic and intimate presence among their constituencies of readers. Even in the late 1860s, when Greeley was consumed by politics, speaking engagements, and outside writing projects, many readers continued to assume that he was responsible for every word in his paper.

The early penny papers were hatched in a nearly premodern economic and social setting. Greeley, like most of the other penny editors, lacked formal

FIGURE 2. Daguerreotype of the *Tribune* editorial staff, ca. 1850, including poet and travel writer Bayard Taylor (seated, second from left), Horace Greeley (seated, third from left), George Ripley (seated, fourth from left), and Charles Dana (standing, second from left). Courtesy of the Library of Congress, Prints and Photographs Division, LC-USZ62-8777.

schooling, began as a printer's apprentice, and emerged from a world where the distinction between a printer (an artisan) and a writer-journalist-editor (a "professional") had not yet been established. Greeley's public career and persona were in many respects fashioned against the original printer-statesman, Benjamin Franklin, who in a similar way materialized out of a family-based craft context to become a reformer, natural scientist, political theorist, and fount of folk wisdom. But the era of the artisan–intellectual did not last. The evolution from an economic system based on individual proprietorship to one based on large corporations was experienced earlier in the world of print, and the *Tribune* appeared at the cusp of the two eras. Greeley founded the *Tribune* out of his own savings with an investment of just a few thousand dollars. Thomas McElrath, shortly thereafter, purchased an equal share in the concern for only $1,500.[15] In its first months, Greeley had trouble disposing of the full run of five thousand copies. But the bad times did not last very long, and within a year circulation had risen to nearly ten thousand. In September 1841, Greeley started a weekly version of the *Tribune* that would circulate nationally and establish the paper's reputation and influence. The *Tribune's* rapid growth reflected the way in which the conditions of print had become radically different by the 1850s. Within a decade of the *Tribune's* founding, the artisanal culture of its founding had given way to virtually modern conditions. Newspaper production became hierarchical and specialized, its ownership corporate, and its consumption democratic. Newspapers such as the *Sun* sold for $250,000, and the *New York Times,* without having published a single issue, attracted an investment of over $100,000. The *Tribune,* along with a few other newspapers, managed to straddle the two eras. With Greeley at the helm until his death, it maintained the personal character of the editor-proprietor period, but adapted in scale to the age of incorporation.

In many respects, the *Tribune* was also a characteristic product of the nineteenth-century's print revolution. Like many of its contemporaries, it was four pages long, about the size of a small blanket, and printed in a miniscule font. Despite the paper's strident moralism, it also featured elements with which readers of the penny press would have been quite familiar. The *Tribune,* though without the sensational zeal of the *Herald* or the *Sun,* published articles on seductions, suicides, crime, and printed advertisements for quack medicines and dubious business schemes. What separated the *Tribune* from its penny counterparts, however, was the extent to which it aspired to cultural influence and was willing to trespass the generic and class boundaries that defined traditional print culture. The *Tribune,* a penny paper targeted to a diverse readership, embraced the democratization of the culture, but it was also an attempt to transcend its limits.[16] In addition to the usual political gossip, foreign news, penny-paper scandals, and commercial intelligence, the *Tribune* also offered democratic audiences challenging reports on religion, science, literature, agriculture, cultural criticism, and European thought. Though about a third of its pages were devoted to the latest news from Washington, the rest of the paper featured fiction, poetry, science, and even social analysis. That the *Tribune* was the first daily newspaper to hire full-time book and theater critics suggests something of the journal's cultural ambitions and catholic format. Launched in the disorderly cultural moment between the aristocratic clubs, churches, and the scientific societies of the eighteenth century and the consolidated professional organizations of the late nineteenth century, the *Tribune* stitched together a vibrant democratic civic culture. Its corps of contributors included some of antebellum America's sharpest minds. The *Tribune* attracted such bright stars of New England Transcendentalism as Margaret Fuller, George Ripley, and Charles Dana, and a diverse coterie of American writers and social critics, including Albert Brisbane, Henry James Sr., John Campbell, George Foster, Stephen Pearl Andrews, Elizabeth Oakes Smith, Bayard Taylor, and James Pike. Through translations, its own American correspondents, and even direct foreign contributions, the *Tribune* also introduced American audiences to radical western European thinkers such as Pierre-Joseph Proudhon, Louis Blanc, and Karl Marx. The *Tribune* was the highest-minded newspaper in American history.

Ideology

Although the *Tribune* was a diverse institution that evolved over time, what held it together throughout nearly the entire Greeley era was its commitment to the cause of labor and various strands of socialism. The significance of the *Tribune*'s socialism has been ignored for a number of reasons. Most important among them was the fact that it was initially based in the communitarian socialism of the French Utopian Charles Fourier. Until recently, most historians have regarded Fourierism as one of the nineteenth century's quack reforms. Among Fourier's prophecies was that the spread of socialist communities, or phalanxes, would inaugurate a new stage in the earth's history. The oceans would turn to lemonade, human beings would grow useful tails, and the planets would copulate. Fourier's more outlandish speculations, however, had little to do with the social movement in America. The Americans called themselves Associationists to distance the movement from its French progenitor, and suppressed Fourier's provocative writings about sex, psychology, and cosmology. And among American Associationists, Greeley was (though vain, unpredictable, and impulsive) particularly pragmatic. His interest in socialist reform was hardly "countercultural." Rather, it was a practical solution to both the alienation and irrationality of a capitalist economy that trapped those willing to work in unemployment and concentrated the benefits of technological progress in the hands of the few. Fourierism's practical character made it a genuine mass movement during the 1840s and it was the germ of various later cooperative efforts that became one of the main demands of the labor movement during the second half of the nineteenth century.

Despite its unquestioned importance, Fourierism's reputation suffered over time. Karl Marx attached the unfortunate label "utopian" to the movement, and even historians sympathetic to leftist movements measure Fourierism, ultimately, against a Marxist standard. Was American socialism class conscious? Was it revolutionary? Did it seek to overthrow the system of private property? According to these Marxist measures, Fourierism came up short. To some, Fourierism was simply too close to the prevailing capitalist system to become a meaningful alternative to it.[17] Indeed, Marx would later write of the very Fourierist *Tribune* for which he labored as a European correspondent that, "under the guise of . . . philanthropic socialistic anti-industrialism," the paper was the voice of the "industrial bourgeoisie," which explains "the secret of why the *Tribune* in spite of all its 'isms' and socialistic humbug can be the 'leading journal' in the United States."[18] What Marx and others missed was the fact that although practical efforts to institute a Fourierist or cooperative order ultimately failed, agitation on their behalf carved out ideological space for a broad, forward-looking critique of competitive individualism and market culture that was of lasting value.

That the *Tribune* advanced what I would call a consistent social democratic program over a three-decade-long period between 1841 and 1871 is of dual significance. In the near term, the *Tribune*'s wide-ranging social democratic critique of the market forces us to conceptualize differently the way we think about nineteenth-century party ideologies. Though the *Tribune* was, as Thomas Wentworth Higginson put it, "the working centre of much of the practical radicalism of the country," it was also immersed in the world of conventional politics.[19] In most cases, the relationship between midcentury labor and reform movements and regular partisan politics was an uneasy one, but the *Tribune* functioned as a bridge between the two.[20] That Greeley was both a key Whig ideologue and one of the main architects of the Republican Party is suggestive of the way the ethos of antebellum reform could cross-fertilize with contemporary political movements and shape their ideologies. The *Tribune* was hardly "representative" of either party with which it was affiliated, but it was hardly marginal either. Its history establishes that no party was entirely coherent ideologically and that internecine conflicts within the parties were always nearly as fractious as those between them. Despite these caveats, the *Tribune*'s reach and influence should also be difficult to ignore when assessing how major Whig and especially Republican constituencies understood the emergence of market society. Its socialism, conservative as it could sometimes be, contradicts traditional historical accounts of party ideology that render both the Whigs and the Republicans the agents of the "business interest" and the bourgeoisie.[21]

I contend instead that the idea of social democracy was rooted in the ethos of reform Whiggery and that the *Tribune*'s efforts to advance social rights were particularly central to its relationship to the burgeoning Republican Party and defined its understanding of "free labor." The Republican Party, a fragile political coalition pieced together from free-soil Jacksonians, modernizing Whigs, abolitionists, and nativists, was in the main a political movement, a revolt against what many Northerners viewed as an aristocratic and rapacious slave power that conspired against popular liberty. Given its diverse origins and constituency, historians have struggled to characterize its ideology and its political-economic program. Some Republicans were promarket capitalists who believed that slavery was an anachronistic obstacle to a positive program of economic development that would unleash the country's productive resources.[22] Others were ordinary workers who feared competition from slave labor in the West, and who, more broadly, must have seen in the commodified labor of the South a disturbing parallel to their own condition. Historians have tried to unify these various strands of thought, feeling, belief, and anxiety under the rubric of a "free labor ideology."[23] The concept of free labor explains how the diverse Republican coalition held together, and particularly elucidates the apparent contradiction between the North's racism and its fierce determination to prevent slavery's growth (the Republican Party, after all, was a slave containment party, not an abolition party). But as an explanatory device, however, the concept of "free labor" has struggled to make clear just what Republicans actually meant when they celebrated free labor, beyond the fact that it was "not slavery."

In the pages of the *Tribune,* the Republican Party's commitment to free labor meant, fundamentally, that producers should own the fruits of their own labor. This was, of course, a relatively conventional idea. Lincoln imagined "free labor" as a an economy where most are "neither *hirer* nor *hired,*" where the "prudent, penniless beginner in the world, labors for wages awhile, saves a surplus . . . then labors on his own account."[24] But what set the *Tribune* apart is that, along with the era's labor movement, it recognized that the prospects for independent producers were threatened not only by foreign and slave labor but by certain tendencies within capitalism itself, and that these might require cooperative solutions. This is how, within this broad nineteenth-century discussion about the organization of labor, that antislavery and socialism intersected. To the *Tribune,* the idea of free labor was fundamentally about self-ownership, but in a broad sense its close association with the socialist and antislavery movements suggests the way in which sectional conflict over slavery and race was connected to a multifaceted national debate over political economy, free, wage, and slave labor, and the nature of individual opportunity within the context of a market society.

Toward Modern Liberalism

In the long term, the central importance of social democracy in the mid-nineteenth-century's leading journal of opinion forces us to rethink the American history of ideology, especially the relationship between liberalism and socialist reform. Until very recently, liberalism's nuanced and historical character has largely been ignored and the influence of various styles of socialist reform underestimated. The overwhelming influence of Marx and his critics, deafening during the cold war but felt even as early as the 1870s, obscures the significant middle ground between traditional laissez-faire liberalism and class-based revolutionary socialism.[25] Traditionally, leftist historians have pondered the question, first posed by Werner Sombart in 1906, of "Why Is There No Socialism in the United States?"; the socialist tradition that did exist has largely been dismissed because it failed to conform to Marx's vision of the abolition of private property, class conflict, and revolution. So-called consensus school historians likewise assumed that the absence of a feudal past and an established church combined with high wages, available land, and abundant quantities of roast beef to ensure the triumph of a liberal tradition that they understood as a commitment to a limited state, private property, and market enterprise. Even latter-day revisionists, who have unearthed such alternative traditions as Atlantic republicanism to refute the persistent American myth that "capitalism," to quote historian Sean Wilentz, arrived with "the first shiploads of white men," end up mirroring consensus-school liberal triumphalism in the sense that their narratives climax with the tragic displacement of some sort of original order—be it communal subsistence or civic virtue—by the market and its attendant liberal legitimation.[26]

In the long term, the *Tribune*'s confrontation with the "social question," and subsequent formulation of more expansive conceptions of freedom and rights, represents American liberalism's deeply historical and contingent character. Liberalism, enriched by the emergence of socialist protest, came to an intellectual crossroads at the middle of the nineteenth century when it had to account for the widening inequalities and deadening alienation of a world remade by the spread of the market. John Dewey wrote of this period as a "crisis in liberalism," a moment when its emphasis on individual liberty and action struggled to cope with the socialization and concentration of economic activity and power. As Albert Brisbane, a Fourierist socialist and sometime contributor to the *Tribune*, likewise put it, "we have in this Country a Republican government, but our Democracy extends only to Politics: it is not *Social*."[27] The *Tribune* represented an initial challenge to liberalism from within to augment its traditional commitments to self-interest, markets, private property, individualism, contract, and limited government.[28]

Today, popular usage of the term "liberal" is usually associated with a set of cultural values that includes secularism, opposition to discrimination, liberation from traditional morality, and in political economy a broad faith in the principles of the social safety net. Among academic historians and political philosophers, though, liberalism remains linked to the ideas of John Locke and Adam Smith. As the intellectual historian James Kloppenberg has pointed out, "liberalism" is "attacked by conservatives outside the university and by radicals inside it" because both are working from alternative understandings of the concept.[29] One might argue that at the core of the liberal tradition are values first enunciated in full form by John Locke that made the individual—self-interested, autonomous, and rational—the center of a political society designed to restrain the exercise of arbitrary power and to maximize material happiness and comfort. But to imagine that even eighteenth-century liberalism spoke with one voice obscures the ambivalence of even such key expositors of the English liberal tradition as Adam Smith, who in *The Theory of Moral Sentiments* wrote his own rejoinder to the free-market materialism of his capitalist primer *The Wealth of Nations*. As Ruth Bloch has put it, liberal political thought may be rightly defined by a commitment to "free markets, individual rights, and constitutional democracy," but it has also always been an intellectual system that has allowed competing and sometimes conflicting discourses to prosper within its "interstices and margins."[30] One such moment included the antebellum United States when liberal Whigs and reformers, who were steeped in the very same aura of Scottish Common Sense philosophy that brought Smith to author his treatise on ethics and moral sentiment, began a not so systematic search for antidotes to the atomizing effects of urbanization, shirtless democracy, and especially the untrammeled individualism and materialism of market culture. In Greeley's case, this search ended principally, but not exclusively, in various forms of liberal socialism. Greeley and his fellow social democrats deliberated on the fate of core liberal values like liberty and property in a world dominated by the market.

Historians use terms such as "liberalism" and "republicanism" to make distinctions and to carve out patterns of thought. American intellectual historians have spent the better part of a generation debating whether the ideological foundation of the United States was properly "liberal" or "republican"; whether, in short, the struggle for independence was rooted in a commitment to, in the former case, property, autonomy, and private interest or, in the latter, virtue and the common good.[31] The republican paradigm that blossomed in the context of that debate has since been extended well into the late nineteenth century, so far and wide that some critics no longer see it as a concept of much value.[32] But what made the republican synthesis so valuable in the first place is that it was an intellectual history that emerged from systematic research in eighteenth-century newspapers and political pamphlets. It was research based in popular thought, which unsurprisingly presented elements adapted from the English "country-party" tradition and others from Locke, and there is little reason to suggest that these traditions are necessarily and uniformly in conflict with one another. The debate itself reveals how ideas function in a fertile political and intellectual environment. Self-conscious intellectual traditions emerge, but they also evolve, fray at the edges, and merge with competing traditions. That the republican synthesis has become a kind of tangled bog drained of precise meaning ("everywhere and organizing every thing," in the words of Daniel Rodgers) also illustrates the depth, diversity, and complexity of historical research on the subject, and ultimately the wide use that varied individuals, groups, and movements made of its common vocabulary.[33] Historians offered up the republican tradition as an alternative founding myth to the liberal consensus outlined in the 1950s at the height of the cold war. In the end, though, the liberal/republican debate ignores the way in which the former offered its own sustained critique of capitalism, a discursive tradition I frame as social democratic liberalism.

Social democratic liberalism, like republicanism, was not a discourse with rigid boundaries; nor was the *Tribune* its sole parent in the United States. Nonetheless, the *Tribune,* and the socialist and labor reformers with which it was allied, represented a crucial development in the history of liberalism. Greeley's *Tribune* epitomized the way in which liberal political economy had diverged into two basic streams by midcentury, one social democratic and another individualistic, and the basis of the split had to do with the way it defined the nature of markets and characterized the relationship between capital and labor. Emerging within or alongside the liberal tradition, social democrats called for social rights, especially the right to an education for all and to labor for those willing and able to do so. Most important, they recognized that the unfettered operation of the market could produce profound inequities, robbing labor of its independence and its real value. In this sense, the *Tribune* and its socialist allies were clearly "social democratic," even using a version of the term to distinguish their reform hopes from the "merely political."[34] Liberal socialists in the antebellum period, adapting language from French political factions, leftist parties, and workers' societies, would at times use terms that approximated "social democracy," such as republican socialism, cooperative socialism, or *démoc-soc,* democratic socialism. The *Tribune's* socialist liberalism thus occupied an ideological middle ground that recognized the interdependence of modern societies and demanded collective solutions to social and economic problems. Nonetheless, it still valued core liberal ideals such as individuality, freedom, and spontaneity. Critical of private concentrations of capital and property, the *Tribune's* socialism expressed the faith that what might seem fixed—institutions, laws, the hierarchy of classes and interests, and even "human nature"—could be altered in ways that would extend human freedom.

The *Tribune's* social democratic critique of the marketplace was part of a wider transatlantic reaction against the social and cultural costs of laissez-faire individualism. Transmitting mostly French social theory to a broad American reading public, the *Tribune* popularized a new way of explaining the effects of complex and abstract social forces on the individual and, more broadly, the notion of society itself as a constellation of diverse interests. The *Tribune's* socialism and, more generally, its politics were instrumental in setting forth the idea that the interdependence of modern economies makes individuals the prisoners—or the beneficiaries—of forces beyond their control, and in ways that bear little relation to individual character. Greeley, like many more conventional Whigs such as Abraham Lincoln, supported aspects of market change—technology, social mobility, cosmopolitan tolerance, obedience to law—but was also vexed by certain destructive social and moral consequences of the market and worried that progress would not benefit everyone equally. He also worried that the culture of the market, particularly its materialism and individualism, elevated swindlers and confidence men to power and created a society held together only by greed. Greeley especially despised the sheer disorganization of large-scale markets. In his view, involuntary unemployment was the problem of the age, and he understood it primarily as a problem of social organization and the exploitation of trade. But unlike radical "Democrats" such as Orestes Brownson, who could be considered a partisan counterpart, Greeley did not think that class relationships themselves were the source of the market's evils. Greeley thought for the most part that capitalists were prudent and hard-working former laborers. He thought the real exploiters were speculators, and those who profited not from work but from exchange.

I use the term social democracy, though, not merely to describe the *Tribune*'s rather singular contribution to liberalism's evolution. Rather, I would also argue that social democracy deserves a history. In its modern usage, the designation social democratic has been merely descriptive and rarely connotes attachment to any sort of self-conscious intellectual tradition. At best, we have a "third way" or what Lee Benson has termed a New Deal tradition of American politics, but these labels fail to capture the way social democracy was both a direct challenge to liberalism and its direct offshoot, a reflection of its discursive complexity, elasticity, and pragmatism.[35] Applicable to a diverse number of thinkers and movements stretching all the way from various antebellum reforms, through the Yankee International, the eight-hour movement, the Knights of Labor, Grange-inspired farmer cooperatives, the nationalism of Edward Bellamy, and even Teddy Roosevelt's "New Nationalism" and Franklin Roosevelt's "Second Bill of Rights," the social democratic impulse has lacked definition, particularly in the United States, which unlike Europe never had a political party take the name or even define itself in those terms. But in this post-Marxist moment, which has witnessed the spread of an increasingly aggressive brand of capitalist liberalism under the banner of globalization, it seems particularly useful and important to carve out an ideological tradition that occupied, however uneasily, a space between class-conscious revolutionary socialism and laissez-faire liberalism. The *Tribune*'s long argument with laissez-faire liberalism, cultural and religious conservatism, and more internationally with revolutionary socialism was at the forefront of this tradition and collectively constituted the first genuine articulation of social democratic principles in the history of the United States.

CHAPTER 1

The Emancipation of Labor

> Phrenology, Mesmerism, and the countless brood of
> novel 'sciences' which have of late years dawned upon
> the world, all agree in this. They all unite in discard-
> ing moral distinctions, in annulling conscience, and
> in rejecting the idea of spiritual laws and even of
> spiritual existences. Every thing is identified with the
> laws of Nature. These laws are revealed sometimes in
> bumps upon the skull; sometimes in the nerves, and
> by means of galvanic action; sometimes in the out-
> ward forms of life and matter: but *always* in Nature.
> The law of Nature is to them the *only* law of God.
>
> Henry Raymond, *Courier and Enquirer*

Reflecting on the first decade of the *Tribune's*
existence, Horace Greeley remarked that his main objective as a reformer
and public intellectual was to be "a mediator, an interpreter, a reconciler,
between Conservatism and Radicalism."[1] For Greeley, the 1840s were a formative period intellectually, and during that decade he labored to harmonize
radical and conservative ideas in ways that would not only benefit his party
politically but also adapt traditional Whiggish values to new economic realities. But for Greeley this impulse to fuse conservative and radical positions
was almost entirely an intellectual one. In his person, he was a divisive figure,
even within the context of his own party. Even though the integration of
intellectual and social opposites was a defining characteristic of Whig political culture, the *Tribune* made socialism the pivot of this project, which outraged
conservative Whigs who insisted that an organic society also be a hierarchical one. When socialism became the *Tribune's* defining marker, Greeley
became an enduring symbol, first locally and later nationally, of the erratic,
unstable, and impractical bent of Yankee reform culture that, to its critics,
would destroy the religious, moral, and familial foundations of the traditional social order. In the end, the *Tribune's* campaign for a socialism that
was theoretically committed to social concord and the harmony of interests
became characteristic of Greeley's tendency to reconcile ideas and polarize
audiences.

When Greeley started the *Tribune,* his platform for labor was in a relatively inchoate embryonic form. His main aim was to demonstrate that Whigs sympathized with labor and to persuade ordinary people that Whig activist government would benefit them. But within the first year of the paper's launch, the *Tribune*'s program for labor became more precisely theorized, embracing in large measure the socialist liberalism of Charles Fourier. For Greeley, Fourierism was a mechanism that could reinforce and advance a Whiggish economic order, one that resisted the atomistic elements of the age and emphasized social harmony, technology, and a mutually sustaining ethos of cooperative self-improvement. Fourierism shared with conventional Whig political economy an affinity for corporate and fraternal bonds, but, more radically, it also imagined a more democratic economic order and a social life governed by uninhibited impulse. By pushing the latter assumptions, the *Tribune* opened up divisions within the culture of Whiggery. Conservative Whigs called for a more orderly capitalism, not a replacement of it. Shaped by a Protestant tradition that valued family and, above all, the individual conscience as the guarantor of moral self-restraint, they conceded the danger of individualism and materialism, but argued that God, family, church, and conscience were the answer, not socialism. Socialism, in fact, became for many conservative Whigs a symbol of contemporary moral decay, synonymous with licentiousness, revolution, moral relativism, and infidelity.

The conservative response to the *Tribune*'s Fourierism was in many ways suggestive of its comprehensiveness. Remembered as a narrow and idiosyncratic Victorian reform, Fourierism actually was indicative of an entire worldview. *Tribune* socialism demanded much more than the material elevation of labor; it was, by definition, profoundly cultural. The Fourierist communities envisioned creative rather than routinized labor, and a new design for public life, one that democratized access to ideas, science, music, and oratory. Fourierist reform, predicated on a liberal, cosmopolitan conception of human nature, eschewed discipline, law, and ascribed status, and celebrated spontaneity, instinct, and freedom. The liberationist component of Association extended beyond the reform of labor and into the most intimate regions of private life. Even though Greeley was a moral conservative and tried to emphasize the practical communitarian message of Association, other socialists on the *Tribune* and within the larger movement were less restrained. Whig conservatives would quickly seize on Fourierism's morally questionable elements in an effort to discredit the movement as a whole. Not dissimilar to their tack in later "culture wars," conservatives countered the *Tribune*'s liberal socialism with a cultural counteroffensive that mobilized traditional Christian and familial values in defense of a hierarchical economic order.

Fourier, Fourierism, and Albert Brisbane

As an international movement, Fourierism was a specific and short-lived solution to economic dislocation, but its basic assumptions would be the mainstay of social democratic discourse for generations. Most important, Fourierism insisted that social inequality was a threat to democracy, that poverty was not reducible to individual character or political corruption, and that economic crises and conflicts could be addressed rationally and collectively through experiments in social organization. What made Fourierist socialism revolutionary was that it understood the problem of inequality and industrial unemployment within a framework of social and economic organization. These basic assumptions are often obscured by the almost cultish outlook that surrounded Fourierism's founder and his apostles.

The route that Fourierist socialism took to the United States was neither long nor indirect, but what it became once it got there was something far different than what its author envisioned. Charles Fourier was born in 1772, and spent most of his adult life as a traveling salesman, drifting from job to job, earning just enough money to survive and write. The things Fourier witnessed as a salesman—speculation, loan-sharking, and artificial shortages—eroded any faith the Frenchman might have had in British political economy and the rational efficiency of the free market. In his early years, Fourier was merely a local crank who hounded provincial officials with his reform ideas, but by 1799 Fourier began to sketch a more comprehensive theory that claimed to solve, mathematically, the riddles of psychology, society, and history. In 1808, Fourier began putting these theories on paper, writing large, "scientifically" complex tomes that promised to transform individual psychology, the social order, and even nature.

Fourier's theory of total reform began with the individual. Influenced by France's Enlightenment heritage of Utopian rationalism, anticlericalism, and perfectionism, Fourier broke with the strain of Enlightenment thought that alleged that consciousness was a blank slate written upon by sense experience. Supplementing sense experience were inborn desires, compulsions, talents, and capacities known as the passions. Though many of the philosophes—including Denis Diderot, Claude Helvétius, Baron de Montesquieu, and Jean-Jacques Rousseau—acknowledged in different ways the role of the passions, Fourier went much further, making innate urges the basis of his entire social system, arguing that their fulfillment was essential to human happiness. Fourier's hierarchy of twelve passions ascended from the senses (or "luxurious" passions) through sociability (the "affective" passions) up to the "distributive" passions, which regulated the lower impulses. Fourier maintained that healthy individual development required the exercise of the full range of passions, that illness was a product of repression, and that an individual's attractions were "proportional" to their destinies (that desire in a well-organized society, in other words, produces its own fulfillment). Believing in humanity's intrinsic goodness, especially if the passions were unleashed and properly channeled, Fourier contended that society could be engineered by grouping and arranging individual psychologies according to mathematical laws, the social-scientific equivalent of Newtonian physics.

Toward this end, Fourier endorsed the organization of phalanxes, planned communities of 1,620 people, centered in a neoclassical phalanstery that would physically symbolize his gospel of social symmetry, balance, and harmony. For Fourier, all of humanity contained 810 personality types. Consequently, he argued that an ideal society, or "phalanx," ought to be composed of 1,620 people, or a representative, for each sex, of the complete range of personalities. With the full range of passional inclinations represented in each community, work would not have to be coerced and perfect social harmony would result. By providing a rational social architecture, Fourier thought he could liberate repressed creativity; in this sense, he fused the twin poles of Romanticism, individuality and social organicism, to Enlightenment mechanistic rationality.

Fourier was not only a socialist. He also considered himself a theorist of nature and the psyche. But it was the French theorist's scheme for the communitarian reorganization of society that appealed principally to most American socialists and especially to Greeley. The Fourier who was popularized in America was, in short, an expurgated one. Fourier thought he had discovered a divine social code. He argued that the planets would create new worlds through intercourse, that humans, after the spread of Association, would grow useful tails. He wrote of the origins of the universe and a history of the earth's "80,000" years. Some of his theoretical works describe the migration of souls between the worlds of the living and the dead. But most dangerously, he held that marriage and sexual relations would be liberated by the laws of passional attraction, and concocted various and elaborate schemes to rationalize the fulfillment of sexual desire. The challenge for American socialists, in their efforts to popularize Fourierism, was to strip it of its absurdities, and more important, of its French "immoralities," without sacrificing the basic outlines of the theory of the passions, which, to them, was the "scientific" basis of social harmony and communal organization.[2]

The main agent who transmitted Fourierism to the United States was Albert Brisbane, the so-called father of American socialism. Brisbane was a complex figure. Monomaniacal and eccentric, he made Greeley look like a

FIGURE 3. Daguerreotype of Albert Brisbane, the so-called father of American socialism. Brisbane partnered with Greeley and the *Tribune* to popularize Fourierism in the United States. Courtesy of the Photography Collection, Miriam and Ira D. Wallach Division of Art, Prints, and Photographs, The New York Public Library, Astor, Lenox, and Tilden Foundations, digital ID 95313.

hardheaded realist. Walt Whitman described him as a "tall, slender man," with "round-shoulder[s]," "deep-set eyes," and an "awkward" manner that made him look as "if he were attempting to think out some problem a little too hard for him."[3] Born in 1809 into a wealthy family in western New York that had made its fortune in frontier land speculation, Brisbane received a fine education, first in New York City and then in Europe where he learned French and studied with such notables as the philosopher Victor Cousin. In both Paris and Berlin, Brisbane mixed freely with the intellectual and radical elite, eventually developing an interest in philosophy and social reform. Initially influenced by Jules Lechevalier and other young reformers, Brisbane became a Saint-Simonian. Comte de Saint-Simon was a liberal who condemned monarchy and aristocracy, but typical of French liberalism he rejected the British laissez-faire model. Although his thinking evolved quite a bit in the decades before his death in 1825, what held it together was a vision of a technocratic society, often quite hierarchical, that wedded scientific progress to a new religious order that would re-create the organic social harmony of an earlier age. Calling for a "New Christianity," Saint-Simon's ideas were influential, certainly more so than Fourier's, particularly among the generations of scientists and engineers that had been trained at the École de Polytechnique. But Saint-Simonianism had also become, by the 1820s, not unlike a religious cult, and while Brisbane was in Paris in the early 1830s the movement split into two bitterly divided wings and then eventually crumbled.[4]

Fourierism, after a fashion, filled the vacuum. Brisbane's friend Lechevalier, purged in the Saint-Simonian factional infighting, joined the growing circle of admirers that surrounded the aging Charles Fourier. Lechevalier, Victor Considerant, and a few others started a Fourierist journal that published summaries of Fourier's ideas that avoided controversial subjects. It was not long before Brisbane, too, became a full-blown disciple.[5] In 1832, Lechevalier introduced Brisbane to Considerant and Juste Muiron, and then finally to Fourier. Brisbane engaged Fourier as a personal tutor at a wage of five francs per hour, studying with him twice a week for six weeks. From that point forward Fourierism became the guiding force in his life.[6]

Brisbane returned to the United States in 1834, but he did little for nearly five years. He stayed in contact with his fellow French Fourierists and boasted of efforts to acquire the necessary capital and land to begin a model phalanx in the New World, but it was not until the late 1830s that Brisbane returned to Fourier in a public way by working on his own translation and summary of Fourier's ideas.[7] Published in 1840 as *The Social Destiny of Man*, it launched Brisbane's own career as a socialist reformer. Noticed in several radical-leaning magazines including the *Dial*, the *Democratic Review*, and Orestes Brownson's *Boston Quarterly Review*, Brisbane's book began building popular American awareness of Fourier beyond the French émigré community. Brisbane reconstituted the Fourienne Society as the Fourier Association of the City of New York, named a predominately American-born board of officers, and not long after the completion of his book began making plans to start a journal of his own. After various fits and starts, Brisbane, along with Cyrenius Bristol and Charles Drake Ferris, backed and launched *The Phalanx*, a weekly magazine and the first Fourierist periodical in America. Both *The Phalanx* and his *Social Destiny of Man* were not exactly popular successes—the former lasted only six weeks—but they did make Brisbane a familiar figure in the world of New York journalism. The book, in particular, introduced Brisbane to Parke Godwin, who was then an editor of his father-in-law's influential Democratic daily, the *Evening Post*. Godwin would become a central leader of the Associationist movement as well as one of the free-soil Democratic founders of the Republican Party. More important, *Social Destiny of Man* also attracted Greeley's attention on the eve of his launching the *Tribune*.[8]

Greeley first noticed the book in a paragraph-long review in the October 17, 1840, issue of the *New-Yorker*. There Greeley pledged, after summarizing the main argument of the book, to "speak further of this work after we shall have considered it more fully." Three months passed before Brisbane's influence became noticeable in the *New-Yorker*. Greeley was long a reformer in the Whiggish mode, but Association very quickly transformed the very language of Greeley's *New-Yorker* editorials. By January 1841 Greeley was arguing that all previous social reform was partial and insufficient. Measures such as labor exchanges, immigrant aid societies, lyceums, and temperance would not transform the "existing organization of society." As was his custom, Greeley here reassured conservatives that Association would not threaten the principle of private property and established conventions regarding the relations of the sexes. He was careful to emphasize the relationship of Association to the system "which has been found so serviceable in Commerce and its handmaids Banking and Insurance, in Manufacturing enterprises, and in the prosecution of Internal Improvements." Despite these cautious qualifications, Greeley for the first time joined his established opposition to competitive individualism with a positive system of collective industry and living.[9]

In late January 1841, Greeley and Brisbane launched a second American Fourierist weekly, *The Future,* which, despite Greeley's astute feel for publishing, lasted only eight weeks. It, however, was only a prelude to what was to come. When *The Future* collapsed, the Fourier Society decided to change strategies. Instead of supporting a separate periodical that was both expensive and preached to an audience of the converted, New York's Fourierists instead decided to issue a popular and Americanized version of Fourier within the columns of a "non-sectarian" newspaper.[10] The *Tribune* was a natural fit. Every week, between March 1842 and September 1843, Brisbane published a column outlining the basic features of Fourier's system. Titled "Association; or, Principles of a True Organization of Society," Brisbane's column was initially a self-consciously distinct part of the paper—Brisbane actually leased the space. But over the course of the 1840s, Greeley and the paper itself became increasingly identified with the cause of what was alternately termed Fourierist, Associationist, or Utopian socialism. The column, too, was reprinted in as many as forty other newspapers and was later published under Greeley's imprint in the form of the 1843 pamphlet *Association; or, A Concise Exposition of the Practical Part of Fourier's Social Science,* selling ten editions of a thousand copies each.[11] Like other disciples of Fourier both in the United States and France who transmitted the ideas of the French theorist to a popular audience, Brisbane did not merely translate Fourier. Instead, he "summarized" and reformulated Fourier in the *Tribune* after the manner of Jules Lechevalier's *Etudes sur la Science Sociale* and Victor Considerant's *Destiné Sociale* (from whom Brisbane borrowed the title of his 1840 volume *Social Destiny of Man*). In these various formats, Brisbane's writings introduced a wide American audience to Fourier's communitarian socialism.

French Fourierism and American Associationism

By 1843, thanks in large part to propaganda in the *Tribune,* twenty-six phalanxes had been founded across America, mostly in the Northeast and the Midwest.[12] Close to two dozen Fourierist clubs met in various Northern cities. Counting actual phalansterians, periodical readers, and society members, the movement counted nearly one hundred thousand adherents.[13] The *Tribune* was the movement's most important organ and Greeley was Albert Brisbane's most important convert. Despite their differences, Greeley and Brisbane's collaboration launched socialism in the United States. When Charles Fourier died in 1837, his death went largely unreported in American newspapers. Seven years later, Fourierism had become one of the most important reform movements in the country, offering antebellum America a third way between the coerced social organicism of the slave South and the individualistic market worship of the capitalist North.[14]

For most American Fourierists, and especially for Greeley, Association was, minimally, a solution to the problems of industrial society. At its most ambitious, Association promised a cultural and psychological cure for the atomization of modern life. The central element that Brisbane and then Greeley borrowed from Fourier was his plan to associate labor and capital within a benevolent community, giving to the former the full product (in both capital and wages) of its work and to the latter security against "social warfare" (revolution). In the United States, and even to an extent in France, Fourier's disciples suppressed his mysticism and his sexual radicalism. They also avoided "scientific and technical terms," and even collectively settled on the term "Association" to separate the American movement from the theoretical extravagance of its French ancestor.[15] In 1844, the American Union of Associationists announced that it advocated only Fourier's theories on the "organization of labor," suppressing any sexual implications of passional theory that might, as one socialist put it later, bring "suspicion upon their intentions."[16]

Stripped of its fantastical elements, Association was an ideological compromise between free market, capitalist individualism and revolutionary socialism, and in the United States, at least until the late 1860s, its vision of society, organized on a township model, was as plausible as an America dominated by corporations, factories, and a restive alien proletariat. Its main goal was to harmonize the relationship between capital and labor by voluntarily, if somewhat radically, instituting within a cooperative framework elements of communal and private property. The interests of capital would not be eradicated, but the communities would balance them against those of labor and talent. Brisbane, like many Associationists, thought the communities would realize a perfect new order without painful disruptions or dislocations. He argued that Association could raise the poor without disturbing the rich, that competition among capitalists and between capital and labor was inefficient, and that contrary to the notions of classical British political economists, was rarely channeled by unseen hands toward a public interest.

Brisbane held that a cooperative economy would produce more wealth in a number of basic ways. He claimed, first, that only a third of the current population was engaged directly in the production of wealth. Association would bring more productive labor into the workplace by collectivizing domestic labor and liberating women from most household duties, fostering full employment for the poor, engaging "playful" labor from children, and by dispensing with occupations that only service civilization's discontents: lawyers, speculators, police, soldiers, and servants. Association would also profit by eliminating poor relief, economic cycles, fraud, monopoly, and duplicated labor. Finally, Association was environmentally rational, promising to restore stocks of fish and game and the basic fertility of the land, increasing the productivity of farming and fishing. By reorganizing labor and bringing more workers into the economy, Brisbane thought socialist communities could produce six times as much wealth, raising the poor without disturbing the rich.[17] Brisbane and Greeley were convinced that under Association, cooperation would replace self-interest and that a dramatic reorganization of social relations could take place peacefully and voluntarily, without painful dislocations and by demonstration.

To some contemporary critics and historians, Associationism's weakness was its conservatism: it was too close to the prevailing order to transform it radically. Ralph Waldo Emerson remarked that the Associationists were mere "describers of that which is really being done. The large cities are phalansteries; and the theorists draw all their arguments from facts already taking place in our experience."[18] Despite its conservative limits, Association-ism made a profound contribution to the burgeoning discourse of American political economy. Though its specific social and economic blueprint was cautious on such basic matters as property, family, and class—and ultimately proved unworkable—its larger ambition to organize, rationalize, and most importantly to distribute the fruits of interdependent economies of scale in more democratic ways stretched core liberal principles on property and markets to their limit. As Brisbane argued, though some claim that the phalanx was merely a joint-stock company in disguise, Association rewards talent, labor, and capital according to a more egalitarian formula, and its "business operations and interests... [would] be managed by Councils, elected annually by all the members."[19] Though Association soberly protected the right of private property, it radically made private property conditional on the right to labor, that is, the right to work for those willing and able to do so. "The Rich complain of revolutionary agitation and excitement against Property," argued an editorial from the London *Phalanx* reprinted in the *Tribune,* "forgetting that Poor Man's only Property—his Labor—has been undermined by silent revolution (by monopoly and privilege, by false competition or indirect spoliation, by monopolized machinery, and by partial legislation) during a half century of anarchy in trade, disguised... by political economists, with epithets of 'freedom in supply and demand.'"[20] To the Associationists, private property, unleavened by the right to labor and monopolized in the hands of a few, not only threatened the social fabric but it also displayed the same weaknesses of the slave economy. "Men who were slow and careless, while working for wages," Brisbane wrote, "become prodigies of diligence as soon as they commence operating on their own account. The first problem of Political Economy consequently should be to endeavor to transform all the hired classes into co-interested proprietors, [who] have an interest in the capital."[21] Association recoiled from class conflict and only tentatively challenged private property and the prerogatives of capital, but it also made class, property, and capital objects of democratic reform. All of which is to say that Association, as a practical solution to the shortcomings of the capitalist economy was perhaps a halfway measure, but its assumptions about the nature of the industrial world and its expansive conceptualization of equality's meaning were revolutionary.

The brand of Association advocated in the *Tribune* also "stretched" the value liberalism placed on privacy, often in radical ways. Associationists were careful to make space for the nuclear family and, more broadly, for private choice, but the very architecture of communitarian living held open the option of a more connected and vital public life. It also, importantly, collectivized domestic labor, to liberate women from the educational and cultural privation of the isolated household and pecuniary dependence on husbands.[22] In certain respects, Association was, for middle-class men, little more than a town or township with a strong civic life. Brisbane himself articulated Association's advantages as the difference between "living in a solitary log-house...half a mile perhaps from any neighbor" and access to "the Arts and Sciences," "extended Social Relations," "Libraries, Reading-Rooms, Baths, the pleasures of Lectures, Concerts" and the "refinements of life." But for women and the laboring classes, Association could, in a revolutionary way, democratize access to a public culture. Association's reform of the conditions of labor, in this sense, gave workers leisure for self-improvement and was bound to an ideal of self-cultural individual realization. Communal living—public culture in the communities—provided intellectual growth, and the rotating character of Associated labor would emancipate labor from the mental dullness of repetitive work.

Association and the Problem of Class

Crafted to curb rootless individualism and even lift the psychological malaise of protoindustrial routine, the *Tribune*'s social democratic liberalism in its Fourierist form aimed as much for individual self-realization as it did for distributive justice. Creative, productive labor and mental improvement would be the foundation of a fully realized existence. The phalanx's design, Brisbane hoped, would harmonize manual and mental labor. "Vigor of body," he thought, "is all-important to richness and vividness of imagination." Labor, for Brisbane, had a double edge, however. The foundation of wealth and individual dignity, labor in its current specialized, unalternated, and coerced "industrial feudal" form was debasing. "Man was not designed for a merely animal, but for a rational, intellectual and moral Existence," Brisbane wrote. "He possessed vast faculties which ought to be developed and trained, but which, in nine-tenths of the Race, are stunted and stifled in the present Order of Society."[23]

To most radicals in the tradition of Marx, Association's flowery emphasis on individual physical and intellectual self-realization—and especially on social harmony and voluntary reform—was bourgeois in its impulses and naively overestimated the extent to which humanitarian goodwill could bring about fundamental social change. The criticism is not disingenuous, but it is also not exactly precise. Even though Brisbane and the *Tribune* did not relish social revolution, and Associative theory and the movement itself were not products of working-class experience, the movement did not shy away from class as a category of analysis. Brisbane and Greeley, for example, were notoriously ambivalent toward strikes, but hardly apologists for the conditions that produced them. In response to striking women in Pittsburgh, Greeley questioned the rationality of the strike, but he also condemned the "tyranny of capital" and asserted the rights of factory women to "food, sleep . . . mental improvement" and "healthful exercise." Most important, Greeley maintained that "industrial anarchy" (which was the title of the editorial) injured both capital and labor; the "adjustment" of the relationship between both "on the basis of perfect Harmony and Justice is the great work of our age."[24] Brisbane similarly balanced sober hopes for class reconciliation with the dim recognition that class warfare was inevitable without some kind of social democratic adjustment. Social democratic reform "will change quietly and by substitution what is false and defective," he wrote. "It will violate no rights, injure no class; it will not impoverish the Rich to enrich slightly the Poor."[25]

Warfare among the classes was the furthest thing from the Associationist agenda. Brisbane argued that social reorganization "must not impoverish a small minority of Wealthy to enrich slightly a vast majority of Destitute, but it must increase Production or real Wealth so immensely that the Prosperity of all Classes can be greatly augmented."[26] Nonetheless, Brisbane recognized that class animus was a given fact of contemporary society, an inevitable by-product of the competitive system. Reassuring readers that "we wage war against no Class or Interest," Brisbane implicitly pointed out that the existing economic arrangements unfairly favored capital at the expense of labor; for the working class, industrialization and higher productivity were counterproductive, resulting in disease, fatigue, routinization, periodic unemployment, intellectual desiccation, and the erosion of happy domestic life. "They are engaged in an employment which absorbs their attention, and unremittingly employs their physical energies. They are drudges," Brisbane wrote, "subject to the prolonged labor of an animal—his physical energy wasted, his mind in supine inaction—the Artisan has neither moral dignity, nor intellectual nor organic strength to resist the seductions of appetite."[27] To forestall revolutionary violence against the competitive system, Brisbane moved instead to democratize capitalist wealth and power:

> The first great aim of the noble-minded men and women engaged in this movement is to show, that Justice and Equity can be introduced in the sphere of Industry—that Labor can be rendered honorable, and the Laboring Classes secured in Intelligence and Social Elevation—that a fair and equitable division of profits can take place—that the Laborer

can become a Capitalist and the Capitalist a Laborer—that machinery may be made to work for the Laboring Classes instead of working Against them as at present—and that these Classes may be united and induced to work together like friends and brothers, instead of being separated, and working against each other like enemies.[28]

Brisbane and Greeley did not ignore class, but they used the menace of conflict and revolution to persuade the public of the necessity of social reorganization, and to challenge more broadly the ideological foundations of the "neutral" free-market economy.[29]

The idea of class, optimistic as the *Tribune*'s Fourieristic formulation of it was, ran counter to prevailing myths of American social mobility and democratic equality. Fourierist socialism, in part a product of the European Enlightenment, was universalistic and cosmopolitan in scope, but American Associationists were careful to adapt the theory to what were understood as particular national realities. Theoretically, Fourierists maintained that world history progresses through inevitable stages that are not culturally specific; social laws discovered in nature and instituted in one township could serve as the model for thousands, just as the "laws of one individual...explain those of the whole Human Race."[30] The shared titles of Considerant and Brisbane's Fourierist tomes (in English, *The Social Destiny of Man*) similarly posited that history progresses according to fixed principles and rational laws. But in the *Tribune,* Brisbane molded Fourierist universalism to predominant myths of American exceptionalism in, as always, simultaneously conservative and radical ways. America, Brisbane pointed out at an 1845 New England Fourierist convention, lacked a "degraded peasantry" and possessed "an intelligent, aspiring, self-respecting and respected working class." Equally important, unique conditions had also produced an egalitarian middle class that is sober and "with every opportunity of intellectual and moral culture open before them," a wealthy class "not tempted by the luxuries, titles, and inherited privileges of an established aristocracy," and a "literary" class "not constrained to seek advancement by servility...[and] free in thought and speech."[31] Associationists, in the *Tribune* and elsewhere, celebrated America as an "open society" whose blessings—its expansive spaces and republican political system—made it the ideal site in which to plant the socialist future, before the exceptional nature of its politics and geography gave way to a European future. Importantly, Brisbane's sense of American exceptionalism was based on historical contingencies and not providence: "If the mass of the population in the United States is better off physically than in Europe, it is because there is an immense extent of soil and a thin population.... But we are moving onward to the misery of the Old World; our present prosperity is temporary." American exceptionalism, in Brisbane's view, allowed, but also depended on, a painless evolution toward socialism; only Association could forestall the laws of historical development and ward off a European future of inequality and class warfare.[32]

Brisbane's agreement with the *Tribune* ended in the fall of 1843. Nonetheless, Fourierism remained a regular feature of the paper, but with a crucial difference. For Brisbane, Fourierism would remain the guiding principle of his life, well into Gilded Age America and after the Utopian moment had passed. Greeley, on the other hand, viewed Association instrumentally, strictly as a utilitarian solution to the economic and cultural dilemmas of labor. "Why may we not give to Labor a republican organization," Greeley begged, "so that workers shall freely choose their own chiefs or overlookers, regulate their own hours of daily toil, and divide the general product according to a preconcerted scale whose sole end shall be mutual and universal justice?"[33] He was, as Brisbane remembered, almost exclusively interested in "the practical side of the questions," in Association's "economies, its order, the proper adaptation of the various functions to the capacities and talents of those engaged in labor." If Fourier's true believers were interested in a "new industrial world," Greeley hoped merely for a better one.[34] Though Greeley helped sponsor an array of Fourierist experiments, he was less wedded to the organizational success of Fourierism except as it fulfilled its promise to instill benevolent social relations between emergent industrial classes and to emancipate labor from the thralldom of wages, poverty, structural unemployment, and intellectual privation.

The Politics of Socialism and Individualism

For Greeley, Association was a component of his democratic economic vision for the Whig Party. To Brisbane and most other Associationists, however, politics was self-defeating.[35] Most Associationists were explicitly antipolitical and the movement in practice involved withdrawal into separate socialist communities. This was not unusual. Hostility to politics and parties was pervasive in reform circles particularly of the Whiggish sort—temperance, abolition, Sabbatarianism—and even dominated the language of third-party movements. The Whig Party itself has sometimes even been interpreted as more a diverse constellation of reform movements than as a party.[36] So, like other reform movements and perhaps even the Whigs, the Associationists envisioned a higher democracy that transcended politics, constitutions, and laws. Brisbane disdainfully asked, "Can a Specie Currency or a Paper Currency, the Right to vote or any other Political Right,—or the establishment even of the best of Governments,—'that which governs least,' do any thing for the real and practical amelioration of the Wretchedness of the poor peasantry of those countries?"[37] Despite Association's explicit antipolitics, its emergence within arguably the Whigs' most influential national organ has a lot to tell us about the ideological dimensions of the second American party system.

Though most Associationists were not nearly as partisan or politically active as Greeley, and although no precise study has ever been conducted of the Associationists' political affiliations, the general tenor of the movement was broadly Whiggish. Greeley claimed, probably with some truth, that the communitarian movement "never fails to give an overwhelmingly Whig majority." Conservative Whigs often charged that Association inevitably led toward class war, but to Greeley they confused causes and cures: "Place men in a condition of assured comfort and thrifty industry, earning what they need and receiving what they earn, surrounded by the means of mental culture and social enjoyment, so as to be above the loathsome temptations of the grogshop, and they will mainly be Whigs, as naturally as water runs down hill."[38] Nonetheless, Greeley's prominence within the supposedly conservative Whig Party and America's first socialist movement has puzzled most historians.[39] This seeming paradox clashes with the traditional portraits of the parties, with the Democrats seen as an institutionally inclusive and culturally populist party that endeavored to legislate economic and social equality, and the Whigs viewed as the party of aristocratic and probusiness ex-Federalists. Even most newer and more nuanced interpretations of the second party system suggest that the parties were ideologically divided in their relationship to an emerging capitalist economy.[40]

The conventional dichotomies that are traditionally relied on to describe the parties—"conservative/liberal," "procapitalist/anticapitalist," "aristocratic/democratic"—fail to square, however, with America's governing liberal consensus. Apart from the conservative post-Federalist wing of the Whig Party in the North and the radical proslavery wing of the Democratic Party in the South, it would be difficult to classify the mainstream of either party as anything but democratic and liberal. Nor should either party be characterized as anticapitalist. Conventional economic debate, even during the ideologically robust Jackson years, rarely questioned either private enterprise or property. Though any overarching description of the parties' political economies is probably overgeneralized, I would argue in a basic sense that the Whigs hoped to diversify and advance capitalist opportunity, but recoiled from the individualism, instability, and materialism of laissez-faire. The Democrats, in turn, prized propertied individualism, but unlike the Whigs were much more

likely to condemn social inequality and to see exploitation in class relationships. Perhaps the best description of party ideology is Parke Godwin's. One
of the few prominent Associationists publicly aligned with the Democrats,
he distinguished the Whigs from the Democrats on the basis of the former's
promotion of orderly capitalism and the latter's appeal to anarchical capitalism: "The Whigs, by the system they propose, would only consecrate by
law those abuses and distinctions which are the evidence and result of our
rapid tendency to a commercial feudality. On the other hand, the Democrats,
by the repeal of all restraining laws, would only give broader field for the
freer development of the elements of disorder—they would only deepen and
widen the breaches in society opened by the operation of the principle of
unlimited competition."[41]

In the end, Democrats and Whigs, ideologically, were products of diverg-
ing strands within liberalism. Democrats, despite their nationalism, embraced
the precepts of British political economy, a rights-based, individualistic, negative liberalism that viewed free markets and the limited state as antidotes to
favoritism and corruption. The Whigs, on the other hand, were in the positive
liberal tradition of continental thinkers such as Wilhelm von Humboldt, Benjamin Constant, Saint-Simon, and eventually Alexis de Tocqueville, Giuseppe
Mazzini, and John Stuart Mill that was profoundly suspicious of the destructive and violent nature of competitive commercial individualism. Advocates of
harmonious personality and society, and arguing for the socially conditioned
nature of individual development, positive liberals were not always statists, but
they required some institution of sociability, often religious, philanthropic,
or moral, as the necessary remedy to individualism and private, inegalitarian
concentrations of power.[42] Greeley thus linked Association's more general
hostility toward industrial individualism to the Whigs' longstanding opposition to free trade:

> A more ruinous, demoralizing, anti-social and anti-Christian principle
> than that of FREE COMPETITION—or, as it should properly be
> termed, *reductive, ruinous and hostile Competition*—was never established
> in Society. . . . People look upon Free Competition as the life of busi-
> ness, and the means of maintaining fair prices in Society. It produces a
> false, jarring and feverish life, it is true, which is disgusting to look at,
> and it cuts down the price of Labor, (and, as a consequence, the Prod-
> ucts of Labor) until the Working Classes are reduced to abject want.[43]

Greeley's pro-labor reform socialism, then, was not antithetical to his Whiggery when we take into account the larger party's ambivalent relationship to
laissez-faire individualism.

French Romantic socialism, traditionally framed, in Jonathan Beecher's words, as a mere "'curtain raiser' to Marxian socialism," was actually part of a much broader reaction in the West against the way in which even early industrialization led to the "breakdown of traditional associations" and the alienation of individuals "from any kind of corporate structure."[44] The revolt against individualism was a widely shared phenomenon that united disparate groups, individuals, and institutions across the discursive spectrum opposed to the culture's seemingly rootless materialism. In the United States, the critique of individualism was also put to both progressive and conservative uses. Evangelicals condemned devotion to money. Newspapers covered suicides, insanity, drunkenness, and murder to the point of obsession. Workers and their intellectual allies bemoaned the decline of skill, repetitive work, and conditions of labor that deprived most workers of the opportunity for intellectual uplift. Proslavery theorists condemned the absence of reciprocal ties in the North. Both Brisbane and Orestes Brownson received a sympathetic hearing from South Carolina politician and proslavery ideologue John Calhoun, and Brownson's quixotic journey from proto-Marxist Transcendentalism to Catholicism is comprehensible within the cultural context of his broadly antimodern search for a more organic communal society. The revolt against individualism was what linked the *Tribune*'s Fourierism and its Whiggery and was the basis of Greeley's self-described ambition to reconcile conservatism and radicalism.[45]

The term *individualism* itself was first used by French disciples of Saint-Simon, and it described a world dominated by specialists, with social ties based on little beyond self-interest and contract. Individualism generally, but more often its symptoms, were resisted by both the Right and the Left. Saint-Simon hoped to construct a new France under the guidance of a scientific elite that would usher in a "new Christian" age of brotherhood and universal abundance. Robert Owen experimented with model factories at New Lanark that would raise the standard of living of workers and, more important, release creative and intellectual energies. Conservatives such as Edmund Burke seemed to be searching for the term in his critiques of the French Revolution. Thomas Carlyle indicted free trade and industrial capitalism in *Past and Present* and elsewhere.[46] In France, post-Lockean liberals blamed individualism for the destruction of an organic society based in the Catholic Church. Lacking fixed hierarchies and vertical attachments, Tocqueville described a United States that was the apotheosis of a kind of liberal individualistic social order that produces a general feeling of social detachment, status anxiety, and anomie. For Tocqueville, the voluntary association was among the only counterweights in the United States against the excesses of individualism, a vision that was shared in an even more comprehensive way by the Associationists.[47]

Brisbane, in his *Social Destiny of Man* (1840), was in all likelihood the first American to use the term individualism in relation to the United States, and its connotation of economic specialization, social instability, and the fragmented self pervaded the *Tribune* essays that followed.[48] "The Ploughman is hardly any thing but a ploughman,—the Mechanic a dexterous instrument," Brisbane wrote in the *Tribune*. "We want an Order of things in which each individual shall be a whole and true Man or Woman,—a fully developed Being,—morally, intellectually and physically."[49] Individualism, as a concept, emerged from the socialist critique of the new economic order, but it resonated with views across the political and social spectrum, and especially with the deeply held Whig commitment to self-culture.

Whig Socialism and the Idea of Self-Culture

Whiggery, as Daniel Walker Howe points out, was less a political party than a culture, a loose ideology whose strands—when followed out—often went in radically different directions. The Whigs built a party machinery, but theoretically the party was fashioned on the principle that politics, particularly organized party politics, was only one way to reform society, often superseded by morality, religion, and literature.[50] Though the means and ends of Whig reform would increasingly become a contested question (most notably over slavery), the overall goal was not. Whig culture was steeped in the Scottish Common Sense philosophical assumption that ethics, conscience, and benevolence are innate, but require education and encouragement. Consequently, Whig reformers pressed for individual and social morality, reason and rationality, and the subordination of passions and desires both within the realm of politics and beyond it. They thus opposed, in particular, laissez-faire political economy in favor of a more directed and moral sort in which the social organism, like the individual, strove to thwart and submerge selfishness, competition, luxuriousness, and violence. The unifying principle of Whig political economy and self-culture was social and psychological integration and harmony.[51] For some Whigs, this meant that a hierarchy of human faculties corresponded with a hierarchy of social ones, with the educated and the intellectual at the "head" of society. Other Whigs, such as Greeley, held simultaneously to the principle of uplift and to the more democratic harmonization of mind and body, of the mental and manual classes.

Though Whig conceptions of order and hierarchy could be marshaled on behalf of conservative commercial interests, a significant fraction of reform or humanitarian Whigs (Greeley was a conspicuous example) battled to expand and democratize Whig values. As a socialist, Greeley called for a form of social organization in which all citizens, scholars and workers alike, would develop and maximize their physical and mental potentials. Challenged by Democrats who claimed that the Whig emphasis on order, national economic development, and cultivation served the class interest of established groups, Greeley and his allies sponsored a wide array of reforms to expand the circle of self-realized citizenship. The *Tribune* advocated, and was itself among, an array of democratic cultural institutions that included working-men's libraries, lyceums, and technical schools, all of which were designed to extend the privilege of education.

The end of the *Tribune's* Whig political economy, as well as its emphasis on popularizing the best of literature, science, and philosophy, was the social application of the principles of self-culture. Self-culture, as the Unitarian minister William Ellery Channing defined it, was the obligation of the individual to "the unfolding and perfecting of his nature."[52] In Channing's hands, self-culture took on a democratic character, and one that the *Tribune* modeled along with other intellectual descendents, namely the Transcendentalists. Channing's 1840 series of lectures to the Mechanic Apprentices Library Association was perhaps the most direct ancestor of the *Tribune's* socialism and the common core of his reform Whiggery; Greeley even reprinted the essay "On the Elevation of the Laboring Classes" in his populist campaign circular, the *Log Cabin*.[53]

Most historians, however, all too quick to dismiss the varieties of anti-capitalism, have read Channing's "Elevation" as the conservative side of an argument with Orestes Brownson's class politics. They characterize calls by Whig reformers such as Greeley and Channing for true and universal social mobility as lending legitimacy to the existing social order. But to Greeley and Channing, mobility was a comprehensive value, quite distinct from its Horatio Alger successor. Social mobility, for them, was not about riches, or a release from toil or manual labor, or a road to luxury, fashion, or consumer abundance. Channing and Greeley valued work—the struggle upward—mostly in the sense that they viewed independent labor, skill, and exertion as vital to the realization of a noble character. It was a worldview that called for, as Channing put it, the "striving of the will, that conflict with the difficult" in which the "alternation of employments" would be "so diversified as to call the whole man into action." True mobility was both economic and cultural. It involved the democratic extension of psychological, social, and physical harmony toward ends that were fundamentally moral and intellectual: education, civilization, citizenship, and participation in enlightenment. The reform Whig conception of the good society had little to do with affluence and abundance at all, but instead worked to avoid a European-style class and industrial system in which material poverty and dependence produced a kind of intellectual poverty, a class cut off from mental stimulation and with little stake in its community.[54]

Channing's call for self-culture and particularly his program for labor was remarkably consonant with the *Tribune's* later agitation on behalf of Utopian socialist communities. Like later socialists, Channing recognized that the modern "division of labor" was not an unmixed good. It brought about "the perfection of the arts," but it also "tends to dwarf the intellectual powers" and makes modern labor "a monotonous, stupefying round of unthinking toil."[55] In the spirit of Channing, the *Tribune's* call for socialist renewal was a comprehensive and, in many ways, a classically Whig response to the social and spiritual threats of an increasingly specialized economy that called upon fewer and fewer mental and physical faculties. The basis of the socialist community was in the call for the education of the whole person, the "harmonious development" of moral, mental, and physical capacities through labor.[56] The socialist manifestation of self-culture, which placed a heavy emphasis on work, dignified the broad middle strata in a critique of passivity and idleness. Post-Victorian intellectuals have tended to view Whiggish derogations of idleness and leisure as a class-driven celebration of the virtue of work and capitalist self-denial—and even disaffected protomodernist intellectuals in the antebellum period, such as Henry David Thoreau and Whitman, celebrated "un-work" in their distrust of "busy" middle-class conformity and inauthenticity. But nineteenth-century democratic Whigs such as Greeley more commonly depended on a sacralization of work that excoriated both an impoverished illiterate mob and, more angrily, an unproductive aristocracy of speculators and slave owners that maintained a parasitical relation to productive labor.[57] The variety of Whig reforms—popular education, protection, temperance—are often represented as the limit of the "conservative" response to industrialization. But working-class radicals shared with reform Whigs a frustration at the failure of mobility, the inability of journeymen to rise to the independent status of master. Self-culture, seen in this context, was quite prescient in attempting to prevent the spread of specialized, degraded labor and its cultural and social consequences—the alienation of classes and the fragmentation of the self.

Beyond the less politicized realm of nineteenth-century self-culture and religious and cultural reform, *Tribune* socialism was also congruent with traditional Whig political economy, which focused on two main issues: protection and internal improvements. Some Associationists, such as Brisbane, ridiculed

Whig reforms as halfway measures, but the central insight of Whig political economy—that unregulated competition is a social war of all against all—mirrored the concerns of American socialists. The central works of Whig political economy emerged from the orbit of Philadelphia publisher Mathew Carey, who was an Irish immigrant (probably the source of his anticolonial economic nationalism) and a disciple of Alexander Hamilton. His natural and intellectual offspring would become the central ideologues of Whig economic nationalism. His son, Henry Carey, worked at his father's firm until 1835 before devoting himself exclusively to political economy. He would become the most important political economist in America before the Civil War. Mathew Carey's other main disciple was Daniel Raymond, a son of New England living in Maryland. Never successful in law, politics, or academia, Raymond was an anomaly in the South, but he did win the patronage of Carey and also helped pioneer the protectionist critique of laissez-faire individualism.

Raymond in particular, as a constitutional theorist and especially as a political economist, shared with the Associationists the notion that the end of the righteous society was solidarity, harmony, and fraternity. The natural state of man was greedy and rapacious and needed to be channeled by law and the state toward socially beneficent ends. Departing from orthodox Smithian free-trade theory, Raymond was, in effect, a neomercantilist, an economic nationalist who argued that the good society protected liberty and opportunity. And unlike the Southern agrarian theorists that dominated American political-economic thought, Raymond cited slavery and the European conquest of the Americas as the embodiment of the anarchical nature of laissez-faire individualism.

Raymond, a proto-Whig ideologue, was hardly a conservative. Like other Whig economic nationalists, he believed in a mixed economy, and supported a positive state that would levy tariffs and taxes, establish a uniform currency, and fund internal improvements. But he was also a critic of inequality, monopoly, and, as an advocate for the laboring poor, strongly supported public education and a fairer distribution of property. On the last, he anticipated later socialists and labor radicals who tried to qualify the absolute inviolability of private property rights. Raymond argued, as socialists would a generation later, that property could only be protected in an absolute sense based on need, productive use, and equal access. The unequal distribution of nature's resources, Raymond maintained, was an unnatural and "legal" monopoly that denied the poor their natural right to God's bounty. In nature, access to the earth's productive resources is unfettered. Human law parcels out access to nature; exclusive possession, then, carries with it responsibilities to the rest of society, which is essentially the landlord to whom the wealthy should pay taxes as social rent. Property then, apart from these limited conditions, was a political, not a natural, right. Raymond, in essence, theorized the artificiality of private property and replaced it with the natural right to labor. Unlike his more radical agrarian intellectual heirs who proposed a general division of land, however, Raymond never followed through on his theoretical insights, apart from a few narrow suggestions to limit and equalize inheritance and to sponsor public works as a means to redistribute income.[58]

The *Tribune*'s political economy was in the tradition of Raymond, but Henry Carey's influence on the paper's "socialist Whiggery" was even more immediate and pronounced. Henry Carey's political economy, though no less democratic, was less morally comprehensive than Raymond's. Carey is most known for protectionism and is (and was) regularly accused of being an apologist for Pennsylvania's manufacturing interests. This critique, however just, overlooks protection's democratic dimensions. Associationists, although they considered protection too narrow a reform, even recognized Carey as something of a fellow traveler.[59] Carey, like the Associationists, believed in the harmony of interests, the importance of community investment in human capital, and the centrality of human institutions (law, politics, education) in the promotion of economic growth. Carey also argued, like the Association-ists, that technology, specialization, and population density on the township model could raise productivity in a manner that would eventually erase class tensions.

It is possible to overstate the relationship of Whig economic nationalism to Association. The socialist *Harbinger,* for example, argued that protection-ism shared socialism's suspicion of laissez-faire, but was not comprehensive enough in its response: "[Even] if we adopted the Tariff policy, and it should bring about all the results he predicts, we should still need Association to perfect the concentric arrangement, and produce those higher spiritual har-monics of which nothing is said.... The difference between our plan and that of Mr. Carey—although they are not adverse—is that he would begin with the action of the Federal government, while we would begin with that of the townships." The Associationists, in sum, were not merely "Carey-ites," but socialism's affinity with Whig economic nationalism makes coherent the relationship between the *Tribune*'s Whiggery and its socialism. Associa-tion, in short, was a specific blueprint for reform, but ideologically it was not antagonistic to the Whigs' traditional economic program. The *Tribune* agitated for socialism because it continued to support what Carl Guarneri refers to as "collective capitalism," a program of national banks, tariffs, and internal improvements to spur modernization, economic growth, orderly progress, and, most important, equal opportunity for economic self-reliance. It was "managed capitalism with a democratic aura by stressing the common purpose of all social groups, the benefits of shared prosperity, and the ease of social mobility."[60]

The *Tribune*'s socialism arguably amounts to the first mature articulation of a social democratic political economy in the history of the United States. During the Early Republic, most American democrats favored an agrarian republic, free trade, and a limited state. Ideologues of Jeffersonian agrarianism argued that the greatest threat to the republic was that government would control all property and wealth and redistribute it to politically corrupting cliques. Their nemesis was Hamiltonian economic nationalism, which used the federal government to advance special economic interests. Through institutions and measures such as national banks, internal improvements, tariffs, and the judiciary, Hamiltonian nationalism created an aristocracy of special privilege that threatened the virtuous independence of the agrarian majority. The laissez-faire principle was also at the center of the political battles of the 1830s, but it was at that precise moment that the spread of the market began to reshape fundamentally the conditions of labor. Once an ideal that purported to protect Northern artisans and Southern yeoman from corruption within an agrarian, decentralized, precapitalist republic, laissez-faire unleashed a commercial system that seemed to many younger reformers to be atomistic and anarchistic. Whig political economy, because it renewed agitation for a more active national state, has often been misinterpreted within the legacy of Hamiltonian antidemocratic Federalism, ignoring the way the Whig Party's two most influential political economists, Henry Carey and Daniel Raymond, wedded economic development with the elevation of labor. Though it was hardly anticapitalist, the moral nationalism of Whig political economy made room for more progressive and even radical critiques of laissez-faire that moved beyond the dilemmas of the preindustrial republican era. By the 1840s, a social democratic Whig such as Greeley was able to articulate a new threat to republican liberty and independence—private concentrations of wealth and property—and proposed both statist and voluntaristic solutions to economic and cultural inequality.[61]

Jeffersonian antistatism was part of a broad, "plain people's" program, but the *Tribune* helped inaugurate a popular reconsideration of individualism and laissez-faire. Along with Northern intellectuals, reformers, and labor, the *Tribune* raised considerable new doubts about the "no government" principle, particularly its capacity to protect labor and the propertyless from the coercive power of private economic interests.[62] In the language of Jeffersonian agrarianism, monopoly, privilege, and aristocracy were the products of a too powerful government. By the 1830s and 1840s, progressive political economy now blamed abstract economic forces for creating what was termed a "new feudalism," a class of economic lords and a subordinate class of economically and culturally unrealized dependents. The *Tribune* asserted the primacy of economic relationships and, like later social democrats, claimed that laissez-faire was less an antidote for aristocracy than it was a recipe for class hierarchies, individualism, and private concentrations of wealth.[63] Even progressive Democrats, bound as they were to their party's traditional commitment to limited government, began to struggle with their party's advocacy of laissez-faire individualism.[64]

Even though some of Greeley's political friends, such as Whig Party boss Thurlow Weed, were suspicious of his Fourierist "delusion" and believed that his association with the movement had "lessened the circulation of his paper, and impaired public confidence in his judgment," the reality was that the *Tribune*'s "radicalism," as its ideological opponents would term it, had little effect on its popular success.[65] Within a year of its founding, it joined the *Herald* as one of the most widely circulated dailies in the city. The *Weekly* edition's large national circulation made the *Tribune* the most influential and widely read paper in the North. The paper's socialism, moreover, must also be counted a success. Associationism had, within just a few years, become a large-scale popular movement. But there were dark clouds on the horizon. Greeley's *Tribune* labored to present socialism as a conservative and sober solution to a dangerous industrial crisis that would threaten all levels of society. And on the ground of political economy, its critique of (if not its solution to) industrial labor and social dislocation did go virtually unchallenged. But on the "culture question"—the way in which socialism challenged what came to be termed "traditional values"—Association provoked conservative dissents so vigorous that they even upset the tenuous balance within the socialist movement itself between emancipatory individualism and communitarian fraternity.

Social Democracy and Conservative Whiggery

The *Tribune*'s strident advocacy of a socialist future placed it at odds with much of its party culture. In 1842, a "Whig farmer" wrote the *Tribune* to praise it for ministering to a "moral and intellectual taste" that shamed "the flood of trashy publications which now administer 'light reading' to the 'light minds' which have been depraved by such fustian 'literature.'" By the middle 1840s, though, the paper and its editor would come to be viewed by much of the religious and mercantile press as an "agrarian," an "infidel," and a

"Jacobin": a threat to the nation's moral and political fabric. Within the culture of Whiggery, socialism would drive the *Tribune* into a series of public controversies that bore the marks of a modern culture war.[66]

As early as 1841, Greeley's "isms" had ruffled conservative feathers within the party. Not long after the *Tribune* started publication of Brisbane's column, one reader objected to the "'jack-o-lantern'...'quagmires'" of social theory in the paper, professing that the answer to economic hardship remained a "family Bible in the corner" and a "church on the hill."[67] Socialism's success as a social movement transformed the low rumble of conservative Whig objections in the early 1840s into an open break by the middle part of the decade. Greeley's break with conservative Whiggery was, however, neither idiosyncratic nor rooted only in his socialism. His political patron, William Henry Seward, also struggled against religious and economic conservatives throughout the 1840s. Seward supported public funding for Catholic schools that instructed children in their native language and faith, and even more radically backed the Hudson Valley's small tenant farmers in their struggle against the landlords during the Anti-Rent rebellion.[68] An ecstatic advocate of Seward's measures, Greeley outpaced his patron, espousing a Whiggery that was culturally pluralistic and democratic. Emblematic of the cultural divide in the party was the 1846 state constitutional convention where Greeley backed two controversial measures, black suffrage and women's property rights, that placed him at odds with conservative critics.[69] In New York, the Whig Party was clearly beginning to crack.

Conservative attacks upon Greeley began in earnest in 1844. The erratic but generally reactionary *Courier and Enquirer* fashioned a conservative-populist critique of Greeley that caricatured the editor as a deluded intellectual whose attachments to the cause of labor were opportunistic and romantically detached from working-class realities. The *Courier* belittled Greeley's vegetarianism, his religious infidelity, and his eccentric appearance, and tried to reformulate the labor question into a debate about values. By the summer of 1845, the *Tribune* was engaged in a full-blown culture war. The Whig *Express* joined the *Courier*'s war on the *Tribune*'s "infidelism," charging that "the Tribune would fain have the Whig party of the North and South become Fourierites, Socialists, Agrarians, Anti-Renters, anti-Capital Punishment people, Repealers, [and] Transcendentalists." The *Tribune*'s socialism, which by the mid-1840s was increasingly wedded to the notion of land reform, threatened "to excite the prejudices of the poor against the rich...to array one class of society against the other."[70] If the conservative papers charged Greeley with infidelism and class warfare, the *Tribune* responded by labeling conservative resistance to any sort of interference by guilds, unions, or associations in the private bargain between employers and employed as "loco focoism."[71] To the *Tribune,* the "'Let us alone,' 'Buy where you can cheapest,' 'Let Trade regulate itself,' maxims of the Free Traders" were alien to the traditions of the Whig Party. "We believe this question of *securing* to every one an opportunity to labor and a just recompense for his work, is the great question of our day," the *Tribune* concluded. "We do not say that its complete solution is within the sphere of Government; but we *do* say that Government should aid in doing it to the utmost of its power, and should at least be careful not to throw any obstacles in its way."[72]

Greeley's battle with conservatives in his own party would culminate in the fall and winter of 1846–47 in his debate over socialism with *Courier and Enquirer* editor Henry Raymond, a discussion that James Parton, Greeley's first biographer, remembered as the "grand climax of the Tribune's Fourierism." In fact, Parton claimed the debate itself *"finished* Fourierism in the United States." Parton no doubt exaggerated, but at the very least the dispute exposed "the nearly unbearable tension between Fourierist principles and Associationist policy," and did so at the very moment that the movement's practical communitarian experiments were unraveling.[73] Nonetheless, the public series of letters between the two editors, later published as *Association Discussed,* illustrated not only cleavages within the Whig Party's political economy but also within American understandings of free labor itself. Though most Americans still held that poverty was either a moral or a political problem, Greeley's support for Association laid out alternative structural social and economic explanations of the causes of inequality.

Raymond and his paper had been trying to goad the *Tribune* into a debate on socialism since August 1846 (and did manage to incite a small exchange with Brisbane, but one that Greeley quickly squelched). By the time Greeley and Raymond did debate, Fourierism as a practical experiment was in a death spiral. But Raymond's motive for engaging Greeley went beyond discrediting socialism. Raymond actually hoped to make socialism an issue in the fall of 1846, because off-year elections were moments when state parties, unconstrained by the need to suppress factional differences for the sake of the national ticket, could vent disagreements within the party in an effort to shape its ideological and institutional future. Given the stakes, Greeley smartly refused extended discussion of the social question until after the election season had ended.

Throughout the 1840s, the Whig Party was internally divided between progressive and conservative wings. Publicly, the former was represented by the *Tribune* and the latter by James Watson Webb's *Courier* and James Erastus Brooks's *Express.* Although both factions supported, in principle, the

FIGURE 4. Daguerreotype of Henry Raymond, ca. 1844–56. Although Raymond was a protégé of Greeley, he would become, as editor of the *Courier and Enquirer* and cofounder of the *New York Times,* his bitter rival. Courtesy of the Library of Congress, Prints and Photographs Division, LC-USZ62-109842.

economic nationalism of Senator Henry Clay's American system, they were divided by issues related to culture and class. The progressive wing reached out to workers, small farmers, immigrants, and blacks, and was friendly to reforms such as abolitionism that mainstream political culture despised. The conservatives were nativists, sympathetic to Southern interests, and defended a rigid social order, all the while waging war against culturally suspect reformers. The progressive Weed-Greeley-Seward wing was clearly the more popular faction of the party, but Whig Party divisions allowed the Democrats to take power in the state, most importantly at the state constitutional convention held that summer. The Webb faction of the party had opposed constitutional revision. Reform Whigs tried to combine with progressive

Democrats in an effort to secure an antislavery, black, immigrant, and Anti-Rent pro-revision majority. This effort failed and Democratic control over the convention all but tabled black suffrage measures (and the issue was later rejected by the voters after it was presented as a separate measure), but internal Whig divisions, exacerbated by the 1846 constitutional convention, carried over into the fall when the Whigs gathered to select a slate of candidates for the forthcoming election. The shape of the party's identity came to a head in the choice of the Whig gubernatorial nominee. In the person of John Young, a Livingston County Anti-Rent Whig, the progressive faction of the party prevailed.

Raymond's war against Association that autumn, then, was an attempt to discredit progressive Whiggery during a period of internal partisan division. As John Young's election would later attest, progressive Whiggery's quasi-populist economic program resonated with voters and threatened to rob the Democratic Party of its identification with democracy.[74] To the conservatives, the success of reform Whiggery counted for very little because they betrayed the party's core commitments: the rule of law, property, and contract. Raymond's goal in the debate over Association, then, was to link the efforts of progressive Whigs to institute a more democratic economic order with cultural radicalism. Association, he would argue, had little to do with the economy at all. Rather, it was an effort to trespass against the sanctity of the traditional family, religion, and even Christian prohibitions against sin.

The rancor between the *Courier* and the *Tribune* was a product of close familiarity. The world of New York newspapers was a small one, and the circle of Whig editors was even smaller; in the competition for patronage and political influence, editorial rivalries were often more severe within parties than without. In 1840, James Watson Webb tried to secure Greeley as a political correspondent in Albany.[75] Henry Raymond, the managing editor of the *Courier* and Greeley's opponent in the Association debate, was formerly Greeley's protégé and had been an assistant editor of the *Tribune* until 1843. Webb himself was one of the more mercurial figures in the history of American politics. He had once been aligned with the Democrats, endorsing hard money, free trade, and a fugitive slave law, and opposing the tariff and a new charter for the Second Bank of the United States. In the service of Tammany, which had close ties to the city's banking, mercantile, and real estate interests, he duly attacked National Republicans, Anti-Masons, and the Working Men's Party. But in 1832, aided by a substantial loan from Nicholas Biddle, Webb abandoned the party of Jackson and its signature causes. Thereafter, the *Courier* became arguably the leading mercantile sheet in the city, but its circulation was dwarfed by the emerging penny papers.[76]

When Webb hired Henry Raymond away from the *Tribune* in 1843, it was not entirely clear that Raymond's relationship to his former employer would unravel to the extent that it did. Raymond had met Greeley in 1838 when, as an eighteen-year-old student at the University of Vermont, he traveled to Albany with a letter of introduction from Rufus Griswold. In 1840, he started a regular correspondence with Greeley that soon landed him a position on the *New-Yorker*.[77] When Greeley launched the *Tribune*, Raymond became its lead reporter on major stories, such as the murder trials of Alexander McLeod and John Colt. He also managed the paper's literary department and covered the city's cultural events. But their relationship was not destined to last. After Greeley struck up a friendship with Albert Brisbane, Raymond's conservatism became more pronounced. When the two launched the socialist *Future*, Raymond was among the conservative Whigs across the city who were shocked, though he presumably kept his opinions private. In correspondence, though, he referred to Brisbane as a "flippant, brainless jackanape" and called Greeley a "delectable ass." To Weed, Raymond opined that Greeley's Fourierism would only jeopardize the "commanding influence which he possesses." Though not overly religious himself, Raymond worried that Greeley "inclines to materialism.... He believed the mind to be the *result* of the body ... and in all his aims seeks only to make the outward condition of his fellows comfortable."[78]

Greeley recognized Raymond's talents, but he also gradually realized that they were ideologically incompatible. As his editor, Greeley modified the "ultra-Federalism" of Raymond's articles; privately, he scolded his apprentice for being "infernally Tory in your leanings, both in Church and State," warning him not to "cut me off ... from the sympathies of the true democracy."[79] In October 1843, James Watson Webb offered Raymond twenty-five dollars a week to help edit the *Courier*—five dollars more than Raymond made at the *Tribune*. He asked Greeley to match the offer and was refused.[80] The *Tribune* publicly wished Raymond well, but only a month would elapse before Greeley's former protégé would be attacking the *Tribune* for its cultural transgressions in ways that would become increasingly common from the mid-1840s onward:

> With Mr. Greeley's Fourierism we have no disposition to find fault, and in truth, no more right to do so, than with his Bran-bread-ism. He has a perfect right to follow Fourier and Graham wherever he pleases, and it is no part of our business to rebuke him; but when as the Editor of a popular Whig Journal he ventures to urge his idle theories upon the Corporation of our city for their adoption, it is our duty gravely to rebuke his fanaticism, and to protest against his folly and monomania being made to attach to the Whig party.[81]

When the Association debate began, Raymond wrote on behalf of the conservative wing of his party that he was unnerved by Fourierism's rapid spread and its theoretical appeal. Throughout 1846, conservative and religious journals, such as the *American Whig Review,* the *Universalist Quarterly,* and the *New York Observer,* published articles that argued that Association threatened Christian values and assaulted conventional sexual and familial morality. Association's most committed activists, too, were drawn into extended discussions of Fourier's "cultural reforms" of church, family, and marriage, the first glimmers of the various lifestyle reforms—dress reform, vegetarianism, free love, spiritualism, and phrenology—that would preoccupy the socialist community in the 1850s. Typical was Parke Godwin. Once one of the movement's most practical-minded coalition builders, he now argued against timid deference to conventional and religious morality: "They never would be with us, and never can, and I should take no pains to conciliate them, rather than state the whole truth." Charles Dana concurred. Though he refrained from "enter[ing] into a minute criticism of society in regard to its sexuality," Dana agreed that "Fourier's sexual theories are an essential part of *his* system."[82]

This mid-1840s drift in the movement toward lifestyle questions unnerved Greeley, and in his view diverted socialism's focus from what he considered the central issues of the era: the relationship of capital to labor, economic opportunity, and the conditions of work. Greeley would always resist novelty on moral issues—the "question of marriage" especially—but the increasingly countercultural bent of the socialist movement could not help but shape his discussion with Raymond from the outset.[83] Raymond had actually hoped to debate Brisbane, knowing that he was more likely than Greeley to be baited into a consideration of sex, religion, and marriage. Greeley's refusal to allow Brisbane to participate and his adamant condition that they debate Association only "as the *Tribune* understands it" exemplifies Greeley's trepidations about socialism's countercultural trajectory, his fear of being "held responsible for whatever the Courier may find in the voluminous writings of a dozen persons."[84] It should come as no surprise, then, that when Greeley opened the debate in late November, he justified "radical Social Reform" in terms set forth in the Old Testament; in his fifth letter, he appealed to the Declaration of Independence.

After some petty and public squabbling, both editors agreed to write twelve letters each on the "principles" and "features" of "social reform," and both promised to publish all twenty-four in both newspapers. Greeley always wrote first and Raymond responded. Both editors also agreed to limit their remarks to a single column, but Raymond, early in the discussion, violated the terms, and it was not long before both editors were churning out letters of two and even three columns. Writing first, Greeley nominally controlled the direction of the debate, particularly at the beginning, but Raymond, in his rebuttals, was able to raise enough questions about the culture of Association that Greeley was lured into an exchange eventually focused on morality, religion, marriage, and family. Though both editors complained of space limitations, the discussion was often repetitive. All told, the controversy lasted nine months, stretching from late August 1846 to May 1847, when Raymond finally concluded the exercise.

Greeley opened the debate on November 20 with an exposition of general principles. He made a case for radical social reform based on a quasi-agrarian conception of land use and property rights. Greeley argued that, because the Creator appointed nature for the sustenance and use of all humanity, private property, without a corresponding system of obligations or compensations, was a legal form of dispossession. "By a law of Nature, every person born in the State of New York had (unless forfeited by crime) a perfect right to *be* here, and to his equal share of the Soil, the woods, the waters, and all the natural products thereof," Greeley argued, but "by law," he complained, "the landless have no inherent right to stand on a single square foot of the State of New York except in the highways." This discrepancy did not lead Greeley to conclude that all landed property is theft, but to insist, rather, that the "only solid ground on which his surrender of the original property of the whole to a minor portion can be justified is that of the Public Good."[85] Private property, in short, was a political rather than a natural right, and one that makes exclusive possession contingent on public welfare.[86]

On the right of property in land, Greeley was emerging from two very distinct traditions. On the one hand, he condemned large holdings and feudal-style land grants, and believed that in a fundamental sense the right of property is derived from labor and productive use. Greeley at this juncture was even in the tradition of more conservative Whig modernizers who had long campaigned for liberal incorporation laws and the right of eminent domain, and who were more than willing to trespass private property if it served the end of capitalist development and progress. Other, more religiously inclined conservatives were also willing to qualify property rights for moral reasons. The conservative communitarian Calvinist Nathaniel Niles declared that God's Creation remained "common property" beholden to the "good of the community" and the "public interest." The radical evangelical Joel Barlow called "society" the "first proprietor" and held that private property is neither a natural right nor would it endure in a more rational social order. In a broad sense, Greeley's qualification of property rights, especially in a condition of monopoly or gross inequality, placed him with John Locke, Adam Smith, James Harrington, Tom Paine, Thomas Jefferson, and James Madison, all of whom, in one form or another, made access to productive property the foundation of a stable social system and the highest duty of political society.[87]

But Greeley also drew from a more radical tradition of political economy that stretched back to the English political economist David Ricardo and his American heirs: Langton Byllesby, Thomas Skidmore, Orestes Brownson, and contemporary land reformers Joseph Campbell and John Pickering. Ricardo and his heirs maintained that a nation's natural resources are limited and that politics shaped the conditions of market exchange between landlords, manufacturers, and labor. Ricardo accepted the market, but argued that as growing populations pressed against natural limits and scarcity, landed political monopolies would inevitably disrupt natural values based on labor.[88] Greeley followed suit. "One inevitable consequence of the prevailing system," he stressed, "is that, as Population increases and Arts are perfected, the income of the wealthy owner of land increases while the recompense of the hired or leasehold cultivator is steadily diminishing."[89] Though some labor radicals such as Thomas Skidmore embraced radical agrarianism—a "general division" and redistribution of all property—Greeley, naturally, never went that far: "The past can not be recalled. What has been rightfully (however mistakenly) done by the authorized agents of the state or nation can only be retracted upon urgent public necessity, and upon due satisfaction to all whose private rights are thereby invaded." Rather than a forced redistribution of land on Skidmore's model, Greeley posited that the right of property, theoretically if not practically suspect, should be made contingent on the right to labor: "The Right to Labor, secured to all, is the inexorable condition of the honest, independent subsistence of the Poor. It must be fully guaranteed to all, so that each may know that he can never starve nor be forced to beg while able and willing to work."[90]

In this early stage of the debate, Greeley's arguments were characteristic of his thought more generally. He was wont to invoke progressive theory as a means to avoid even more radical alternatives. The right to labor, Association, land reform, and the ten-hour day were reforms designed to restore congenial social relations, elevate and refine the working class, and encourage proletarian investment in an orderly and lawful society. Greeley prized orderly reform as an alternative to violent revolution. Association, thus, was a modest response to the era's ills. It merely substituted for "the present Township"—or "whatever the smallest Social Organization above the Family"—a system of communal life that would secure and guarantee housing, education, subsistence, work, fair "wages," and cultural uplift. It could be instituted without revolutionary upheaval or trespassing on traditional rights. Its efficient use of land and its economies of fences, fuel, transportation, household labor, technology, education, and commercial exchange would raise the productivity and wealth of the entire community. Addressing the problem of social inequality but without painful dislocations, Association, in Greeley's mind, was true to the values of the Whig Party's liberal wing. Association, Greeley hoped, would "level upwards."[91]

Raymond's response to Greeley took two basic tacks. In a general theoretical sense, he rejected the qualification of the right of property upon which the entire socialist project was based. To Raymond, property was a natural right and the foundation of a civilized social order, and Greeley's efforts to circumscribe that right placed him in the same company as "Fanny Wright" and the "most radical and ignorant portion of the Loco Foco party."[92] Though Greeley was convinced that his socialism and his Whiggery stemmed from the same moral source, Raymond insisted that socialism rendered "one of the ablest, most adroit, and most influential leaders of the Whig Party" no Whig at all. Socialism colored the *Tribune*'s "whole System of Politics and Morality," "its notices of common events," and "its political theories... [and] measures," and it threatened, prophetically, to "convert the political party with which it acts, into a new party, made up from all existing parties."[93] But when Raymond responded more specifically to Greeley's general outline of Association, he posed questions that would dominate the remainder of the debate and, in essence, the course of noncoercive socialism: "In whom is the property to be vested? How is labor to be remunerated? What share is capital to have in the concern? By what device are men to be induced to labor? How are moral offenses to be excluded, or punished?"[94]

Greeley initially greeted Raymond's questions as if they were simple inquiries. Moral offenses would be punished traditionally and through the mechanism of shame, which would be heightened in the close-knit and intimate associated community. Property, in Association, would be vested in capital. Labor, capital, and skill would be remunerated by a fixed ratio in relation to the total product. Greeley defended Association from charges that the associated community was merely a joint-stock company by explaining that the original investor of capital would not receive the entirety of the added value that was derived from labor and improvement. Greeley estimated that an original $50,000 investment would yield a phalanx worth $500,000. The original capitalists would receive a just proportion of the phalanx's added value, but nine-tenths of the improved phalanx's value would be distributed proportionally to labor and talent. Association, in short, would generate productive workers on the principle of free labor; guaranteed a share of the total product, labor would have the same incentives as the capitalist. Labor, moreover, relieved of repetitive monotony and performed in a festive cooperative social environment, would be spurred into even greater productive spontaneity and creativity.[95]

To Marxists, Association was too close to the standing order to transform it radically; to conservatives, Association threatened the foundations of civilization: private property and the family. At various stages of the debate, both Greeley and Raymond tried to have it both ways, which suggests in one respect communitarian socialism's amorphousness but in other respects could be indicative of its virtue as a middle way. Not long after comparing Greeley to abolitionist and feminist Fanny Wright, Raymond countered that Association actually augmented the power of capital; that under Association, the "men who have Capital," by paying a fixed percentage of the total product to labor and talent, merely replicate the "relation subsisting between... *Landlord* and *Tenants.*" The "Tribune seeks to substitute for that now existing," Raymond mocked, the "essential features... by which all the large estates in the *Anti-Rent* districts have always been held. The property in those estates, just as in an Association, is vested in the men of capital. The laborers upon them... receive a fixed *proportion* of the products of their labor."[96] Greeley responded in kind, cheering Raymond's new and "decided objection to 'extending and perpetuating the [Manorial] system of Land Tenures,'... I shall bear it in mind upon the great question of shielding forever our yet unsold Public Lands from the possibility of being so perverted." But in the same letter, Greeley suggested that Association, with its greater degrees of social interdependence and complexity, was based on the very system of social organization it purported to reform. "Manufacturing Capitalists," he pointed out, "have done more than any other class to demonstrate the vast economies and efficiency of Organized Industry."[97] Without realizing it, Greeley and Raymond had argued themselves into an odd sort of agreement. Raymond attacked Association on the grounds that it replicated an economic arrangement that he and especially his paper had long vigorously defended: the quasi-feudal landlord-tenant relationship that was provoking so much controversy in upstate New York throughout the 1840s. Greeley defended Association on the grounds that it hardly challenged the economic system already in place.

The debate, however, took a crucial turn in mid-December. Until that point, Greeley managed to direct the controversy toward questions of economic justice. About a third of the way into the planned discussion, though, Raymond began to bend the discussion in the direction of culture and morality. Initially, Raymond merely suggested that "social evils"—social evils that, in his view, the *Tribune* exaggerated—"grow out of the defects or vices of individual character, and are only to be remedied by individual and personal reform."[98] Whereas Greeley contended that "the organization of Society" was largely responsible for unemployment and inequality, Raymond maintained that the moral and individual failures of the poor were responsible for their own condition.[99] Raymond held, moreover, that the prospect of private gain was the sole possible spur to hard work, productivity, and efficiency. Social and economic life, he believed, required both incentive and discipline. Given these assumptions, Raymond questioned whether labor could be organized on a cooperative and democratic basis, and without compulsion, power, or economic and social hierarchy.

In many respects, Raymond's perspective on the relationship between labor and discipline reflected widespread ambivalence about how laissez-faire individualism could actually function in practice. Most moderate and conservative procapitalist Whigs were convinced that the lure of self-interest would compel people to work in this new social universe of free labor. But self-interest depended on social mobility, and always looming in the background was the specter of a permanent wage-earning class. If proletarian England was the future, it was one that threatened the sustainability of the free-labor model. Mainstream Whigs argued for protection so that wages would remain high enough to enable workers to make the leap to individual proprietorship.[100] Like them, Raymond also prized the productive efficiency of incentive, but feared that, for subordinate groups, the economic and moral order could not be sustained without various forms of discipline and coercion. For workers, he insisted on the inward spur of poverty and starvation, and the outward constraints of traditional religion and the patriarchal family. In all, Raymond suspected that socialism would emancipate workers, women, and other subordinate groups from long-established restraints and the result would be anarchy. In this respect, the debate over culture, individual morality, marriage, and the family that ensued, while distinct, was also intimately connected to the question of political economy and the social order.[101]

Starting in January, Raymond accelerated his attack on Association's "moralities." Raymond avowed that Association was hopelessly naive about the "inherent vices... [and] essential *selfishness* of man," and ignored the fundamental human frailties "at war with the essential principles of Association": "While men continue victims or imperfect, while they are governed or influenced by prejudice, passion, or self-seeking in any of its forms, they can not combine and carry forward such a community as that proposed." Raymond was striking at a one of antebellum reform's central dilemmas: Could social reform precede individual reform? This question was particularly central to Fourierists, and many of them wavered.[102] Greeley admitted earlier in the debate that quarrelsome persons "must have a new spirit breathed into them before they can comprehend and act upon the vital principles of Social Unity." Raymond even quoted the damning testimony of Transcendentalist activist and reformer Charles Lane: "Manners which are quite passable in individuals become intolerable in association.... Thus the conclusion at which most men have arrived, is that... a superior race of human beings is requisite to constitute a superior human society."[103]

Raymond pointed out that Association's promise to be both the cause and the effect of individual reformation was logically untenable. Convinced of the precedence of individual moral reform, Raymond defended traditional values, threatened in his view by Association's romantic spontaneity and moral relativism. "The personal reform of individual men must precede Association," he argued, and the "agency" of individual renewal "is Christianity": "We have a right to insist that Reformers shall *commence* their labors by making individual men *Christians:* by seeking their personal, moral transformation. When that is accomplished, all needed Social Reform will either have been effected or rendered inevitable."[104] Raymond's assertion of a Christian reform alternative to Association was intimately tied to his defense of the traditional family. Association, he charged, collectivized the care of children and, in a basic way, threatened "*the authority and control of PARENTS over their children.*" Worse still, children and wives would no longer be pecuniary dependents on their fathers and husbands: "A wife, if the term be then retained, will keep her own name, retain her liberty of heart and of action, and be in short entirely independent of her husband in all respects. Will that be the relation recognized as that of husband and wife in the Word of God! Will it be any thing more than a copartnership for certain purposes between the two?"[105] This early attack was overshadowed by what followed in March, when Raymond made an all-out assault on Fourierist passional theory, pushing beyond the family into the realm of marriage and sex.

Raymond argued correctly that the Fourierist edifice was built upon the theory of the passions, which he defined as the "*feelings, [and] free impulses of Man [that] point out to him the path on which he should walk, the relations he should form, the labor he should do, the functions he should discharge, and generally, the whole course of life which he ought to pursue*" (Raymond's italics). He also quoted Parke Godwin's more succinct depiction of the how the passions operated within an associated system. "Reason and Passion," he wrote, "will be in perfect accord; duty and pleasure will have the same meaning; without inconvenience or calculation, *man will follow his bent;* hearing only of Attraction, he will never act from necessity, and *never curb himself by restraints*" (Raymond's italics). For some time, Raymond had attacked the relationship of Association to family discipline and authority. He also repeatedly prodded Greeley on the question of labor discipline. Greeley was able to answer both charges with reasonable persuasiveness. Earlier in the debate Raymond also had gestured to the free rein given to the affections under Fourier's theory, but here, finally, he did not euphemize:

> How will it [i.e., passional theory] guide and control...the relations of the sexes.... What does the theory of the System require? When a man has a special passion for a dozen kinds of work, he joins a dozen *groups.* When he has a special passion for a dozen kinds of study, he joins a dozen *groups.* So, if the System be carried out, if its fundamental principle be not abandoned as a System—if a man comes to have a *passion* for a dozen women, *there must be a dozen different groups for his full development and gratification.*[106]

Until this point, the debate had been primarily about political economy and the labor question, and to this extent it pitted Raymond's Christian individual moral reform against Greeley's structural interpretation of the social origins of poverty. Here, though, Raymond transformed the terms of the debate. Greeley only recognized socialism as a solution to the labor question, but Raymond recast it as a scheme to reorganize the family and as a movement for sexual liberation.

Greeley had long bragged of Association's theoretical comprehensiveness, but Raymond made Fourier's social and psychological reach its greatest danger. He revealed the way in which Fourierism, because it rejected power, discipline, and coercion, was underwritten by a Romantic proto-Freudian sense of the psychic costs of repression—a sensibility that in Fourierist form seemed to countenance free love. "This is the great principle which Fourier discovered, and upon it are based the whole theory and practice of Association," Raymond concluded. "All the passions of Man, it is held, are divine in their origin, and good in themselves. Evil flows only from their repression or subversion. Give them full scope, free play, a perfect and complete development, and universal happiness must be the result."[107] Association, he argued, counseled a moral relativism explicitly forbidden by "the teachings of the Bible." Where Association obeys the "law of nature," Christianity implores humanity to rise above its passions, "to repress, deny, and subject to the higher law of conscience the passions and appetites of his nature." Association, instead, refuses to "admit the existence of *Sin,* except in the form of suffering. Nothing, in its view, is good or bad, right or wrong, intrinsically, but only as it produces happiness or misery.... It recognizes no absolute distinction between right and wrong."[108]

Raymond's charges rendered Greeley apoplectic. He attempted to return the discussion to the basic questions of political economy: property rights and the monopolization of land, the oversupply of labor, falling living standards in an age of skyrocketing productivity, and the inefficiency of the competitive system.[109] Despite recent controversies on the marriage question in the pages of the *Harbinger* and the religious press, and even his own long efforts to conceal the sexual implications of passional theory, Greeley seemed unprepared to answer Raymond's charges that socialism abolished monogamous marriage. From the beginning of the discussion, Greeley had hoped to cordon off any reference to marriage and sex. He declared repeatedly that he would only defend "Association as I understand it." In his eighth letter, he referred to and quoted the general resolution from the first convention of the American Union of Associationists that distanced the American movement from the more "conjectural" theories of their French master. Ultimately, Greeley resisted making any response to Raymond's charges on "Love, Marriage, [and] Conjugal Duty," beyond that "*I* have propounded no such theory; much less asserted that such Attraction is to be universally followed." "Human beings," he insisted, "will no more desire change in the conjugal relation than to be continually swapping children with their neighbors."[110] But in the end, Greeley abandoned Fourier's theory of passional attraction altogether:

> Fourier's idea that God governs the Universe throughout by Attraction— that this is the law of life and health for all intelligent beings—is a grand and inspiring one: it may possess great practical value when we come to fully understand and apply it. But, when he conceded that there will be human beings truly educated and living in a wisely ordered Social State, who will deliberately abandon a life of purity to wallow in incontinence and sensuality, he proves, not perhaps that his Law is fictitious, but that he knows not how to apply it.

Defensive and defeated, Greeley had lost ground. Reduced to personal attacks, he represented himself as a martyr to a truth, a truth even he was no longer willing to defend.

Greeley's efforts to suppress the familial implications of Association were to no avail and somewhat disingenuous. For Raymond and Greeley, and for conservatives and socialists more generally, the debate over the family was tied intrinsically to debates about political economy and the market. Not only was the character and function of the family a kind of metaphor through which Americans questioned, what, within an economic system increasingly designed around mutual self-interest, their obligations to one another. But more broadly, the family had always been the principal framework within which most economic activity was carried out; as socialists particularly sensed, the modern nuclear family was the midwife of a bourgeois value system that made a market society possible. As such, even outside of their dialogues with their conservative critics, American socialists were divided in their views on the family. Association's corporatism, in one respect, was intended to replicate familial ties. But more radical Associationists and other communitarian socialists viewed the nuclear family itself as a symptom of modern individualism. Robert Owen maintained that the nuclear family represented the selfish instinct at its worst, a system of social organization that reflected the tyranny of competitive society and its system of private property. The aforementioned Charles Lane, for example, eventually ended up in a Shaker community where he thought abstinence would instill Christian fraternal feeling. Brisbane wrote in the *Social Destiny of Man* that "the family spirit, which, tending to selfishness, should be absorbed by corporative ties. A man, connected from passion with thirty groups exercising divers branches of industry, will be as strongly attached to the interests of these thirty groups as to those of his family."[111]

Unlike his more culturally radical brethren, Greeley's critique of the family was more limited and rested on pragmatic rather than moral grounds. Greeley maintained only that present conditions of want made ideal family life impossible. Industrial individualism, in his view, was not the extension of familial selfishness. Instead, he argued, modern economic conditions rendered the corporate defense of the nuclear family inadequate. Unlike countercultural Associationists who were drawn to cooperative theory as an alternative to middle-class moral conventions, Greeley maintained that capitalist and familial values were antagonistic, and that the cooperative basis of Associative life was based in the spirit of familial love. This sensibility made him an outright conservative on questions such as divorce, but it also allowed him to endorse public education, companionate marriage, women's property rights, communal child care, and to attack without qualification the "practical slavery of the Wife to the Husband," the "pecuniary" dependence of women, and Raymond's implicit assertion that the basis of the family is economic subjection rather than love.[112] While Raymond believed that Christianity and the family undergirded an economic system based on propertied individualism, Greeley viewed socialism as an extension of Christian and familial principles and as being explicitly opposed to the materialism and atomism of the market.[113]

When the debate concluded, Fourierism was already in eclipse, but Raymond's moral attacks made it, as an orthodox body of theoretical doctrines, heretical in many quarters. Nonetheless, Association's more general indictment of industrial capitalism had in the end also been left virtually uncontested. Raymond even conceded, in the end, the existence of "social evils," even if he termed Greeley's solution "so radical, so sweeping...[and] silently poisoning the public mind with false notions of natural rights and of personal obligation." Raymond simply never mounted a forceful challenge to the more general principle that capitalist inequality, and the social problems it precipitated, required some kind of active intervention. He managed to discredit socialism, but it is not as if his neo-Federalism—his defense of a conservative, organic, and hierarchical order—carried the day either. Even he, despite his opposition to Jacksonianism, would abandon it, becoming over the course of the 1850s and 60s an unabashed proponent of a laissez-faire, liberal, contractual society: in short, a proto–Gilded Age Republican.[114] Greeley, in this debate and elsewhere, had demonstrated that industrial society was slowly progressing toward a social crisis. He established the fruitlessness of private charity and of individual moral reform, as well as, moreover, the social causes of poverty. Even more broadly, he had successfully articulated a more expansive framework of liberal natural rights and principles—among other things the right to labor, education, and the social origin of poverty and crime. Although it is probably true, as Greeley's contemporary and biographer James Parton concluded, that the Greeley-Raymond debate *"finished Fourierism in the United States,"* Fourierism's larger indictment of capitalist inequality signaled a transformation of the democratic mentality that was as significant as the Jacksonian political revolution of the 1820s and 1830s.[115]

CHAPTER 2

Transcendental Cultural Democracy

> For see this wide society in which we walk of labor-
> ing men. We allow ourselves to be served by them.
> We pay them money & then turn our backs on them.
> We live apart from them & meet them without
> salute in the streets. We do not greet their talents, nor
> rejoice in their good fortune, nor foster their hopes,
> nor in the assembly of the people vote for what is
> dear to them.
>
> Ralph Waldo Emerson, *Journal*

Henry Raymond's assault on socialist moral-
ity unsettled Greeley. Raymond had introduced a line of attack that would
contribute, along with the failure of the communities themselves, to the
diminished scale that American socialism would take from 1848 onward. It
would also effectively separate the labor question from the paper's broader
critique of American culture. However fantastical, Fourierism was guided
by a commitment to social transformation that combined political economy
with institutional cultural reform—music, lectures, conversation, and science.
Over the course of the nineteenth and twentieth centuries, social democratic liberalism would become increasingly statist and abandon its moral
and self-cultural element. The seeds of that shift were planted in the 1840s
and 1850s. And it was not that reformers lost interest in cultural experimentation and renewal, but rather that conservative attacks such as Raymond's
made it difficult to sustain both moral and economic reorganization within
a single movement. The paper's comprehensive Fourierist mix of countercultural radicalism and labor populism, in short, became separate tributaries.
Despite this theoretical division, the *Tribune*'s ongoing discussion of literature,
marriage, and the family continued to be informed by its social democratic
analysis of the market and its values.

Socialism was not the only source of the *Tribune*'s commitment to democratic
self-culture. New England literary radicalism played an equally important

role. No figure, in fact, embodied the *Tribune*'s cosmopolitanism and its profoundly political understanding of culture more than Margaret Fuller, the paper's literary editor from December 1844 to August 1846.[1] Even before Fuller's arrival, Transcendentalism had profoundly influenced the *Tribune*'s idea of a revitalized democratic society. Transcendentalism, itself a transfigured expression of a certain kind of Yankee religious sentiment, offered the period's most trenchant critique of diverse aspects of market culture. During the 1840s, its preoccupations merged in many ways with those of the socialists. When the Transcendentalists became public intellectuals in the 1840s, they, like the socialists, pondered the fate of American civilization under the shadow of the new economy. They diagnosed and critiqued the country's materialism and anxiety, and lamented the gender, racial, and class inequalities that produced segmented neighborhoods, churches, and public institutions. Though the Transcendentalists were divided in response to socialism itself, the movement shared with Associationism the broad sense of contemporary crisis. To Greeley, the relationship between Transcendentalism and socialism was obvious. The editor remarked in a deceptively Victorian sounding lecture, "The Formation of Character," that he owed whatever was "forcible or striking" in his "views" to the "free-spoken, profound thinkers of our age; and foremost among them to Ralph Waldo Emerson and the little band of earnest, clear-sighted spirits who are more commonly known by the contemptuous appellation of *Transcendentalists.*"[2]

The *Tribune,* in turn, played a central role in the spread of Transcendentalism. Recent work in literary history has demonstrated the extent to which the Transcendentalists, especially Emerson, Thoreau, and certainly Fuller, owed their national reputations to the publicity they received in the *Tribune.* The *Tribune* was, throughout the 1840s, the main source of information about the Transcendentalists and it became the chief outlet for many of the movement's central figures after the collapse of its literary magazine, the *Dial,* and its literary turned Fourierist commune, Brook Farm. As Richard Teichgraeber put it, the *Tribune* was "the single most important source of popular knowledge of Emerson's name and ideas." Greeley "nationalize[d] Emerson's reputation well before any of his publications had gained any significant commercial success" and "his notices of Emerson's early publications and lectures" supplied "the continuing publicity needed to make and keep Emerson's name and writings visible in American culture at large."[3]

Greeley believed that one of the *Tribune*'s special missions was to cultivate and disseminate American literature and thought, and the Transcendentalists were an important component of that mission. In addition to efforts made on behalf of Fuller, Emerson, and Thoreau, the *Tribune* would later employ

George Ripley as its literary critic and fellow Brook Farmer Charles Dana eventually as associate editor. In the 1850s, Dana would become, next to Greeley, the single most important figure in the early history of the newspaper. The *Tribune* also lent vigorous support for corporate Transcendentalist enterprises such as Brook Farm and the *Dial*. But the *Tribune*'s first Transcendentalist refugee was Fuller and her connection to the paper *as a Transcendentalist* was singular. On the *Tribune,* Fuller mediated between Transcendentalism's aspirations for popular democratic reception and influence and the *Tribune*'s desire to translate its socialist critique of the excesses of the market into the realm of literature and culture, broadly understood.

Fuller and Greeley

Both her intellectual background and her sex made Margaret Fuller's decision to join the *Tribune* an unlikely one. She first met with Greeley at the beginning of 1844, but he did not formally offer her a place on the paper until the summer of that year and she, in turn, did not accept immediately. Throughout the summer she debated the offer with herself and Transcendental confidants, and even after she committed to the prospect, confessing to her brother that she finally felt "clear now about doing this," she nonetheless only committed in her own mind to "try it, at least for some months." To another friend Fuller admitted that the "arrangement" was not "seducing" but hopefully could "be turned to much good." Fuller's feelings about the opportunity were clearly mixed. When Fuller began considering the prospect of popular journalism, she had already taken several significant steps toward literary professionalism. She was the first editor of the Transcendentalist magazine, the *Dial*. In the spring of 1844, she published *Summer on the Lakes,* which Greeley termed a "peculiar and eccentric" book, but one rooted in an established travel genre familiar to a mass audience.[4] Nonetheless, newspapers were something different. Even though Fuller respected Greeley's talents, the quality of the paper, and, more vaguely, the project of cultural democracy, she still viewed the prospect without genuine enthusiasm. She feared that Greeley would not be "free from the usual foibles of Editors" and that even if she did manage to do quality work for such a publication, her merit would be swallowed up by the anonymity of the metropolitan journal. Most of all, Fuller dreaded the taint of the penny daily, which was widely considered a low instrument. Partisan, sensational, and vulgar, the newspaper had never been a vehicle through which the great questions of morality, philosophy, religion, and culture had been debated.[5]

FIGURE 5. Margaret Fuller, the noted Transcendentalist, was the *Tribune*'s literary critic and one of its foreign correspondents. Photograph © 2009 Museum of Fine Arts, Boston. Courtesy of the museum, accession number 43.1412.

Despite the draws of audience and income (she had been the main source of support for her family after her father died in 1835), Fuller naturally viewed the *Tribune* with the ambivalence that was typical of the Transcendentalists. Male Transcendentalists, at times, viewed popular journalism and lecturing as a matter of coarse necessity, a degrading compromise with the demands of the new literary marketplace, and their biographers consequently imagine public scholarship as evidence of a literary career winding down toward comfortable gentility. The Transcendentalists themselves regularly vented about losing purity in the popular marketplace of ideas; even Fuller once worried about the idea of "walking forth alone to meet that staring sneering Pit critic, the Public at large, when I have always been accustomed to confront it from amid a group of 'liberally educated and respectable gentle-men.'"[6] During the 1840s, print's mass audience was yet in its infancy, and many regarded the newspaper as a sphere of low-minded sensation-driven drivel, the embodiment of mass democracy's worst excesses. Emerson once dismissed rural readers of the "Try-bune," as it was commonly pronounced in the Midwest, for learning "everything they know for $2 per year," and his own episode as a religious pariah (particularly the controversy surrounding his Harvard Divinity School address) had taught him to be wary of the press's attraction to trivia and scandal: "The newspapers of course will defame what is noble and what are you for but to withstand the newspapers & all the other tongues of today; you do not hold of today but of an age, as the rapt & truly great man holds of all ages or of Eternity. If you defer to the news-paper, where is the scholar?" Though Emerson, and later Ripley and Thoreau, held Greeley in relatively high esteem, most viewed newspaper work as "a very poor use to put a wise man & a genius."[7] So despite the *Tribune's* lofty reputation, writing for mass circulation was in some ways a step down for Fuller. It forced her to surrender the safety of her avant-garde marginality and obscurity, which had given her a small but collegial readership, and put in its place a print medium that was more democratic, public, and anonymous than the traditional Transcendentalist outlets.

Still, the *Tribune's* attractions were many. The *Tribune* offered Fuller regular pay, "a chance at half a hundred thousand readers," and an opportunity "to aid in the great work of popular education." "I never regarded literature as a col-lection of exquisite products," she explained, "but rather as a means of mutual interpretation." The *Tribune,* moreover, was a journal of high repute.[8] With the *Tribune,* Greeley was trying to raise the character of the commercial press; Fuller went a step further by raising the character of the *Tribune.* Before Fuller's arrival, the *Tribune's* commitment to formal culture rested on announcements of upcoming lectures and events, travel narratives, the occasional series on history or science, and book reviews that were rarely critical. All of which may seem unremarkable, but given the paucity of cultural coverage outside of the segmented audiences of high-priced periodicals, the *Tribune's* achieve-ment, even before Fuller's arrival, was significant. Moreover, its pre-Fuller reform commitments—its antinativism, its support for the expansion of suf-frage, its sponsorship of woman's rights, its friendship with labor and popular education—worked toward ends that were at bottom cultural.

Fuller's most important impact on the paper was that she brought it a critical edge that had been lacking. Greeley believed in uplift as an unmixed good. He rarely made distinctions and was a bit of a dilettante; Emerson called him "no scholar but such a one as journals & newspapers make, who listens after all new thoughts & things but with the indispensable New York condition that they can be made available."[9] Although by the mid-1840s Greeley's purported "isms"—his socialism, vegetarianism, abolitionism, and agrarianism—had made him a figure of radical infamy in conservative Democratic and Whig journals, he personally despised conflict and tried to harmonize his reform ideas with his partisan commitments and the broadest range of public opinion. Fuller had few such concerns. Fuller was a genuine intellectual, vigorous and confrontational. More aggressive in tone than Greeley, Fuller's *Tribune* writings complained of the cultural tyranny of commerce and middle-class respectability, and she would express her alienation from middle-class convention by identifying with marginal populations—blacks, immigrants, women, prostitutes, the insane—in ways that sharpened the paper's voice.

Despite their difference in temperament, the editor would become one of Fuller's central professional mentors. Unlike Emerson, who had always considered Fuller more a conversationalist than a writer and had his doubts about New York and the emerging literary marketplace, Greeley encouraged Fuller's popular ambitions. He published under his own imprint Fuller's groundbreaking feminist essay, "The Great Lawsuit," in pamphlet form as *Woman in the Nineteenth Century*. As he would with Thoreau and later Charles Dana and George Ripley, Greeley sought out audiences for Fuller and genuinely believed she deserved one. Greeley called her the "best instructed woman in America" and, with Emerson, the "rarest, if not ripest fruits of New England's culture"; he wrote to fellow editor Rufus Griswold of *Woman in the Nineteenth Century*, "Margaret's book is going to *sell*. I tell you it has the real stuff in it. . . . It is not elegantly written, but every line talks."[10] Fuller embraced cultural democracy in New England, but it was not until she met Greeley that she found a practical model of democratic and political engagement. "I like Mr. Greeley much," she confided to Samuel Ward. "He is a man of the people, and outwardly unrefined, but he has the refinement of true goodness and a noble disposition." Mostly, she praised his close attunement to the interests and values of "the people," with their "life and manners," and even as their personal and professional relationship became strained by familiarity, Fuller reflected that Greeley "teaches me things" that her previous friends, mentors, and acquaintances had "prevented me from learning." Rid, for a time, of metaphysics, abstraction, and the tangled web of Romantic self-understanding, Fuller entered the "'stream of life.'"[11]

The *Tribune* was more than a destination for Transcendentalists in search of a practical vocation; it, in many ways, manifested in practice what we might call an Emersonian vision of a high-minded yet democratic public

culture. At bottom, Transcendentalism, socialism, and even the *Tribune* itself
were united by a shared commitment to a philosophy of liberal self-culture
that aimed to institutionalize democratic access to ideas and self-expression.
All pleaded for a more intimate and harmonious union between the mind
and the body, between the scholarly and laboring classes. By 1848, conservative newspapers and Southern critics would lump the *Tribune* together with
various heresies that included Transcendentalism, socialism, and other radical
reforms, including free love, agrarianism, Irish nationalism, and opposition
to capital punishment.[12]

Transcendentalism and Radical Self-Culture

Transcendentalism, in many respects, was a product of many of the same
impulses that gave rise to Fourierism. It began as a small revolt by a group of
radical Unitarian ministers with largely religious implications. For the Transcendentalists, this revolt initially took the form of a religious dispute, but it
reflected broad dissatisfaction with the place of the ministry in an America
overtaken by the market revolution and the "consumer-led" religious culture
of the Second Great Awakening, which reduced the status of the learned
ministry. Once the head of an official culture, the liberal ministers turned
their backs on the vast social changes swirling around them, and in so doing
they became little more than the dispensers of comfort and emotional reas-
surance for their wealthy congregations. Though currents within Unitarians
gave rise to Transcendentalism, to its contemporary and historical detractors
Boston's liberal ministers "had sacrificed the Puritan notion of a covenant
with the community as a whole for a class compact with the rich," and had
become, as a result, detached, elitist and "irrelevant."[13] Institutional Unitarianism, to its disaffected radical progeny, reflected the worst aspects of the age.
It resisted the democratic vitality of the Great Awakening and, as a result of
disestablishment, succumbed to the moral disintegration of a now atomized
community. The Unitarian ministry, in the eyes of most Transcendentalists,
turned a blind eye to the social and cultural consequences of the market revolution and became merely a servant of New England's new commercial elite.
Theodore Parker and Ralph Waldo Emerson marked these changes bluntly.
The minister-scholar had become, in Parker's words, a "mild, inoffensive
man, who hurts nobody." To Emerson, he had become "a placid smiler, a
demure inoffensive reader of such books as the newspapers applaud, to be
helped over a fence when he walks with a man, as if he were a girl, (like my
dear Rev Mr Armstrong). I see not how he is better than a lackey hired to
read instead of one hired to wait on table or to polish boots."[14]

As a response to this new religious culture, as well as to the social and economic changes that produced it, during the 1840s the Transcendentalists embarked on a series of experiments in social and communal reform. Some, such as Thoreau's Walden or Brook Farm, are widely known, and others, such as Bronson Alcott and Charles Lane's vegetarian commune Fruitlands, or even Emerson's own domestic experiments, are more obscure, but they were all experiments in new styles of living. There were also, in addition, an important series of intellectual experiments. Alcott, Fuller, and Elizabeth Palmer Peabody, for example, all launched efforts in educational reform. Peabody became a publisher and opened a radical bookstore. Emerson embraced the lyceum movement. Virtually all the Transcendentalists contributed to the *Dial,* the movement's counterculture magazine. Among the most important of these intellectual experiments in democratic scholarship was Margaret Fuller's tenure as a member of the daily press—the eventual destination, I might add, of most of the leading Transcendental socialists of the 1840s. This second series of reform experiments, like the first, were attempts to transform and deepen the relationship between that emerging social type—the intellectual—and a democratic public. There was, moreover, a connection between the experiments in living and the experiments in thinking, one that went beyond the fact that at some point virtually every Transcendental communitarian also joined the movementwide effort to fashion a hybrid democratic high culture. All of these experiments, I would argue—communitarian and intellectual alike—sprouted from an ideological soil that had already been well fertilized by Emerson.

In a series of major addresses in the late 1830s and early 1840s ("The American Scholar," the "Divinity School Address," "Man the Reformer," and "Self-Reliance"), Emerson outlined a vision of personal and cultural renewal that would be the basis of Transcendentalism's experiments in both democratic scholarship and communitarian social reform. Two Harvard addresses—"The American Scholar" and the "Divinity School Address"—were Emerson's broad considerations of the role of the intellectual in a democratic and modern society. In the "Divinity School Address," Emerson catalogued the failures of the contemporary ministry. Emerson complained, for one, about a liberal religion left unregenerated by the democratic vitality or the intuitive boldness of the Second Great Awakening. More generally, Emerson's jeremiad was directed at a ministry so trapped in ritual, form, and ceremony that it evaded its responsibility to preach vigorously and prophetically to its congregation—a church that was no longer a universal community in which "the best and the worst men in the parish, the poor and the rich, the learned and the ignorant, young and old, should meet one day as fellows in one house."[15]

Emerson's clearest manifesto, however, of a reformed intellectual life was the "American Scholar," an essay in which he attempts to reconcile the intellectual's moral authority—his or her claim to stand above a "society [that] lives to trifles"—to a style of intellectual endeavor that willingly condescends to a democratic public on questions of civic import. Although Emerson delivered his "American Scholar" address to the Phi Beta Kappa Society at Harvard, his use of "scholar" did not refer merely to the "bookish" class or even to college professors, whom he viewed skeptically as mere commentators. One of his recent biographers suggests that by "scholar," Emerson meant "something of what we mean by *student,* something of *intellectual*...[or] *writer,*" but perhaps the closest translation into our own idiom would be "public intellectual"—"American Scholar" and "public intellectual" reflect both the democratic engagement and the thoughtful independence of a reconstituted thinking class.[16]

Emerson was one of a host of midcentury critics of individualism, American Fourierist socialists among them, who argued that American materialism had produced a nation of specialists, amputees who "strut about so many walking monsters,—a good finger, a neck, a stomach, an elbow, but never a man." This specialization, reflected in the segmentation of social life, was particularly dangerous for the "American Scholar":

> There goes in the world a notion that the scholar should be a recluse, a valetudinarian,—as unfit for any handiwork or public labor, as a penknife for an axe. The so-called "practical men" sneer at speculative men, as if, because they speculate or *see,* they could do nothing. I have heard it said that the clergy,—who are always more universally than another class, the scholars of their day,—are addressed as women: that the rough, spontaneous conversation of men they do not hear, but only a mincing and diluted speech. They are often virtually disfranchised; and indeed, there are advocates for their celibacy. As far as this is true of the studious classes, it is not just and wise. Action is with the scholar subordinate, but it is essential. Without it, he is not yet man.

Emerson's solution to this crisis was manifold, comprehending both the experiments in living and thinking that followed. On a basic level, he counseled physical invigoration, bringing manual and mental natures into harmony. In "The American Scholar," for example, he argued that "there is virtue in the hoe and the spade, for learned as well as for unlearned hands," and in his later address, "Man the Reformer," he advocated economic and moral self-sufficiency and suggested that manual labor and the pride in craft were the "basis for our higher accomplishments, our delicate entertainments of poetry and philosophy." "We must have an antagonism in the tough world for all the variety of our spiritual faculties, or they will not be born," Emerson concluded. "Manual labor is the study of the external world." For the scholar-intellectual, the vocational counterpart of physical self-renewal was scholarly engagement with the community. Just as the physical discipline of labor would bring mental vitality, contending with a diverse society would deliver a healthy mental antagonism. Both impulses were implicit aspects of experiments in democratic scholarship such as Fuller's newspaper work and communitarian experiments such as Brook Farm.[17]

Traditionally, Emerson's consistent pronouncements about the importance of labor—and laborers—and his regular accountings of the psychological, cultural, and social costs of market individualism have counted for little among historians and literary critics because he did not join the Utopian community at Brook Farm. He claimed that "the ground of my decision is almost purely personal to myself," but few since have believed that his reasons were not ideological. As Perry Miller put it, "henceforth there were two opposing poles in Transcendentalism—the associationists and the Emersonian individualists," and this imagined division has been applied writ large, especially to Fuller.[18] And yet, on closer scrutiny, the "official meaning" of Brook Farm as well as the way the community functioned in practice were hardly antagonistic to Emersonian principles.

There were, of course, subtle doctrinal differences within Transcendentalism, but Emerson's plea for the renewed union of both manual and mental labor, and the manual and mental classes, coheres precisely with Brook Farm's effort, in the words of George Ripley, "to insure a more natural union between intellectual and manual labor... guarantee the highest mental freedom, by providing all with labor, adapted to their tastes and talents, and securing to them the fruits of their industry... thus to prepare a society of liberal, intelligent, and cultivated persons, whose relations with each other would permit a more simple and wholesome life, than can be led amidst the pressures of our competitive institutions."[19] Brook Farm, in short, was merely one effort, if the largest and most "demonstrative," among a variety of Transcendentalist efforts to challenge the cultural consequences of the market. Provoked initially by the failure of the institutional church to counteract the class segmentation of the community, Brook Farm critiqued the hegemony of competitive capitalism and proposed to counteract the specialization of scholarly and manual work, to reestablish the relevance of intellectuals, and to use manual labor both to reverse the alienation of intellectuals and to organize their populist cultural politics. Brook Farm was, in effect, an attempt to embed Emersonian principles in a communal practice.[20] The same might be said of the various Transcendental experiments in democratic scholarship, particularly Margaret Fuller's journalism.[21]

Fuller's popular-newspaper work mirrored the intentions of Brook Farm in the sense that it brought her into experiential contact with a variety of classes and opened a dialogue with a larger portion of the reading community. But it was also a departure in very significant ways—ways that would provide a model of longer-lasting and steadier significance for intellectuals with democratic commitments. What distinguished Brook Farm from Fuller's tenure with the *Tribune* (and Emerson's career as a public lecturer for that matter) was less a difference between individualism and socialism than between two distinct institutional solutions to the problem of class segmentation. In similar ways, Transcendental self-culture demanded institutional and cultural reform to unfold the intellectual and spiritual possibility of individuals; Brook Farm, like other progressive Whig social experiments, hoped to reintegrate both the manual and intellectual classes by bringing the mental and physical sides of individuals into natural and harmonious relation. Emerson had held that the democratic realization of American intellectual life required, first, the scholar's physical restoration, and, second, his engagement with the public on questions of shared import. The former, which was the direction Emerson's other main disciple, Henry David Thoreau, took, depended on a constellation of values associated with manhood—independence, self-reliance, power, and vitality. These values were largely unavailable to Fuller who was likely the most feeble of the Transcendentalists, plagued by headaches and poor eyesight throughout her life. She was also, of course, among the least manly, despite condescending admiration of her "masculine mind." Democratic engagement was also traditionally unavailable to women, but by the 1840s it was less so given the flurry of female reform activity, and it would be the impulse driving her increasingly public literary career beginning with the *Dial* and culminating in the *Tribune,* with both publications aspiring to the high-toned populism outlined in Emerson's manifestos.

The launch of the *Dial* in 1840 was a turning point in the history of Transcendentalism and it provides an important contrast to Fuller's career on the *Tribune.* The Transcendentalists started the *Dial* at a time when controversy froze them out of most major religious and literary magazines—magazines that the Transcendentalists viewed, in Bronson Alcott's words, as "destitute of life, freshness, independence," and as emblematic of the Federal-style intellectual culture that they themselves had already rejected.[22] The introduction of the *Dial* marked both a generational and aspirational transition from the ministerial preoccupations of the 1830s to the "cultural awakening" of the 1840s. This is not to say that all along visions of a reformed and democratic culture were not an integral aspect of the religious controversies of the 1830s, but from 1840 forward the debate over culture was finally stripped of religious and theological dress; as such, it signaled a transition among the movement's core from disaffected minister to modern intellectual. Fuller was at the head of a surge of nonministers and women into the movement. She was the principal and most assertive voice among a group of young disciples who had gathered around Emerson and "looked to Transcendentalism," as Charles Capper has suggested, not to rouse "a new theology or church, but rather...a cultural awakening." She became in 1840 the first editor of the *Dial*, a magazine that along with the lyceum were halfway steps toward letters as a modern profession.[23] Transcendentalism became America's first avant-garde, and its organ, the *Dial*, reflected the inherent tensions within a project of that sort. The *Dial* was Fuller's—and Transcendentalism's—first major institutional step toward democratic scholarship, but it simultaneously reflected their long-standing frustrations with mass conformity and the popular culture of the marketplace. The tumultuousness of Jacksonian culture had made traditional forms of intellectual authority irrelevant, but in the *Dial* the Transcendentalists had to figure out a way to preserve their moral autonomy in a culture where the value and status of learning were no longer assumed as a given. In effect, the very issue that drove the Transcendentalists from the pulpit—fashioning a sphere in between traditional patrician elitism and modern watered-down, emotionally laden, and consumer-dominated popular culture—also shaped the history of the *Dial*.[24]

The *Dial*'s contradictory goals, which crystallized the Transcendentalist longing for both democratic energy and learned authority, materialized almost immediately. In the first issue, both Emerson and Fuller wrote a prospectus for the magazine, with the latter's submerged, after some discussion, into her "Short Essay on Critics." In his letter to the reader, Emerson announced that the journal sought a democratic audience among those who were not usually counted among the educated: "In lonely obscure places, in solitude, in servitude, in compunctions and privations, trudging beside the team in the dusty road, or drudging a hireling in other men's cornfields, schoolmasters, who teach a few children rudiments for a pittance, ministers of small parishes of the obscurer sects, lone women in dependent condition, matrons and young maidens, rich and poor, beautiful and hard favored." Emerson, as he had in his two Harvard addresses, proclaimed the infallibility of private intuition and the universality of truth, and in ways that could not account for the marginality of aspiring prophets in an age when popular spectacles, such as those of P. T. Barnum, increasingly ruled supreme. Fuller, on the other hand, was more comfortable with the idea of literature as dialogue, but figured culture in strenuously hierarchical terms, with critics standing between divine artists and common readers. She proclaimed that critics "must not tell him [readers] what books are not worth reading," but at the same time she declared to Emerson, on the eve of the *Dial's* founding, that she would never write "mutilated" prose "dictated to suit the public taste." Her artistic and intellectual ambitions, she said, could never be subordinated to the lure of "lucre." Despite subtle differences between them, the Transcendentalists were neither comfortable with the pretension or exclusion of traditional hierarchy nor with the tyranny of popular taste, and the tension between the two impulses shaped the history of the magazine.[25]

In practice, the *Dial's* elite aesthetic and radical cultural politics were irreconcilable and ultimately it struggled to close the gap between its populist pretensions and its avant-garde marginality. In the end, with a circulation only in the hundreds, the *Dial* became a virtually private medium; its contributors were very nearly the journal's only direct audience. After it became obvious that the *Dial* would never find a mass audience, Transcendental populism (which, of course, was never *so* populist that it adapted itself to popular expectations and tastes) occasionally drifted into elitist scorn for vulgar democracy. Emerson hoped "our Dial will get to be a little *bad*.... enough so to scare the tenderest... Conformity," and Parker also worried that the journal was too genteel, like a "band of men and maidens daintily arrayed in finery to a body of stout men in blue frocks, with great arms and hard hands and legs." Bronson Alcott, the most thoroughgoing democrat of the regulars at the Transcendental Club, and who had once passed out copies of his "Orphic Sayings" to unlettered farmers, cautioned that "vox populi is not vox Dei" when those very sayings became subject to myriad popular parodies after their publication in the *Dial*. Ironically, the journal's difficult jargon, which very few could understand, reproduced an older, antidemocratic ideal of aristocratic enlightenment—that knowledge, culture, and learning would become the exclusive possession of preeminent and narrow cliques. The philosophical and linguistic obscurity of the Transcendentalists, combined with their claims to serve as the oracles of democracy, resulted in a paradox not lost on contemporaries. Oliver Wendell Holmes, weary of what he viewed as a hypocritical mixture of populism and didacticism, snorted that "the transcendental nose was one that stretches outward and upward to attain a fore-smell of the Infinite." The *Dial's* populist critical commitments were thus divorced from reality. Without a genuine popular audience, the *Dial's* democratic credentials were articulated in a cultural vacuum, with an audience that would remain, as it was rendered in the first number, a fantasy. The *Dial's* populism, mixed with a curious elitism, was of an imagined and symbolic sort; a perspective and not a practice, it was a counterculture in which disaffected elites identified with the "manual" classes as a kind of literary protest against commercial materialism and bourgeois respectability.[26]

To imagine the *Dial's* audience in the hundreds as the complete story of its influence, though, is to misunderstand the role of the then developing mediating institutions, namely lyceums, periodicals, and newspapers. It was within these kinds of cultural institutions that Transcendentalism's avant-garde "democratic high culture" amplified its voice, and principal among these for the 1840s Left was the *New-York Tribune.* Middlebrow journals such as the *Tribune* produced a critical aura that gave the Transcendentalists the power and the freedom to pursue a unique vision while preparing an audience, anxious for self-improvement, to be challenged, provoked, and uplifted. The *Tribune* regularly scolded the public that in the age of "Popular Literature," that it had made no room for the *Dial,* "that an original American work, costing but $3 per year...has been published four years in the midst of our hundred thousand liberally educated men, ten thousand professed scholars, and over one hundred colleges and 'universities,' without winning more than *three hundred* subscribers?"[27] The Transcendentalists used the *Dial* to make their national reputations. Their prestige, in the end, was less a direct product of the *Dial* and more the work of advocates such as Greeley who publicized and republished their work and, ironically, a result of the various parodies of Transcendentalism's airy idiom that appeared around the country in popular magazines and newspapers. Popular parody and popular criticism let the public know that the Transcendentalists were important. Critical appreciation, along with the Transcendentalists' obscurity, their indifference to commercial success, and their removal from party politics, was the preliminary capital that endowed the Transcendentalists with the moral and cultural authority to claim fame and, in the long term, a professional, critical readership. Remaining studiously "above" the popular audience, they eventually acquired the independence to reach the best of that audience and on different terms. So, even if the Transcendentalists were not read directly in the *Dial,* they were noticed and read in the *Tribune,* which gave them sanction, and in a kind of shadow reading familiarized the public with their work, or at least with their presence. Popular criticism and biographical notice created the institutional skeleton that lent coherence to a public conversation and that elevated, and gave shape to, a new social type: the intellectual.[28]

If the *Dial* experience taught Fuller one lesson, it was that the task of producing a high-toned, radical, and experimental magazine, in an indifferent cultural environment, extended far beyond writing programmatic statements about the nature of an ideal journal. But this realization did not bring her closer to a democratic audience. That privilege would fall to Horace Greeley. Greeley became acquainted with Fuller's intellect though the *Dial* (even though, in public notices, he associated the magazine's genius almost wholly with Emerson), but he had known of her for years through his wife who had attended Fuller's Conversations. The Conversations were a program of serious literary and philosophical discussion for women and in some respects a small-scale model of a noninstitutional, communal, and democratic intellectual life that would flower in a more comprehensive manner in the *Tribune*. Fuller's audience for the Conversations—well-educated, religiously liberal, heterodox women associated by marriage or birth with reform Whiggery and New England's older merchant elite—was in no small measure the audience of the *Tribune* as well.

The Star of the *Tribune*

Transcendentalism and the *Dial* shared with socialism and the *Tribune* a politico-cultural sensibility and aspired to a common vision of democratic self-culture, but institutionally they were distinct. On the *Tribune,* Fuller joined the brawling world of popular politics and New York journalism. She was expected to write frequently and for unmixed audiences. Eventually, Fuller would write over 250 pieces for the *Tribune* on a diverse number of topics, most of them signed with a star (★). Anonymity was common among nineteenth-century newspaper scribes, but Fuller's identity was an open secret. Her first piece of writing for the paper hinted pretty heavily at her background. It was a review of Emerson's *Essays: Second Series,* a column that not only illustrated the connection between her New England past and her New York present but that moreover occasioned public meditation on the relationship between democracy and the scholar, a theme that had been percolating among the Transcendentalists for the better part of a decade and was at the heart of Fuller's decision to join the *Tribune*. She wrote of Emerson that "here is undoubtedly the man of ideas, but we want the ideal man also." Emerson, she claimed, had "raised himself too early to the perpendicular" and cut himself off from the "conflicts on the lap of mother earth" and from harder democratic realities. Oft-quoted, Fuller's reservations about Emerson's idealism are too often, though, taken as emblematic of her growing hostility to a disengaged Transcendentalism. A paragraph in a long review, they do not reflect the general tenor of the essay, which was less an effort to distinguish her from the New England literary culture she had left behind than an attempt to outline a vision of engaged intellectual life. This vision, impressed upon the figure of Emerson, justified her own publicly oriented literary and cultural criticism within a democratically circulated newspaper. For Fuller, Emerson's dominant quality was not his superior cultivation or genteel "ethereal lightness," but his willingness to "admonish the community" and "arouse it to nobler energy." Despite concluding sentiments that hoped Emerson could push further, the main thrust of Fuller's review makes a claim for Emerson as the embodiment of a new style of intellectual culture that would abandon parlor finery for combative relevance as a democratic prophet.[29]

Fuller's review is significant because for the first time a Transcendentalist directly and self-consciously acknowledged the usually unpaired conflict between the movement's aesthetic, emotive, and cultural populism, such as Emerson's editorial preface to the *Dial,* and its hostility to the banality and superficiality of poplar culture, expressed most often in the pose of the marginal Romantic artist. At the outset of the review, Fuller notes that America's most representative and democratic intellectual had found his most sympathetic audience in aristocratic England. America's narrow devotion to "bringing out the material resources of the land" and its limited "early training for the enjoyment of books" diminished the character of public life and rendered culture merely one of a variety of superfluous luxuries imported according to the dictates of English fashion. The United States, she argued, presented peculiar obstacles to literature. Most notable among them was that the very democratic openness that provided the freest scope for the intellect also presented an institutional formlessness that made it nearly impossible to channel popular attention. The cultural marketplace insisted that "writers and speakers" must "lend all their efforts to flatter corrupt tastes and mental indolence." Nonetheless, given the fact that she viewed literature as a vehicle of mutual interpretation and intersubjectivity, the relationship between the artist and the audience remained central. As she wrote later of Norwegian violinist Ole Bull, "It is not vanity that makes the plaudits of the audience so necessary to performers even of undoubted genius. It is because they need the assurance of sympathy to fan into flame the coal of enthusiasm, and without it, can no more do themselves justice, than one of their instruments can make its vibrations felt, if the atmosphere or shape of the apartment be calculated to deaden it." Emerson, as a representative and prophetic intellectual, symbolized the possibility of, and the first step toward, a deeper kind of democracy, beyond politics. Fuller, then, proposed through the figure of Emerson an ideal of public intellectual life that would counteract the apathy of pervasive materialism and direct the energies of an audience now capable of only passive stimulation:

A man who has within his mind some spark of genius or a capacity for the exercises of talent should consider himself as endowed with a sacred commission. He is the natural priest, the shepherd of the people. He must raise his mind as high as he can toward the heaven of truth, and try to draw up with him those less gifted by nature with ethereal lightness. If he does not so, but rather employs his powers to flatter them in their poverty, and to hinder aspiration by useless words and a mere seeming of activity, his sin is great: he is false to God and false to man.

Ultimately, she sketched Emerson as nothing less than a heroic national "representative of the claims of individual culture" made democratic and universal; it was also, however, a kind of self-portrait that justified her own publicly oriented journalism.[30]

Fuller, more than any other Transcendentalist, ventured into a modern intellectual arena, one shaped by the publishing revolution and the national literary marketplace it created. There, the traditional intimacy of the "gentlemanly" audience was replaced by a nameless public. Fuller, ironically, had roots in the old order. From her father she had received a patrician's classical education with extensive training in languages; had she been a man, and had she lived in a previous era, she would have been ideally suited to assume a position of public leadership. Even for a man, though, her education was somewhat anachronistic, and the revolt from within by first-generation Transcendentalists—Ripley, Emerson, Alcott, and Frederic Henry Hedge—against the genteel detachment of liberal Christianity formally brought the era of amateur letters and patrician cultural leadership to a close.

Fuller's classical education and her gender had prepared her for a world that existed only in the past and the future. In the present, faced with the rise of cheap print and literary professionalism, she faced an entirely new set of dilemmas. Unlike first-generation Transcendentalists, Fuller, in the *Tribune,* did not square off against a narrow sectarian nemesis. Instead, she faced a largely indifferent culture, where ideas were exchanged as a commercial transaction and where the intellectual's relationship to the public was detached and anonymous. For some women, the emergence of literary professionalism was an unalloyed good; sentimental literature was among the most profitable in the field. But Fuller's learning resisted the leveling effects of popular literature.[31] Though influenced by women reformers whose writing was colored by sentimentalism, Fuller largely rejected mass culture, but from a radical angle. Fuller self-consciously embraced the role of avant-garde critic, what she once called the "extreme left of the army of Progress," and later "that advanced guard in all liberal opinions." The main target of Fuller's contempt, then, was shallow respectability, gentility, and middle-class conformity in literature and the culture at large. Fuller became, in short, a highbrow populist, viciously denigrating conventional taste and lauding "outsider" perspectives. Fuller's review of artisan-poet William Thom's *Rhymes and Recollections of a Handloom Weaver,* for example, lambasted literary "excellence" as the crumbs of "rich men's tables." Literature, she wrote, ought to be a "great mutual system of interpretation between all kinds and classes of men...an episto-lary correspondence between brethren of one family, subject to many and wide separations, and anxious to remain in [the] spiritual presence of one another."[32]

For Fuller, the antithesis of both Thom and highbrow populism gener-ally was Henry Wadsworth Longfellow. Though Fuller had modest respect for Longfellow's talents, she had long thought that he and his fellow Fireside poets were a pale imitation of cultivated English aristocracy. While preparing to launch the *Dial,* Fuller wrote in her journal that Longfellow's poems were "a melancholy monument of the evils of culture for the sake of being culti-vated, not of growing." Later, as editor, she wrote Emerson that "Longfellow sent us his poems, and if you have toleration for them, it would be well to have short notice written by some one (*not* me)." And her review of Long-fellow's poems in the *Tribune* was squarely in the tradition of countercultural attacks on what would come to be figured as the genteel tradition. Longfel-low's poetic dexterity, Fuller argued, was neither innovative nor imaginative, but the methodical translation, through established literary conventions, of orthodox, borrowed feeling. Though she thought Longfellow an educator of democratic readership, he did not possess bold originality: "He has no style of his own growing out of his own experiences and observations of nature. Nature with him, whether human or external, is always seen through the windows of literature." Longfellow was, at best, a technician, conscious of the "rules of versification" but never able to penetrate "that soul from which metres grow as acorns from the oak." He represented the timidity of the new middle-class reader, "a man of cultivated taste, delicate though not deep feel-ing, and some though not much poetic force."[33]

Fuller's attack on Longfellow could be read as part of a broader Transcen-dental effort to liberate intellectual life from its association with femininity and respectability. Literary contempt for gentility and femininity was a way of describing and condemning class segmentation, safety, and conformity, which women came to symbolize in their role as the guardians of bourgeois taste and morality. In attacking Longfellow, Fuller identified both with Emerso-nian calls for masculine renewal through labor and with the socialists' broader demand for less socially segmented modes of living. The segmented self, the segmented society—as Emerson put it in "The American Scholar," the "good finger, a neck...but never a man"—were defects of market society rooted in middle-class parlor society.[34] Fuller, like Emerson, was opposed to all that was "conventional"—to a literature that was an expression of the values of the parlor—and she was equally fearful that culture was becoming an irrelevant and genteel diversion, divorced from politics and power, and reflecting the specialized character of the marketplace. But for Fuller, the consecration of labor, even as a trope within a larger critique of genteel respectability that relied on antifeminine/domestic metaphors, was largely unavailable.

Fuller was no sentimentalist, but she was happy to allow literature to become "woman's work." But where Emerson and Thoreau had their gardens and the Brook Farmers had their plow, Fuller battled similar cultural and experiential alienation by agitating on behalf of undomesticated women, subordinate ethnic and racial groups, and the poor. Her estrangement from middle-class convention, moreover, led her to impose a constellation of counter-values upon the ethnically and racially marginal. In her articles on the Irish character, for example, Fuller referred to stereotypes such as their "generous bounty," "indefatigable good-humor," "ready wit," and "elasticity of nature." Flirting with romantic racial essentialism, Fuller went even further when she celebrated Frederick Douglass as "a specimen of the powers of the Black Race" and rejected his conformity to "white" standards of literary excellence. In the end, however, a figure such as Douglass embodied her hope for a mongrel America, one that could "assimilate" the low and "peculiar element" of the "African Race" and the higher elements of "those imported among us from Europe." The combination, she thought, "would give to genius a development, and to the energies of character a balance and harmony beyond what has been seen heretofore in the history of the world. Such an element is indicated in their lowest estate by a talent for melody, a ready skill at imitation and adaptation, an almost indestructible elasticity of nature." Cultural pluralism, the dialectic between high and low, was, in effect, the social corollary of Emersonian self-culture; just as an individual's moral education required an encounter with nature, culture and national self-realization, for Fuller, required cosmopolitan engagement between self and other.[35]

Fuller's theory of mind and culture depended on multiple perspectives to the point that she approached intellectual and moral relativism. Fuller practiced two types of criticism, one, universalist in spirit, that "tries by the highest standard of literary perfection," and another, Romantic and subjective, "which enters into the natural history of every thing that breathes and lives, which believes no impulse to be entirely in vain, which scrutinizes circumstances motive and object before it condemns, and believes there is beauty in each natural form, if its law and purpose be understood." In the spirit of the latter, her review of the report of the United States Exploring Expedition,

a government-funded naval survey of the Pacific, counseled distrust of missionary and trader reports "because their minds are biased towards special
objects": "Would you speak to a man, first learn his language!" It was in this
spirit of romantic subjectivity that Fuller approached New York's diversity.[36]
The varied subject matter of Fuller's *Tribune* writings suggests how expansive Fuller's conception of literature really was. In addition to her reviews
and translations, Fuller's *Tribune* cultural criticism included urban sketches
and reform columns, articles that served as a pretext for excursions into the
city and fostered Fuller's burgeoning politics. Fuller's accounts of her urban
encounters promoted a cosmopolitan ideal, and suggested that an authentic
American culture would be a product of racial and ethnic mixture, of the
"low and the common."

On the surface, Fuller's sympathy with the marginal, especially given the
Tribune's progressive Whiggishness, placed her within an established feminine
reform discourse. In many respects, the model for Fuller's *Tribune* writings
were Lydia Maria Child's "Letters from New York," which were published in
the *National Anti-slavery Standard,* the *Boston Courier,* and later in book form.
Fuller had even praised Child's "Letters" as "lively," "interesting," and "true,"
and the author for her "acquaintance with common life." Both Child's "Letters" and Fuller's columns were based around a series of morally resonant
anecdotes, and both women focused on social outcasts, such as criminals,
prostitutes, the poor, and the insane, and progressive means of redeeming
them. But unlike Child, Fuller, even in her most explicitly reformist columns,
was less directly interested in the plight of the marginal than in critiquing the
larger society that excluded them.[37]

Fuller's interest in class meshed naturally with the *Tribune*'s efforts to
democratize the Whig Party. But whereas Greeley hoped to extend the blessings (education, property ownership, economic independence, civic equality, and culture) of middle-class life, though often in ways that offended
hierarchy-conscious conservative Whigs, Fuller brought to the *Tribune* a
countercultural perspective that at times renounced bourgeois values. In
"Prevalent Idea That Politeness Is Too Great a Luxury to Be Given to the
Poor," Fuller criticized the "missionary" mentality that supposes "pecuniary position" justifies "insolent rudeness." Her account of the Bloomingdale
Asylum's annual report, likewise, lauded more patient-centered treatments
of the insane and figured the mentally ill as the inevitable by-product of a
repressive and overregulated culture. In Fuller's view, the traditional cures for
insanity—restraint and fear—replicate its cause; Bloomingdale's alternative
of "religious services, school, lectures, and amusements" embody the sort of
public culture that Fuller long thought should counter America's diseased

materialism.[38] Fuller embraced reform causes typical of her Whiggish host, but mostly to assail bourgeois materialism and respectability. Her accounts of New York's charities—Bellevue Alms House, the Farm School, the Asylum for the Insane, and the Blackwell's Island Penitentiary—defined criminality, poverty, and insanity not as the product of a sinful nature but of a society that denied dignity, education, and productive employment to its lower classes. Arguing that "public charity" made the poor "feel themselves . . . paupers" and not "men," she cautioned against a style of charity that did not develop individual capacities. Fuller proclaimed, like most reform Whigs, that poverty's origins were social and not individual, and that a society that denied people work denied people the means toward the full realization of their physical, moral, and spiritual faculties—a goal consonant with both Utopian socialism and Emersonian self-culture. Charitable institutions, in Fuller's view, ought to function almost like socialist phalanxes, rationally unleashing productive economic energies while also elevating and nourishing the life of the mind:

> There should be instruction, both practical and in the use of books, openings to a better intercourse than they can obtain from their miserable homes, correct notions as to cleanliness, diet, and fresh air. A great deal of pains would be lost in their case, as with all other arrangements for the good of the many, but here and there the seed would fall into the right places, and some members of the downtrodden million, rising a little from the mud, would raise the whole body with them.[39]

In this vein, Fuller argued that the children of wealthy parents ought to have "useful labor mingled with their plays and studies," poor children ought to be educated in such a way that "study is associated with labor," and that prisons ought to have a "higher object than the punishment of fault" by mixing "instruction" with a physical life, a "sanitary system, which promotes self-respect . . . [and the] health and purity of the body."[40]

Greeley's *Tribune* was one of the most vigorous critics of market individualism and materialism, but Fuller went further than most on the paper in arguing that respectable morality, religion, and middle-class culture itself were responsible for the very excesses it imagined itself restraining. Bourgeois culture, tied implicitly to Protestant individualism and anti-institutionalism, resulted, in Fuller's view, in a fragmented culture. To Fuller, the erosion of sympathy and mutual understanding between classes was both an intellectual and institutional problem. As such, she envied Catholicism's social architecture in which "rich and poor knelt together upon their marble pavements," and condemned fashionable religion in America, symbolized by the city's luxurious new Grace Church, in which the "claims of the poor"

were addressed in a "side chapel."[41] Fuller's endorsement of religious tradi-
tionalism, so overwhelming in her holiday occasional pieces—"New Year's
Day," "Thanksgiving," and "Christmas"—was figurative, but it was a way
of describing the way American materialism had made culture, even sacred
culture, little more than an ornamental expression of class hegemony.[42]

Popular journalism has often been framed, in histories of socialism and
Transcendentalism alike, as a retreat from radical engagement with direct forms
of reform. Henry Golemba, one of George Ripley's biographers, laments his
subject's post–Brook Farm flight into the culture of "letters." Carl Guarneri
describes Ripley and Charles Dana's tenure on the *Tribune* as the embodiment of the "genteel tradition."[43] But Margaret Fuller's career with the *Tribune* suggests something different. Although it is true that newspapers, even
their antebellum incarnations, tend to divide the world into "departments,"
Fuller brought to the *Tribune* a more complex sense of literature's importance.
Before Fuller's arrival, the *Tribune*'s literary department housed a simple form
of criticism: it announced and summarized recent publications under the
ethereal assumption that the literary world was not a contested realm. For
Fuller, however, literature was a form of social criticism, and although her
columns generally remained on the "outside" of the paper—on the front
page, separated from the *Tribune*'s editorial matter—they were imbued with
the reform spirit of the paper and constituted its literary critique of the culture of the market.

Fuller's decision to join Greeley's *Tribune* was also a solution to a long-
standing vocational problem, one that she shared with her fellow Transcendentalists. Fuller's previous efforts to engage a world beyond the "mountainous
me" had met with qualified failure. The Transcendental magazine, the *Dial,*
brought her the prestige and the confidence of a professional and public
writer, but it tyrannized her with overwork and, more significantly, failed
to find a broad and democratically anonymous audience. The *Dial,* not
unlike her previous literary outlets, was not nearly public enough and it
did not bring her contact with a genuine readership. It was, with the New
England intellectual world that produced it, intellectually cosmopolitan but
institutionally circumscribed. The *Tribune* was something in between. Writing short pieces, meeting deadlines, and approaching general audiences, the
Tribune's upward-reaching daily journalism offered both a sense of purpose
and of relevance, an intellectual and professional architecture within which
ideas could find effect. Journalism, as Ann Douglas suggests, helped Fuller
find "a subject outside herself" that in essence released Fuller's spontaneity
and, paradoxically, her subjectivity: "Finding a form of indirection, she found
direction."[44]

The link between Transcendentalism and the *Tribune* was personal and intellectual, but it was also ideological. The *Tribune* was, in a narrow way, the midwife of the Transcendentalists' emergence as literary professionals and public intellectuals. But the *Tribune* was a comfortable institutional home and a suitable vehicle of national promotion because it shared with the Transcendentalists a common reform spirit. Transcendentalism and *Tribune* socialism offered complementary, comprehensive quasi-countercultural views of contemporary society. They both connected the labor question and the broader effects of the new economy to an equally wide-ranging vision of a reinvigorated self and expressive culture. In an age of market transformations, the Transcendentalists and the socialists posed semiradical alternatives to the ethos of competitive capitalism, particularly its specialization, its materialism, its inequalities, and its alienation. The specific alternatives were diverse. Emersonian Transcendentalists, individualistic and spiritual, recoiled from Fourierism's mechanistic and communal commandments. Nonetheless, as Fuller's career demonstrates, the Transcendentalists and the socialists insisted on the tie between ordinary experience and transcendence—both hitched their wagons to the stars.

Fuller did not remain in New York, but she did continue with the *Tribune*. When Greeley hired Fuller as literary editor, her original focus was to be on European literary currents. Her output, ultimately, was wide ranging. Still, Europe remained in her thoughts, and when offered the opportunity to go there in 1846 by the wealthy socialists Marcus and Rebecca Spring, she jumped at the chance. The Springs offered to pay some of Fuller's expenses in exchange for her tutoring their son, but Fuller still needed money and her experience in New York left her convinced that the *Tribune*'s "sincerity and generosity of purpose...has never been surpassed...by any journal."[45] So Fuller contracted with Greeley for a series of twelve European letters; she eventually wrote thirty-seven. Fuller's European travels culminated in Italy where she documented, and participated in, the tragically ill-fated revolts in 1848 and 1849 that attempted to unify Italy and end Austrian domination. In Italy, Fuller's transformation as a public intellectual, activist, and socialist was completed. Though Fuller remained a writer for the paper until a shipwreck took her life off the coast of Long Island in 1850, her presence on the *Tribune* became somewhat more peripheral. Not only did she write less frequently, but the principal subject she wrote about—Italy—was less central to the subjects that gripped the *Tribune* during those years: social revolution in France and the free-soil revolution at home. Italy's nationalist revolution was at the tail end of a wave of European revolutions that had erupted after 1848, but within the world of the *Tribune* it was little more than a dark coda to what had already unfolded in France. It was France, whose revolution was produced out of a complex mixture of liberal, nationalist, and socialist elements, that raised in the most direct way the question that preoccupied the *Tribune* throughout the Civil War era: What are the rights of labor and how can they best be defended?

CHAPTER 3

The French Revolution of 1848 and the Radicalization of the *Tribune*

> We cannot conceal the fact that the great battle between the Bourgeoisie and the Proletariats is not yet fought to an end. What took place on the 24th of February was only a sortie—a surprise.... The people, who in the joy of victory suffered themselves to be disarmed, stand with weaponless hands, and no defense but the consciousness of the justice of their cause. But, notwithstanding these appearances, the cause of the people will triumph, and the bourgeoisie will fall and fall forever, this time entirely destroyed.
>
> Henry Börnstein, *Weekly Tribune,* July 1, 1848

The final years of the 1840s were dark times for American Fourierism. The movement had spread like a wildfire but after just four years the "Age of Fourier" was coming to a close. Critics mocked the communitarians as "four-year-ites." Phalanxes began to fail as early as 1845. In the spring of 1846, Brook Farm, which had only recently reorganized itself on Fourierist lines, lost its recently constructed and uninsured phalanstery to fire. Despite the efforts of generous New York stockholders—Greeley among them—America's most important communal enterprise disbanded. Throughout the fall, winter, and spring of 1846–47, Greeley engaged Henry Raymond in what turned out to be a self-destructive theoretical dialogue that exposed Fourierism's distance from conventional moral values. By 1848, with nearly all the major communities disbanded and both the American Union of Associationists and its organ, the *Harbinger,* on the brink of extinction, the movement no longer generated much popular excitement or interest. From the perspective of European Fourierism, the prospects for the American wing of the movement looked positively promising. While the American communities were failing, nearly all Europe was on the precipice of political and social revolution, and in these clashes of classes and nationalities, the Fourierists were largely on the sidelines. To leftists, Fourierism proved incapable of addressing the ever-deepening divide between capital and labor; to its critics on the right, Fourierism was merely part of an undifferentiated mix of Jacobin theories that threatened property and a stable social and moral order. But despite these losses, Fourierism had an afterlife.

To many historians of antebellum reform, the collapse of the varied 1840s reform movements—and the almost total absorption of reform energy into the antislavery cause—made the 1850s the parent of a more conservative America. To John Higham, the decade "witnessed a subsidence of the radical hopes and reactionary fears of the early nineteenth century and the formation of a more stable, more disciplined, less adventurous culture." Now associated with "the threat of socialism" and radicalism, "the very idea of revolution lost much of its luster."[1] To an extent, socialism's reconfiguration during the 1850s does parallel the larger story of American reform. It became more modest and rejected the millennial aspirations of the previous decade, and in particular it sundered the link between social and cultural reform, the way in which Fourierism in particular wedded economic justice to more comprehensive ends—namely, a promise to realize individual psychological, creative, and emotional capacities. But the socialism that emerged from the crisis of the late 1840s was also arguably stronger, and it would begin to evolve into the cooperative form that would define the aspirations of American labor reform into the 1890s when it was finally supplanted by bread-and-butter unionism. Moreover, as socialist experiments wound down, as the relatively isolated experiments in communal living depopulated, and as the low-circulation Fourierist journals finally stopped publishing, socialist reformers moved from demonstrative reform, which was largely local, personal, and voluntaristic, to a more ideological, public, and nonsectarian activism on the model of their putative publicist Horace Greeley.

During the 1840s, Fourierism was a reform principle not unlike temperance or abolition. It was a philanthropic venture, a practical but limited demonstrative experiment. Its narrow reach was symbolized by the separation of Brisbane's column from the rest of the paper—as an extended advertisement. And Brisbane's *Tribune* series was Fourierism in its most public form. Despite considered efforts to strengthen alliances with workers' movements, Fourierists published in "sectarian" journals, renounced politics, and gathered in socialist communities well apart from the workers who bore the brunt of "competitive society." In the course of agitating for Fourierism throughout the 1840s, however, socialism's more general indictment of "competitive society" began to transcend the movement. It came to model a way of interpreting public problems and events, becoming a kind of social science. Socialism, consolidated as a general set of assumptions after 1848, made it linguistically possible for William Seward, a decade later, to frame sectional political rivalry as an "irrepressible conflict" between two social systems.

The death of Association as a practical blueprint of reform was in certain respects discouraging, but within its remains was the ideological skeleton of a serious and more practical social democratic indictment of the nature and excesses of free-market political economy. This sustained indictment of the market and its related call for social rights for labor became particularly manifest in the *Tribune's* response to the French Revolution of 1848. France's 1848 revolution was, ideologically, a transnational event that helped, in the United States, to broaden the popular currency of a socialist vocabulary, making class and social organization part of the very language of American politics. Although the year 1848 signaled the practical death of Fourierism, it hardly destroyed the idea of social democracy. To Greeley, the European revolutions, in combination with the first stirrings of popular domestic political revolt against the advance of slavery in the form of the Free Soil Party, seemed to open up "boundless vistas," signifying the "uprising which *must* come."[2]

France and the 1848 Revolutions

A wave of revolution swept Europe in 1848, and, as in 1789, French politics in particular would unearth latent ideological conflicts in the United States. In the first four months of 1848, there were nearly fifty instances of political violence in Europe, but from the point of view of the American left, these were small ripples until they reached France, where the question of social democracy was raised most distinctly. Word of the February Revolution did not reach America until mid-March, and when it did most Americans were reflexively inclined to view the struggle as the renewal of France's jagged progress toward a liberal republican government resembling that of the United States. Greeley's ecstatic response to the news was not unusual. Across the political spectrum, Americans greeted the revolution as the dawn of a new political age. The American foreign minister almost immediately recognized the provisional French government, Congress voted in late March to "congratulate" the French people on the birth of their new republic, and in April President Polk extended the official blessing of the American people to the new French government. Apart from the Whig *National Intelligencer,* the newspapers of both parties were nearly unanimous in their support.[3]

The initial consensus did not hold. News that the provisional government had abolished slavery sparked some sectional controversy, but surprisingly it generated less heat than reports about the creation of national workshops, which provided state jobs for the unemployed and raised the specter of socialism and communism. For radicals in America and France, the workshops were the salient fact in a new kind of revolution, one that would institute both political *and* economic rights. As Margaret Fuller put it in a March letter to the *Tribune,* "The political is being merged in with the social struggle; it is well; whatever blood is to be shed, whatever altars cast down." Boston's *Advertiser,* however, was more typical in its response, nervously accusing French progressives and their American supporters of "legislating the details of life." The *Courier* was even more alarmist: "The lightening has *struck. Socialism* in France is seen to be something more than a mere *abstraction....* It has life, and power, and may do infinite mischief." Most dangerously, socialism, the *Courier* warned, taught "the poor,—the ignorant,—the degraded...that they were the victims of a *false society.* Their sufferings and their vices were charged to the account of the social organizations.—They were taught that society owed them employment, with ample wages;—and that they would never enjoy their rights until the present order of things should be overthrown."[4]

The *Tribune,* virtually alone, saluted the socialist nature of the revolution— embraced its "right to work" slogan—and was heartened by the fact that the revolution was not limited to self-government, but included "The Rights and Interests of Labor, the Reorganization of Industry, the Elevation of the Working-Men, the Reconstruction of the Social Fabric." In an April editorial, "Democracy—in France and here," the *Tribune* argued that French democracy had progressed fifty years beyond any nation on earth. Greeley viewed French reforms—a national bank to aid industry, the regulation of specie-payment, and the abolition of slavery—as a version of his own "socialist-American System." With an activist government pledged to promote the economic welfare of its citizens, France, in Greeley's mind, represented a democratic future wholly counter to the American Democratic Party, which "glories in the negative, let-alone, do-nothing axioms of Free Trade Economists, which condemn Public Charity, and are used to justify the worst exactions of Absentee Landlordism." Once the worker uprisings of April and May made even clearer the social nature of the revolution, the "indomitable *Tribune,*" as the *Harbinger* called it, became the public voice of the Left.[5] Throughout the 1840s and even after, Greeley remained opposed to class violence and even strikes for the most part; they were the very things that he and other American Fourierists hoped that Association could prevent. Still, France had demonstrated that certain circumstances could make revolutionary violence a lamentable necessity. "Revolution is the only resource left," he argued, "the more speedy its outbreak, the more sudden and complete its success, the better for mankind."[6]

For most of the *Tribune*'s European commentators, the European revolutions represented inevitable historical progress from revolutionary liberty and individualism to democratic fraternity and equality. Charles Dana noted when he arrived in Germany later that year that all of its republican parties were also socialist. Albert Brisbane reported that German radicals respected the United States, but rejected it as a model for their own revolution. They wanted a "Social" rather than "a Bourgeois Republic, as you have it in the United States, where Labor is the prey of Capital, where free competition ruins the laboring classes, where you have the same distinctions of classes in Society, the same contrasts of wealth and poverty that we have here." Socialism in Europe was a response to conditions that will one day exist in the United States, wrote one of the *Tribune*'s German-language correspondents, where "the sparseness of the population prevents the appearance of the evils which belong to the principle of Individualism, and otherwise we should have our Laborer's Riots and Revolutions."[7]

French Socialism after Fourier

In the 1840s, while American socialists were preoccupied with various quasi-Fourierist communal experiments, French radical thought had proliferated. The revolution would expose the *Tribune* to this broader, more practical, and class-bound stream of French socialism that had been largely ignored in the United States. Before 1830 and as in America, most French labor unrest was expressed in the language of the past. French critics of the new order often blamed machines rather than the capitalist class that employed them, and often appealed to an older corporate guild ethos to protect them from the depredations of the free market.[8] Like American workers' movements, French radicals of the 1830s also had not yet moved beyond republican critiques of "aristocracy" and "monopoly."[9] In France, it was not until after the 1830 Revolution that the working class became aware, in the words of one historian of French labor, "of the incompatibility of bourgeois and worker notions of 'freedom' in industry" and self-aware with the rise of a "new discourse about the 'working class' to which popular activists now had access."[10] After 1830, many workers in France began to contend that the bourgeoisie was forming a new aristocracy with its own distinctive set of rights and privileges. There was a proliferation of books and pamphlets from the Left offering a variety of solutions to the problems of the new economic world. Worker periodicals such as *L 'Artisan* and thinkers such as Philippe Buchez began to scale back the utopian schemes and millennial hopes of Fourier and Saint-Simon, and offer in their stead more class-bound and practical plans for labor. In 1839 and 1840, Etienne Cabet published *Voyage en Icarie,* Pierre Joseph Proudhon *Qu'est-ce que la propriété,* and Louis Blanc *Organisation du travail.*

Ranging from the centrist programs of progressive liberals such as Adolphe Crémieux and Alphonse de Lamartine to the insurrectionary platforms of Louis-Auguste Blanqui and Armand Barbès, the laissez-faire bourgeois order was under assault. Though their programs were wide ranging, most of these reformers proposed that workers seize control of their economic fates by pooling capital to create cooperative workshops. Workers would thus collectively own the means of production and share in its profits.[11]

The most influential of these French reformers was Louis Blanc. As a central figure in the unfolding drama of revolution, Blanc the ideologue was subordinated to Blanc the political leader, but nonetheless his *Organization du travail,* published in 1840, shaped the *Tribune's* understanding of the role of socialism and social conflict in 1848 and it was quite sympathetic with its overall point of view. Blanc, unlike the violent insurrectionists on his left and the class "conciliationists" on his right, was a state socialist who naturally viewed the revolution as a moment of political possibility in which the French government, elected by universal suffrage, could direct the economy toward an Associationist future. For Blanc, the social revolution would be based in a state-directed associated economy of producer cooperatives that would be underwritten by cheap and available credit and direct state purchases.[12] The popularity of the *Organization of Labor* and Blanc's prominence as the representative of workers and the Paris left made his writings, for American observers, the official word on the social revolution.

Blanc's *Organization of Labor* offered both a solution to the "social problem" and provided the Left with a new vocabulary through which it could interpret and critique emerging capitalist social relations. On a practical level, Blanc sought a social republic in which universal suffrage would institute a cooperative economy that would eliminate ruinous individualism, unbridled competition, and class conflict. Blanc parted ways with established social theories in his reliance on politics and the state. Unlike most Christian and Associative socialists, Blanc thought that it was impossible to reform society outside of the state and he recognized that it would require some degree of power and organized force. Blanc's plan was for the government, through a commission of democratically elected representatives, to supply capital to an array of social workshops that would gradually limit, and then ultimately eliminate, competition. Profit from cooperative industries would be set aside for the cooperative development of other industries, and would eventually be the basis of a system of social insurance, a welfare state. But beyond their reform blueprint, Blanc's writings laid out a set of general assumptions about labor, political economy, and social change that would become commonplace after 1848: that history progresses through the contestation of economic interests; that law and politics legitimate the hegemony of economic elites; that capitalism was a "system of extermination," advancing inexorably toward monopoly, ever-more extreme inequality, and moral/social decay; and that the political and social organization of the proletariat could produce a future of cooperation and fraternal love. Blanc also proclaimed what would become the Left's mantra during the revolution: the "right to work." Most importantly, Blanc helped popularize the idea of a social science—the idea that the problems of society can be rationally identified, critiqued, and reformed.[13]

It was not until the 1848 revolutions that the central ideas of non-Fourierist radical French social reformers were widely circulated in the United States and the main organ of their transmission was the *Tribune*. The revolution accelerated a process whereby American reformers called upon an entirely new vocabulary; as the Associationist *Harbinger* pointed out, "'Organization of Labor,' 'Unity of Interests,' [and] 'social Science,' are henceforth destined to be common words in all prints...with all editors and all who minister to public opinion."[14] Typical was the *Tribune* series, "Philadelphia in Slices," which, modeled after George Foster's more widely noted series on New York, began its description of the city's "Bourgeoisie" with the apology, "the last few months have rendered all readers of newspapers familiar with this word, although we do not undertake to say that even the Editors themselves who are most in the habit of using it know what it means."[15] The revolution brought to the surface various treatments of what French radical intellectuals self-consciously called "social science" and the "social question," which made its core subject the relationship of individuals to the institutions, laws, and practices that govern their lives. In particular, they investigated "the problem of labor and its organization."[16] Ultimately, 1848 would unearth an immense variety of French and European radical discourse; as a result, the *Tribune* diversified its coverage of socialist ideas. But more than that, socialism itself became not simply a mode of reform but also, significantly, of explanation, a way to interpret events. Fourierism was a sectarian movement, and it failed, but along with the revolution it cleared the way for a new language and a new political mentality through which American progressive intellectuals perceived and critiqued their social and political world.

Henry Börnstein's Revolution

If the language of social revolution was French, the *Tribune*'s translators of the revolutionary events of 1848, and the texts that undergirded it, were German.[17] The *Tribune*'s first correspondent on the ground in Paris and perhaps America's most influential and incisive eyewitness of the 1848 events in

France was Henry Börnstein, a German émigré and, eventually, the paper's link to Karl Marx and a more class-conscious radicalism that would emerge in Europe during the 1848 revolutions and in their aftermath. Börnstein was the product of the same Parisian radical expatriate milieu as Marx, but he has remained at the margins of recorded history. He signed his letters to the *Tribune* with the anonymous "H.B.," and referenced himself in the title of his memoirs as a "nobody" or an "unimportant person." If Börnstein is remembered at all, it is as part of the great migration of "Forty-Eighters" who played such a key political role in Civil War–era cities such as Saint Louis. He was a sharp writer and a perceptive observer, but not an original thinker, and the combination demonstrates all the more strongly the speed and extent to which socialist ideas were permeating the literate West—he was truly a representative figure. Though largely unknown today, Börnstein was arguably America's sole chronicler of the social revolution who was thoroughly steeped in, and sympathetic to, the radical social theory that underlay it. A participant observer in both the 1848 revolutions and the American Civil War, his life suggests the way in which the two events were connected generationally and ideologically.[18] Both promised to transform the organization of labor and society in the name of liberty, freedom, and emancipation at the very moment when the meaning of those very concepts had been transformed by industrialization.

Börnstein was born in Hamburg in 1805 to a Protestant mother and an Austrian Catholic father, and his life was a reflection of the revolutionary upheaval of the period. Once a medical student, then an actor and translator, Börnstein moved to Paris in 1841 where he eventually became a correspondent for a variety of German newspapers before censors banned his work in 1844 and he was forced to found his own cultural and political review, *Vorwärts*. It too was soon outlawed throughout much of Central Europe, but, despite restrictions, it became popular with German speakers around the world. It also became one of most important radical journals in all of Paris for reasons that had little to do with Börnstein.

At the very moment that Börnstein's *Vorwärts* began encountering political hostility, its future became wedded to the *Deutsche-Französisch Jarbücher*, a radical journal of philosophy and politics started by another circle of German refugee insurgents that had gathered around Arnold Ruge and Karl Marx. As a publishing concern the *Deutsche-Französisch Jarbücher* was short-lived. Financially unstable, and without any regular French writers, the *Deutsche-Französisch Jarbücher* was also monitored closely by the German secret police who banned it after only a single double-issue in February 1844 and issued warrants for the editors.[19] Even so, its publication signaled decisively the transition of Marx and Engels to communism and historical materialism, and the debates that were launched there defined the larger evolution of social-ism. And after its collapse, the entire circle of revolutionary intellectuals who launched it would move on to *Vorwärts,* swallowing it whole and making it one of the pivotal journals in the history of the revolutionary left.

Within the context of *Vorwärts,* Marx abandoned academic philosophy and, driven by the practical necessity of journalism, absorbed a decade of French socialist theory. With dizzying rapidity, Marx embraced class struggle as the engine of history, marked the proletariat as the rising class of the nineteenth century, and began self-identifying as a communist. It was also in this one-year period that Marx first met Friedrich Engels and made his first efforts, with Mikhail Bakunin and the rest, to organize the worker societies of Paris. Their efforts were monitored closely by French and Prussian secret police who reported that a "few intriguers are misleading the impoverished German workers... [toward] regicide, abolition of property, down with the rich, etc." "We must," the police contrived, "prevent such people as Marx, Hess, Herwegh, a Weil and Börnstein [from] continuing to lead young people to disaster." After *Vorwärts* cheered an assassination attempt on the king of Prussia, Prussian diplomats complained to French foreign minister François Guizot about the paper and he successfully called upon the Interior Ministry to shut it down. Despite its ignominious 1844 end, *Vorwärts* presided over something historic: the melding of German philosophical debate to cosmo-politan and practical agitation. It was the moment when Marx became a Marxist.[20]

Börnstein was never one of the leading minds on *Vorwärts,* and his account of his conversion to socialism in his memoirs is somewhat shallow. Marx and Engels thought of him as little more than a business agent, and later believed him an "informer" for the French authorities. Nevertheless, he did absorb the ideas that were percolating in the radical expatriate community, and he would play an important role in disseminating those ideas in the United States, first in the German language press and then more broadly during the crisis of 1848. Börnstein's first American outlet was the *Deutsche Schnellpost,* a German-language newspaper published in New York that had a relatively small circu-lation of 1,150 subscribers, as well as a dynamic staff of radical contributors. The *Schnellpost* was the *Tribune's* neighbor and both suffered through a fire that consumed their offices in 1845. Originally edited by Wilhelm Eichtal, the journal's leading and most controversial figure was Karl Heinzen, a radical socialist and acquaintance of Ferdinand Freiligrath, Ruge, and Marx. When Eichtal died in 1847, Heinzen, who had only recently immigrated to the United States, took over the paper. The *Tribune,* which almost always had someone fluent in German on staff, had regularly reprinted *Schnellpost* articles and actively promoted the paper while it lived. Margaret Fuller, while still in the New York phase of her *Tribune* career, noticed it four times in her column, describing it as a "journal... conducted with great spirit" and as a must-read for all "who desire fresh intelligence from the liberal party abroad." The most important of her columns on the *Schnellpost* was "The Social Movement in Europe," which was a translation from the paper's correspondence—most likely Börnstein's—and was probably the first English-language mention of Marxist socialism in America. In it, Börnstein opined that equality had a wider meaning than citizenship, and that he "would give not a farthing for political revolutions, even if as radical as those of 1793... that leave the poor poor, the hungry hungry, the ignorant ignorant, and all kinds of miserables as they were before." Politics, he maintained, could "correct neither the faults nor vices of individuals nor the errors of the masses, nor the false relations of our present society, nor the woes that spring from them, and that we must have grander, wider, more comprehensive principles on which to base a new order."[21]

In 1848, the *Schnellpost* faced financial difficulty. The *Tribune* solicited public aid to keep the German paper afloat, but when it failed, it benefited from the *Schnellpost*'s suspension. At some point in 1847 or early 1848, Greeley wrote Börnstein to offer him ten dollars per letter to become the *Tribune*'s Paris correspondent. With Fuller in Italy, Greeley offered Charles Dana and Bayard Taylor as translators. Börnstein accepted, and gladly. "I have to admit that my reports won a great deal through the translations of Dana and Taylor," he remembered, "which is not usually the case of translation. Both were well versed in the way things were in both Europe and America... [and] therefore [it was] only natural that the reports won through this elegant English form." Börnstein's American letters, which began to arrive in early May, were a personal and professional success. "For the first time," Börnstein recalled, he was able to write "without censure," and as a result his dispatches "became a sensation and were reprinted in all of the German papers."[22]

Until Börnstein began writing for the *Tribune* in April 1848, most of the information coming out of France was filtered through conservative English newspaper reports, sources that few American reformers trusted. Börnstein's reports were not only a fresh perspective on the events but, by transmitting the more radical and violent class-based socialism of the Paris streets to American audiences, they were a link to more radical forms of social criticism that had largely been unavailable on the American side of the Atlantic during the age of Fourierist Association. Börnstein's *Tribune* reports on the ebb and flow of the revolution in France modeled a style of journalism that wedded news to social criticism. In doing so, they reflected American socialism's post-Fourier evolution from a sectarian reform movement to an outlook and a vocabulary, a broader complex of mental conventions and dispositions that gave shape to the current of events. Armed with an explanatory ideology culled from the *Vorwärts* circle and a decade of French social criticism by figures such as Louis Blanc, Börnstein covered politics as a contest of social forces. Years later, he understood the shift from "news" to "analysis" as merely a consequence of technology, but his own reporting in the late 1840s anticipated this transformation of style. "Correspondents now have to talk about other topics besides political events because these topics are outdated," he wrote. "Now they have to provide the 'big picture' about what is going on in Europe. Explain the reason for events to supplement the dry telegraph reports."[23]

Börnstein's first letters began to arrive at the *Tribune* just as the radical nature of France's 1848 revolution was starting to emerge. At the outset of the revolution, opposition to the monarchy had united a diverse coalition of republicans, but as the spring wore on France and especially Paris divided along class lines. Soon after the February Revolution established a provisional government, radicals announced plans for "National Workshops" modeled after Louis Blanc's manifesto, *The Organization of Labor*. Blanc himself, though a member of the provisional government, left the practical application of his plan to subordinates, while he continued theorizing as the leader of the "Workers' Commission." The National Workshops, unfortunately, were a near total failure. Instead of creating a series of legally protected and state-subsidized producer and consumer cooperatives, the National Workshops became, in essence, a public dole that did little to reform the economy structurally. As a result, French politics became increasingly polarized.

Börnstein's letters, first published throughout May in the national weekly edition of the *Tribune,* celebrated the revolution's radical trajectory. Delirious in their excitement, they celebrated the destruction of the old order with a vigor that was clearly distinct from the "harmonic" and antirevolutionary sobriety of the Fourierist *Tribune*. "Hurrah! How gaily it burns," Börnstein's wrote. "I am still giddy, still all bewildered. Every day comes fresh news, each thing more astonishing than the next." Initially, Börnstein's letters made Greeley fearful that the radicalism of the workers' parties in France would discredit the Associationist movement in America. In Börnstein's second letter, which detailed the split within the provisional revolutionary government between the republicans and the socialists, Greeley inserted a note within Börnstein's column: "In this term Socialistic, our correspondent does not include the large body of professed Associationists of Paris. They, as we understand, do not act with [Alexandre] Ledru-Rollin and the ultra-revolutionists, but are steadfast supporters of law and order." Two weeks later, after the conservative Whig *Express* attacked Börnstein's letters for their "ultra-Revolutionary and War-invoking sentiments," Greeley all but apologized: "We do not engage correspondents to reecho our own opinions on all points, but to increase the aggregate of information afforded by our columns. We have engaged 'H.B.' to let our readers know what the ultra-Radical party of Europe are meditating and doing, which is neither fully nor fairly set forth through the other channels of information accessible to us. We have a large class of readers who are not satisfied with seeing France and Europe presented through British Conservative spectacles." In the next issue of the *Weekly Tribune,* Greeley labeled Börnstein's letter the "Radical Correspondence of The Tribune."[24] The New York *Evening Express* praised the *Tribune* for distancing itself from its radical Paris dispatches, but added, in a rather backhanded way, "How happens it always, that there gathers around the Tribune all the Robespierres of the day?"[25]

Just before, and even during the first few months of Börnstein's letters to the *Tribune,* the paper's editorial line continued to insist that the goal of social reform was the reconciliation of capital and labor, but gradually, as events in France became radicalized, the paper followed suit, becoming ever more resigned to class violence. In late April, it still referred to communism as "the most mistaken" of the various "solutions of the social problem"— even Börnstein once contended that "Communism... [is] as despotically hostile to freedom as [the] old Absolutism"—but it also began to concede that "revulsion," "bankruptcy," and "bloodshed" was a necessary prelude to "a vastly improved social order." Social progress, the paper admitted, could be "accelerated by the Revolution of the Laboring Class," a far cry from its traditional Whig-Fourierist harmony of interests.[26]

It should come as no surprise that conservative papers failed to distinguish between social democratic reform and insurrection, and despite Greeley's best efforts to distinguish between the two, his own correspondent had made the line increasingly blurry. Events in the working-class districts of Paris would make it even more so. Throughout his May and June correspondence, Börnstein predicted "that the great battle between the Bourgeoisie and the Proletariats" was coming. He regretted only that the workers' parties trusted the good intentions of middle-class "republicans" and "suffered themselves to be disarmed." Börnstein acceded very early on in the revolution to the principle that Marx had outlined four years earlier in *Vorwärts*—"the state is the organisation of society," and particularly during moments of social and economic crisis, it could not serve as a neutral arbiter of an objective public good. The situation, Börnstein concluded, had unraveled to the point that "the government remains only in name. Stationed between the two parties of the *Bourgeoisie* and the *Proletarists,* every energetic measure which it originates, must offend one or the other of these important classes."[27]

Though the prescience of Börnstein's analysis of the French political and social scene was unmatched, his millennial expectations of proletarian triumph were just that. During the first week of June, he promised that the cause of the people was "justice," and that justice would "triumph." As he put it, "The bourgeoisie will fall and fall forever, this time entirely destroyed."[28] He could not have been more mistaken. In response to continuing worker protests, the new popularly elected assembly announced on June 22 that the National Workshops would be closed. Barricades went up once again throughout the city. Unlike in February, however, when Louis Philippe's bumbling monarchy was easily overthrown, the new bourgeois-led government was ready to act, and with cruelty. After three days of fighting, fifteen hundred people were dead, and afterward, three thousand more were executed, forty-five hundred were deported, and twelve thousand were arrested.

To conservative and even moderates in United States, the June Days fully discredited the new social theory. The *Express* claimed that "nearly all the principles which *The Tribune* teaches are calculated to lead to the same war of classes in this city and country that have broken out and consumed no small portion of Paris." Its editorial "Parisian Fourierism and its Fruits" labeled the *Tribune's* sympathy with the insurrectionists a "defense of... butchers" and blamed Greeley's "pet theory" for "most of the bloodshed and barbarity." The *Courier* joined the *Express* and other conservative journals in deriding the French "mob" that allegedly equated liberty with idleness. Ignoring the desperate position of the Parisian unemployed, the *Courier* cheered the reaction and tied the uprising to "the influence of *Socialism*" and the misguided state effort "to provide workshops, in which workmen were hired and paid out of the Treasury." Even the Democratic but free soil New York *Evening Post* abandoned the revolutionary cause in France. Committed only to a limited Democratic paragon of political democracy and laissez-faire, the *Post* condemned the June uprising as "madness" and a "dreadful slaughter": "They [French socialists] are sometimes called ultra-democrats," the *Post* editorialized. "We do not understand what sort of democracy that is, which denies the majority the right to frame its own government.... Such men as these are not democrats in any sense."[29] Greeley's eventual response to such criticism from "progressive" Democrats was to point out the parallels between his own brand of Whig socialism and the working-class democrats of France. "It is remarkable that the Progressive Democracy of France and that which aspires to the like distinction in this country," he wrote, "are at direct issue on nearly every element of practical legislation. The anti-Tariff, Hard Money, anti-Public Works, *Laissez Faire* notions of *our* self-styled Democracy have scarcely an adherent among Progressives of France."[30]

Charles Dana and the Rise of Practical Socialism

Börnstein's reports throughout the spring had already framed the ongoing conflict in France as a social revolution, but his letters on the culmination of those events—the June Days violence—marked the end of his tenure as the *Tribune*'s regular Paris correspondent. Charles Dana, who would later become in the 1850s what today we might call the managing editor of the paper, arrived in the city and took over the reporting the very day the Assembly closed the National Workshops and Paris went up in flames. Dana remained in Europe for the better part of a year, issuing correspondence from Paris, Frankfurt, and finally Cologne, where, no doubt armed with an introduction from Börnstein, he met Marx. The meeting resulted, in 1851, in Marx's decadelong employment as European correspondent for the *Tribune*.[31]

Dana's 1848 reporting illustrated perfectly the revolution's ideological impact both on the *Tribune* and social democratic reform more generally. Dana argued that although 1848 had discredited Fourierism, "the man who should say that the idea of Association had made no advance during this period would be mistaken." In the context of 1848, he contended, Association "yielded to necessity" and "passed from abstract theory into practice"; thereafter, social democrats would not entirely abandon the goal of social harmony, but would more often seek more practical and class-bound solutions to the labor problem.[32] Dana himself was at the forefront of this transformation, and the very fact that the initiative for the *Tribune* to move in this more pragmatic direction came from him demonstrates the dramatic ideological impact of the French '48. Dana, more than anyone on the paper, had been a committed Fourierist. Dana's *Tribune* work was preceded by five years at Brook Farm, which he viewed as the "last hope of Divine Providence" on earth, or literally as "heaven on earth."[33] He was Brook Farm's secretary, helped to direct the community's educational program, and brought to the settlement's finances his valuable experience from his six-year apprenticeship in his uncle's Buffalo dry goods shop. Despite his youth, Dana played a leadership role that was second only to George Ripley, Brook Farm's founder (and future *Tribune* literary editor).

At Brook Farm, Dana was drawn at once to the practical and to the utopian, and had little sense of how to compromise between the two. He joined Brook Farm because he favored its political economy and because he thought associated living could bring about spiritual growth. He also needed physical exercise and a place to live after an eye problem effectively ended his college career at Harvard. While living in the community, he often wrote for the *Dial* and the *Harbinger,* but when fire destroyed any hope that Brook Farm could continue, he went into the newspaper business. His first major position was with Boston's *Daily Chronotype,* an intelligent paper but one whose readership was primarily composed of orthodox Congregationalists and conservative Whigs. There he filled columns, clipped items from other newspapers, and even edited the paper when editor Elizur Wright was absent. In February 1847, Greeley offered him three times the pay to work on the *Tribune's* city desk, and Dana jumped at the chance. But he did not remain happy in the job for long. Proficient in a number of languages (Carl Schurz once remarked that Dana spoke better German than any nonnative he had ever met) and interested in European culture, Dana longed to travel in Europe.[34] More than that, like most members of the *Tribune's* socialist circle, Dana viewed the European revolutions as a historical turning point and he was anxious to witness them firsthand. Greeley initially resisted. He had hoped Dana would bring stability and talent to the operations of the paper, and he was satisfied with the European correspondents he already had.[35] Dana eventually prevailed, but Greeley exacted a price. Offering Dana only ten dollars for a weekly letter, Greeley forced him to negotiate separate agreements with four other publications. Dana, newspaper historians often note, became out of necessity the first "syndicated" columnist in the history of American journalism.[36]

Dana, who would become the most powerful voice on the *Tribune* next to Greeley, left New York on June 10 and arrived in France on June 23, just as the June Days violence erupted. When his train pulled into Paris at five o'clock on Sunday morning, there was so much chaos in the city that porters hesitated to unload bags from the train. Soldiers were already visible on every street and all France was in an uproar. Dana had not even been able to sleep on the train through the din of "La Marseillaise" and "Mourir pour la Patrie." Leaving his bags at the station, Dana hastened to the working-class districts, but soldiers made movement between districts difficult. Finding the one available unguarded bridge, Dana and his guide finally managed to pass through to the scene of the fighting. Along the way, with cannon and musket fire echoing throughout the city, Dana and his attendant were repeatedly searched and forced to account for their presence on the streets.[37]

Thanks to Börnstein, when Dana arrived in Paris, he was met by an already established network of contacts that helped him slip into the working-class districts.[38] Still, Dana's initial account of the June insurrection was more than a sensory account. Among prominent American Associationists, Dana had already come the closest to endorsing class conflict and revolutionary violence. His first letter from Paris argued that the insurrection was the spontaneous work of the laboring classes; it had not merely been encouraged by socialists, journalists, and other publicly oriented theorists and intellectuals. He also maintained that the working-class communities resented the manner in which the bourgeoisie had appropriated the meaning of the revolution and usurped the provisional government, replacing a tyranny of birth with a tyranny of capital. To Dana, what was unfolding before his eyes was a lost opportunity to transform the social and political order, a "glorious chance to do something immortal." With all resistance—monarchical, aristocratic, bourgeois—swept away, the revolution afforded France the opportunity to make a political democracy simultaneously a "Social one." And social freedom—the freedom of labor—meant to Dana that workers could become their own employers: "To secure to them all the advantages of buying necessaries at wholesale, of preparing their food on a large scale, of lighting and warming their houses and workshops on a more unitary and economical plan."[39]

Though Dana would spend the next several months outlining the various theoretical factions in the capital, he came to believe that doctrine was of little consequence, except in the most general sense. To Dana, the insurrection was a populist uprising and the radical parties had little control over the course of events. Communists, such as Cabet, were "not fighting [men]" and had little "influence among the workingmen." Dana's own party, the Associationists, was not aligned with any practical political faction; they merely petitioned the revolutionary governments to make the protection of labor a priority. In inverse proportion to the miniscule consequence of doctrinal disputes among the radicals, however, was the general effect of socialist agitation on public discourse. Thus, he maintained, even as particular socialist schools were discredited by the June defeat, public opinion came to understand proletarian resistance in sociological rather than in moral terms. "Socialism is thus not conquered nor obscured in France by this desperate attempt... but strengthened," Dana wrote. "It is no longer Fourierism, nor Communism, nor this nor that particular system which occupies the public mind of France, but it is the general idea of Social Rights and Social Reorganization. Every one now is more or less a Socialist."[40]

Dana, who had once shared the Brook Farm hope for the restoration of a more "natural union between intellectual and manual labor," now lauded what he called "practical Association," worker and consumer cooperatives, based largely on the writings of Proudhon, that promised a "radical change in the relations of Capital and Labor." In 1849, Dana penned a series of articles for the *Tribune* on Proudhon that reflected the decline of the *Tribune's* trust in Fourieristic "goodwill" between the classes. Though the *Tribune* would never go so far as to argue that capital and labor are inevitably antagonistic, the paper now argued that labor needed to replicate the action of capital. Their interests, the *Tribune* finally admitted, could not harmonize voluntarily. "Our idea," the *Tribune* announced, "is that Labor needs not to *combat* but to *command* Capital." Only cooperative reform on the part of labor, independent of the actions of capital, could achieve meaningful social change. Private property was, in effect, both the cause of, and a solution to, the problem of wage exploitation—labor needed to "command capital." After the decline of Fourierism, Dana, Greeley and the *Tribune* began an eclectic search for various mutualist schemes that could either secure the independence of labor from the market or, at the very least, elevate its position within it.[41]

Dana, in particular, developed an abiding interest in and sympathy for France's radical communist parties. In a closely watched National Assembly debate between Proudhon and Adolphe Thiers on the closing of the National Workshops, Dana not only sided openly with Proudhon against his reactionary critics but all but linked Fourierism with the latter.[42] "The 'Fourierists,'" Dana conceded, "have not a more thorough antagonist than M. Proudhon; and the special grounds on which he denounces them are their pacific tendencies and their constant defense of the right of private property." Though referring only to France, Dana finally concluded that the "Right of Labor could not exist with the royalty of money, with aristocracy of capital. One of two things must then happen—either the Republic would abolish Property, or Property would abolish the Republic."[43] Dana arrived in Paris as the social revolution was winding down. Although he left the city in October, he never really abandoned the questions raised by conflicts in that city. Disappointed with the outcome, Dana left heartened by the fact that although factions and parties could be defeated, the rights of labor, even in the darkest days of reaction, were the central issues of the revolution.[44]

From Association to Cooperation

In the aftermath of the June Days, the *Tribune* neither abandoned social democratic reform nor embraced revolutionary socialism. Rather, its reform principles came to recognize, in a moderate way, the inherent antagonism between capitalism and labor. The *Tribune* instead advocated a form of democratic "capitalism" that did not repudiate Fourier entirely, but did introduce more class-specific forms of cooperative organization. Embracing a materialism of sorts, the *Tribune* realized that the marketplace's "laws" would have to be dealt with in a way that did not rely on the benevolence of capital. Without much fanfare or introspection, the *Tribune* evolved during the early 1850s from a Fourierist organ to one that was distinctly less sectarian, although it promoted worker associations in a vaguely Proudhonist way. The "Proudhonist" solution, as the *Tribune* translated it, involved little more than worker cooperation in both production and consumption. The *Tribune's* "Proudhonism" meant two basic things. First, it dispensed with its hope for the harmonization of capital and labor. Second, it deserted comprehensive reform—a vision of a socialist future that involved the direct reorganization of cultural and social life. The *Tribune's* "Proudhonism" was instrumentalist and never became a comprehensive theory of society, work, or personality. It was a scheme to empower labor, and eventually became wedded to land reform principles that had little to do with the French socialist.

It was Dana who outlined this new "Proudhonist" blueprint when he returned to the United States in March 1849. Dana was determined to energize America's dwindling socialist movement by transmitting more recent French ideas about class-specific cooperative reform. Back in the United States, Dana continued to follow events abroad, particularly the surviving worker associations in Paris, with an eye toward their demonstrative value in America. But most important, that spring he began a series of six articles on the then obscure (to Americans) Proudhon in which he outlined a new, and narrower, solution to the problem of industrial labor.[45] Dana's series of articles on French postrevolutionary socialism signaled the *Tribune's* Proudhonist turn. They were, in some ways, Dana's and the paper's post-1848 answer to Brisbane's earlier series on Fourier.[46]

Before Dana's *Tribune* series, Americans had heard little about Proudhon. New York City in the 1840s had witnessed a few efforts at cooperative reform that were in the spirit of the French "mutualist." John Bray's *Labour's Wrongs and Labour's Remedy,* a widely read critique of wage labor and land speculation, led to a variety of land and producer cooperatives. George Ripley, who would become the *Tribune's* literary editor, had been urging cooperative reform in the pages of the *Harbinger* as early as 1845. George Henry Evans's 1844 National Reform Association, also in the spirit—if not under the influence—of Proudhon, attacked banking and credit institutions within a broader program of democratic land distribution. Still, in the mid-1840s most American socialists and labor reformers continued to dream of a distinctly Associationist future.[47]

For Dana, Proudhon's political economy had a number of core principles. Proudhon argued that the contradiction between the scale of modern industry and the individualistic way prices and wages are negotiated worked to the detriment of workers and consumers. Maintaining, like most socialists, that labor creates all value, Proudhon emphasized that the "collective force" of large-scale production was exponentially greater than the work of individuals, but labor accrued only a fraction of the surplus. Proudhon was also a critic of property, but in a more nuanced manner suggested by the aphorism for which he is popularly known, "property is theft." He distinguished between "possessions," which were productive property—actual tools, land, and machines that produce wealth—and accumulated capital, rent, interest, and all forms of what he called proprietary property or investment capital, which is idle and appropriates surplus value. The latter was what he considered a form of theft. On this theoretical bedrock, Proudhon hoped to ensure that labor, not capital, accumulated profits by banning interest and rent. Naturally, his solution to what he referred to as "the social problem" went directly to this conflict between labor and possessive property on the one side and capital and speculative property on the other. Claiming that capital creates no value, Proudhon attempted to create a cooperative workers' bank, a Bank of the People, in order to reduce the rate of interest to cost. Ideally, Proudhon hoped that his bank's legitimacy would be based on popular participation, but he gradually evolved toward a position in which his People's Bank, at the behest of the state, would take over the assets of the Bank of France. By suppressing interest and rent, Proudhon also expected that his banking scheme, by disengaging currency from specie and private banknotes, would transform the system of exchange from one based on supply and demand to one based purely on the cost of production.[48]

Dana identified with Proudhon both personally and politically. They shared a humble upbringing and both bridged practical reform (Proudhon created an actual cooperative bank, while Dana was an officer at Brook Farm) with theoretical writing and regular journalism. "Great as is the influence Proudhon's books have exercised upon opinion in France, it is as a journalist," Dana wrote in admiration, "that he has come most in contact with the people. His paper had a very large circulation . . . [and] this was due to him alone, for none of his associates had the talent to gain so wide a circle of readers."[49] Dana even seemed to model his at times skeptical and confrontational post–1848 journalistic style after Proudhon.[50] Like Dana and the Fourierists, Proudhon was not an egalitarian leveler. He did not value all labor equally, but argued instead that the system of exchange had produced inequalities of value that failed to account for "talent and industry." Proudhon valued competition, innovation, and private industry, but he recognized that the emergence of extended global markets and large-scale capital-intensive manufactures required cooperative mechanisms that would level the playing field. Proudhon hoped to create a system of financial institutions and property laws that could mediate between the extremes of free-market and communist absolutism, between individualism and the slavery of community. Unlike the Fourierists (though, like Dana, Proudhon was also once briefly a disciple of Fourier), Proudhon did not advocate communal living, which he thought denied women "a position worthy of society or herself." He also believed in the family insofar as protecting the right of inheritance (once again, what he termed possessive rather than speculative capital/property). Characterized disdainfully by Marx and Bakunin as a petit-bourgeois social-ist, Proudhon worked, at bottom, to protect the independence of small pro-ducers and was the product of a nationalist-protectionist tradition that shared with the *Tribune* a sort of socialist mercantilism that called upon nation-states to protect labor from becoming undervalued by global commerce and trade.[51]

In his summary and translation, Dana remained largely faithful to Proud-hon's economic theories. Dana opened his account of Proudhon's work with the apology that "whoever seeks in Proudhon's books for a complete system will be disappointed. Hitherto his writings have been critical more than con-structive." Dana, however, ignored Proudhon's early "transcendental specula-tions" and fixated on his plans for the practical emancipation of the laboring classes: "Our business is to try to get at his political economy."[52] Proudhon's virtue as a political economist, to Dana, was his simplicity and realism, quali-ties that were particularly appealing in the aftermath of Fourierism's failure.

Dana explained that Proudhon, like Fourier, rejected violence, but he real-ized that some mechanism beyond love—some "higher philosophical truth," "universal formula," or "comprehensive social principle"—was required so that "discord" and "antagonism will disappear."[53] The basis of Proudhon's, and now Dana's, system was a critique of capital and the financial system that sustains it. Fundamentally, they argued that capital is unproductive—only labor creates wealth—though capital, defined as surplus labor, makes labor more productive. Unlike some radical workingmen and Jacksonians who hoped simply to do away with banks, Proudhon and Dana hoped to harness their cooperative power to benefit the working classes. "In such an organi-zation credit is raised to the dignity of a social function," Dana summarized, "managed by the community; and, as society never speculates upon its mem-bers, it will lend its credit, not as our banks do theirs, so as to make seven per cent or more out of the borrowers, but at the actual cost of the transaction."[54] Equally important, Proudhon and Dana advocated the elimination of specie, which financiers and industrialists consolidate and becomes the means by which "labor is kept in subjection."[55]

Despite Dana's ringing summary and endorsement, it would be a mistake to conclude that the *Tribune* became in the 1850s anything approaching an explicitly Proudhonist organ. Even during the 1840s, the paper's socialism was not limited to the exposition of Fourier's principles, and their failure only made the *Tribune's* socialist sectarianism less pronounced. In the spring of 1850, the *Tribune* admitted that although "no theorist has yet truly solved the great problem of the harmonious and beneficent combination of Labor, Skill and Capital, it is none the less palpable that this problem *must* be solved, and that Society fearfully suffers while awaiting the solution."[56] Proudhon's influence was even less direct than Fourier's had been. Even so, the *Tribune* looked optimistically toward Proudhonist-style workingmen's associations in Paris, Brussels, London, and the United States. In New York, Greeley pressed for the establishment of a labor exchange, where workers could trade directly with one another, and even public works. "An able-bodied and willing man or woman is *not* a proper object of charity," he wrote, "but should have instead simple Justice—that is, Work. Let the State provide work for all willing and able to do it who can find none for themselves; let the Alms-House engulph [sic] only those who are too young, too old, too imbecile or too ill to work."[57] In an editorial statement of its "Isms," long the signifier of its offense against a conservative moral and economic order, the *Tribune* outlined a general social democratic platform the included the right to labor, the right to education (mental, physical, and industrial), and just wages.[58] Throughout the 1850s, the *Tribune* lobbied for the creation of a "People's College" in New York "in which Labor should be taught, required, and practiced," elevating the status and productivity of industrial and agricultural science.[59] It also continued to advocate a legal limit to the length of the workday, particularly for minors.[60] In New York State, Greeley agitated successfully for a homestead exemption for bankrupt farmers.[61] Like the strike, however, all of the above reforms from Greeley's point of view merely relieved the distress of wageworkers temporarily. His larger goal was to make every wageworker a "capitalist"—independent of the labor market itself. For the next two decades, this imperative, in a vaguely Proudhonist way, would issue forth in regular calls for worker cooperatives.

Worker cooperation was rooted narrowly in Proudhon but also was the natural outgrowth of the failure of Fourieristic "goodwill." Proceeding from the assumption that labor's emancipation was predicated on the availability of capital, the *Tribune* proposed with increasing frequency that labor ought to organize by and across trades, so that "non-employed or half-employed laborers" could furnish "each other with bread, shelter, coats and shoes" directly. Like Fourierism, but more modestly, cooperative labor would harness industrial productivity to the welfare of workers: "Why *should* it be difficult for organized Associations of Carpenters, Shoemakers, Hatters, &c. to effect exchanges of labor or of products with and for each other."[62]

Consistent with the view that a permanent wage labor class and social justice could not coexist, cooperative industry was a solution to the labor problem that did not rely on either benevolence or ignore the laws of supply and demand. For the latter reason, the *Tribune* advocated worker cooperatives rather than strikes. During the decade's many strikes, the *Tribune* never contested "the right of workmen in any trade to combine for the enhancement or maintenance of a special rate of wages." "Aside from the notorious fact that employers continually combine to *reduce* wages," the *Tribune* reasoned, "we see no other mode in which Labor can possibly protect itself against the overwhelming power of Capital than by this very method of Combination."[63] Nonetheless, the *Tribune* regarded the strike, though a natural right, as ineffective.

Writing about Philadelphia's striking carpenters, Greeley characteristically cautioned against strikes, not because they offended morality or the sacred right of individuals to bargain freely in the labor marketplace, but because they did not address the root cause of low wages and economic inequality. Strikes, to Greeley, surrender to the logic of supply and demand, neither challenging it morally nor overthrowing it altogether; how many striking journeymen, Greeley asked, "ever paid a poor widow a dollar a piece for making your shirts when you could get them made as well for half a dollar." "Strikes or Combinations...may sometimes be necessary, but they are the last dire resort," the *Tribune* editorialized. "A scale of prices so established is a stone rolled up a mountain; the first jar sends it headlong down again." Without securing some sort of collective independence from wages, "there is no rational hope of a permanently improved condition of the Laboring Class except through the exercise of unusual forecast, frugality, diligence and mutual confidence on their own part." The *Tribune,* then, never opposed the formation of industrial unions, but it did argue that they could serve a new and more constructive purpose. Workers must pool savings to effect their "elevation *out of the* thralldom of the Wages System....Unless the Laborers can combine to work for themselves, their combinations *not* to work for employers...will exert no influence."[64] Through the cooperative principle, Greeley tried to sustain his basic Whiggish view that class antagonism was artificial and avoidable, even if he embraced new methods that dispensed with cross-class benevolence. Recognizing that no natural harmony of interests existed between capital and labor, Greeley hoped to reform the latter out of existence through cooperative action.

Practical Socialism and the *Tribune* Career of Karl Marx

It was within the post-1848 context of the *Tribune's* search for alternative strains of socialist thought that the *Tribune* would reach out to Karl Marx to become one of the paper's European correspondents. Marx's tenure on the *Tribune* would end up lasting for more than a decade, and encompass some 487 articles, about a quarter of them written secretly by Engels. Though Greeley was said to be lukewarm about Marx's work, Dana considered him one of the paper's most "highly valued" talents and made him "one of the best-paid contributors to the journal." *Tribune* literary editor George Ripley thought enough of his correspondence to arrange for Marx (and Engels) to write for his *New American Cyclopaedia* at the lucrative rate of two pounds per page. For Marx, it was the most regular employment he held in his entire life, and even though he thought little of "newspaper muck," his articles were polished and engaging. Marx thought highly of the "outspoken," "witty," and "straightforward" "gentlemen" in the *Tribune's* "foreign department," and was proud that his articles were "read with satisfaction by a considerable number of persons, and are widely reproduced." Marx valued some of his American journalism enough that he imported some of it directly into *Capital*.[65]

Marx wrote on a broad variety of subjects for the *Tribune*. He wrote wide-ranging articles on European politics, war, and diplomacy. He wrote about international economics and imperialism in India and China. He even penned biographical sketches of important statesmen. Although it is clear in retrospect that Marx was ideologically and temperamentally more radical than Greeley and the *Tribune*, his correspondence was not by any means out of place in the paper, and unlike Börnstein he provoked little comment from readers or from other newspapers. And the articles, both those of Engels and his own, were identifiably "Marxist." Of Germany just before the 1848 revolutions, for example, Engels wrote that the era of political "superstition which attributed revolutions to the ill-will of a few agitators have long passed away. . . . Wherever there is a revolutionary convulsion there must be some social want in the background, which is prevented by outworn institutions from satisfying itself." More astonishing is how neatly Marx's interpretation of European and imperial politics coheres with the Radical Republican analysis of sectional antagonism. Marx and Engels' depiction of Germany on a revolutionary precipice was eerily similar to Radical Republican portraits of both the South's "antagonistic interests" and the larger "irrepressible conflict" between slavery and free labor.[66]

Even though, in a broad and abstract manner, the *Tribune* shared with Marx a sort of socialist sociology—a tendency to view politics and law through an economic and social lens—they clearly occupy distinct traditions. Marx was at times contemptuous of the paper's humanitarianism. "Under the guise of Sismondian philanthropic socialistic anti-industrialism," Marx wrote of the *Tribune* in 1853, the paper was the very voice of the "industrial bourgeoisie," which explained "the secret of why the *Tribune* in spite of all its 'isms' and socialistic humbug can be the 'leading journal' in the United States." Marx had actually contracted with the *Tribune* without realizing that it was a pro-tectionist organ, and at times he and Engels waged war on the paper's Carey-ite, nationalist political economy, if in ways too subtle to attract Greeley's notice or interest. In "The British Rule in India," Marx strikes what would have been a familiar note for *Tribune* readers in reporting that the "British principle of free competition" has "broken down the entire framework of Indian society." To Marx, however, English despotism was a welcome devel-opment because it eradicated the "economical basis" of the "semi-civilized," traditional village community, which was "contaminated by distinctions of caste and by slavery," by "unspeakable cruelties," and was generally "undig-nified, stagnatory, and vegetative." From Marx's perspective, the article was a swipe at the "*Tribune*'s 'leaders'" because in his mind the backward Indian village alluded to the protectionists' model for the associated township's mix-ture of community, household industry, and agriculture, a vision that was the basis for American "petty bourgeois" protectionist campaigns to preserve the small producer against British political economy, "centralization," and global trade. Nevertheless, Marx never really attracted much notice editorially from other newspapers, or from readers, and did not really shift the paper's point of view.[67]

Marx's mostly private contempt for the *Tribune*'s ideological immaturity and incoherence rehearsed later transatlantic conflicts within the Interna-tional Workingman's Association between orthodox Marxists and the more far-flung and diverse spirit of "Yankee radicalism." At the core of such conflicts was Marx's contempt for the eclectic character of much of the Anglo-American anticapitalist Left during the Civil War era, and particu-larly its basic commitment to the democratization of property rather than its abolition. Despite important differences, however, Marx's presence on the *Tribune* during the long 1850s was representative of the paper's post-1848 turn toward more class-bound and pragmatic strains of socialist thought.[68] Marx's American presence did not mean that either Dana or Greeley made class conflict or class consciousness the basis of their political economy. In fact, in politics and on the labor question, the *Tribune* followed a similar course to Marx's opponents within the main leftist parties in France, a path carved out by Alexandre Ledru-Rollin, Proudhon, and the workers' societies and newspapers that was alternately termed republican socialism, cooperative socialism, or *démoc-soc,* democratic socialism. Nonetheless, the consequences of 1848 made it increasingly clear that permanent classes were a natural result of labor markets, and moreover that forceful intervention was necessary to ensure that those who labor own and control the fruits of their efforts.

Despite postrevolutionary demoralization, the *Tribune*'s foreign correspondence demonstrates the continuing influence of socialist ideas upon the paper into the 1850s. Throughout the decade, the paper employed some of the West's leading radical minds. Margaret Fuller, as noted earlier, finished her career at the paper at the outset of the 1850s writing quasi-socialist dispatches on behalf of the Italian nationalist movement in which she was also a participant.[69] Louis Kossuth and Central European national liberation movements also remained familiar subjects in the pages of the paper. In the early part of the decade, Charles Lane and Jules Lechevalier wrote letters from London and the Continent, respectively. The English socialist Hugh Doherty carried the Fourierist mantle into the 1850s, insisting that Associationism remained the right middle road between "spurious" "Red socialism" and "National exclusivism and *patriotic* hatred." But for most of the decade, the *Tribune*'s attentions were primarily national: "Cosmopolitan fraternity has many obstacles to overcome before it can become a living, practical reality."[70]

At key moments during the first one hundred years of American history, events in Europe and especially France had a decisive impact on domestic politics, culture, and ideology. During the Federalist era, French revolutionary passions played an important role in early party formation and more broadly became a symbol through which Americans debated the meaning and range of their own revolution. During Reconstruction, the Paris Commune also became a canvass upon which Americans projected and then interpreted the significance of their own labor, racial, and sectional conflicts. And so it was for 1848. In 1848, Americans witnessed a failed attempt in France to realize a true social democracy. This effort came about at the tail end of one of the most dynamic decades of reform activity in the history of the United States. Traditionally, cultural historians of the antebellum period have argued that the defeat of radical revolution abroad had a sobering effect on this side of the Atlantic. Communal experiments disintegrated. Urban life and popular culture became increasingly disciplined and segmented. Economic forces began the process of consolidation. Radical reformers, they argue, retreated from profound democratic engagement with the problems of industrial society into a comfortable gentility. Intellectuals either abandoned reform entirely, or were diverted by middle-class "lifestyle" reforms such as vegetarianism, marriage and sex reform, spiritualism, and health. In Carl Guarneri's words, "in much the same way that the 'Me Decade' succeeded the turbulent 1960s, utopians during the prosperous 1850s turned from advocating broad structural reform to preaching changes in personal life-style." He added that "this strategy of retreat and its promise of fulfillment for the enlightened few" diverted the focus of American socialism "from socioeconomic to personal issues and collectivistic to individualistic solutions." The one major reform movement that remained—free-soil antislavery—implicitly endorsed a limited, bourgeois conception of liberty, equality, property, and mobility.[71]

In their laments for the lost 1840s, historians have underestimated two things. First, and most important, was the persistence of the labor movement's interest in cooperative reform. In the crisis atmosphere of failing phalanxes and 1848, socialists refined Fourier's comprehensive blueprint. Though the United States would experience communal surges at various moments of its history, after 1848 social democrats embraced a stripped-down version of Fourierism that focused principally on a more practical style of worker association termed cooperation. Fused to various instrumental reforms such as the eight-hour day, worker cooperation became the central demand of the labor movement into the Gilded Age. The second thing that historians have ignored was the way that post-1848 reform—the debates over slavery, land, sex, and the family—was rooted in earlier debates over the organization of labor. Moreover, antislavery sentiment and lifestyle reform themselves were connected to many of the same economic anxieties that contributed to the emergence of socialism. Disputes during the 1850s over sex, marriage, and slavery all derived from a common source: the manner in which the new economy had upset and overturned traditional modes of social organization.

CHAPTER 4

Marriage, Family, and the Socioeconomic Order

> We maintain that the isolated family is not the most
> perfect form of the household.... We maintain that
> for Woman, from infancy a toy or a slave, so often
> condemned to mercenary or loathed marriages, or
> a useless and joyless loneliness, by an education and
> by Social usages, which deny her means of essential
> independence, there is no hope but in a true Social
> condition, and enlarged opportunities for Knowledge,
> liberal Culture, and Industrial usefulness.
>
> Horace Greeley, *Hints Toward Reforms*

During the 1840s, American socialism was uni-
fied behind a brand of Fouricrism that was both practical and comprehensive.
Structurally, Fourierism aimed to recalibrate the structural inequalities in the
relationship between capital and labor, but it was also based on a psychological foundation—the passions—and committed to a broad agenda of cultural
reform. Libraries, lectures, music, and even communal living were essential
parts of its appeal. Nonetheless, American Associationists were fundamentally uneasy with the way in which Fourier's writings broached the subjects
of family, marriage, and sexuality. The first major American distillations of
Fourier's thought suppressed his sexual extremism. Albert Brisbane acknowledged that he deliberately "separate[d] his [Fourier's] doctrines into two distinct parts: his personal intuitions and speculations, and his deductions from
the Law of the Series," the mathematical code that combined individuals and
working groups in a manner that would maximize personal and collective
fulfillment. Greeley was even more adamantly opposed to any discussion of
familial and connubial experimentation, and when challenged on those issues
by conservatives such as Henry Raymond, he insisted that sexual novelty was
not a core part of Fourier's system. Other leaders followed suit. Parke Godwin, an early and influential Fourierist convert and propagandist, remarked
that "the policy of the Societary School" has been to treat the marriage and
family question with "reserve" even though it "has brought suspicion upon

their intentions." Though in private Godwin was less squeamish about Fourier's passional theory, he worried that deliberate misinterpretation by Association's opponents would discredit the movement with the public. Critics, of course, were less bashful, and by the end of Fourierism's run as a live, intact, reform option, sexual and familial issues came increasingly to the fore.[1]

The 1850s was a decade of women's rights agitation and free love scandals, ranging from New York City's "Free Love League" to Robert Dale Owen's vigorous advocacy of divorce toward the end of the decade. These private and public debates over the nature and meaning of marriage and the family eventually engrossed Fourierist leaders who, liberated from the practical defense of actual communities, began publicly debating the marriage question for the first time. These debates revealed inherent tensions within socialist theory, between women and men, and between individualists focused on personal emancipation and communitarians centered on the reconstruction of a more organic and reciprocal community life. Fourierism clearly challenged traditional Christian conceptions of human nature and family values, but within the Left itself socialism wavered between two antagonistic ideals. It hoped to replace competitive individualism with a corporate society bound by ties of fraternity and love. At the same time, Fourier's theory of passional attraction seemed to license a kind of anarchistic individuality that was radically emancipated from any and all moral conventions. Throughout the nineteenth century, socialists would debate the relationship of the family to the capitalist social order, but this was particularly true in the United States in the aftermath of failed revolutions at home and abroad. In the *Tribune,* these issues became particularly acute in the early 1850s when Greeley was pushed into an exchange on marriage and sexuality with Henry James Sr. and Stephen Pearl Andrews that became known popularly as the "Free Love Controversy."

To some scholars, the antebellum Left's preoccupation with sex, marriage, women's rights, and the family—often grouped further with vegetarianism, spiritualism, and other "lifestyle" reforms—diverted the energy of reformers from the more pressing necessities of the labor movement. Greeley might have agreed. As Greeley wrote Paulina Davis, "To my mind, the *Bread* problem lies at the base of all the desirable reforms which our age meditates. Not that the Bread is intrinsically more important to man than Temperance, Intelligence, Morality, and Religion; but that it is essential to the just appreciation and healthful acquisition of all these."[2] To Greeley, although free love and related reforms invoked Fourier's passional theory, they were, in the end, its perversion. In Greeley's view, "free love" had little to do with socialism at all, and instead originated in the rootless, anarchical individualism that he had long spent his political and cultural energies combating. "The farthest he [Greeley] seems ever to have seen into the magnificent speculations of Fourier," Stephen Pearl Andrew once lamented, "is to the economy to be gained by labor done upon the large scale, and the possibility of the retention of profits by the laborers themselves by means of association."[3] During the 1850s, Greeley's pragmatism became even more pronounced, and many in the movement went with him in this direction. Other Fourierists, however, moved in the opposite direction, embracing a moral and cultural radicalism that was inherently individualistic. Reformers, such as Andrews, Marx Edgeworth Lazarus, and Thomas and Mary Gove Nichols, openly engaged what Associationists in the 1840s had, to an extent, skirted: sex, family, and marriage. As we have seen, this turn was hardly a distortion of Fourier, but it nonetheless represented a notable change in the American movement's posture on these issues.

The Political Economy of the Family

The prominence of the "free love moment," as well as the *Tribune's* discussion of marriage and the family, was the product of broader historical currents. Throughout the early nineteenth century, the institution of marriage itself had been evolving slowly from an austere, utilitarian economic relationship to a more individualistic, romantic, sentimental, and companionate form based, ideally, on the spiritual and emotional affinity of its partners. The glacial pace of marriage's emotive and institutional transformation was dramatically accelerated during the 1840s as conceptions of sex, marriage, and the family underwent systematic and popular critique. The burgeoning woman's rights movement, engaged in such diverse reforms as divorce and dress, subjected marriage and sex generally to public debate. Health reformers, led by the publishing house Fowler and Wells, made, moreover, the scientific discussion of sex somewhat commonplace. Sexual conservatives, such as Greeley, and more conventional conservatives both pushed for laws that would punish seduction and adultery. Liberals (and Greeley could be counted among their number as well) advocated the extension of property rights to women to protect them against abandonment and from the debauchery of intemperate husbands. Mormons and Christian perfectionists challenged the conventional nuclear family, sometimes with plural marriage and sometimes with abstinence. Conventional bourgeois marriage was thus a ripe subject for reform for a dizzying array of critics.[4]

Changes in family discourse as well as actual changes in the structure of the family were not only intimately connected to changes in the economy, they were mutually reinforcing. It is tempting to imagine that the new economy led deterministically to the modern family. But equally important was the way in which the family, as one scholar put it, was the "cradle" of the new economy and the new middle class that served it. Companionate marriage and smaller nuclear families followed the spread of the capitalist market, but smaller families, evolving gender roles, and new child-rearing patterns and practices also helped create market culture by conditioning younger generations to survive and prosper within a radically new economic environment.[5]

Among the reformers who eyed the rise of market capitalism with unease, there were profound disagreements about the relationship between "family values" and the vast social changes taking place around them. The *Tribune* was one place where these disagreements came to a head because it was one of the few places where socialists, feminists, and religious conservatives could debate the marriage question openly and in concert. What made the marriage question so discomfiting to voices across the political spectrum was that everyone agreed that the family institution bore some relationship to the emerging bourgeois order, but there was little consensus about what exactly that relationship was. Marriage and the family, of course, were at the center of middle-class life. It was for that reason that socialist critics of individualism critiqued the family institution—the isolated household—as the source of a pervasive and socially destructive egotism. The individual household and the ideal of privacy also formed, in a sense, a bulwark against various antebellum attacks on the sanctity of private property. On the other hand, the modern nuclear family, as it was emotionally and economically constituted, was an evolutionary development of the eighteenth and nineteenth century. Though the nuclear family educated its offspring for life within a hostile and anonymous marketplace, the family and the sentimental discourse that rose up around it was also one the marketplace's severest critics. The ideal sentimental family was everything the marketplace was not. The most central of bourgeois institutions, ironically, called forth a host of what might be called counterbourgeois values. Benevolence, love, obligation, intimacy, care, protection, transparency, and community were all ideals that had little place in the bourgeois marketplace.

The conventional modern family's relationship to the new economic order was complex and contradictory. Equally so was that of the nuclear family's radical, free love critics. In the nineteenth century, "free love" meant a variety of things. Few free lovers openly avowed hedonism—pure sexual freedom—but rather condemned traditional, indissoluble marriage as an anachronism. What they proposed to put in its place varied widely. Nevertheless, most free lovers rejected the main beliefs that respectable middle-class Victorians held sacred: Christianity, feminine virtue, and the moral channeling of physical appetites. But, at the same time, free love was also a natural product of other aspects of middle-class culture. Like the emerging consumer culture, it made happiness and self-fulfillment the central ends of existence. Free love discourse was also steeped in the language of sexual purity; only spiritual unions were divinely sanctioned and a perpetual and loveless marriage was a form of slavery or prostitution. The free love movement, then, reflected a broader middle-class search for authentic and emotional relationships over the course of the antebellum period.[6]

The contest over marriage also relied on some of the same vocabulary used to debate political economy. Just as Whig economic nationalists celebrated the "harmony of interests" between society's economic orders, a moderate feminist such as Elizabeth Oakes Smith would call for reform of the marriage institution to "harmonize" the "sexes."[7] Conservative Victorians, likewise, often thought of sexual indulgence in economic terms—of spending and saving. To conservatives, familial discipline, authority, and hierarchy was the natural counterpart, and indistinguishable from, that of the workplace. Little notice, however, has been taken of the relationship between radical political economy and the discussion of sex and marriage.

Fourierism and the Free Love Controversy

Fourierism, as I have noted, promised a progressive intervention within the social, cultural, and psychological realms, in addition to its reforms of industry and the organization of labor. So it is not surprising that when industrial reform failed, countercultural radicals would continue to uphold the banner of Fourier's critique of conventional bourgeois culture, especially that of marriage and morality. In 1848, C. J. Hempel, in *The True Organization of the New Church,* announced that sexual experimentation was an integral aspect of Associative theory. Soon afterward Thomas Low Nichols, recently married to fellow sex radical Mary Gove, published *Woman in All Ages and Nations* in which he argued that permanent marriage was a form of barbaric prostitution and that "true marriage" was the perfect spiritual—and dissolvable—union of self-reliant equals. Henry James Sr. (father of novelist Henry James and philosopher-psychologist Williams James) also weighed in by anonymously translating Victor Hennequin's *Love in the Phalanstery,* an abridged version of Fourier's sexual theories. Subsequently, James engaged in a long discussion of marriage in the *Harbinger* that embroiled him in controversy with religious conservatives.[8] These controversies were largely ignored in the *Tribune* until George Ripley joined the paper informally in 1849 and became the editor of the paper's literary department in 1850. Ripley was friendly with James and attentive to his writings, and as a result steered the paper toward the burgeoning discussion of sex and marriage in the radical community.

Ripley was one of the founders of Brook Farm and was among the last members to leave. He never really repudiated its goals and continued to agitate for socialist reform.[9] When the community dispersed in 1847, Ripley first devoted his efforts to making the socialist *Harbinger* America's radical journal of record, but by the spring of 1849 it too went bankrupt, so Ripley turned to conventional journalism.[10] Much like Greeley, Ripley was instinctually conservative in temperament and bearing, but receptive to radical ideas. On the basic questions of economic reform, Ripley rejected out of hand common ownership of property and hoped ultimately that cooperative association would defend artisanal independence and self-reliance from the pressures of the market, namely the tendency toward specialization and consolidation.[11] But for Ripley, even more than for Greeley, economic reform was meant to serve higher cultural and spiritual ends. Given those interests, along with the more prosaic fact that Brook Farm's demise was itself the most important sign that the practical age of Fourierist association had come to an end, Ripley helped unleash discussion of the marriage question in the paper.

Within Fourierism, there was genuine tension between its impulses toward corporate fraternity and anarchy. Greeley emphasized the former, of course, but many of the sex reformers—the Nicholses, Lazarus, and Andrews—gravitated to the latter, and not a few of them were disciples of the original American anarchist, Josiah Warren. Warren, born in 1798, was with Robert Owen at the New Harmony settlement in the 1820s. Nonetheless, his work appealed to younger sex reformers such as Stephen Pearl Andrews who believed that Warren's *Equitable Commerce* got to the root of socialism's failures: its tendency "*to regulate* men *by legislation,* instead of trusting to men to regulate themselves and their relations to each other *by a knowledge of principles.*"[12] In 1851, Warren and Andrews founded the Modern Times commune on Long Island, and it was both an extension and repudiation of Associative socialism. Modern Times aimed to build a society in which all economic exchanges were based on labor notes or direct exchange. It outlawed profit, interest, and speculation. But mostly it was a community based in the "sovereignty of the individual"—that "no organization, no indefinite delegated powers, no Constitutions, no laws nor bye-laws, 'rules' or 'regulations' but such as each individual makes for himself."[13] Warren's libertarianism was primarily an economic doctrine. He resisted the transformation of his libertarian individualism into a theoretical license for sexual emancipation, but in the hands of disciples Andrews, Thomas Low Nichols and Mary

Gove Nichols, and especially Marx Edgeworth Lazarus, it gave birth to free love principles.[14]

In 1852, Lazarus published *Love vs. Marriage,* a book that was a cross between a health manual, a hygienic guide, and a free-love promotional handbook. Lazarus had been involved with health reform movements such as vegetarianism, water-cure, and homeopathy, throughout the 1840s, and claimed the title of "Doctor." Fowler and Wells issued *Love vs. Marriage* as part of a larger project linking marriage, sex, and health to social reform.[15] Though Lazarus had once written for the *Harbinger,* had lived at the North American Phalanx, and was well known to more orthodox Fourierists, he clearly was a postmortem product of the movement. His book is littered with Fourierist terminology—"isolated households," "passional affinity," and "attractive industry"—but the argument has little to do with the central issue identified by 1840s Associationists: the harmonization of capital and labor. Lazarus, in fact, had little interest in the problems of labor at all. Instead, it was marriage, he believed, that was the source of human unhappiness and an institutional arrangement whose true nature was not unlike prostitution or slavery. Wedlock, he wrote in terms borrowed from Josiah Warren, violated the spirit of "self-sovereignty."

When George Ripley became literary editor of the *Tribune,* he invited Henry James Sr. to review *Love vs. Marriage.* When James wrote the review his idea of marriage was in a state of transition. Most of James's early writings advocated the free love position. It was implicit in his translation of *Love in the Phalanstery* and in modified form in his quasi-perfectionist *Moralism and Christianity.* In April 1850 he published a series of letters that advocated the liberalization of divorce, starting on the same day that the paper published a glowing review of Nathaniel Hawthorne's novel of marriage, spiritual affinity, adultery, and sin—*The Scarlet Letter.* James argued that marriage enslaved the passions, and when a man and woman cease to love one another, they are, in reality, spiritually and emotionally divorced. To require them to remain married reduces the institution to an economic relationship: to, in effect, prostitution.[16] James's various writings on marriage in the paper scandalized some readers—one wrote the paper that "he could not consent to have the sacredness of Marriage discussed, pro and con, in any work which he allowed to be read in his family"—but Greeley remained firm that his paper's usual practice was "to let every body know what every body else is thinking."[17] Despite, at times, vicious disagreements with James, Greeley intermittently opened the paper to him, and James in turn would invest $10,000 in the *Tribune* in 1851. In 1852, the *Tribune,* approvingly, counted James with Emerson as "decidedly the two profoundest and most sweeping radicals of our time."[18]

Despite James's history of sympathy with the free love position, his autumn 1852 review of Lazarus's *Love vs. Marriage* was almost unremittingly hostile. In it, he all but declared independence from the burgeoning free love movement.[19] James lambasted the book as a "needless affront to public decorum" and took exception especially to the title, which suggested that "a commerce of the sexes regulated by social needs necessarily excluded love, or as if true manhood stood in a profligate abandonment." Less than one column of a nearly three-column review, however, was devoted to the book. In the rest, James outlined his new view on the marriage question.[20] Marriage, James argued, was both a divine and a social institution. The divine marriage "embodies the most humane, and the highest... idea of the sexual relation." But marriage, as it was actually practiced, was strictly a legal and social institution, a "ratification" of a union, no longer voluntary, that consists of a set of privileges and especially obligations. When James had endorsed free love principles during the 1840s, he was inclined only to endorse the divine ideal of marriage as a perfect and spiritual union. Now James was also ready to defend marriage in its lower form. "The germ of society," he argued, "is the family, and the family has no bulwark but marriage." Although marriage, like "all the institutions of Society," is "purely finite" and removed from "absolute or divine realities," James was now receptive to any institution that regulated humanity's inherently selfish and degraded passions. "We can easily conceive that in a perfect society, where man's essential or inward divinity is reflected in all his institutions, that marriage will then confess itself the ratification of a purely spontaneous or spiritual tie between the sexes," James wrote. "But until that time comes, the less that is said of 'following the divine clue of charm,' and turning men over to the guidance of sensual instinct, will be, in our opinion, decidedly the best for the community."[21] James, in the end, was never a careful or consistent thinker, and his vagaries and contradictions are representative of the way in which midcentury socialists struggled to frame the relationship between the family and the new economic order.

After James reviewed *Love vs. Marriage,* he was hit from all sides. From one side came Greeley, who invoked biblical law to oppose "inflexibly... any extension of the privileges of divorce." "But," he added, "we are *not* opposed to the discussion of the subject."[22] Greeley's position hardly appeased the conservative press, particularly the *New York Observer.* The *Observer* acknowledged that Lazarus's book "is not reviewed favorably by the philosophers of the Tribune School," but insisted that "they have a theory of their own on marriage," which is "a specimen of poisonous and covert infidelity" designed "for the gradual subversion of the religious faith of the young and unsuspecting." Outraged by James's suggestion of human divinity, the *Observer* urged

Christian readers to quarantine the *Tribune* from their homes. "It is nothing more and nothing less than the most subtle and dangerous form of modern infidelity, meanly but industriously insinuated in a political newspaper," the *Observer* concluded. "Are we wrong in saying as we do, that 'the Tribune is the most mischievous paper in the English language.'"[23]

The *Observer*'s "assaults" provoked a series of letters in the *Tribune* between November 1852 and February 1853. The *Observer*, which naturally lacked the *Tribune*'s liberal commitment to the free exchange of ideas, refused to publish James's replies to its attack, so he was forced to publish his responses in Greeley's paper. James, in his original response to the *Observer*, claimed that he was not in any way opposed to the institution of marriage. "The drift of your assault," he complained, "is to charge me with hostility to the marriage institution. This charge is... far from being true." Instead, James merely "aimed to advance the honor of marriage by seeking to free it from certain purely arbitrary and conventional obstructions in reference to divorce." His argument was a simple one: the virtue of the institution did not require permanence. As long as men and women insulated the state from the care of affected children, divorce should essentially be granted on demand. From James's perspective, divorce would not "weaken... respect of marriage," but "plainly strengthen it." Laws against divorce, in his view, subvert marriage by suggesting that the only "security for the faithful union of husband and wife... dates from the police office." James proposed, in accordance with what historians of gender and marriage now conclude was a Victorian shift in sexual and familial values, that marriage be regulated not according to "legal bondage," but by "reciprocal inward sweetness or humanity."[24]

The *Observer*, of course, was not swayed by James's defense. In an editorial, "Marriage and Reformers," the *Observer* noted that the "very fact that it [marriage] is found so directly across the path of most radical and fanatical tendencies, shows it to be the very heart of all sound conservatism." Marriage, in a trinity with the church and the state, was the "fountain of law-abiding" society and a bulwark against tyranny and despotism. "The socialist knows [this] instinctively," continued the *Observer*, and "the first step" toward the subversion "of established political society, is the utter breaking up of these domestic obstacles." James's argument with the *Observer* continued into December, but meanwhile the tenor and course of the discussion changed directions radically.[25] James's original intent in his *Tribune* review of *Love vs. Marriage* had been to renounce publicly his former endorsement of Fourieristic sexual spontaneity. As was made clear by the *Observer*, religious conservatives thought any suggestion that civil marriage was anything less than a divine and permanent instrument jeopardized both society and religion. But soon after the *Observer's* "assaults," James faced another sort of antagonist, Stephen Pearl Andrews.

Andrews, Greeley, and Sexual Individualism

Andrews, a free love anarchist and Lazarus sympathizer, was modest about his intentions when he entered the controversy. He claimed that James's argument with the *Observer* merely "piqued" his "curiosity," and that the new "positions assumed by Mr. James" had driven him "to a sort of 'hope-I-don't intrude' propensity to ask questions." By year's end, he would proclaim that the "Social dogmas" of "Philosophers, Politicians, and Theologians...must give way before the sublime principles of a new and profoundly important Science, which determines exactly the true basis of all Social relations."[26] Andrews, not unlike Greeley, was an advocate of woman's rights, a critic of wage labor, and a spiritualist of sorts.[27] He had also spent his early adulthood in a dangerous and somewhat quixotic effort to abolish slavery in Texas.[28] Like Greeley, Andrews tried to combine reform with entrepreneurship, and though both were products of a New England upbringing and sensibility, Andrews's was of a Calvinist sort. Andrews's youth was morally austere, and after making a painful break from it he became in due time a marriage reformer: "I conceived a dread of marriage at that early day which had in it something of the prophecy of the bold and critical investigations I have been led to make of the claims of that institution later in life." Andrews's feminism was further sharpened by his experiences in the South. There, both he and his brother had been threatened and attacked by mobs, which in his view were rooted in the brutish code of Southern honor. This code, he thought, was not only the basis of white supremacy but its exaggerated masculinity also maintained a sexual order that isolated unmarried women from any possible defaming mixture with society.[29]

Andrews was among the reformers who, like Lazarus, used Warren's economic principles to critique conventional domestic relations. Even so, when Andrews entered the controversy, he pretended to "third party" neutrality, "quite indifferent" to any party and invoking "the Socratic privilege of propounding difficulties and seeking for further information." Though he alluded somewhat wryly to the new "ferocious morality" of a onetime sexual radical (James), the focus of Andrews's first contribution to the free love controversy was a series of questions designed to expose the untenable logic of James's efforts to carve out a middle ground between indissoluble marriage and free love. In the most basic sense, Andrews wondered, what exactly is the difference between liberalized divorce and no marriage institution at all?

The only legal obstacle James supported at this point on the right of divorce was the guarantee of perpetual and private care of offspring. To Andrews, this made little sense. Why, he asked, "if the maintenance of the unswerving constancy of husband and wife can be safely intrusted to the guardianship of 'their reciprocal sweetness or humanity,' with no 'base legal bondage' super-added—why may not the care and maintenance of the offspring be" commended to "that same 'inward sweetness or humanity?'" If marriage, echoing James's language, is degraded by its dependence on "the police office," why is not the care of children? "Why," probed Andrews ultimately, take "the trouble and expense of maintaining a police office at all?"[30]

To Andrews, the only logical outcome of James's position on the liberalization of divorce was a morally neutral free-love position similar to his own. Andrews argued that if the "dissolution of Marriage" should be left entirely to the contracting parties, then it only made sense that individuals should be free to pursue alternative forms of marriage such as polygamy. "We are aware," he wrote, "that men have differed in theory and practice in divers ages and nations—between Monogamy and Polygamy, for example—and with all restraints, both of custom and of law removed, possibly they may differ in like manner again.... Who is to be the standard of proprieties?"[31] Both James and Greeley were repulsed by the extent of Andrews's relativism. James suggested that "Mr. Andrews's queries need [not] detain us" and refused to respond. Greeley, however, allowed Andrews to join the conversation, but on a limited basis. Andrews thus provoked Greeley's participation in the discussion.

Greeley had any number of philosophical objections to Andrews's position. Though Greeley was an advocate of sexual, ethnic, and racial equality, at an instinctual level he simply could not tolerate sexual libertinism. Nor did he agree with the basic assumptions on which Andrews based his free love ethic: that there were few if any innate differences between men and women, and that marriage was an institutional impediment to the emancipation of women. Temperamentally and morally opposed to divorce, Greeley, who was married, worried that "marriages *would be* contracted and dissolved with a facility and levity now unimagined. Every innocent young maiden would be sought in marriage by those who now plot her ruin without marriage, and the facility of divorce would cover the arts and designs of the libertine." For this, the conservative *Observer* praised the *Tribune* for its "progress in the right direction." "We cannot but recur to the time," it wrote, "when this same paper sowed... the seeds of Fourierism in this city and the country, a system that would convert society into a nightly brothel, and make the relation of the husband and the wife unknown in the family of man."[32]

In a deeper sense, though, Greeley's resistance to divorce rested on the same intellectual foundation as his socialism. It reflected his profound and abiding distrust of market individualism. Greeley thought that free love, however much it subverted the selfish and privatizing tendencies of the nuclear family, was an expression of the very individualism that he hoped socialism would overcome. It was, in effect, sexual laissez-faire. Free divorce, promulgated under the principle of "the Sovereignty of the Individual"—in Greeley's view, the "right of every one to do pretty nearly as he pleases"—was merely an extension of "free trade" sophistries, the very same that resisted measures of public uplift such as temperance and tax-supported schools. "The State does not exist for the advantage and profit of this or that individual," Greeley protested, "but to secure the highest good of all,—not merely of the present, but of future generations also.... We insist, then, that the question be considered from the social or general rather than the individual standpoint."[33] Alongside the period's conventional sentimental defenses of the family, Greeley insisted that the marriage institution's virtue rested on the extent to which it served to curb the individualistic excesses of the culture. The family was the antidote to the market, a separate sphere. To Greeley, Andrews and the like obliterated the line between market competition and domestic obligation. Even James's more moderate position mirrored the values of the market: all human relationships rest on no firmer or spiritual basis than a contract, revocable at will. But Greeley could hardly be placed in the sentimental camp either. He hoped rather that socialism could implement familial principles, namely benevolence and reciprocity, within the larger society.

The free love controversy continued intermittently until February 1853, but it did not cover much new ground. When Andrews published his pamphlet collection of the controversy that year, he complained that the *Tribune* had "abruptly...closed [its columns] to me, in the midst" of the debate and that Greeley, "owing to the want of consistency in his own mind," was a dishonest moderator. Greeley, Andrews concluded, is the "leader of the Reform Movement in America," but he lacked a philosophical temperament. "He sees broadly over the surface," Andrews asserted, "but never down into the center of things."[34] James, on the other hand, was publicly mortified by the debate. He complained about the impropriety of the *Observer's* "unmannerly allusions to my private history" and only reluctantly engaged Andrews's provocations. But the close of the debate also found James a popular intellectual. During the winter of 1852–53, James lectured to packed houses on the subject of "Woman and the Woman's Movement." The lecture, which was later published in the recently launched *Putnam's Magazine,* revealed the extent to which the free love controversy had transformed him. James had become, in short, an opponent of sexual equality, arguing that the woman's movement was unnatural and promoted an ideal of womanhood at war with her fundamental nature. "The 'Woman's Movement,'" James contended, only "furnishes another and a striking commentary upon woman's incapacity as a legislator or leader in human affairs."[35]

Free Love and Feminism

James's reactionary sentiments prompted a stinging response in the pages of the *Tribune* that served as a sort of postscript to the free love controversy. The anonymous author was almost certainly Elizabeth Oakes Smith, who, during the tail end of the free love controversy, published a set of parallel letters in the *Tribune* on woman's rights, marriage, and divorce, but they neither engaged nor were engaged by Greeley, Andrews, or James. In 1849 Smith had also published a series of articles in the *Tribune* on "Woman and Her Needs." In the *Tribune* she had been a consistent advocate for women's civil equality and rights. She demanded for women equal compensation for equal work, a voice in lawmaking including the franchise, fair access to education, and the privilege to enter a profession. To those such as James who claimed that it was a natural "fact" that "Woman is by nature inferior to Man," Oakes Smith responded, "Why are you not content to leave the matter where Nature placed it? Why enact laws at Albany and Washington to fortify Nature's resistless fiat?"[36]

Like many early feminists, though, Oakes Smith opposed divorce, but on grounds quite distinct from those of Greeley or religious conservatives. In all of her *Tribune* letters on the subject, she rarely mentioned Christian sanctions against divorce and was dismissive of marriage as a spiritual union:

> I admit I have taken an external view of marriage, because I contend that that is all which can be reached by Legislation. The true spiritual marriage is what the laws do not inquire into, and cannot therefore provide for spiritual contracts nor divorces. Society, it is acknowledged, is corrupted, imperfect. . . . Marriage, like all other institutions, is imperfect, because all human institutions are imperfect. But when we say there is no Marriage except in its interior sense of compatibility, companionableness, congeniality, we in fact deny Marriage altogether; for this trueness of spirit can be reached only by a very few, and it may be even by those only for a limited period of life, and that not the earliest part of life, at which time marriages are mostly solemnized.[37]

She argued, in short, that a true and spiritual marriage is only possible if it is one that unites independent and equal partners. Until the time comes that women do not have to "marry for support," women will remain a "sort of household chattel." "Marriage," she wrote, "can never be fully chaste and holy till Man recognizes fully the social equality of Woman." Oakes Smith's opposition to divorce was based, then, on the inequality of women and the pessimistic sense that sexual relations between unequal partners was so hopeless that couples should not expect love, happiness, or nearly anything beyond mutual division of care and support.[38] Oakes Smith, in the end, opposed divorce on precisely opposite grounds from those of Greeley. Greeley viewed marriage and the family as upholding a broader communitarian ideal of society. Because Oakes Smith viewed a pure spiritual union as an unlikely blessing in an age of sexual inequality and beyond the purview of the state regardless, she defended perpetual marriage as among a host of rights extended by the liberal state for the protection of individuals in their persons and property.[39] Her position reflected the extent to which feminists, like socialists, were divided on the question of marriage and divorce. Antoinette Brown, one of Greeley's loyal correspondents, also opposed divorce, advising instead permanent separation. Both she and Oakes Smith thought that the institution of marriage's demands for monogamy in theory protected women from sexual impurity and male lust. Other feminists, on the other hand, such as Elizabeth Cady Stanton and Ernestine Rose, believed that liberal divorce laws could emancipate women from abusive men, and it was a perspective that meshed well with conservative moral reform movements such as temperance that made masculine appetites the most common source of marital conflict.[40]

Throughout the decade, however, the *Tribune* would revisit the "woman question," which, broadly construed, was a general discussion of sex, marriage, individualism, and even political economy. In 1854, the *Tribune* exposed and condemned Andrews's "Free Love League." As late as 1860, Greeley once again publicly debated the divorce question with another refugee from communitarian socialism, Robert Dale Owen. The *Tribune*'s engagement with the "woman question" was both philosophical and political. Philosophical debate over the nature of "womanhood" was paired with a more strident advocacy for such progressive measures as married women's property rights and the extension of suffrage, as well as more paternalistic measures that outlawed alcohol and seduction. But in the broadest sense, the woman question was directly connected to the debate over individualism and the values of the market, the subject that had consumed the paper since its inception.

Like many historians since, Greeley contended that the "bread question" was largely unconnected to, and should take precedence over, "culture," particularly the divisions that had erupted around the status of women, marriage, and in a broad sense the family. But ever since the family, over the course of the nineteenth century, surrendered its economic function, Americans have been contesting its character and structure. In only a few cases, however, have they drawn an explicit link between the discourses of the family and political economy. Greeley viewed the moral and cultural challenge from both the Right (Raymond) and the Left (Andrews) as an unnatural distortion of socialism's pragmatic response to the perils of the market. But what he ignored was the way in which the structure of the family and even "human nature" were at stake in any comprehensive consideration of the socioeconomic order. The character of the family was a key metaphor through which nineteenth-century reformers considered the responsibilities and duties that individuals owed one another. This was particularly true in the nineteenth century when the diffusion of the market meant that the rural and largely subsistence economy organized around the obligations of kinship gave way to the specialized and differentiated economic system structured around individual self-interest and contract.

The rise of the market brought with it a revolution in values and law that challenged the communalism, violence, and patriarchy of traditional rural life. Along with the spread of ideas and commodities came a new form of social organization that historians came to regard as the liberal tradition, a political economy and a cultural framework that rested principally on the values of individualism, contract, and rational self-interest. Among the clearest signs that a new liberal order was emerging was the vigorous debate taking place in the popular press over the structure of marriage and the family. Prior to the nineteenth century, under English and American law, married men and women were one person—effectively, the man. Designated by the law as under the protection of her husband, married women did not have a legal identity of their own. She could not, for the most part, make contracts, could not sue, could not draft a separate will, and she could not own property independent of her husband or without his consent. These legal disabilities reflected powerful dependencies and inequalities, but also the mutuality of the traditional patriarchal family. In the premarket universe, the family had been an all-encompassing social and economic entity, but in response to the demands of the new market economy, the structure of the family, the meaning of the home, and new patterns of child rearing came forth to contend with a world in which all individuals had to make themselves anew.[41]

Not only did the market transform the roles of fathers, mothers, and children, but it altered relations between them. Political theorists and social critics from across the political spectrum recognized this shift. Karl Marx and

Friedrich Engels wrote famously that what "distinguish[ed] the bourgeois epoch from all earlier ones" was that a revolution in the "instruments of production" had transformed "the whole relations of society": "All fixed, fast-frozen relations, with their train of ancient and venerable prejudices and opinions are swept away, all new-formed ones become antiquated before they can ossify."[42] The ambivalent liberal Alexis de Tocqueville observed likewise that under the premarket aristocratic regime, society was organized in a way that "had made a chain of all the members of the community, from the peasant to the king; democracy breaks that chain and severs every link of it." Among the things he observed when he visited the United States was the way in which democratic individualism had relaxed the lines of authority within marriages and families.[43]

In the realm of the family, the most visible manifestations of the new liberal individualism that both Tocqueville and Marx described were social movements and public debates over the status of women and the nature of marriage such as the ones witnessed in the *Tribune*. Along with the debates over marriage, some of the clearest markers of the emergence of liberal individualism were campaigns for married women's property rights and efforts to end coverture, married women's invisibility in the eyes of the law. Each proceeded on the liberal assumption that women were free, rights-bearing individuals.[44] Perhaps even more than the marriage question, the battles over women's property rights were central because they took on a political dimension in state legislatures throughout the 1830s, '40s, and '50s. These legislative struggles suggested further the extent to which women and the family were registers of political-economic values in a period when marriage was shedding its patriarchal dimensions in favor of a companionate model, and when the role of women was being reshaped along class lines, with some women enmeshed in the most advanced industrial work of the period and others taking control of households that were increasingly private and superficially divorced from economic endeavors.

Fundamentally, contention about the nature of marriage was a means to discuss the nature of social relations in a market society; it reflected pervasive uncertainty about the relationship between market and family values. Could a market economy based on self-interest, materialism, individualism, and competition coexist with the emotional economy of the family rooted in Christianity, obligation, self-sacrifice, and love? In the realm of property rights, feminists questioned whether the unequal condition of parties to the marriage contract undermined its legitimacy and fairness. Some even pushed the logic farther by arguing that inequity, exacerbated by legal disabilities, made marriage an economic necessity because law and convention forced it upon them; as a result, marriage was not all that distinct from prostitution. Such arguments shared the logic, in certain respects, of labor advocates who characterized the wage relationship as a form of slavery. Paulina Wright Davis complained of married women being "partners in toil, not in profits"; Lucy Stone and Elizabeth Cady Stanton likewise warned women against the dangers of economic dependence, and encouraged them to seek the security and the psychic rewards of self-reliance.[45] This rhetoric mirrored the efforts of labor reformers to respond to worker dependence and dislocation with schemes to democratize property and raise the position of workers in the labor market. Historians of American socialism and the 1850s have complained that the post-1848 turn toward antislavery and lifestyle reform diverted attention from more pressing economic concerns related to the rise of capitalism. What that critique ignores, ultimately, is the degree to which economic and social relationships were rooted in familial and marriage relationships; any discussion of one directly impinged on the other. As the historian of women and marriage Norma Basch put it, "Marriage was (and is) a metonym for the social order."[46]

On marriage, Greeley was on the conservative side of the equation, but he did for once have the merit of consistency. In both the private and public realm, he was a critic of individualism. Nonetheless, Greeley's conservatism was slightly out of step with the paper. Moreover, that he even allowed the free love debates to take place at all would forever associate the paper with counterculture radicalism. Despite Greeley's protests, all through the 1850s free love would remain linked to both socialism and the *Tribune,* and rightly so. Both socialism, and the market values it condemned, contested social and economic relationships at all levels. Debates over culture, in short, were intimately connected to debates over political economy. Given the *Tribune's* mélange of cultural and economic reform, Greeley more than likely intuited this point even if he resisted some of its more threatening implications.

The failure of Fourierism during the late 1840s gave rise to a social democratic sensibility that was more pragmatic, interventionist, and consumed by questions of economic organization and class; the new socialism, in short, separated cultural reform from its systematic assault on the "bread question." On behalf of the latter, the 1850s *Tribune* would advocate a series of piecemeal reforms, such as state regulation of the hours of labor, the restriction of child labor, and the creation of agricultural and technical colleges, many of which were destined to become the Republican Party's program for labor and a constituent part of its political economy. All had roots in the socialist indictment of competitive society. But land reform stood above them all. Land reform was an instrumental reform, a less comprehensive reorganization of society and economy than full-blown Fourierism, but that may have been part of its appeal, particularly to workingmen. Initially, orthodox Fourierists opposed land legislation as a partial reform, but as Associationists reached out toward labor, many began to see the two movements as complementary. In the early 1840s, socialists argued that property rights should be contingent on the right to labor, and this helped lay the intellectual groundwork for a land reform movement that was, arguably as early as 1846, the leading object of organized labor.

Self-conscious socialism may have unraveled, but its separate threads became the basis of a new politics. Cooperation and land reform galvanized labor, and the latter became the basis of a decadelong process of political realignment. Beyond that, what emerged from the wreckage of 1848 was a new socialist method of interpretation, which articulated the role of interest and class in the political struggle between and within the sections, and it became part of the available vocabulary that Americans used to understand the political and industrial conflicts of the 1850s, at the center of which were questions that the socialists had already raised about property rights and the organization of labor. These questions only became more pressing after 1848, culminating in the creation of the Republican Party. "The call of the time was for a new democracy—one that should be social and economic rather than political," the early historian of labor John Commons mused, and "Horace Greeley was the prophet."[47]

CHAPTER 5

Land Reform, Pragmatic Socialism, and the Rise of the Republican Party

> We are strongly attached by convictions and sympa-
> thies to the Whig Party, and have acted with no other
> since this had an existence.... There are *men* in the
> Whig Party with whom we have little sympathy, and
> tendencies sometimes evinced by it, through their
> influence, which we feel bound to resist; but, viewed
> as a whole, we regard the Whigs as the party allow-
> ing the ampler tolerations of Ideas; the larger liberty
> in Political Action; the freer play to the reformatory
> and humanitary impulses which inspirit and honor
> our age.... But, though belonging to none of the
> distinctively Anti-Slavery factions or sects, we are
> profoundly hostile to Human Slavery, and in part for
> reasons just indicated.
>
> *New-York Tribune,* June 12, 1852

In the spring of 1846, Horace Greeley exulted that a political revolution was imminent. It would "dissolve and recombine," he hoped, the Jacksonian party system "so that the old Hunker Whigs and Loco-Focos shall be put in one file and liberal Progressive Whigs and Demo-crats go together." "The basis of union of the True Democracy," he wrote to one New York free soiler, "is to be *Land Reform,* not alone as applied to the Public Lands but to all Lands. With this goes *Labor Reform* or the Ten Hour regulation. To these articles I hope another will naturally attach itself—viz. *Abolition of the Army and Navy."* To Greeley and his allies, "there were con-servatives and radicals in both parties," and this worked to the advantage of timid partisan professionals. The radicals, Greeley reasoned, "should act in harmony and be true to their political convictions, no matter what became of the old parties."[1] But these were private sentiments. Not only were Gree-ley's hopes for political realignment premature but the increasingly powerful New York editor played a leading role in ensuring that the traditional party framework remained in place despite pressure from reformers.

From the mid-1840s on, Greeley was perpetually on the cusp of political revolt, but the prospect of abandoning an election to the hated Democratic Party always brought him back to the Whigs. It took nearly a decade for Greeley to abandon his party, and those familiar with his post–Civil War campaigns for sectional reconciliation might wonder whether he ever truly foreswore Whig values. For Greeley to leave the Whig Party, he had to abandon three basic tenets, some directly and some loosely connected to his political economy. First, he had to give up his absolute faith in the harmony of interests, and the notion that reform could somehow restore an organic social order. Second, he had to surrender his belief in the neutrality of the law and the state, and, by extension, the viability of reason and persuasion in democratic politics. Finally, he came to accept, shaped by the failures of 1848, the role of power, interest, necessity, and violence in social and political change. The issue that drove this radical evolution was land.[2]

Premised on the principle that it was unrealistic to expect the voluntary reconciliation of capital and labor, land reform was one of the piecemeal, pragmatic, and interventionist reforms that the *Tribune* adopted after Fourierism's post-1848 decline. Initially, land reform clashed with the *Tribune*'s dual commitment to socialism and Whiggery. To orthodox Fourierists, what was variously called "land reform," "agrarianism," or later "homesteads" was a "partial reform"; orthodox Whigs opposed population diffusion on the frontier, and the Whig Party staked its political economy on urbanization and human development. Since then, land reform also has been dismissed by historians as a "bourgeois reform" because of the emphasis it placed on the democratization of property, autonomy, and self-reliance. As Eric Foner rightly points out, the "homestead idea was defended in middle-class, capitalistic terms," yet in the largely pre-Marxist context of the 1840s, '50s, and '60s, the question of property was not yet the polarizing litmus test it would become, and most labor radicals viewed the democratic extension of property, rather than its destruction, as central to labor's emancipation.[3] Not surprisingly, the idea of land reform emerged not from the Right but from the Left, and like many nineteenth-century reforms it possessed a characteristic mix of "conservative" and "radical" assumptions. By Marxist or even Fourierist standards, the homestead concept was a partial reform, but from the point of view of the artisan republicans who agitated on its behalf, it was an attempt to guarantee the right of property in labor.

Even though Greeley was a product of that artisanal world, he was, like many Associationists, somewhat slow to embrace the movement.[4] Like the land reformers, Greeley and the Associationists had always argued that landed property was a political right, contingent on a socially guaranteed right to labor. This issue was, in fact, the very one that launched his notorious debate on socialism with Henry Raymond. The land reformers also shared Association's social democratic assumptions. Committed to economic rights, land reform was among the first initiatives that explicitly promoted the state as an agent of economic welfare and wealth redistribution. The Fourierists tried to strike a balance between the interests of property (or capital) and labor. The land reformers hoped to curtail property rights paradoxically by democratizing the ownership of property. As one historian recently put it, the land reformers thought that westward migration would challenge "imbalances in resources and power . . . [by] fashioning circumstances whereby American wage earners cast off their dependence on their employers."[5] It was the latter principle that made land reform so successful. It did not require complicated mathematical formulas or a mastery of French theory. Instead, land reform resonated with distressed workers and farmers alike, and its wider appeal lay in its simplicity and its adherence to the long-held agrarian assumption that the foundation of American republican virtue was a broad distribution of property.

Land reform's popularity and eventual adoption (and modification) by the Republican Party obscures the movement's radical roots. Land reform's modern genealogy in the United States stretches back to New York City's labor battles in the 1830s when agitators began probing the relationship between the condition of labor and the availability of land. By the late 1840s, land became the centerpiece of a mature ideology that linked the political fate of Western lands to the rise of a "new feudalism," both Southern and industrial. To land reformers, the reservoir of land in the West, protected by the federal government from speculation and slavery, would be the sole effective antidote to the oversupply of labor in the East. Land reform, thus, also became the vehicle through which antislavery became a popular political cause. Before the 1840s, even committed reformers regarded the abolitionists as hopelessly myopic and blind to the economic injustices in their midst. Margaret Fuller remembered them as "so tedious, often so narrow, always so rabid and exaggerated in their tone."[6] But land reform recast antislavery as a populist movement with a stake in the social and economic future of white labor, and in doing so it restructured the existing party systems and political institutions.[7] Eventually, the *Tribune*'s commitment to land reform and the West as a solution to the labor problem dramatically reoriented its politics. More apt to embrace statist solutions to the mounting stratification of the wage economy, the *Tribune* came increasingly to view the South and slavery as the principal obstacles in the way of a realized social democracy. Pushed left by 1848, the central Whig and Fourierist notion of a "harmony of interests" gave way to a more radical style that shaped its sectional politics. Emerging from the struggles of New York's labor parties, land reform, thanks in no small measure to wide publicity in the *Tribune,* became the basis of a national movement that culminated in the Republican Party.

Anti-Rent and the Land Question

The *Tribune's* political pivot on the land issue can be traced back to an event that came to be known as the Anti-Rent rebellion. In 1839, a century-old conflict between tenant farmers and landlords in New York's Hudson Valley erupted in violence, and the ensuing political struggle over how to settle it raised the issue of land, monopoly, and property rights in a way that initially galvanized New York politics and eventually the entire country. New York's Hudson Valley, the scene of the Anti-Rent movement, had a peculiar history with settlement patterns outside the mainstream of American development. Initially part of New Netherland, the English took possession of the area by the end of the seventeenth century, but most of the fertile lands along the Hudson that had been acquired from the native population remained at the disposal of Dutch lords. Once the English took power, they recognized the grants and even mimicked the practice. The land grants were massive—the Van Rensselaer family controlled the largest tract, twenty-four miles long and forty-eight miles wide—and their royal origin made them a point of contention in what became republican America. Generations of farm families occupied the land and were bound to their landlords through perpetual leases. The leases dictated yearly rents, required the tenants to perform services for their landlords, and restricted merchant activity, which forced tenants to grind grain at landlord mills and sell produce through landlord middlemen. Worst of all, the landlords owned any improvements a farmer might make, be they houses, barns, or shops. These conventions, which essentially created a landed aristocracy, formed an anomalous reminder of feudalism that survived the Revolution and persisted into the middle of the nineteenth century. To the tenants, the perpetual rents were a remnant of feudal servitude, contrary to republican ideals, and by 1839 tenant farmers were resisting their servitude with violence.

The Anti-Rent movement began as a "rent strike" on the 726,000-acre Manor of Rensselaerwyck and quickly spread to other estates in the Hudson Valley. In January 1839, the so-called good patron, Stephen Van Rensselaer III, died, and his more ambitious sons were determined to collect back rents and evict those who refused. The tenants resisted, and the scale of the revolt overwhelmed local officials. In December 1839, Stephen Van Rensselaer IV conscripted a posse of seven hundred in an attempt to provoke violence and thus provide an excuse for crushing the strike, but soon the situation spiraled out of control and the local sheriff, essentially an agent of the landlords, was forced to petition the governor, William Henry Seward, to dispatch the state militia to the region. Seward complied, but in his annual message the governor sided with the tenants, recommending legislation that would "assimilate the tenures in question to those which experience has proved to be more accordant with the principles of republican government and more conducive to the general prosperity and the peace and harmony of society."[8] Seward's message provided a kind of official sanction for the movement, and by 1845 the insurrection involved eleven counties, ten thousand tenant farmers, and 1.8 million acres of farmland.[9]

Although he offended conservatives in both parties, Seward's handling of the situation was masterful. In a reversal of all we have been taught to expect from Jacksonian politics, Van Rensselaer and the landlords enlisted the aid of the Albany Regency, the Democratic political machine, and its organ, the Albany *Argus*.[10] Seward, on the other hand, was widely hailed as the farmer's friend and he began to establish a national reputation as a liberal and a political comer. Seward convened a legislative committee to investigate, and possibly end, land tenure. It concluded that the manorial system injured public welfare, that the leases were not made in good faith, and that the landlords had not fulfilled their terms. More important, the committee concluded that the right of eminent domain would allow the state to force the sale of lots to tenants at a just price. The movement made strange allies and enemies. Conservatives of both parties, but especially Democrats, stymied progressive efforts to resolve the issue at the state level. Populist figures, on the other hand, lauded the governor's course. James Gordon Bennett, the editor of the *New York Herald* and frequent ally of the Democrats, mocked that "none but the educated, the refined, the financial, the brokers, the great commercial interests of society have a right to suspend their just debts."[11] He was joined by New York City reformers including Thomas Devyr, a long-time Irish radical, former Chartist, and recent ex-communicant of the Democratic Party; George Henry Evans, veteran of New York's 1830s labor struggles; and, of course, Greeley.[12]

Though Anti-Rent farmers were fighting only against a semifeudal system of entail, their occasionally violent attack on vested interests polarized New York politics. Most of the antebellum political battles over land involved "unoccupied" public lands, but the ownership and monopolization of land in New York posed far more fundamental questions. As such, Greeley walked a delicate line on the issue. Without exception, he condemned the movement's violence, but he credited the tenants' complaints and questioned the justice and legitimacy of large landed holdings. Vast tracts of land, he argued, granted by monarchies or seized in marketplace speculation were unjust, immoral, and not conducive to republican nationhood. "There should be *some* limit," Greeley maintained, "to the legal right of one man to acquire exclusive possession of the Soil from which the sustenance of all must be derived," and that land titles contrary to social justice ought to be "negotiated" out of existence.[13] Conservative papers such as the *Express* accused the *Tribune* of agrarianism and, more pointedly, of obscuring the difference between land limitation as a *moral* and a *legal* principle. But Greeley held firm to what was, in fact, a traditional view that only labor could claim a moral right to property:

> By virtue of their [i.e., New York poltroons and Western speculators] "grants," they are enabled to appropriate an area greater than that of Kentucky or Ohio respectively to a mere hunting-ground if they choose, and punish any man who shall venture to settle thereon, though all earth beside were occupied and the settler unable to earn elsewhere a meal to ward off starvation. Is this politic? Is it right? Has one generation a *right* thus to cede away from posterity the soil which nobody wants or uses?[14]

On Anti-Rent, Greeley was trying to strike a balance between the justice of the tenants' claims and respect for the law.[15] In the end, Greeley proposed no forced redistribution of land or wealth, but he also suggested that "we would so shape the legislation and policy of the country as to discourage the *future* concentration of land into vast estates or manors and encourage its division into small freeholds."[16] The end Greeley had in mind was, as always, social harmony.

The actual Anti-Rent farmers were hardly radical agrarians. They fought merely for a bourgeois notion of individual, fully alienable property and their eventual victory involved no forced redistribution of resources. Tenant agitation and state intervention only compelled landlords to grant fee-simple leases, and eventually the large landholders disposed of their property roughly according to market values. It was a paradoxical and modest victory. What the farmers eventually won was an essentially capitalist entrepreneurial conception of property rights.[17] Nevertheless, the movement itself was in many respects a rehearsal for future battles over slavery and even Reconstruction. Like later battles over the status of slavery in the West, the Democratic Party defended an agrarian aristocracy against the united assault of small farmers, politically conscious urban workers, and commercial modernizer Whig nationalists alarmed by the deleterious effect of land tenure on economic development. And, as during Reconstruction, Greeley's supportive but cautiously muddled response to the Anti-Rent insurrection anticipated both the idealism of the Republican free-labor commitment to a broad distribution of productive property and its paralysis when confronted by an economic order in which one class had already consolidated control over most of the region's productive resources.

The Anti-Rent rebellion was all but settled by 1847; for the most part, it was a conflict of mostly local importance. But the rebellion, in triggering a more general discussion of land, monopoly, and property rights, was a gateway to more radical reform movements. As the conflict continued into the 1840s, state politics married the struggle of tenant farmers to New York City's reawakened Working Men's movements. The interest of New York's labor advocates in the plight of rural farmers transformed the debate over land and property from a discourse rooted in the Jeffersonian agrarian republican tradition into a movement for a more modern industrial democracy. Though Anti-Rent farmers were largely conservative and resisted association with socialism, social reorganization, and New York's labor radicals, their struggle inspired others outside the movement to question the absolute sanctity of private property and monopoly and—ideologically—to link the lands question in New York and eventually the entire West to the fate of urban workers. The concurrence of land and labor movements in New York during the 1840s became the vital foreground to the formation of the Radical Republican worker/farmer coalition of the 1850s.

The Anti-Rent movement precipitated dialogue on property rights and land, questions that had long roots. Though land reform and homesteads as national issues came to prominence along with the rise of free-soil politics in the mid-1840s, the issue of land itself had long been a contentious question in political economy. Overpopulation and landed monopoly were preoccupations of political economists Thomas Malthus and David Ricardo. Artisan egalitarians such as Thomas Paine had condemned landed monopoly as a source of political corruption in the late 1790s. Paine argued in *Agrarian Justice* that it was absurd that, in a "civilized state," people were "worse off" than those in a so-called state of nature. Paine claimed that the right of private property—a right to the exclusive use of the soil—ought to be a conditional one that came with social obligations and debts that should be satisfied in the form of a cash payment to the landless. Thomas Jefferson, also a fount of inspiration to the land reformers, argued that cultivation of the land was a mainspring of public virtue (though his other oft-repeated remarks that cities and manufactures were the germ of vice also made him a slightly dubious figure for the urban wing of the movement). Between 1815 and 1837, the distribution of land was a political lightning rod, as nearly as divisive as the battles over banks and tariffs.[18]

But the more direct intellectual and political sources of the nineteenth-century land reform movement were on the other side of the Atlantic, ironically where the ratio between available land and the supply of labor was radically different. The most radical of England's first generation of land reform agitators was Thomas Spence who argued that all land should be held in common and redistributed every generation. When conservatives in the American press vented about the danger of "agrarianism," they were likely thinking of Spence. But the discussion of land in England also fostered conservative contributions. William Ogilvie, an opponent of republican-ism and modernity, called for public acquisition of landed estates, which would be divided into small farms for the impoverished. On these public estates, Ogilvie hoped to construct a new feudalism by binding lot holders to the land, fostering paternalism and reciprocity, replicating a traditional social order built on service and hierarchy. This Enlightenment discussion of land and property would eventually fertilize land reform movements on both sides of the Atlantic. During the 1830s and '40s, English Char-tists in particular coupled republican political demands with cooperative efforts to remove excess industrial labor to small farms on the countryside, and over the course of those decades not a few Chartists made their way across the Atlantic, joining labor movements in New York State and New York City.[19]

In the United States, it was the Working Men's movements of the 1830s that both resurrected the writings of Enlightenment thinkers who questioned absolutist conceptions of property rights and marshaled more recent English writings on the distribution of land. Though largely devoted to unionism, education, and politics, the Working Men of the 1830s early on linked the distribution of Western lands to the fate of Eastern workers. Both Langston Byllesby and Thomas Skidmore denounced the right of property in land and, particularly after the decline of labor unions in the late 1830s, called for a general distribution of property.[20] Skidmore, in particular, shared Spence's radicalism, but the majority of the Working Men were put off by his attacks on private property, a right they were trying to extend to their own labor. Most of the Working Men thought the interests of "masters" and "workers" could be reconciled, at least to the extent that they dreamed of a day—and a social system—in which all men could be their own masters. After the 1837 depression, however, the Working Men's movements of the 1830s went into hibernation and with it the theoretical discussion of land and property dis-tribution. The Anti-Rent movement revived it.[21]

Vote Yourself a Farm

Greeley's support for the Anti-Rent farmers placed him in unusual company for a Whig. The Anti-Rent movement renewed Working Men's agitation on the land question, and it eventually coalesced under the leadership of George Henry Evans.[22] Throughout the early 1830s, Evans had been a prominent figure in New York's labor movement. He published the *Working Man's Advocate* and, in 1835, led a faction of radical workingmen out of the Democratic Party. Evans's political movement failed, and after the 1837 depression, organized protest in New York City all but ceased. Evans himself retired to a New Jersey farm.[23] But when the Anti-Rent movement seemed to reenergize the Left, Evans returned to New York in 1844.

Evans's experiences as a labor organizer during the 1830s had brought him ideologically closer to Greeley. He concluded that labor's independent political organization was futile, and also that strikes were effective only in times when labor was scarce. Evans eventually reasoned that government land policy and speculation deliberately oversupplied the labor market by crowding workers into the cities. Evans's solution—that the federal government could relieve urban distress by making Western lands available to urban workers—seemed realistic given his own experience as a New Jersey farmer.

Evans had accepted the necessity of land reform by the early 1830s, but it was not until the mid-1840s that he became devoted enough to the cause of land reform to revive the *Working Man's Advocate* under a new name, *Young America.* In conjunction with *Young America,* Evans organized a political movement called National Reform that, attempting this time to work within the established party system, petitioned candidates to pledge their support for homestead legislation. The National Reformers littered the city with handbills bearing their infamous slogan "Vote Yourself a Farm." Even so, National Reform barely stirred public opinion in its first year. Evans had established a constitution for the National Reform organization, encouraged the formation of local societies, and made plans for yearly conventions, but the movement was ridiculed in the conservative press and ignored by workers who perhaps initially struggled to understand the relationship of Western lands to their own interests and aspirations. By 1845, however, the movement had spread from New York City and into other Northern states, and conservatives began to take notice.[24] Evans's proposals were far less radical than those offered by his old rival, Thomas Skidmore, who, while leading a faction of the Working Men's Party, revived a strain of Paineite artisanal leveler radicalism by proposing a "General Division" (or redistribution) of all property and the abolition of inheritance as early as 1829. Nonetheless, the *Courier and*

Enquirer labeled the movement a "menace." Its proposed reforms, the *Courier* argued, were of an "infamous and abhorrent character," threatening changes "so wild, so utterly senseless, so fatal to society" that they would destroy "all social and civil interests."[25]

Within a couple of years of his return to the city, Evans had organized an effective and committed cadre of reformers. Lewis Ryckman lectured in upstate New York, Thomas Devyr labored in Anti-Rent counties, Fourierist H. H. Van Amringe lectured in the Great Lakes region, novelist George Lippard organized Philadelphia, Alvan Bovay (an important future Republican) lobbied in New Jersey, and even traditional labor leaders joined the group. Evans's New York organization eventually united with the New England Working Men's Association to form the Industrial Congress, which gathered in yearly national conventions from 1845 to 1856 to coordinate a comprehensive reform agenda for labor. In addition to a homestead law, the Industrial Congress demanded a ten-hour day. The movement also received ideological justification with the publication of John Pickering's *Working Man's Political Economy,* a popular work that challenged English and Democratic Party free trade orthodoxy. Despite these efforts, Greeley's backing would be crucial in amplifying the cause beyond the parochial world of labor reformers. Most important, the *Weekly Tribune* had the potential to propagandize land reform and the National Reform movement in the agricultural Midwest where homestead proposals resonated with farmers in the Great Lakes region.[26]

Greeley was a reluctant convert to the land reform movement. He read Evans's *Young America* attentively, attended meetings, and had espoused the principle of land reform as early as 1845, but he was hesitant to embrace National Reform as an organization in a public way. It was a difficult decision. On the one hand, Greeley had been advising distressed mechanics to head west since 1837. Greeley considered Thomas Carlyle, who advocated emigration and government distribution of land in *Past and Present,* the greatest mind of the nineteenth century. Nevertheless, land reform violated any number of fundamental Whig principles; most important, it promoted the diffusion of population, which to the Whigs retarded economic and cultural development. Like most modernizing Whigs, Greeley thought loose land laws jeopardized the balance between agriculture and manufacturing, which was so central to both Clay's American System and even Associationism. A dispersed population not only slowed the progress of towns and manufacturers but also denied the federal government revenue that could be applied to internal improvements or distributed to the states to develop a system of public education. Previously, Greeley had supported Henry Clay's land policy, which had the virtue of limiting speculation (unlike Democratic plans) but restricted the speed of settlement by maintaining land prices and granting few rights to squatters. Clay too hoped that the profits from land sales would accrue to future generations in the form of internal improvements and education. But over time, as the increasing scale of the market made it ever more difficult for small farmers and artisans to achieve propertied independence, Greeley began to view public lands in a different way: as an escape valve for pauperized labor.[27]

Greeley would not join the National Reformers unreservedly until 1846, but even his earlier hints of sympathy for the organization made Seward and Weed uneasy and almost completely alienated his Whig Party brethren. The *Express* and the *Courier and Enquirer* branded Greeley a "Fourierist, an Agrarian, and an Infidel." Greeley responded that the principle of legal exclusivity was a moral wrong when "land becomes scarce and subsistence for the landless scanty and precarious."[28] In a November 1845 editorial, Greeley called for open discussion of the land question. Without yet fully endorsing the movement, he praised the National Reformers' basic indictment of the current management of public lands: that speculation and monopoly denied pauperized workers the opportunity for economic self-sufficiency. The rapid influx of Irish immigrants and the economic slump of 1845–46, concurrent with the decline of Association as a viable reform option, overwhelmed Greeley's remaining reservations on the matter of land reform. Conceding that surplus labor resulted in downward pressure on wages, Greeley faced a choice: he could either advocate immigration restrictions or lobby the government to facilitate the emigration of workers to the countryside. For Greeley, nativism was never an option, and he came to view the reservoir of land as the antidote to class conflict and prejudice, as "the great regulator of the relations of Labor and Capital, the safety valve of our industrial and social engine."[29] In January 1846, Greeley finally declared "the plan" of "the little band who have taken the name of 'National Reformers'... the best that can be devised." By May, Greeley was a determined homesteader. "The freedom of the public lands to actual settlers," he wrote, "and the limitation of future acquisitions of land to some reasonable amount, are also measures which seem to us vitally necessary to the ultimate emancipation of labor from thralldom and misery."[30] In a July address to the New York Constitutional Convention, Greeley asked for free land grants for the poor and, more radically, that the state constitution "forbid future aggregations of great Landed Estates... by breaking up... those which now exist in our state."[31]

The principle of land reform, as the *Tribune* understood it, was more radical than the homestead proposals that would eventually take root within the Republican Party. The *Tribune* had three basic policy commitments. First, it called for "land limitation," which would cap the amount of federal land a single individual could own, restrict the sale of federal land to actual settlers, restrain the alienability of land grants so they would not fall into the hands of speculators, and even limit the size of inheritances. Second, the *Tribune* endorsed "homestead exemptions" to protect small farms from speculators and seizure for debt. Greeley's position was controversial within a party of creditors, but nonetheless in 1850 a homestead exemption became law in New York and several other states. The final component of land reform, as Greeley understood it, involved grants of 160 acres of public land to actual settlers without cost.

Greeley's turn toward land reform coincided with the decline of Fourierism, but he was not inclined to surrender the notion of comprehensive reform. He thought it unfortunate that the National Reformers had little to say about the character of life on the land after workers dispersed from the cities. Greeley tried to wed the concept of association with land reform by encouraging emigrants to pool their capital and to migrate communally. If collective living was not an option, homesteading could at the very least be undertaken in a way that recognized the importance of community and be based on the township model of traditional New England. Many of the leaders of the land movement—Lewis Masquerier and Lewis Ryckman, for example—were, in fact, communitarians who likewise advocated emigration in the form of densely settled townships, which would foster mutuality, cultural self-improvement, sociability, and local markets.[32] Greeley also tried to blend the basic principle of land reform—free land for actual settlers— with traditional progressive Whig ideas about economic development. Hiring Solon Robinson and other agriculture editors, Greeley made the *Tribune* into an organ of scientific farming. In his own (and endlessly parodied) *What I Know of Farming,* Greeley counseled farmers to raise the productivity of their land through crop rotation, manuring, and irrigation. He also called for agricultural colleges and a federal department to propagate, and further, farm science. Two visions of political economy had long contested America's economic future: one dreamed of a republic of agriculture and small property, while the other imagined an economy that balanced commerce, manufactures, and farming. By linking land reform to the Whig tradition of human development, Greeley hoped to marry the two; the result, he thought, could also be the basis of a progressive political party.

Under the aegis of the *Tribune,* the Industrial Congress, and National Reform, land reform became part of the basic vocabulary of Northern political life, uniting intellectuals, workers, and small farmers across the region. The platform appealed to a Jeffersonian ideal of a nation of small farmers, but it also implied a basic commitment by the national government to intervene in the economy on behalf of beleaguered workers. In so doing, it fused the political economies of the progressive wings of both established parties. Conventionally, the Democrats held that western expansion was the key to American prosperity. In the spirit of David Ricardo, an English free trader in the tradition of Adam Smith and the most influential political economist in America, many Democrats believed that an inevitable by-product of population growth was diminishing returns for labor. The Ricardian framework supported global trade, regional specialization, and posited an economy that functions as a static whole with contending interests: namely, wages, profits, and rent. Population growth makes land scarce and drives down both wages and profits. Ricardo's framework was one, in sum, that viewed the political and economic realm as a sphere of contending classes and interests; naturally, it was rejected by most Whigs. To the Whigs, the interests of landed capital, labor, and industrial capital were not inherently antagonistic, and most hoped that, with the application of science and human ingenuity, progressive societies could avoid Ricardo's pessimistic scenarios. Instead of relying on perpetual western and imperial expansion, Whig progressives and protectionists thought that investment in human capital (i.e., education), technology, and infrastructure—in productivity—would maintain high wages and profits.[33] Greeley, after his conversion to land reform, ended up mixing the Democratic emphasis on cheap land with the Whig emphasis on human development. Land reform was thus, like Association, a characteristically American attempt to construct an egalitarian utopia without violence and class conflict.[34] Without the use of strikes and without abolishing the principle of private property, land reformers hoped to redress the power imbalance between employers and workers by the very market mechanisms that employers defended. Though critics of British political economy, land reformers worked within its laws to diminish the oversupply of labor and to provide an independent agricultural competence to workers removed from the labor market. At the same time, land reformers challenged the absolute protection of vested property rights. They argued that land is a shared and inalienable endowment of nature, and that rights of property are dependent on a socially guaranteed right to labor.

From Greeley's perspective, land reform may not have been a comprehensive response to modernity's ills, but it did redress the imbalance of power between workers and employers. Equally important, it, unlike Association, worked through the political system. Making matters uncomfortable for Greeley, though, was that land reform was largely out of step with the traditions of his party. Association, Anti-Rent, and land reform all challenged in an indirect but fundamental way the twin pillars of conservative Whiggery: property and religion. Greeley reasoned, though, that land reform as an issue would redound to the Whigs' benefit. In addition to its basic merits, the issue of Western lands could also divide the Democratic Party by exposing the latent conflicts between planter and yeoman agrarianism long concealed and suppressed by the evasions of Jeffersonian republicanism.[35] Initially, land reform was loosely associated with the remnants of New York City's Loco Foco Democrats, and Evans, for a time, even merged his *Advocate* with Mike Walsh's Democratic *Subterranean,* but the alliance did not last. National Reform, by pressing the interests of New York labor in a national context, exposed sectional and ideological divisions within the Democratic Party. In New York State, many reform Democrats were dismayed when Southerners scuttled the presidential candidacy of native son Martin Van Buren. Party regulars seemed ever more willing to subordinate the interests of New York workers to the political interests of Southern planters. One-time allies such as Mike Walsh became Northern apologists for the slave South and eventually dismissed National Reform as the elitist distraction of "some twenty aliens, Fourierites, moral suasionists and bran-bred philosophers."[36] Land reform, in short, spurred political realignment, making fast allies of progressives from both parties. The questions that it raised about labor, the West, and eventually the expansion of slavery would dominate American politics into the Civil War and even after.

Land, Slavery, and the Second Party System

Party realignment would not come in New York until the 1850s, but the origins of the 1850s political revolution stretched back to the 1840s. The Whiggery of Greeley's formative years was ideologically incoherent in many ways, but its internal contradictions would not become manifest until land reform, the battle over the extension of slavery, and Greeley himself pushed certain assumptions far enough that the fissures became visible. Ideologically, Greeley essentially wedded two of the main political tributaries that made up the Whig Party—Anti-Masonry and National Republicanism—even though both factions had disappeared by the time he had entered public life. Like most in the Anti-Masonic movement, Greeley was born into the world of economically marginal farmers of Yankee origin, a culture that despised the social disorder that accompanied the spread of the market, wanted virtuous republican government, and, though not always evangelical, sympathized with campaigns of moral regulation, such as temperance.[37] Greeley's entrée into organized politics was made possible by Thurlow Weed, the Whig Party boss who had once been an Anti-Mason. Greeley's early cheap campaign newspapers—the *Jeffersonian* and the *Log Cabin*—targeted distressed farmers and artisans who resented the arrogance and corruption of the political and commercial aristocracy. These democratic journals served as reminders to members of his own party, even Weed, that "the men who enjoy most of the hatred of the Aristocracy are the very men whose names will go best before the People."[38]

At the same time, Greeley dedicated his *Tribune,* throughout the 1840s and beyond, to the cause of National Republican economic nationalism. Until Clay's death, Greeley would press for the presidential candidacy of the Kentucky Whig, regarding his American System as the basis of the Whig Party. To Greeley, internal improvements, a national bank, and tariffs were part of a democratic economic program that would raise wages, reduce unemployment, and bring prosperity to a broader class of citizens. The American System, not surprisingly, also facilitated the spread of the market. Anti-Masonic populism coexisted uneasily with the economic nationalism of the American System, and even within Greeley himself.

Given his ideological contradictions, Greeley would never find a comfortable place within the high councils of Whiggery, despite the fact that his *Tribune* quickly became the party's most important national organ.[39] The history of Greeley and the *Tribune's* relationship with Whiggery was characteristic of the ideological disunity of the parties during the age of Jackson and Clay. Although it was clear to Greeley by 1846 that both parties had factions that were ideologically incompatible, his private longing for a progressive political union was belied by his publicly aggressive Whig partisanship.

Greeley's fusion of populist Anti-Masonry and National Republican economic nationalism is representative in certain ways of the ideological prehistory of the Republican Party. By the mid-1840s the parties of Clay and Jackson were ideologically divided, and New York State seemed to be a singular place where divisions within the national parties erupted in local factional struggles. Before 1848, both parties were comprehensive and multifaceted, and various blocs within them competed to impose their wills on the national party. The Democratic Party included haughty planters, humble yeoman, and urban workers. The Whigs, even in the North alone, were similarly complex, representing commercial, financial, and manufacturing interests, as well as anti-immigrant populists, religious traditionalists, and a variety of conservative and radical reformers working on behalf of temperance, Sabbatarianism, abolition, women's rights, and socialism. Westward expansion brought a party system already strained by factional differences to a breaking point.

Western expansion had been a potent force in American politics ever since the Missouri crisis but the issue took on renewed intensity during the 1840s. For close to a decade, Northern reformers had opposed American expansion into the Southwest. But starting in the early to mid-1840s, land reform had given the question of Western expansion and slavery new force, and at the very moment when proexpansion forces had become that much more aggressive. This was particularly true for New York's Democrats after 1844, the year a coalition of Southern and Northern conservatives manipulated convention rules to deny Martin Van Buren, the architect of the party of Jackson, the Democratic nomination for president. In the minds of many, the triumph of the imperial wing of the party severed its link to the party's original economic populism, making it a party dedicated to imperial expansion at the behest of slavery.[40] The first sign of danger was the annexation of Texas, which raised the ire of both abolitionists and Whig reformers, but the Mexican War was even more destabilizing politically because it eventually raised questions about the status of slavery in the acquired territories. The Mexican War brought both parties to a breaking point as it became increasingly clear that the political and economic viability of slavery depended on territorial acquisition and imperial expansion at the same time that land reformers had begun to convince Northern labor that its economic future depended on an available reservoir of land in the West. It was at the outset of the Mexican War that Greeley began to flirt with the idea of a left-liberal or progressive fusion party.

The war, in a basic way, transformed the basis of American politics.[41] Prominent Democratic leaders justified it on racist grounds. President James Polk's treasury secretary, Robert Walker, referred to Mexicans as "ignorant and fanatical," Secretary of State James Buchanan offered that blood mixing had produced an "imbecile and indolent Mexican race," and the most prominent Democratic newspaper in Illinois argued that the racially mongrel Mexican was "but little removed above the Negro."[42] Democratic ideologues, such as John L. O'Sullivan, hailed the U.S. invasion of Mexico as the "advance guard of the irresistible army of Anglo-Saxon" progress and tried to silence dissent by attacking the war's critics as "Anti-American."[43] Even Walt Whitman called for Mexico to be "thoroughly chastised" and in an editorial, "Abetting the Enemy," denounced Greeley, "the black mouthed libeler," for his "blasphemous" and "anti-American" opposition to the war.[44] Stoked by the popular press, prowar rallies were held in large cities in the Northeast and many Americans came to view the war as a modern crusade of Christian virtue against barbarism and vice.[45]

Critics of the war became part of an embattled Left as war fever swept the country. Radical abolitionists, at a meeting of the American Anti-Slavery

Society in May 1846, instituted a policy of noncooperation and resolved that the war was one "of aggression, of invasion, of conquest, and rapine." William Lloyd Garrison led antigovernment resistance to the war by disrupting enlistment drives and organizing tax protests. Thomas Corwin, a Whig senator from Ohio, hoped publicly that the U.S. Army would be welcomed with "bloody hands and hospitable graves" (in appreciation, Greeley began to speculate on his presidential prospects).[46]

Whigs in Congress abetted the war with their votes. Their caution in opposing the war was reflected in the mainstream Whig journals, which denounced the war, but sometimes in less than forceful ways.[47] Greeley, on the other hand, rebuked his party's tentative opposition to the war, and thundered daily against it:

> People of the United States! Your Rulers are precipitating you into a fathomless abyss of crime and calamity! Why sleep you thoughtless on its verge, as though this was not your business, or Murder would be hid from the sight of God by a few flimsy rags called banners? Awake and arrest the work of butchery ere it shall be too late to preserve your souls from the guilt of wholesale slaughter! Hold meetings! Speak out! Act![48]

The *Tribune* publicized antiwar rallies that were held throughout the North. It seemed even to relish reports of American deaths and published poetry sympathetic to the Mexican struggle for liberty against the imperial tyranny of the slave South.[49] It became even more strident when an obscure Pennsylvania congressman named David Wilmot attached a proviso to a war funding bill that barred slavery from all lands acquired as a result of the Mexican War. David Wilmot was a Pennsylvania Jacksonian Democrat, but in a region dominated by New England emigrants. Versions of his bill were repeatedly passed in the House, but were stymied by Southern opposition in the Senate.[50] Nonetheless, for the *Tribune,* and the progressive wings of both parties, the Wilmot Proviso would become a kind of declaration of independence from increasingly decrepit institutional politics.

The Wilmot Proviso and the Politics of Free Soil

Though destined to become the wedge that split apart both parties, the Wilmot Proviso initially provoked almost no comment. The *Tribune* was one of the few newspapers or journals to recognize immediately the significance of the Wilmot Proviso.[51] But the following winter, when both the appropriations bill and the Proviso were reintroduced, there was an immediate uproar. This time, debate raged for a week. Preston King, a New York Democrat, declared that "if slavery is not excluded by law, the presence of the slave will exclude the laboring white man." Walt Whitman exclaimed that the Proviso pitted "the grand body of white workingmen, the millions of mechanics, farmers, and operatives of our country, with their interest on one side—and the interests of the few thousand rich...and aristocratic owners of slaves at the South on the other."[52] As the free-soil *New York Evening Post* put it, the central political question was whether "the principle of our government be aristocratic; if it be instituted for the sole benefit of the class of slave holders...[or] the less favored class of whites, who toil for themselves."[53] With help from the *Tribune,* the notion that the future of Northern workingmen depended on the freedom of Western lands had percolated up from the labor movement and into the political sphere. Antislavery had become a populist issue.

The main effect of the Wilmot Proviso was to bring the latent divisions within both parties out into the open. The clearest manifestation of the Whigs' intraparty ideological cracks was in Massachusetts where the split between the business and reform wings of the party was commonly articulated as a division between "Cotton" and "Conscience" Whiggery. A similar dynamic was at work in New York where the liberal Weed-Seward-Greeley wing supported the Proviso openly and enthusiastically. Conservative Whigs, though suspicious of Southern Democratic designs on the continent and fearful of populist despotism, distrusted the Proviso party and viewed anti-extension as the product of an agrarian populism that threatened the social order. James Watson Webb labeled anti-extension as the radical political outcome of progressive social schemes that pandered to the working class. It was, he claimed, the embodiment of Greeley's faction of "Anti-Renters, vote-yourself-a-farm men, Fourierites, Radicals, and Abolitionists."[54] But unlike in Massachusetts, the New York Whigs did not formally split, in large part because Empire State Democrats had already beaten them to the punch.

In Ohio, Massachusetts, and New York, renegade Whigs and Democrats bolted their parties for the Free Soil Party, a political movement based almost entirely on support for the principles of the Wilmot Proviso. The *Tribune* flirted with the third party movement and it resonated, obviously, with its recent interest in land reform, but it could not make the decisive leap. Greeley attempted to back a free-soil West from within the Whig Party. It was a pragmatic decision, yet it was the first sign that he was moving, however slowly, toward a break from Whiggery. In 1844, the *Tribune* had condemned the abolitionist Liberty Party because Greeley thought it divided the "reform" vote and gave the election to the Democrats. He even implied that the abolitionist party was a front for "Polk men." In 1848, however, the *Tribune* termed proslavery "factional." Opposing slavery, expansion, and militarism, Greeley claimed to be defending the original mission of his party:

> The Whig Party must ever be, from its composition, character and traditions, in the noblest sense Conservative—not as opposed to Reform, for we appeal to our National history for proof that it has done its full share in promoting beneficent Reforms—but as standing inflexibly opposed to the sway of popular passion, the lust of conquest, and the intense craving of hot blood for wild adventure and lawless gratification.[55]

Despite Greeley's protests, slavery and the war loosened, but did not break, the *Tribune*'s ties to mainstream Whiggery.

When the Whigs nominated Louisiana slaveholder and Mexican War hero Zachary Taylor at their June convention in Philadelphia, Greeley alternated erratically between resignation and defiance. Taylor's supporters offered little beyond their candidate's popularity, and never even affirmed what was, in Greeley's view, the fundamental tenet of Whiggery: that government "is bound to do all that is fairly within its power to promote the welfare of the People—that its legitimate scope is not merely negative, repressive, defensive, but is also affirmative, creative, constructive, beneficent."[56] Short of bolting the party, Greeley did everything he could to prevent Taylor's nomination. He lobbied publicly and privately for a Whig candidate who favored the Wilmot Proviso and who opposed the war. The Whigs, he complained to whoever would listen, were becoming a party of military chieftains, and his opposition to war and standing armies made him reluctant to support another general. After Taylor's nomination, Greeley followed what Thurlow Weed termed a policy of "semi-neutrality," and refused to endorse Taylor.[57] "For our own party, we shall take time for reflection," the *Tribune* concluded. "If it shall appear to us that the support of Gen. Taylor is the only course by which the election of Cass can be prevented, we shall feel bound to concur in that support. If, on the contrary, the developments of the next few days shall prove that the Free States are now ripe for the uprising which *must* come sooner or later, and which this nomination has done very much to precipitate, why then *we* are ready."[58]

The *Tribune*'s very public reluctance to endorse Taylor strained its relations to other factions of the party. Conservative Whig papers labeled Greeley everything from a party apostate to an outright infidel. The Boston *Atlas* accused the paper of "bad grace" for turning the convention into a farce. The Trenton *State Gazette* ridiculed the contradictory logic of the *Tribune*'s complaints about the weakness of Taylor's affiliation to the Whigs and the paper's own recent wavering. The *Express,* condemning elements in the Whig Party for wandering "from their moorings in pursuit *of isms* and idealities," scolded the *Tribune* for "plotting the disruption of the Whig party."[59] Webb, in the *Courier,* chided Greeley for his hypocrisy, quoting *Tribune* editorials from the early 1840s in which Greeley had attacked Van Buren as a creature of spoils and a "Northern Man with Southern Principles."[60] The *Tribune* would not finally endorse Taylor until October 7 and it did so only because, as Greeley explained to Joshua Giddings, he lacked faith in the free-soil Democrats: "The truth is, there is *no* deep devotion to Principle among a large faction of the American people. Each man has a keen regard for his own rights... but for the rights of 'niggers' who cares?... Many of the leading Barnburners were among the bitterest opponents of the right of poor Blacks to vote, all through 1846. Do you think they are more careful of Human Rights in New Mexico than in New-York?"[61]

Thurlow Weed rewarded Greeley's loyalty by nominating him to fill out the term of a vacant congressional seat. It was a small plum, but Greeley made the most of it. Greeley's session in Congress was eventful to say the least. In only ninety days, Greeley introduced broad legislation on protection and homesteads. He tried to abolish flogging (and alcohol) in the navy, to end the funding of army recruiting, to outlaw slavery in the capital, and even attempted to change the name of the United States to "Columbia." More controversially, he offended his congressional colleagues by attempting to reduce franking privileges, governmental pay, and especially mileage bonuses that were paid to Congress on the basis of outmoded distances between their districts and the capital. Most important, Greeley authored legislation that would provide any American a modest plot of land without cost. When a fellow congressman from the West inquired why a representative from New York City was so interested in the distant public domain, he replied that "he was interested because he represented more landless people than anyone else in the House."[62] For his efforts, he was very nearly expelled from the House.

Greeley's independence, however, was further fortified by the growth of the *Tribune.* By the 1850s, the paper had nearly two hundred employees. With twelve editors, twenty domestic correspondents, and eighteen foreign correspondents, it was clearly the most influential and important journal in the North. The very qualities that alienated conservatives and party functionaries made the paper and its editor wildly popular with contributors and the public alike. In 1850, the *Tribune's* circulation reached 18,600 for the daily edition and 41,400 for the weekly. In 1854, those numbers grew to 27,360 and 112,800 respectively. By 1860, the paper's combined circulation among its daily, weekly, semiweekly, and California editions would reach

247,000, the largest readership in the country.[63] The *Tribune's* success did not accrue to Greeley alone. Organized on "associative" principles, the *Tribune* in 1849 divided its ownership into one hundred shares valued at $1,000 each. By 1851, each share had doubled in value. The paper's crusading moralism and occasional radicalism had, in short, only solidified the loyalty of its readership.

Still, Greeley was caught off-guard by the Free Soil movement. Greeley had been in discussions with politically like-minded friends for some time about the formation of a radical fusion party, but he viewed the 1848 election, wrongly as it turned out, as a last opportunity for progressives to make a final "desperate, concerted struggle for the control" of the traditional parties. He had hoped the Whigs would nominate a Proviso candidate and that the Democrats could have nominated an "anti-southern man," such as Van Buren.[64] Failing that, Greeley was prepared to dispense in the future with the Jacksonian party system and to construct a new democratic coalition of labor, independent farmers, and reformers. Greeley's reluctance to bolt the Whig Party was validated in some respects by the result of the 1848 election.

As a national movement, Free Soil was a failure. For the most part, it played a spoiler role, particularly in New York. There, Free Soil helped shift the state's electoral votes to the Whig column by dividing the New York Democratic Party in half. Elsewhere, Free Soil factions did manage to seize certain states, but failure at the national level moved most who had embraced the splinter party to consolidate their popularity at the local level by retreating back to familiar partisan alignments. New York, in this case, was typical. The Whig victory made the state's Democratic factions, Hunkers and Barnburners, anxious for compromise. Van Buren retired from politics and by 1849 the Barnburners had conceded to Hunker demands that anti-extension no longer figure in the nomination of candidates. By 1852, Greeley's suspicions were confirmed when the entire New York Democracy backed pro-Southern New York Democrat William Marcy for president. In Ohio, Salmon Chase folded his organization back into the Ohio Democratic Party, sacrificing most of its principles to political expediency and his own political ambitions. In Massachusetts, the Free Soil coalition held the balance of political power after 1848 and the movement broke Cotton Whig domination of the state, but the movement's only long-term success was Charles Sumner's election to the Senate. In Congress, even those who remained loyal to the Free Soil movement were either too timid or too stubborn to make much of a difference, and most merged with the minority parties in their states.[65] The Free Soil Party was just enough of a success that leaders from the traditional parties worked feverishly to produce some sort of compromise that would settle the slavery question and safeguard their political bases. The ultimate result was the Compromise of 1850. That said, although the Free Soilers did not carry a single state in the presidential balloting, elected just thirteen congressmen, and received only 10 percent of the vote, the party's formation signaled an ideological and cultural reorientation of both the parties and American public opinion. Though Greeley and the *Tribune* participated only in a peripheral way, the door had been opened for a progressive coalition in a manner that would bear fruit in the 1850s.

From Land Reform to Homesteads

The surprising political success of the Free Soil Party's anti-extension agenda solidified land reform as a permanent part of the *Tribune* and the nation's political agenda in the 1850s. When the *Tribune* lobbied on behalf of National Reform in the mid-1840s, it was accused of "agrarianism," but by 1850 the inherently pastoral nature of the "homestead" made the land issue somewhat respectable. The homestead movement was able to capitalize on American agrarian myths, and its antiurban and anti-industrial message gathered supporters because it promised to "return" the United States to a simple and sturdy rural republicanism. By the early 1850s, the only opposition to homesteading left standing was largely Southern. In these early years of respectability, the movement combined the reassuring myths of a "virgin land, free labor frontier" with more radical assumptions about the nature of property rights; the latter were among the reasons homestead legislation required some two decades of agitation before achieving its eventual if modified success.

Some of the movement's first successes came at the state level. In New York, land reformers pushed through the assembly a homestead exemption in 1850 that protected small property from seizure for debt. In 1847 and 1851, the New York Assembly instructed the state's congressional delegation to push for legislation that would limit the size of holdings in public land.[66] The *Tribune* and its labor allies, however, had less success at the national level with more radical provisions such as limitation or alienability restrictions, which challenged traditional property rights and raised the specter of "agrarianism." In 1850, Greeley opposed Stephen Douglas's land measures, which provided a quarter section of public land to anyone who would settle on it for four years but did not limit speculation. "In the rear of the vast army of squatters which this bill would inevitably call into existence would march a corresponding army of Speculators and Monopolists," Greeley feared, "buying up quarter-sections for the price of a barrel of whiskey.... No bill with respect to the Public Lands ought to pass which does not plainly embody and stringently enforce the principle of Land Limitation."[67] In this context, Greeley's worries were unfounded because the Southern caucus was able to block any form of land reform in the Senate, radical or otherwise. Nevertheless, throughout the decade the *Tribune* never lost sight of land reform as class legislation and as a social welfare measure. And unlike some of his land reform allies who emerged from the labor movement in New York, Greeley resisted the inherent individualism of land legislation.

Greeley would never become reconciled to naked individualism, and in his land proposals he advocated communal organization within settlements, imagining a scenario in which squatters could combine their economic and cultural resources. Free land was his primary objective, but Greeley hoped that homesteaders would pool their capital, and thus make new farms more productive, while ensuring that the frontier retained some attachment to society, religion, civility, and learning.[68] Greeley hoped that provisions that limited the cost, size, and alienability of public land would encourage sociability among homesteaders. Cheap or even free land, the *Tribune* argued, would actually allow populations to concentrate: "The great majority of settlers choose to locate where they shall have some sort of neighborhood where they may hope to send their children to school, and where they can reach some kind of assemblage for Divine worship." Unfortunately, "Land Speculation" under the present system acquires "nearly every available acre" and "thus Speculation is perpetually operating to scatter, to retard and barbarize our pioneer settlements."[69]

That homestead legislation, a central plank of the Republican platform and an important component of the party's appeal, was a product of a radical indictment of land monopoly in the 1840s was a fact not lost on land reform's enemies. As late as 1860, President James Buchanan warned that land legislation would "demoralize and repress" labor's "noble spirit of independence" and "introduce among us those pernicious social theories which have proved so disastrous in other countries."[70] Though homestead legislation appealed to long-standing agrarian and republican articles of faith, the *Tribune* took few pains to conceal the radical philosophical justification for the principle. By curtailing one right—the absolute right of property—the *Tribune* claimed that others could be democratized. When an 1852 homestead bill passed the House, for example, the *Tribune* was heartened; but the paper was not without its misgivings because the bill failed to embody the principle of limitation:

> The imperfection of this bill is freely admitted by its friends. It fails to give full effect to the vital principle on which it is based, and whereby alone it can be justified—namely, that unappropriated, unimproved

> Public Land is by the law of Nature and of Social Right the portion of
> those who, claiming no other portion of Man's heritage, are willing to
> improve and cultivate. The bill is defective in that it fails to interdict
> and prevent the further buying up of the Public Lands by men who do
> not need and will not improve them, for the purpose of selling them at
> a profit to those who *do* need and *will* cultivate them.[71]

Land reform was absorbed into the political mainstream by the late 1840s,
and this was possible because it resonated with so many deeply held American
values; even its radical opposition to accumulation echoed Jeffersonian-
Jacksonian suspicions of speculation, monopoly, finance, luxury, and favoritism, and their faith that republican virtue rested principally on the shoulders
of American yeoman.[72] Its complex and simultaneous embrace and critique
of property rights, capitalism, and the promise of social mobility were characteristic of social democratic liberalism. To Greeley and his allies, homestead legislation curtailed the right of property by limiting accumulation,
and relied on the state to redistribute economic resources. At the same time,
a more limited form of homestead legislation, one that made a small section
of unoccupied and fully alienable land available at a low price, appealed to a
more conservative and bourgeois form of liberalism. Throughout the decade,
homestead bills passed the House easily, with near-unanimous support in the
North. By 1850, even the *Courier* was calling for a narrowly conceived homestead bill. But to the labor radicals, limitation was as important a principle as
free land. What the *Tribune* wanted was rooted in its socialistic labor theory
of property and value. "Our present Land System," the *Tribune* editorialized,
"*virtually compels one set of men to do the work by which the bulk of the Public Lands
are enhanced in value . . . and enables another set to secure and enjoy the wealth thus
created.*" Settlers, by improving their land and the community, raise the value
of speculators' land without the latter investing any labor. "We do not blame"
the speculator, the *Tribune* continued, "we blame only the vicious laws which
foster this injustice, and the law-makers who will not perceive, or perceiving,
will not correct it."[73] What, in short, is remarkable about the *Tribune* position
was not its investment of all value in labor. That was a relatively common
perspective. Instead, the *Tribune's* outlook was unique because it indicted the
market as the very mechanism of inequality, and lobbied for positive economic legislation that would overcome it.

Land reform originally aimed to empower ordinary workers by interven-
ing in the market for labor, but in the end it would fall prey to conventional
bourgeois assumptions about opportunity and American exceptionalism and
the link between hard work and social mobility. As the movement drifted out

of the hands of the original National Reformers and toward respectability, the paper was an increasingly lonely voice pressing for the essential anticapitalist elements of the reform. When, in July 1862, the Civil War exodus of Southern congressmen made the Homestead Act finally possible, Greeley dutifully praised it even though it lacked elements designed to curtail monopoly and speculation. Sadly, by the time it passed, as Jamie Bronstein points out, there were few labor radicals "left to greet the measure with rejoicing." In fact, when mainstream politicians embraced land reform, not a few labor radicals abandoned politics to launch associated communities in the West.[74] Poignantly, in 1870 Nathan Meeker, a former Fourierite and agriculture editor at the *Tribune,* founded an associated agrarian "Union Colony" in Colorado, just south of the Wyoming border, halfway between Denver and Cheyenne. The community named its town center Greeley, after its most enthusiastic booster.[75]

By calling upon traditional republican hostility to aristocracy and monopoly, the combination of land reform agitation and the 1848 Free Soil political revolt linked the question of slavery to the fate of the Northern working class. The salience of the land and slavery issues eroded the *Tribune*'s relationship to institutional Whiggery along with its core principles. Not only did Greeley abandon the conservative land policy of the Whigs and his political champion Henry Clay, but in a deeper, ideological sense his socialist sympathy with labor was beginning to come into conflict with his traditionally held faith in the harmony of interests. Land reform is often remembered as a somewhat limited bourgeois reform—and it was in its final iteration— but it had its roots in a more radical agrarianism that contested the right of speculation, the large-scale accumulation of landed capital, and even, at its most extreme, demanded a form of capital redistribution. Despite land reform's limitations, perhaps the best question to ask of it was the same one a conservative New Yorker asked about the movement with an eye toward discrediting it: "Who asks for it?... Certain associations, called 'Industrial Congresses'—offsprings of the German school of socialism, and of the American school of 'higher law' transcendentalism—partly political partly agrarian."[76] That the imbalance of power between capital and labor required forceful intervention became a given of protoindustrial life to socialist reformers in the 1850s. Though the extent of available public land allowed the *Tribune* to stop short of supporting any radical disruption of established property rights, the very idea that the federal government would institute policies to redistribute resources to the poor was revolutionary in and of itself. To conservative Whigs, the very idea of land legislation was "infamous and abhorrent," "wild," "utterly senseless," and "fatal to society... [and] all social and civil interests."[77] As part of a larger program for labor that included cooperation, the regulation of the hours of labor, the restriction of child labor, and the enlargement of educational opportunity in the form of industrial and agricultural education, land reform was the signature element of the *Tribune's* "loco foco Whiggery" and it became central to the Republican alliance of reform Whigs and Jacksonian populists.

By the late 1840s, Greeley and the *Tribune* were already bywords for radical reform—for dangerous "Isms"—even though the editor and his paper remained loyally Whig. Indeed, it was by pressing the usual Whig objective of a harmonious social order to its logical extreme that Greeley and the *Tribune* ended up as what could only be described in the context of the times as ideologically radical. Greeley was always ambitious for a harmonious society, a kind of national compact or commonwealth. During the 1840s, he had been convinced that the principal source of social disorder was the unregulated market—laissez-faire. But by the early 1850s, he came to view poverty and social conflict as the by-product of something more insidious. After the simultaneous failure of the 1848 revolutions abroad and the Fourierist communities at home, Greeley came to believe that it was more than the abstract mechanism of the market that produced poverty and social conflict—that certain economic and social interests were fundamentally antagonistic. Greeley's socialist Whiggery dreamed of rational, technocratic solutions to industrial unemployment, poverty, and social immobility; that a better world could be realized without hard choices, without winners and losers. Though it would always remain a formative and reflexive component of his political and reform instincts, the 1850s forced Greeley to qualify the dream of Whig concord. His Whiggery, in effect, carried him to his socialism, and his socialism carried him to Whiggery's repudiation. The dissonance between the Whig ideal of the harmonious Utopia and the increasingly pressing Radical Republican real-world sense of the fundamental nature of antagonistic social and economic interests made the *Tribune* from the 1850s forward both politically and intellectually unstable. This tense mixture of conservatism and radicalism, of idealism and pragmatism, made Greeley's political course both unpredictable and idiosyncratic but it also was, in a curious way, representative of the Republican Party's ultimately diverse ideology and mixed political achievement. As a former Chartist put it, Greeley would become, not unlike the Republican Party he slowly but finally embraced, a "bound Samson," a cautious revolutionary.[78]

Whig to Republican

Land reform was the bridge from 1840s socialism to the overriding political question of the 1850s: the status of slavery in the Western territories. The post-1848 pragmatic contraction of the original Fourierist vision into narrow, interventionist reforms such as cooperation and homesteads became easily wedded to the larger free-labor vision of the Republican Party. The other main element that socialism contributed to the emerging Republican movement was its vision of politics as a contest of social forces, at times even violent. During the 1850s, the battles over slavery's expansion, launched by the Mexican War and culminating in "Bleeding Kansas," thoroughly radicalized the *Tribune,* which more and more viewed the political process as merely a means to power. During the 1850s, the South, hostile as it was to a free-labor West, became the principal obstacle to labor's emancipation, even more than the market itself. The *Tribune's* developing sectionalism, in short, further eroded the paper's commitment to Whiggery's articles of faith: the neutrality of the law, the harmony of interests, and the primacy of political compromise. After the domestic and international events of 1848, the *Tribune* lost confidence in the capacity of reason and democratic compromise to resolve social conflicts, and became increasingly resigned to sectional and class antagonism and to the role of violence in bringing about fundamental social change.

Greeley's repudiation of Whiggery was, in many ways, painfully slow. Over the course of the 1850s, Greeley and the *Tribune* followed an intermittent course away from the Whig Party and toward radicalism.[79] The first stage of Greeley's slow repudiation of law, compromise, and Whiggery itself, both as an institution and as an intellectual system, was the political storm that erupted after the Mexican War. In the 1848 election, Greeley's party, if not his candidate, captured the presidency, but the issue that gave rise to the Free Soil movement did not abate: What would be the status of slavery in the West? As Zachary Taylor assumed office, Texas and New Mexico were contesting their border to the point of civil war, and more importantly California was poised for statehood, an issue made pressing by its isolation from the main body of the United States and the discovery of gold within its borders. The new president proposed immediate statehood for a free California, but when the South revolted a political stalemate ensued. Eventually, Henry Clay would propose a massive bill designed to settle not only the status of slavery in the territories acquired from Mexico but every lingering sore point on the slavery issue that had been polarizing American politics. Clay's grand compromise effort also failed, but when Stephen Douglas of Illinois broke Clay's omnibus bill into its eight separate components, he was able to craft eight separate majorities for each provision. Greeley's winding course on what came to be called the Compromise of 1850, as well as the various proposals that preceded it, was emblematic of the weakness of his party affiliation, and his growing independence from former sponsors William Henry

Seward and especially Thurlow Weed.[80] Nonetheless, in the context of vigorous congressional debate over the status of slavery in the Mexican cession, Seward delivered a speech that signified the way in which radical reform was eroding traditional Whig values.

William Henry Seward's "Higher Law" speech was arguably the most important piece of political oratory during the 1850s. Delivered to protest the concessions that Henry Clay's omnibus bill made to the slave interest, it symbolized the growing radicalism of the North and even the way in which a kind of political antinomianism was supplanting the traditional Whig devotion to reason, law, and social harmony. In the speech, Seward moved beyond the basic political questions at hand, contending radically, and in the spirit of Transcendentalist and abolitionist commitments to the moral conscience and civil disobedience, that there was a "higher law" than the Constitution that mandated human liberty. The speech symbolized the contradiction within Whig culture between what Daniel Walker Howe refers to as the "claims of stability" and "social conservatism," on the one hand, and the "claims of morality" and "ethical absolutism," on the other.[81] The Whig Party owed its birth to a coalition that opposed the spirit of nullification, debt repudiation, mob violence, and Jackson's usurpation of judicial and legislative prerogatives. No longer. In a profound sense, Seward's "Higher Law," despite its affirmation of a kind of religious principle, disavowed the Whig faith in the orderly and reasonable adjustment of the law. Later commentators have taken pains to point out that Seward was not a radical immediatist; he thought that slavery could be eradicated only "under the steady, peaceful action of moral, social, and political causes...removed by gradual, voluntary effort, and with compensation." But to invoke a "higher law" was to invoke the rule of unchecked passion. Whatever his more conservative intent, the "higher law" was an invitation to anarchy and violence, and anticipated later extralegal agitation against the slave power.[82]

Most conservatives responded to the speech's anarchical implications and accused the New York senator of baiting civil war; Southerners viewed the "higher law" doctrine, naturally, as "monstrous and diabolical." Naturally, and despite Greeley's growing personal distance from Seward, it electrified the *Tribune*. What made it so central was that it seemed to articulate values that now rivaled, though they did not permanently supplant, his core Whig principles. "We cannot but feel," Greeley wrote, "that Gov. Seward has in the main spoken the word that Ages will balm and Eternity approve."[83] Afterward, a new radicalism began to creep into the *Tribune*. The *Tribune* had always recognized the right of revolution, particularly after 1848, but for the first time these revolutionary sympathies were turned toward the United States. The struggle against the slave power and its conservative allies in the North took on an insurrectionary character. Seward's legal antinomianism was nothing less than the clarion call of a new sort of radical antislavery politics.[84]

Throughout the early 1850s, New York Whigs remained as divided as ever. Liberal Whigs organized around Seward's leadership and a platform of land and labor reform, protection, free schools, and antislavery. The "Cotton" Whigs, as the *Tribune* took to calling them, broke with Seward, refusing to commend his Senate record or commit the party to opposing slavery's extension. During the 1850 state elections, conservatives in New York City and the Hudson Valley who had long complained of Seward's agrarianism and abolitionism demanded a pro-Compromise plank in the state platform, which, they thought, would implicitly condemn the "higher law" doctrine. When the Sewardites successfully resisted, the conservatives walked off the floor. Despite efforts to mend the breach, wealthy New York merchants, the financial backbone of the Whig Party, refused to endorse the antislavery trajectory of the party. When gubernatorial candidate Washington Hunt denounced the Fugitive Slave Act, city merchants withdrew their support for his candidacy and called for a nonpartisan pro-Compromise ticket composed of both Democrats and Whigs. Greeley seemed to welcome the rupture. Although publicly he espoused party unity, privately he argued that the conservative exodus from the Whig convention, coupled with their public renunciation of agrarianism and reform, would solidify the democratic credentials of the Seward Whigs. For the first time, Greeley and the *Tribune* began to push beyond narrow electoral political pragmatism to engage "the great battle of this generation, between Freedom and Slavery."[85]

The dissolution of Whig unity in New York in 1850 continued into the 1852 presidential season. Then, the *Tribune* remained formally aligned with the party, and even made one last effort to make protection a unifying issue, but it was a hopeless cause.[86] In the midst of these ideological conflicts, Henry Clay died, and with him passed the primal tie of Greeley and that of many others to the party's liberal economic nationalism. The *Tribune* endorsed the Whig presidential nominee, Winfield Scott, but called the party platform an abomination.[87] "That Hunker Platform," as Greeley referred to it, officially pledged the Whig Party's "acquiescence" to the Fugitive Slave Law and "deprecate[d] all further agitation of the [slavery] question thus settled, as dangerous to our peace." The Whig Party's repeated obfuscations and evasions on the issue of slavery's extension and its more general failure to take up the mantle of reform drove Greeley finally into public, free-soil radicalism.[88] The party's internal divisions were reflected at the polls. Scott and the Whigs were crushed. Conservative Whigs despised Scott and progressive Whigs despised the platform. Attachment to the party, traditionally a coalition of opposition factions, was always flimsy. After 1852, all was lost, and almost immediately after the election Greeley and the *Tribune* declared political neutrality. Few conservative Whigs complained. "If a party is to be built up and maintained on Fourierism, Mesmerism, Maine Liquor laws, Spiritual Rappings, Kossuthism, Socialism, Abolitionism, and forty other isms," the *Republic* remarked, "we have no disposition to mix with any such companions."[89]

Throughout 1853, Greeley devoted the paper to a series of nonpartisan instrumental reforms. He fought for the passage and enforcement of temperance laws in New York, continued to fight for homestead legislation and a "People's College" that would combine agricultural and industrial instruction, and, at the risk of aligning himself with the nativists he despised, Greeley took on the Catholic Church's opposition to free public schools throughout the state. Greeley also enlarged the *Tribune,* which cut into the paper's profits but solidified its democratic credentials. The paper's enlargement placed it in the same class as the aristocratic *London Times* but at a fraction of the cost. When it announced the expansion of both its daily and weekly editions, the *Tribune* repudiated its partisan identity:

> It [the *Tribune*] has ever supported, with the force of earnest conviction, those principles of Political action distinctively termed Whig, because it has recognized therein the basis of a perfected development to Industry, of rapid and vast improvement in Intercommunication, and realization of a lofty and benignant National destiny through the general diffusion of Intelligence, the just reward of Labor, the perpetuity of Peace, and the purification of Morals.... Whatever may be the fate of the Whig organization... the *Tribune* has not been and never can be a mere party organ.[90]

It was a risky moment for the *Tribune.* Though long identified as a liberal paper associated with labor, it was also required reading for committed Whigs. But Greeley was satisfied that popular loyalty would sustain its advertising base, despite its increasingly public free-soil radicalism. As he wrote Seward, "Though the hostility of the wealth and commerce of our city work hard against us... the People are in good sort with us; and, if our circulation goes up as I hope, cotton will advertise with us as freely as it trades with slave drivers—because it will make money by it."[91] But at least one dark cloud loomed on the horizon. The *Tribune's* apostasy occurred not long after the launch of a more sober, and more conservatively reliable, *New York Times* by Greeley's longtime antagonist Henry Raymond.

Raymond's *Times* appeared in September 1851 and it was designed to be a conservative substitute for the *Tribune*. A firsthand witness to Greeley's nearly immediate success with the *Tribune*, Raymond had been planning a new journalistic venture for some time with George Jones, also a former *Tribune* employee.[92] Capitalized by American and European investors at a phenomenally large sum of $100,000, the launch of the *Times* signaled the end of the editor-proprietor era in journalism. Journalism and print more generally had entered the "age of capital." Not surprisingly, given its backing, the *Times* indeed became the respectable alternative to the *Tribune*, an organ of the Northern merchant and industrial class. Its prospectus promised conservatism in "political and social discussions," "devotion to the Union and to the Constitution, obedience to law," and, alluding at least obliquely to the *Tribune*, pledged "to check all rash innovations and to defeat all schemes for destroying established and beneficent institutions."[93] As an 1855 biographical sketch of Raymond in the *New York Family Journal* pointed out, the "success" of the *Times* was due to the fact that its editor "seldom permits the columns of his journal to be devoted to the propagation of the abstract opinions of individuals." The "practical character" of the *Times* confined itself to "errors as they exist" and "urges only such remedies as promise cures. It runs no tilts against imaginary evils—proposes no theoretical curatives."[94] The *Times*, in short, distanced itself from radicalism, especially antislavery and labor reform. The *Times*, moreover, inaugurated a new, more neutral journalistic style, which was a sweeping departure from the tradition of partisanship and especially the reform engagement of a paper such as the *Tribune*.[95] As a result, Raymond became the lead journalistic confidant of Seward and Weed, and the reliable *Times* replaced the *Tribune* as the mouthpiece of the putatively liberal Seward-Weed Whigs.[96] New York now had three major newspapers. The *Herald*, with its spicy writing and sensational stories, still captured the majority of the city's readers. The *Times*, thorough and "informative," became the newspaper of the city's merchant and financial elite. The *Tribune* continued as more of a national than a city paper, and remained in a broad sense a voice of reform.[97]

Violence and the Death of Compromise

Without a party or a political patron, the *Tribune* carried on in a radical direction and events in the American West would only accelerate its movement. In January 1854, Stephen Douglas introduced legislation that would organize the Nebraska territories on the basis of "popular sovereignty"; it was an explicit repeal of the Missouri Compromise and it would revolutionize the political landscape. The *Tribune*'s opposition was immediate and unwavering. It referred to the measure as a "National Perfidy" and exclaimed that Douglas and his allies "doomed themselves to be immortal in the detestation of mankind as the most noxious things that ever vegetated on the dung hill of political corruption."[98] The *Tribune* opposed popular sovereignty on a variety of grounds, but in a broad sense the *Tribune*'s response to the Nebraska bill bore all the marks of the degree to which, after 1848, the paper had become resigned to social and economic antagonism and had adopted a broad sociological conception of historical and political conflict.[99] After Kansas–Nebraska, the *Tribune* became, for the first time, openly and aggressively sectional. Its critique of the South formed the basis of what would become a well-established sectional vocabulary; it was lazy, backward, unrepublican, tyrannical, and immoral. Gruesome accounts of violent and lustful masters became regular staples in the *Tribune*.[100] Though hesitant to commit to a new partisan identity, eventually the paper embraced the organized anti-Nebraska movement, coalescing under the "simple name...'Republican.'" It was a label that evoked the idealism and the revolutionary legacies of both 1776 and 1848.[101]

Land reform, which was an extension of the paper's newly pragmatic socialism, had made the *Tribune* interested in the fate of the West, but Kansas completed its radicalization. The salient difference between the *Tribune*'s Whiggery and its emergent Republicanism was the erosion of its former faith in political compromise, social harmony, and the disinterestedness of the law, all of which became particularly manifest during the Kansas crisis. Popular sovereignty, as the *Tribune* had predicted, did not create even an illusion of democracy. Every major election in the territory was marred by fraud and sectional violence. Initially the *Tribune* hoped that the state's free-soil majority would control the nascent political process and thus avert armed struggle, but when that failed it would no longer even look for political substitutes to civil war. By 1856, it openly identified with free-soil armed resistance in Kansas and eventually elsewhere.[102] The Kansas crisis created what was essentially a revolutionary party. It launched a political movement whose aim, as the *Herald* fumed, was "the destruction of the social system of the Southern States, without regard to consequences."[103] The rhetoric that accompanied the Republican Party's creation brooked no pretenses. Republicans planned nothing less than to seize the national government and to oppose slavery to an extent limited only by their own interpretation of the Constitution. It was conservative, certainly, in the sense that it promised a "restoration of original principles," but it was a party that, unlike the Whigs and despite efforts by its more moderate and conservative elements, resisted the very notion of reconciliation and compromise. Less than a decade earlier, the Whig *Tribune* had condemned violent elements within the Dorr Rebellion and the Anti-Rent movement almost without hesitation.[104] But in Kansas, though it preferred a congressional repeal of the Nebraska law, it also openly supported the organization of an "armed force in the Territory" to "repel" a slavocrat "invasion." Contemptuous of pragmatic politics, law, and compromise, the *Tribune* alleged that "the great want of Kansas" was not order but "revolvers and other weapons."[105] The paper even cited Jefferson's justification for revolution in his letters on Shay's Rebellion: "If they [the people] remain quiet under such misconceptions, it is lethargy, the forerunner of death to the public liberty. What country can preserve its liberties if its rulers are not warned from time to time that the people preserve the spirit of resistance."[106] Kansas, the *Tribune* hinted, was an American 1848.

The final blows to the *Tribune's* faith in political compromise, social harmony, and the legitimacy of America's republican institutions and even the law were the Dred Scott decision and John Brown's invasion of the South. The Dred Scott case was heard, of course, in the midst of the Kansas crisis and the legal issues it presented directly addressed the central political and constitutional question of the Civil War era: Did Congress have the authority to outlaw the spread of slavery into the Western territories? The court's ruling became a subject of speculation in Washington in mid-December 1856, in the *Tribune* not long after, and the new president, James Buchanan, even mentioned it in his inaugural address, insincerely announcing that he would "cheerfully submit" to the eminent tribunal. Given the composition of the court and the rigidity of sectional politics, a pro-Southern outcome was largely predetermined.[107] When the court indeed ruled on behalf of the most extreme Southern position on the rights of Southern property in slaves, the *Tribune* concluded that the only viable course left open to Northern progressives was disobedience to the law. "You may 'cheerfully submit'—of course you will—to whatever the five slaveholders and two or three doughfaces on the bench of the Supreme Court may be ready to utter on this subject," the *Tribune* groused in an open editorial letter to Buchanan, "but not one man who really desires freedom over Slavery in the Territories will do so."[108]

When the decision was announced just days after Buchanan's inauguration, it reaffirmed the bankruptcy of the *Tribune's* old Whig faith in a neutral constitutional order immune from politics, interest, and popular passion. "This decision," Greeley wrote famously, "is entitled to just so much moral weight as would be the judgment of a majority of those congregated in any Washington bar-room." Terming the court's ruling "treason to the principles of Democracy, treason to the principles of Republicanism, treason against humanity, treason to the cause of justice, truth, and progress," Greeley called for a kind of constitutional overthrow of the court by making it a representative body proportional to population. Greeley refused "to submit slavishly to fraud and usurpation."[109] Compared to some of his correspondents, Greeley's approach was measured. James Pike, the *Tribune's* abolitionist correspondent, wrote from Washington: "Let it be everywhere understood that the oligarchs have at length fully emerged from all obscurity as to their policy and designs.... There is nothing left for the people of the Free States but to confront and break down this insulting domination over their rights and their interests. The only question left for the consideration of those who do not intend to recognize the legitimacy of this revolution in the administration of the Federal Constitution is, what is the true mode of resisting."[110]

If Dred Scott tested the *Tribune's* Whiggish devotion to law and its orderly adjustment, John Brown's Virginia insurrection challenged even more sacred Whig principles. After John Brown launched a revolutionary invasion into Virginia, the *Tribune,* not unexpectedly in the context of its development, joined Brown's chorus of defenders. The *Tribune* endorsed what the paper itself conceded was "the work of a madman." On the surface, the *Tribune* still clung to the Whiggish premise that the "way to Universal Emancipation lies not through insurrection, civil war and bloodshed, but through peace, discussion, and the quiet diffusion of sentiments of humanity and justice." But by excusing and even justifying Brown's actions, the paper seemed to encourage slavery's violent overthrow. "There will be enough to heap execration on the memory of these mistaken men," the *Tribune* responded in the immediate aftermath of the uprising. "We leave this work to the fit hands and tongues of those who regard the fundamental axioms of the Declaration of Independence as 'glittering generalities.'" "They dared and died for what they felt to be right," boasted the *Tribune,* "though in a manner which seems to us fatally wrong. Let their epitaphs remain unwritten until the not distant day when no slave shall clank his chains in the shades of Monticello or by the graves of Mount Vernon."[111]

In the controversy that followed Brown's capture, the *Tribune* moved even further toward extremism. It was enraged by the treatment of the insurrectionist's corpses and accused the Virginia militia of firing upon men flying the flag of truce. The *Tribune* now began, in concert with antislavery radicals, the canonization of John Brown. But the *Tribune* rendered Brown less as a religious martyr and more as a product of political struggle; in the end, it wrote, "President Pierce and Judge Douglas are...the real authors of the late insurrection."[112] Though the *Tribune* still insisted that it was committed to working within the political process, it excused Brown's uprising and seemingly encouraged others. "War has its necessities, and they are some-times terrible," the *Tribune* declared, "[and] there are eras in which death is not merely heroic but beneficent and fruitful." "The essence of crime is the pursuit of selfish gratification in disregard of others' good; and that is the precise opposite of Old Brown's impulse...to benefit a despised and down-trodden race," the *Tribune* concluded, all but advocating revolution in the South. "Let none doubt that History will accord an honored niche to Old John Brown."[113]

Despite the *Tribune's* ever-increasing radicalism, the paper's revolutionary sentiments also had their limits. From this point forward, through the war years and after, the Whig ideal of a political and reform culture rooted in an ideal of social harmony would be in almost constant tension on the paper with a more radical mode of politics and reform that was reconciled to the role of interest and even violence in social change. In the midst of the country's post–John Brown descent into disunion and civil war, the *Tribune* was among the few voices on the radical margins of a polarized political cul-ture yet still calling for peace. Just days before Lincoln's victory, the *Tribune* allowed that if the South was determined to "fight, they must hunt up some other enemy, for we are not going to fight them." "If they insist on staying in the Union, they must of course obey its laws," the *Tribune* proclaimed, "but, if the *People*...of the Cotton States shall ever deliberately vote themselves out of the Union, we shall be in favor of letting them go in peace.... We will buy it [cotton] and pay for it, just as other nations do—just as we do now."[114] "We hold, with Jefferson, to the inalienable right of communities to alter or abolish forms of government that have become oppressive or injurious," the *Tribune* granted. "The right to secede may be a revolutionary one, but it exists, nevertheless." As long as the process was deliberative and "fully can-vassed before the people," peaceful secession was preferable to both war and the late efforts at a compromise movement led by Constitutional Unionists, Northern Democrats, and conservative New York financiers and merchants who feared economic ruin.[115] "We mean to remain in and be loyal to the Union; we shall gladly see all do the same," the *Tribune* avowed, "but we will hire nobody, bribe nobody, pay nobody, cajole nobody, to remain in it."[116]

The *Tribune's* support for peaceful secession has been understood in a vari-ety of ways and seems on the surface to run counter to its 1850s radicaliza-tion. The paper's contradictory violent and pacific tendencies prompted one major Civil War historian to conclude that Greeley's calls for peaceful seces-sion were insincere, a crafty attempt to appease the South's political passions and especially to calm Northern moderates who repeatedly gave concessions to the South in the face of threats.[117] But Greeley's opposition to social and political war during the secession crisis was hardly singular; when examined within a longer context that includes a Reconstruction history in which he advocated both radicalism and reconciliation, Greeley's promotion of both peaceable secession and aggressive war in 1860–61 becomes somewhat more comprehensible. The paper's post-1848 radicalization never supplanted its earlier Whig notions; rather, it coexisted with them in sometimes improbable ways. At times, these intellectual vagaries could seem like the foolish inconsistencies of a shallow mind. But in others, they were the contradictory elements of deeply held views.

With regard to the South in the immediate crisis of secession, Greeley's faith in free labor was so profound that both radical and reconciliatory impulses sprang from it. In the years leading up to the war, the *Tribune* helped propound the widely held Republican view that there was a latent free-labor majority within the South that was poised to reform the region from within. During the John Brown controversy, the *Tribune* even claimed the insurrection revealed the tenuous nature of the South's slave-based social order and its dependence on the "forces of the General Government" to sustain it. Even earlier, the *Tribune* played a central role in publicizing Hinton Helper's *Impending Crisis of the South,* an incendiary tract first published in 1857 and republished in a cheap pamphlet form in 1859 by Greeley and some other leading Republicans.[118] Helper's main message, an inflammatory one, was inflected with if not directly shaped by socialist-style accounts of how contending social forces shape contemporary politics: Helper was, in some respects, a Southern Louis Blanc. He argued in the various iterations of his book that the South's slave interest subordinated its democratic white majority—a majority that was primed for revolution. In embracing Helper's vision, the *Tribune* agitated, in effect, for an internal Southern revolution, one in which independent yeoman farmers would overthrow the region's ruling planter aristocracy.

Helper put a radical twist on mainstream Republican political economy but, in a fusion not unlike the *Tribune's* own, his ideas also resonated with older Whig notions as well. In a basic political-economic sense, Helper echoed the antislavery arguments of sober-minded former Whigs such as Henry Carey. Both argued that the containment of slavery was a political and economic goal; not only was slavery inimical to basic liberal political values, but it also arrested the economic development of the South. Slavery, they insisted, trapped the South in a kind of free-trade, colonial agricultural dependency, and the slave regime compounded the problem by blocking measures that promoted mixed economic development, most notably by resisting investment in human development. But in a deeper sense, Helper's thesis also manifested, beneath the more obvious revolutionary sentiments, a deeper Whiggish commitment to social harmony and reconciliation, a quality that must have connected with Greeley on an instinctual level. Helper did prophesize the overthrow of the South's social order, but he also implied that the conflict between the free North and the slave South was artificial, that without the conspiratorial interference of a powerful interest—the slave system—free labor would blossom across the region and the sections would be naturally reconciled.

In the early years of the war, when Helper's supposed latent free-labor majority failed to realize itself, the *Tribune* nonetheless continued to waver between bellicosity and pacifism, conservatism and radicalism. Greeley's position on secession and the war effectively represented the culmination of his two-decade-long development and especially the contradictory nature of his mind and motives. His commitment to a reasoned, peaceful secession— always holding out the promise of reconciliation—represents the persistence of his Whiggery. That said, by 1860 Greeley's Whiggery had also been tempered by a more fundamental and revolutionary sense that slavery and freedom were inherently antagonistic and destined to clash. His Whiggish faith in reason and the harmony of interests would never entirely recede (and it would surface again during Reconstruction), but it was hopelessly muddled by an equally powerful socialist sense that society was composed of a diverse collection of dissonant interests.

The *Tribune's* discordant mixture of Whiggery and socialist Republicanism made for particularly unstable policy, unsuited for the crisis of disunion or the challenges of reunion. During the course of the Civil War, Greeley's reversals became ever more frequent, exaggerating what William Cullen Bryant referred to as Greeley's "vagaries," his petulance and instability.[119] Throughout the 1850s, Greeley complained of the Whigs' political caution, but in the 1860 election Greeley first backed Edward Bates and then Lincoln rather than the putatively more radical Seward. In 1860–61, within the space of a year, the *Tribune* would advocate first peaceful secession and later, in a series of infamous "Forward to Richmond" editorials, aggressive war. After the humiliating defeat at the First Bull Run, the *Tribune* once again pushed peaceful reconciliation. And throughout the remainder of the war Greeley's pacifism would reemerge in moments of crisis and defeat, sometimes in such a pronounced way that he became a self-appointed mediator between the North and the South in several failed attempts at private diplomacy. All the while, the *Tribune* also became the public voice of Radical Republicanism, the North's most vigorous critic of Lincoln's early unwillingness to make the war a crusade against Southern slavery and its concomitant social order.

Whigs of every ideological stripe had once prized stability, order, morality, and the rule of law. Much of the Whigs' social policy could be understood as an effort to reduce the amount of, and tolerance for, violence in society. Whig antipathy toward social conflict and violence manifested itself, for example, in reform campaigns against capital punishment, flogging in the navy, lynching, Native American removal, alcohol, war, dueling, and slavery. The primacy of rationality and the moral conscience accounts for the paramount importance Whigs placed on free discussion and education. Opposed to anarchy and mob rule, Whigs viewed government as the mediator and harmonizer of faction and passion, often protecting the weak from the strong. The Whigs campaigned, in short, against what Horace Bushnell invoked as a "bowie-knife style of civilization"—language that also could have been clipped from the early *Tribune*.[120]

But for reformers of the *Tribune*'s ilk, revolution abroad and post–Mexican War sectionalism at home challenged the basic tenets of the Whig political culture, and with Seward's "Higher Law" speech a new sensibility started to emerge that bore bloody fruit four years later in Kansas. Culturally, Seward's invocation of a "higher law" was hardly revolutionary in a predominantly Protestant nation that prized the individually examined moral conscience, but his sentiments seemed to encourage civil disobedience and to question the rule of majorities and constitutions.[121] The notion of a "higher law" raised the specter of a radical assault on established institutions and norms: property, religion, law, family, and majoritarian democracy. Greeley had defended Seward's principle despite a long history of opposition to legal antinomianism. Whiggery, at its very core, eschewed extrapolitical, extralegal resistance to the law, and its great antagonists throughout the period—mob violence, popular passion, lynching, debt repudiation, nullification, disunionism, social and economic anarchy—were all antithetical to the party culture's faith in the orderly and reasoned resolution of public conflicts. But in the case of slavery, Greeley, like Seward, was forced to contemplate the law, written not as an impartial public-minded arbiter, but as a tool that served a powerful and rapacious interest. After the Kansas-Nebraska crisis, Greeley could no longer believe unreservedly in the harmonious adjudication of political conflicts, and his misgivings were part of a loudly resonating discourse within the culture of Republicanism: "We are not one people," he wrote in 1855. "We are two peoples. We are a people for Freedom and a people for Slavery. Between the two conflict is inevitable."[122] Intellectually, the war had begun.

When Whigs such as Greeley abandoned their faith in the law and political compromise, they abandoned the values that sustained the party. A decade of socialist social criticism and the failure of the 1848 revolutions had carried

Greeley to an ideological position where, in the aftermath of Kansas-Nebraska, he was now ready to put into practice the assumption that politics was a contest of antagonistic interests. Though Greeley's radicalism would continue to ebb and flow based on locally contingent circumstances, the Republican political revolution in which he was a central participant proceeded with the fundamental understanding that politics and political economy were areas in which power was disputed rather than rationally arbitrated. As Greeley had concluded after Seward's speech, "When the Law becomes the ally and the instrument of oppressors... [it] defame[s] and villif[ies] the great body of Law, whose vital aim is Justice betwixt man and man."[123]

CHAPTER 6

The Civil War and the Dilemma of Free Labor

> Bodily slavery, that which gives one man a property in the body and talents of another, is the worst, the most outrageous and baleful form of the wrong, but by no means the only form. It is rather its outer husk which, when removed, discloses still more subtle and concentrated growths within.
>
> *New-York Tribune,* June 29, 1850

For two decades, Greeley had called for economic reforms that would democratize property, diffuse the benefits of technology and specialization, and protect labor from the ravages of competition with chattel and foreign labor. Most of all, he encouraged workers to form cooperative associations in response to the increasing consolidation of capital. Throughout the 1850s and during the Civil War, the *Tribune,* like most Republican organs, predicted that the defeat of slavery would result in a golden age for labor, but few anticipated the extent to which the Civil War would accelerate the changes associated with the market revolution. This entirely new world was symbolized in many respects by Greeley's own New York City, which had become a surging, modern capitalist metropolis, the financial center of the emerging industrial economy. The city's size and its extremes of wealth and poverty were staggering. The rapid expansion and contractions of the money and debt markets allowed a single operator to clear hundreds of thousands of dollars in a single transaction. "Wall street grows every day richer and more commanding, though fortunes are made and lost there every year that would buy the broadest dukedoms of Europe," an observer remarked. "Whatever of energy and enterprise, financial daring and reckless speculation, lust of commercial power and mania for money-getting there is in the land seems compressed into Wall street for half-a-dozen hours of the twenty-four." Amid the glitter of postwar prosperity, there remained stubborn poverty. New York had become a mature metropolis, suffused with "caste-feeling." "No society in the world has more divisions and sub-divisions than ours," said one New Yorker, "more ramifications and inter-ramifications—more circles within circles." Of the city's more than seven hundred thousand residents, two-thirds lived in tenements, most of them without light and stuffed to the brim with families. Despite the grim condi-tions, rents doubled within a year of the war's end. When the *Tribune* sent a reporter to investigate working conditions, he found that unskilled workers still earned the same wage that they had earned in 1860—three to five dol-lars a week—even though the cost of living had doubled. Women workers employed by army contractors made half that much. While the majority of New Yorkers lived in poverty and ignorance, upper-tier Republicans orga-nized themselves into Union Clubs and reform committees whose answer to urban problems was to cleanse the city of filth and corruption.[1]

The Civil War marked the transition toward mass industrial America. Before the war, there were only a handful of manufacturing firms that were not family run and almost all employed fewer than a hundred workers. And yet the changing nature of work was already apparent. The social reorgani-zation of work preceded large-scale mechanization when, during the first half of the nineteenth century, the relationship between capital and labor—employer and employee—lost its familial character and was increasingly ruled by the temporary ethos of cash and contract. Work itself became less skilled; with specialization, many workers lost autonomy and self-respect. This novel universe of capital and labor had always been particularly visible to Greeley, lodged as he was in New York City, the epicenter of the new America, and in an industry that had achieved a level of scale and mechanization that would not become common in other industries until after the war.

In many respects, the ideological and actual war against slavery left Repub-licans unprepared to grapple with the challenges of the postwar social order. Republican optimism was fueled both by the progress and growth of the war years, but also by the fact that the long war against the slave system had blinded many Northerners to the shortcomings of their own society. His-torians have described the North's worldview in the years leading up to the Civil War as shaped by a "free labor ideology," a consensus vision particularly in Republican circles that wedded the party's economic vision to its critique of slavery.[2] At its core, free-labor ideology was a defense of the North's contractual, incentive-based economic system and a critique of the South's reliance on violence and coercion. The free labor thesis explains why most Republicans simultaneously opposed, passionately, the expansion of slavery while exhibiting few moral or ethical objections to white supremacy or even to slavery where it already existed. It elucidates, in short, why Northerners opposed slavery's growth without becoming abolitionists, without any sort of commitment to black citizenship or racial equality.

As much as any journal, the *Tribune* was the bible of this free-labor culture. In the immediate aftermath of emancipation, the *Tribune* looked forward to the quick emergence of a color-blind society where "manual labor will be as respectable in South Carolina as in New England." It imagined that in the postwar world, the "artificial degradation of practical production will pass away; . . . [and] the color of the producer will be the last thing which the employer will think of" when contracting for labor. It voiced the broadly shared Republican expectation that without a Southern check on the dynamism of the national government, their party's idealistic fusion of Hamiltonian economic complexity and Jeffersonian economic democracy would triumph in a climate of unbridled nationalism. The national government would now have free rein to introduce a positive economic program—internal improvements, a national financial system, and protection—that would bring about a mixed and largely self-sufficient economy rivaling those of Europe. Heirs of Jefferson as much as Hamilton, it was also a Republican article of faith that the vast Western expense offered a limitless economic vista, one that would guarantee the promise of opportunity and social mobility. Lincoln was the product of the most optimistic vein of this nationalist developmental tradition, which argued that once the country was emancipated from the shackles of slavery, all Americans would have the right to rise and would be in control of their economic futures.[3]

Most early Republicans had regarded the marketplace for labor as a largely neutral one, and more importantly they believed that the United States was exempt from the most vicious aspects of its laws. Even so, Republicans also saw the expansion of slavery and the unprecedented growth of European-style immigrant-dominated industrial cities as a threat to the dignity of American labor. Together, slavery, immigration, and global competition augured a bleaker future dominated by widespread wage-earning dependency, which ran counter to the basic Jeffersonian economic vision of labor's independence and autonomy.[4] Within the broad Republican free-labor coalition that came together to preserve the Union, there were yet real divisions about the causes of poverty, which explains why during Reconstruction, when Republicans were in control of the government and had to consider the meaning of freedom, equality, and citizenship, there was robust disagreement even within the Radical wing of the party about the nature of work, property, and the market.[5] Some prominent Republicans, such as Henry Raymond and Frederick Law Olmstead, understood poverty as moral deviance; in the

United States, they thought, poverty is a reflection on character, a sign of sloth and moral turpitude. For them, the debate with the slave South legitimated capitalism by contrasting bondage with the efficiency of free labor's incentives and promise of social mobility. But there was another brand of Republicanism, associated primarily with labor and reform movements, that viewed the outcomes of market competition more warily, and regarded chattel slavery as an advanced manifestation of the condition of labor under monopoly capital. Greeley was with this latter group, treating slavery not merely as a check on the market's limitless perfection but instead as an extension of the market's inevitable tendency toward monopoly, inequality, and aristocracy. For Republicans in the Raymond mold, the end of the war meant closure. For Republicans of Greeley's cast, the end of the war meant the resurrection of the labor question, which had been overshadowed during the war by the more pressing crusade against slavery. For socialist reformers and the labor movement, the end of the war revived the antebellum debate over the nature of market relationships and the hidden coercion that underlay contracts struck between unequal partners.

Within the Republican Party and without, the death of slavery and the explosion of industrial capital fueled the labor movement and a broader debate over liberal political economy. The emergence of a genuine proletariat in the wake of emancipation meant, as labor leader and Civil War officer Joseph Weydemeyer wrote, "the modern labor question—the question of hired labor, which is better known under the euphemistic name of 'free labor'" could once again lose its "secondary character which heretofore adhered to it on this continent."[6] Within this new political and ideological context, Greeley would be challenged in a vigorous way by voices both to his right and to his left. As historian Jonathan Glickstein has pointed out, Greeley had always been searching "for a formula that somehow would supplant the market mechanism—the source of economic 'anarchy' as well as class antagonism—while preserving other attributes of American capitalism that he deemed truly valuable. These attributes included private property itself together with a differential-reward system."[7] The Reconstruction North, however, was a new economic landscape, and whether meaningful reform could avoid trespassing the sanctity of private property became an increasingly open question. As productive capital consolidated in ever fewer hands, the private property principle, traditionally regarded as the mainspring of liberty and independence, became to an escalating number of voices in the labor movement an obstacle to the freedom of labor. So as workers collectively began to petition government to refashion the rules of political economy in their interest, the labor question—the "organization of labor" as the socialists had put it a generation earlier—became the central focus of politics during Reconstruction in the North as well as in the South.

Journalism and the Civil War

However much it was the actual agent of the vast changes in the mid-nineteenth-century American economy and society, the Civil War has long been a convenient marker, dividing the age of entrepreneurial capitalism from its industrial successor. The newspaper business, as much as any other, was representative of the vast scale of the new industrial economy. The *Tribune*'s own institutional history was emblematic of many of the economic trends it wrestled with as it labored to adapt its antebellum free-labor vision to the realities of the postwar age of capital. When Greeley started the *Tribune* in the 1840s, he had been an artisan printer. By the 1850s, major newspapers were capitalized at tens and even hundreds of thousands of dollars. The Civil War would accelerate this trend even further, and remake the business of journalism both structurally and ideologically. Namely, extensive war reporting was so demanding and competitive that it required vast resources; in the process of reporting on the war, newspapers became more anonymous and fashioned themselves as "objective" conduits of facts and information. In a variety of ways, the economics of journalism transformed its character. Over the middle part of the nineteenth century, journalism experienced a "news revolution," as one historian described it, and it was one of both structure and content. This "news revolution" shifted the focus of the major metropolitan dailies from editor-statesmen to correspondents in the field who gathered facts and reported stories. Circulation now depended on information and speed—on "beats" and "scoops" in the contemporary vernacular. Even though the telegraph was hardly new, its influence was increasingly felt in the overall feel of newspapers when the meandering, epistolic character of antebellum correspondence gave way to the new wartime journalism's more consolidated, lead-driven, modern format of reporting.

The staggering logistical challenge of reporting on a massive modern war would revolutionize the newspaper business and in many respects render Greeley an increasingly marginal and archaic figure, in the antebellum mode of the editor-crusader. Even the appearance of major newspapers had changed during the war.[8] The front page, once covered with advertisements, weeks-old letters from abroad, and transcripts of important speeches, was now given over to the latest news. Though the *Tribune* maintained a mostly bland look (advertisements, for example, were printed in the same font as the regular content), other newspapers such as the *Herald* highlighted the importance of the most recent reports by using headlines and laying the stories out against a backdrop of visually arresting woodcuts. The *Tribune*, behind both the *Herald* and the *Times,* would not move the latest news to the outside front page until its twenty-fifth anniversary in 1866. It was one of the last of the major dailies to do so. Of the great editor-proprietor dailies, only the *Evening Post* held to the traditional format. The new layouts of the information-driven newspapers of the Civil War era were, in effect, literal representations of the new division between reporting and opinion and the escalating importance of speed and technology.

When Greeley founded the *Tribune,* his "leading idea was the establishment of a journal removed alike from servile partisanship on the one hand and from gagged, mincing neutrality on the other."[9] But the *Tribune's* effort to wed "news" and "opinion" would make it increasingly outdated, and crusading public intellectuals of Greeley's sort would flee to opinion magazines such as *The Nation.*[10] The Civil War's "news revolution," with its emphasis on speed, information, and, most of all, "scoops," elevated reporters and their pursuit of facts above the editor-crusader, and their decline reflected the new scale of New York's newspaper giants. Though many readers continued to identify everything in the paper as coming from Greeley (including the advertisements!), in 1861 the *Tribune* had some 212 employees and twenty-eight editors and reporters. Greeley joked that every morning he "opened the paper... [in] a terror as to what they [the night editors] might make me say after eleven o'clock."[11] "The *Tribune,*" Greeley once said, "would rather be right than popular."[12] It was a sentiment that Greeley could sustain in the 1840s when he practically wrote, edited, and printed the paper himself, but it was not one that could survive the competitive pressures that marked the heavily capitalized business environment of the Civil War.

Amid the *Tribune's* dramatic growth, control of the paper largely passed from Greeley's hands. During the war, Greeley filled columns in the *Tribune,* the *Continental Monthly,* and the *Independent,* and kept up a vigorous speaking schedule. After the war, Greeley contracted to write a two-volume history of the war that kept him working late into the evening. In 1867, he spoke openly about retiring from the paper, and throughout much of the decade he spent a great deal of his time either in Washington or on the lecture circuit. In the late '60s, he added a career in politics to an already overcrowded schedule, running unsuccessfully for Congress in 1866 and state comptroller of New York in 1869. Gradually, the paper passed into the hands of a new generation of writers and editors. The paper's antebellum generation became either too old or too affluent to put up with the odd hours and difficult work of daily journalism. Some moved on to other positions with competing publications and others took positions in the government or private industry. Reporter Charles Hill became the U.S. consul in Zurich in 1865. Longtime news editor John Cleveland took a job with the Treasury Department. Washington chief Adams Hill returned to Harvard as a professor of rhetoric. Two other *Tribune* reporters, Henry Villard and Sam Wilkeson, were absorbed by the robber baron culture whose imprint on postwar America was becoming so noticeable. Wilkeson became a publicist for financier Jay Cooke, and Villard, a fellow reporter in the field, became a financier and industrial magnate. Generous to a fault, Greeley lost any semblance of financial control over the paper. In an age of corporate consolidation, the *Tribune* remained an employee-owned association. The head of the composing room owned as much of the paper as Greeley, typographers earned as much as the reporters, and the compositors were organized into "phalanxes."[13]

By the end of his journalistic career, Greeley was a shell of himself. Plagued by poor health, his body was often covered in boils. Stories circulated about his "eccentric[ity]" and "absent-mindedness." He supposedly employed "a boy...especially to inform him...whether he has eaten dinner, and what his name was when he entered the office."[14] Worst of all perhaps, the Yankee spirit of his reform moralism, always slightly out of step in New York City, seemed entirely misplaced amid the glittery materialism of the surging postwar metropolis. The entire *Tribune* operation seemed to be an aging artisan shop in the new industrial age.[15] Greeley was dwarfed by the new universe of corporate journalism, and his ever more anachronistic relationship to the newspaper business mirrored the way he and other antebellum reformers were ill-equipped to respond to the new industrial realities of postwar America.

A Radical Republican Gazette

Throughout much of the Civil War era, Greeley and the *Tribune* were aligned politically with the Radicals, the party's "antislavery vanguard." One historian of Civil War journalism called the *Tribune* the "official gazette of the Radicals."[16] Greeley's paper gave unflagging support to Union officers such as John Fremont, Benjamin Butler, and David Hunter who, in advance of federal policy, gave sanctuary to self-emancipating slaves, who were flooding into their lines as refugees. It joined the Radicals in Congress in criticizing Union commanders with Democratic loyalties, implying that they fought passively and tentatively because they sympathized with slavery and the rebellion. For the most part, the *Tribune* advocated vigorous prosecution of the war and expansion of its meaning: namely, that the war should become an emancipationist crusade, and that the emancipated slaves ought to be armed. When Lincoln explained in his first State of the Union message that he was doing everything he could to prevent the war from becoming a "remorseless revolutionary struggle," Greeley was embittered that conservatives had taken over the administration—despite the fact that Lincoln was following the very policies Greeley had once suggested to maintain hold of the border states.[17] And during the war's 1862 turning point, Greeley and the *Tribune* acted with the "Jacobin" party in Congress—Charles Sumner, Ben Wade, George Julian, Joshua Giddings, Zachariah Chandler, and Thaddeus Stevens—to press Lincoln into making the destruction of slavery a fundamental war aim. In August, Greeley penned what was perhaps the most important newspaper editorial in American history, the "Prayer of Twenty Millions," which called upon Lincoln to make emancipation an explicit war aim. In Lincoln's forceful response, he explained one month in advance of his already planned Preliminary Emancipation Proclamation that any decision he might make about slavery was secondary to his efforts to save the union. Greeley's radical credentials served, ultimately, as a useful foil to Lincoln as he sought conservative grounds to transform radically the meaning of the war.

Though Greeley's mood and pronouncements shifted back and forth throughout the war, to the public he was the symbol of Radicalism, the "nigger's friend." This popular perception became tragically manifest during the 1863 New York City draft riots, when the city's immigrant and working-class communities violently protested conscription and the war in a three-day rampage that left more than one hundred dead. Greeley and the *Tribune* were icons of Radical elitism and the "unnatural" abolitionist crusade to elevate the status of blacks at the expense of the white immigrant working class. The *Tribune's* main wartime rival, the *Herald,* stoked working-class resentment, proclaiming Greeley a "crazy, contemptible wretch, who now asserts the equality of white men and Negroes, [and] formerly asserted," in the name of "Fourierrieriteism [sic], phalanxism, and free-loveism that all men should have property in common," the family should be abolished, "[and] that all women should be common prostitutes."[18] Explicitly linked both to the riots' more narrow precipitant—the Republican war—and its larger one, Protestant missions, "colored" orphanages, liberal boardinghouses, prostitute's asylums, and all the various manifestations of elite humanitarian reform, the *Tribune* building became the focus of not less than three violent protests.[19] Octavius Frothingham, a Unitarian minister sympathetic to Transcendentalism, noted the irony that Greeley, who became the main target of "the rage of the populace," had also "been the steadfast friend of these very people who hungered for his blood."[20]

FIGURE 6.   During the New York City draft riots, mobs attacked the most visible symbols of abolitionism and the Union war effort. These included Greeley and the *Tribune* offices. Courtesy of the
Picture Collection, The Branch Libraries, The New York Public Library, Astor, Lenox, and Tilden Foundations, image ID 809562.

Despite his association with the Radicals, Greeley, from the dawn of the
secession crisis through the last years of the war, wavered between pacifism
and belligerence, and the former foreshadowed the break he would make
from Radical principles in the final year of his life. Despite the way post-
1848 domestic and international politics had radicalized him, Greeley never
entirely let go of his Whig faith that there was a natural harmony of interests
in society. As a long-time pacifist, Greeley often pressed for peace as vigorously as he pressed for emancipation, particularly during moments of crisis.
After publicly advocating peaceful secession, Greeley instigated not less than
five separate campaigns for peace during the war, all of which would have
effectively secured Southern independence. All told, Greeley's "peace efforts"
belied his reputation as a Radical and a fanatic. More basically, they illustrated
the way instinctual conservatism always lurked beneath his commitment to
radical reform. This conservatism would persist throughout the period of
Reconstruction, from the moment when he bailed Jefferson Davis out of
jail in 1867 all the way through to his 1872 presidential campaign when he

promised to institute both Southern home rule and black rights. Greeley's "gyrations" and contradictions persevered to the last.[21]

Despite his quixotic interventions in government and diplomacy, the war and its aftermath actually changed very little about Greeley's politics. Throughout the postwar period, Greeley tried to do what historian David Blight has termed the impossible: combine the rhetoric of rights and reconciliation, rights for former slaves and reconciliation for former Confederates.[22] From the outset of Reconstruction, the *Tribune* proclaimed two great principles, "Amnesty" and "Impartial Suffrage," and in spite of subsequent violence, that position would not change.[23] The logic of the combination was rooted in political instincts nurtured before the war. In a basic way, the *Tribune's* Reconstruction policy was driven by a revived Whiggish faith in the harmony of social and economic interests. The *Tribune's* conviction was that various national and Southern regional interests could be reconciled and that the South's ongoing racial conservatism represented the views of an artificially sustained minority determined to uphold the social system of the Old South.

As was conventional in Republican circles, the *Tribune* held that freedom was natural and that slavery was artificial, sustained only by political conspiracy and despotism. Remove the irrational obstacle of slavery and free labor would transform the South and usher in a new era of prosperity without social conflict. In 1866, it predicted the rapid triumph of Northern values in the South. "The time is coming," the *Tribune* foresaw, "when manual labor will be as respectable in South Carolina as in New-England": "The artificial degradation of practical production will pass away... [and] then the thankless business of legislating for classes will become simply impertinent; for, with acknowledged usefulness, will come admitted power and men without distinction of hue will be able to take care of their own interests without let or hindrance of the selfish and unjust."[24] The *Tribune* proclaimed, against the public doubts of Southerners such as William Sharkey who thought that black shiftlessness would render them extinct without slavery, that "Blacks *will* work, provided they can be reasonably assured of fair payment" and that "the badly reconstructed Rebels and their Copperhead allies will refrain from wantonly killing them." From the *Tribune's* perspective, the major question facing the South was "Will the *Southern Whites* work?"[25] Eliminate the "threat of the whip" and stop treating the "freedmen as serfs" and the natural logic of free labor will unleash the region's latent wealth, "as the past prosperity of the Southern planters proves."[26] Greeley, always a moralist, believed in the redemptive virtue of work and self-reliance, and during the early stages of Reconstruction he assumed that freedom would have the same impact on blacks that it had on whites: "If the negroes are idle, they must go hungry and ragged; if they steal, they must be punished—not as negroes, but as men. If they have not yet learned that 'freedom means freedom to work,' the winter just coming on will teach them—with a good many others—that wholesome lesson."[27]

In the aftermath of the war, the *Tribune* tried to provide a realistic portrait of the promise and limits of free labor in a post-emancipation plantation society in the most politicized environment imaginable. Many of the *Tribune's* Southern reports recognized that slavery had lingering effects and that the mutual suspicion between the classes and races made nearly any labor system unworkable. Blacks naturally refused to work in gangs. A wage system was problematic in a cash-poor economy and, moreover, it hardly held out the promise of independence. Blacks and whites quickly and mutually turned to the share system, but as the *Tribune* correspondent pointed out, contrary to free-labor dreams of the harmony of interests, it was nearly impossible for planters and former slaves to cooperate in a yearlong endeavor that involved some risk. The allowance made to black labor was so scanty that "he cannot live more poorly under any circumstances unless he actually starves." Naturally, former slaves do not "like the discipline, the working in gangs" or any remnant that "savors too much of Slavery" and prefer the "smaller but safer" and less humiliating "business of odd jobs and tilling little plots of land on their own account." The convulsive effects of the passage from one social system to another, the correspondent concluded, meant that the Northern hope that the plantation system could be maintained within a system of free labor was misplaced. Rather, the future of free labor in the South, according to the *Tribune* correspondent, was a fragile one that was dependent on labor shortages created by "keeping the women at home and sending the children to school." Labor scarcity would ideally force the "plantation" and its "aristocracy" to "give way to the small farm"; "in this way," he finished, "the laborer will find the attainment of land of his own within the reach of his ambition, and so be stimulated to work beyond the mere needs of the hour; villages will follow, and the wealth of the region, though distributed in the hands of more people, will in the aggregate be greater than before."[28]

Throughout the first five years of Reconstruction, the *Tribune* presented the news in a manner aligned with a Radical narrative. The *Tribune* blamed conservative whites for most of the postwar violence in such Southern cities as Mobile, Memphis, and Galveston.[29] The *Tribune's* diverse correspondence emphasized the recalcitrance of former rebels and the noble restraint of former slaves. "Walter" in Savannah wrote that the only decisive action being taken in this "utterly paralyzed" land was that of confiscated land being

returned to liberated Confederate prisoners. During Presidential Reconstruction, reporters in Norfolk, Jackson, South Carolina, and Georgia wrote
of various forms of reenslavement and of daily assaults and even murders
being committed by whites against blacks, and the reappearance of "those
twin relics of barbarism, the chain-gang and the whipping-post."[30] During
Reconstruction, every incident in daily life had political overtones and value-
neutral reporting was next to impossible. Knowing that much of the coverage of the region was corrupted by the "Southern agents of the Associated
Press... either Rebels or Copperheads," the *Tribune* made it its mission to
provide an alternative point of view.[31]

On the political and racial conflicts of Reconstruction, the *Tribune* was
allied with the Radicals, almost all the way up to the 1872 election, but
there were shades of difference that would become more pronounced over
time. In the spring of 1866, President Johnson vetoed two bills, acts that led
effectively to his excommunication from the Republican Party. The first was
an expansive Civil Rights bill designed to counter early efforts by Southern
conservatives to restrict the practical scope of emancipation by defining a
sphere for blacks between slavery and full-blown freedom. The second was
a bill to extend the life of the Freedman's Bureau, a federal agency created to
manage the transition from slavery to freedom, grapple with the humanitarian crisis that came with the end of the war, and negotiate the many legal
and economic conflicts that arose between the races. The Civil Rights Act
put the force of the federal government behind a conventional slate of liberal
political rights, but the Freedman's Bureau did something almost entirely
new. Whatever its limits, the Freedmen's Bureau was the first federal agency
charged with caring for the social welfare of citizens; grounded in the idea
of social rights, it was naturally quite controversial on ideological grounds.[32]
Despite overwhelming support in Congress, Johnson opposed the Bureau,
claiming that humanitarian relief would undermine the "character," "prospects," and self-reliance of the freedmen.[33] The *Times,* which was allied with
Johnson and had been pushing a proto–social Darwinist brand of laissez-faire
liberalism for more than a decade, argued likewise that the Bureau reduced
"the negro" to a condition of dependency, approximating "that of a *minor.*"
The *Tribune,* even though it would only hesitantly endorse the idea of government charity, termed the *Times*'s hostility to the Bureau "sophistry" and
totally indifferent to context. To the *Tribune,* market absolutism applied to
the formerly enslaved was the equivalent of their being "shut up in a dark
cellar... [for] forty years... and then liberated only to be told, 'You have no
business with daylight because you can't see.'" "Deplorable necessities of
the Blacks result from their life-long subjection to cruel social and political

disabilities," the *Tribune* insisted. "Give the Blacks their honest due to-day, and they as a race would need none of your alms."[34]

On the land question, the *Tribune* struck a similar balance between conservatism and radicalism. It advocated the extension of the Homestead Act to blacks and to various parts of the South, yet it stopped short of confiscation or special measures for "any particular class." Throughout Reconstruction, there were voices on Greeley's left that carried forward in practice the socialist critique of American democracy, arguing that the only way any semblance of equal citizenship could be achieved would be to redistribute landed capital among the freedmen. Greeley's instinctive Whiggery, however, made him blanch at the prospect of confiscation. As he had long counseled Northern workers, Greeley encouraged Southern blacks not to "cling desperately to pavements," but to pursue self-reliance by emigrating to open lands: "Go South—go West—go East if you will.... Strike at once for the open country!"[35]

In resisting confiscation of Confederate lands, Greeley opposed the emergence of a racially neutral, class-based party dedicated to the redistribution of a landed property and to serving the larger needs and aspirations of the region's poor. Instead of a biracial Southern workers party, like many centrists he backed a revived Whiggery in the existing Republican Party that resisted open class warfare and was predicated on prodevelopment economic policies that set aside racial conflict and postwar bitterness.[36] He continued to recognize undue concentrations of land and wealth as a threat to republican values, but he could not conceive of a means to address the problem in a manner that would not destabilize society in an even more dangerous way. As he had in the 1840s, Greeley deluded himself that a new economic order could materialize without social conflict or costs:

> Let me speak for myself only as to the general policy of Confiscation. If half the vagrant, waste lands of the South could be *instantly* distributed among the landless, I have no doubt that the effect would be beneficent.... But, when you come to the practical work of Confiscation... all industry would be paralyzed by the prospect and the process of confiscation.... The inevitable evils of Confiscation are too great to justify an experiment of this character. In my judgment, any general confiscation will produce general bankruptcy and famine.[37]

Even though Greeley recognized that "allotment of a small farm to every poor man would do good," and that, without land or some other kind of independent economic competence, the formerly enslaved would inevitably become once again a subject population, he still shied away from forced confiscation. It is the gap between his recognition of the relationship between economic dependence and inequality and the moderation of his solutions that is the true riddle of his, the *Tribune*'s, and perhaps liberalism's history.[38]

Liberalism and the Postwar Republican Party

Greeley's difficulty in grasping the immense challenges faced by former slaves in the Reconstruction South mirrored his vacillations in the face of postwar industrialization, and this despite the fact that journalism was one of the first crafts to be transformed by technology and the new economies of scale brought forth by the expansion of markets. Greeley, like many Whigs, had long been ambivalent about the moral and psychological consequences of capitalist enterprises and the division of labor, and, as was the case in jour-nalism, the postwar period accelerated these tendencies. During the 1830s and 1840s, the paternalist and regulatory ethos of factory communities such as Lowell reconciled conservative Whigs to the emerging capitalist order. During the 1850s, former Whigs such as Abraham Lincoln, who were at the ideological center of the Republican Party, could still legitimately imag-ine an economic world where wage labor was merely a temporary stop on the way toward full-blown propertied independence. Slightly to the left of Lincoln and the general run of modernizer Whig-Republicans, Greeley had his doubts all along about the spread of capitalist specialization and scale, but as a reformer he still dreamed of a democratic version of the Whigs' moral community based principally in his case on worker cooperation. But after the war, the Whig tradition of Christian, reciprocal capitalism and the ante-bellum Republican insistence on social mobility within a free society were supplanted by the triumph of a stripped–down and stark version of laissez-faire liberal individualism that aggressively asserted the impersonal mecha-nisms of market relations as a reflection of natural law. It was a vision that for the first time justified the existence of a permanent wage-earning class. Like many of his generation, including the mainstream of the postbellum labor movement, Greeley continued to push for a cooperative order based on the principles of social mobility, self-reliance, and the widespread diffusion of productive property. But his update of a traditional near-Jeffersonian vision of universal propertied self-reliance struggled to cope with the complex and powerful economic forces that came into play during the 1860s. In Greeley's midst, then, the very ruthless competitive system that he had made a career of opposing suddenly surrounded him and there was little he could envision that would stop it.

For the first time in its existence, the *Tribune* had become an organ of a ruling party that was virtually unchallenged. But in the aftermath of the war, the Republican Party ruled over a diverse constituency. The Republican coalition included capitalists and financiers, farmers and workers, all of whom hoped that the state and national governments would intervene in the economy in ways that would advance their interests. Even more, the party's Southern wing was dominated by ex-slaves who required an even more powerful state presence to protect their rights as citizens, workers, and even as human beings. These practical pressures once again made the assumptions of liberal political economy the focus of political discourse, forcing Republican ideologues to define what exactly they meant by free labor. It was a challenge that the amorphous character of Republican free-labor politics was ill-equipped to answer.

The political and partisan roots of the party only added to its diversity and complexity.[39] Some in the party had once been free-soil Democrats, others nativists, and still others Whigs of various stripes. Even when there was vigorous two-party competition in the North, both parties were often bitterly divided internally. As a result, when the detritus of the Jacksonian two-party system poured into the new Republican Party to fight the expansion of slavery, the result was a party that was even more ideologically diverse than its predecessors. It was united by free labor, a negative, anti-extensionist principle; as a positive program for labor, however, it was virtually empty of meaningful content. Just as in the antebellum era (and perhaps even more so), there was very little agreement from state to state and faction to faction on questions of political economy, even on very traditional issues such as currency and protection that had once bonded the Jacksonian party system together. And astride the kaleidoscopic character of Civil War–era partisan politics was the labor movement, which, like the parties it hoped to influence, remained a patchwork of both organizations and beliefs. It complicated the political picture even further by standing aloof from partisan politics in some cases or making temporary alliances with parties and leaders in others. Making Reconstruction politics and ideology even more intricate was the fact that the period witnessed for the first time the emergence within the Republican Party of a Liberal wing devoted to the sanctity and inherent justice of market relationships.[40] Liberalism was a political movement and would be a vital reform force throughout the remainder of the century. Closely associated with the world of print, many leading public intellectuals were at the forefront of the movement, including second-generation *Tribune* writers and editors. For a brief moment Greeley even became its putative leader, despite the fact that as a movement it proclaimed a set of values that largely repudiated everything he had stood for throughout his career.

The novelty of the Liberal position on labor and political economy can easily escape notice. The postwar Liberal vision of individual self-reliance, much like the idea of free labor, resonated with deeply ingrained American values. The Whig and the early Republican parties—Greeley among them— had long hosted voices committed to self-reliance and social mobility. Yet, for many Whigs and Republicans these precepts were leavened by a simultaneous commitment to a moral economy, a distrust of the competitive system, and a more general suspicion of greed and self-interested individualism. They were also sentiments forged in a radically different economic context. Even so, before the Civil War the most aggressive antebellum advocates of laissez-faire were, in fact, Democrats in the tradition of Jefferson, but even they represented not the most advanced form of bourgeois liberalism, but rather what we might call prebourgeois interests: planters, subsistence farmers, and unskilled immigrant labor. Their viewpoint was a carryover of a traditional republican outlook that inequality was a product of special privilege, government favoritism, and corruption. So although the Liberals' insistence on the sanctity of property, limited government, and individual self-reliance overlapped with aspects of traditional political economy, the mainspring of their movement was radically new: the Liberals embraced the market unreservedly, depicted it in scientific terms, and believed it was an ideal and natural framework within which to organize social and economic relationships in an industrial society. Postwar bourgeois Liberal Republicans, in effect, seized the mantle of laissez-faire liberalism and marshaled it on behalf of an industrial system radically different from the agrarian and artisanal order imagined by Jefferson and his direct political heirs.[41] These new laissez-faire Liberals added yet one more perspective to the postwar cacophony of voices within the Republican Party that made its position on the labor question and political economy almost hopelessly muddled.

Cooperation

Before the full-blown emergence of the Liberal movement in the early 1870s, Greeley and the *Tribune* continued to stake out an ideological middle ground between laissez-faire liberalism and Marxism by aggressively advocating worker cooperation. Worker cooperation represented a social democratic alternative to both market individualism and the abolition of private property; along with the eight-hour day, cooperation was the key plank in the labor movement's postwar agenda. It reflected the broad Lincolnian Republican faith that self-reliance and owning the fruits of your labors were the desired ends of a just political economy. Most of all, Greeley's support for cooperation reflected his long-standing belief (shared with many Republicans) in the incompatibility of self-ownership and the wage economy. Greeley's opposition to the existence of a permanent wage-earning class had deep roots in the formative moralism of 1830s Whiggery. Then, Whig capitalism had been profoundly patriarchal and colored by a Christian reciprocal ethos, when most wage laborers were, in fact, either women or children and early factory life was modeled ideologically on the artisan workshop. Early factories imposed a high degree of social control that the *Tribune,* when reflecting on the history of labor over the last generation, fondly recalled as a "system of patronage" that, despite its "destructive" flaws, at least "provide[d] for the higher mental and social culture of working people" by providing "literary institutions," "reading-rooms and schools." For the *Tribune,* capitalist paternalism had its virtues, but the paper did not fall completely under the sway of conservative nostalgia. Meditating on French social reformer Louis Reybaud's recent ruminations upon the "blessings… of patronage" for labor in the *Revue des Deux Mondes,* the *Tribune* also maintained that paternalistic "alms" rob labor of self-respect and sustain "the idea that the capitalist and operative are not the same kind."[42] Searching for an alternative to both patriarchal patronage and class division, the *Tribune* continued to insist that a third way was possible, that worker cooperation "might deliver us" from all-out social warfare.[43]

The *Tribune* renewed its support for cooperation during Reconstruction for a number of reasons. As noted above, it was embedded in its opposition to the wage economy. Its hostility to wage labor was not dictated, however, by any sort of class-conscious hatred for capital. Like most that were sympathetic to the labor movement, the *Tribune* continued to believe that labor created all value, including capital, which it defined as savings or past labor. It opposed wage labor, then, not "on the assumption that journeymen were inadequately paid," but because "the wages system… [is] not calculated to foster habits of thrift, foresight, and providence." Wage labor fails to elevate character.[44] Cooperation, in short, was a higher form of free labor. The *Tribune's* critique of wage labor was in fact nearly identical to the antebellum Republican portrait of slavery. Cooperation promised to emancipate wage workers from the slavery of wages and restore the "workingman's self-respect." It saved labor from dissipation ("less money will be squandered at gin shops… and places of ruinous pleasure") and strengthened labor's moral fiber. Just as slavery was inferior to free labor because it robbed workers of incentive, so also was wage labor compared to the more highly emancipated labor that was realized by cooperation. "The feeling of proprietorship in lands, houses, corporations, accumulations of invested wealth," the *Tribune* pronounced, "to have an income from funded property, an interest in well-conducted institutions, is to feel oneself a man; and to be sensible of being an organic part of such an institution is to be sensible of personal responsibility and character."[45] Cooperation seemed the next logical step up from both slavery and wages. "Work for Wages," naturally, is superior to slavery; "with all its faults," the paper reasoned, "the laborer for wages is measurably free; he has a choice of pursuits and of employers; he has some voice in fixing the compensation of his service... he has the stimulation of hope." But as with slavery, the *Tribune* finished, "the wages system has this radical vice—*it does not adequately interest the laborer in the perfection of his work.*"[46] To antebellum reformers such as Greeley, an equal distribution of wealth was important, but it remained subordinate to an ideal of economic freedom and self-reliance. Social mobility, in this sense, was not a precursor to the cult of the "self-made man," but an alternative vision of political economy, one willing to sacrifice economies of scale for independence and self-ownership.[47]

Though cooperation rejected the idea of a wage economy in a pretty radical way, the moderation of its presentation betrayed its humanitarian Whig origins. The *Tribune* continued to hold that a new order for labor could be brought about without social disruptions of the sort that doomed slavery. In the *Tribune*'s view, the primary source of injustice was not the relationship between capital and labor, but the process of exchange. "The Happy day of the universal abolition of usurers and 'middlemen'" was the main goal of the *Tribune*'s brand of cooperation, to hasten "the reconciliation of many of those differences which have brought Capital and Labor into false and damaging antagonism."[48] The *Tribune* relished, in short, the idea of shoemakers trading directly with carpenters.

Nativism and Protection

Republican unease with the falling status of labor and the general spread of the exchange economy was expressed politically through three main platforms: cooperation, protection, and nativism. Nativism had long been the most divisive politically. During the 1850s, white, native-born workers feared competition from various sorts of degraded labor that they believed would drive down its price and status, and nativism offered to many a viable explanation for the eroding condition of American labor. As a protectionist and antislavery organ, the *Tribune* argued that such reforms were necessary to protect Northern labor from foreign or enslaved competition; nativists, in effect, took that argument one step further, claiming that degraded labor threatened artisanal dignity whether it was in South Carolina, New York, or Manchester, England. For the *Tribune,* however, equal citizenship and tolerance were basic foundations of its liberalism. Through the 1840s, the paper had supported Seward's controversial efforts to allow Catholics to withdraw from New York's Protestant-inflected educational school system and to use public funds to build their own schools. In 1852, the paper reaffirmed its opposition to imperialism and ridiculed the pretensions of expansionists who relied on the fiction of "extending American human rights" as a pretext for slaveholders to acquire territory for slavery in the Caribbean and Mexico.[49] And it opposed, during Adm. Matthew Perry's expedition, forcing open the Japanese market.[50] At home, the *Tribune* suggested that Irish attachment to the priesthood was due merely to the fact that "priests... are about the only educated and intellectual class who evince any sympathy with the peasants' needs and sufferings." Nativism would only "aggregate these faults [clannishness] where they exist and tend to produce them where they do not."[51] In contrast, the paper promoted a cosmopolitanism that viewed the "proscription of foreigners" as a "token of barbarism... [and] ignorant national pride." Great nations "encourage the subjects of other States to reside among them, confer privileges and employments upon them, and thus abstract from other nations their best arts, their most cunning inventions, and their highest ideas," the *Tribune* concluded. "In fact, no nation is received into the comity of good society until it outgrows its snobbish exclusiveness, its vulgar arrogance of superiority, and is able to appreciate the virtue, the heroism, and culture of other nations."[52]

Before the war, Republicans exploited workers' fears, campaigning against the extension of slavery and convict labor; some Republicans extended that critique to immigration and free trade. After the war, threats to the price of labor included the "four millions of recent slaves," women workers (who were discriminated against in regular trade organizations and were sometimes used as strike replacements), and especially Chinese labor. Chinese immigration, in particular, vexed California Republicans when the national party was debating universal suffrage for the South, but for the *Tribune* the question became more pressing when Massachusetts shoemakers in North Adams, organized into the Knights of St. Crispin, saw their jobs being filled by imported Chinese labor during the summer of 1870. Labor groups throughout the country protested the move. Liberals such as *Nation* editor E. L. Godkin lauded it; nativism interfered with freedom of contract in precisely the same way as strikes or tariffs. New York's labor organizations rallied in sympathy with the Crispins and the Tammany organization helped fund the protests to shore up its working-class support. Tammany's record on the issues that mattered to labor organizations was lukewarm, but the use of

Chinese strikebreakers was just the sort of polarizing issue that meshed well with the party's traditional racism.[53]

Even though it made more compromises with nativism than it did before the war, the *Tribune* remained convinced that immigration restrictions countered one evil with another. No such doubts, though, plagued its support for protection. In the *Tribune,* protection, as an issue, returned with dramatic force during Reconstruction. The paper was filled with reports on the status of degraded labor in Europe: on Belgian ironworkers who labored eighteen hours a day for less than two dollars and on "half-starved children" as young as three years old who worked in match factories for just pennies a day. The *Tribune* characteristically objected "that American Manufacturing Labor should compete unprotected with this half-paid, pauperized labor of Europe."[54]

In 1870, Greeley published a series of essays on political economy in pamphlet and book form that revived antebellum campaigns against laissez-faire, economic anarchy, and globalization. What this meant in practice was, in the spirit of his Whig-socialist roots, pushing for social mobility through economic development: initiatives such as railroad construction, Western homesteads, land grant universities, cooperative living, and especially tariff protection for home industry. Though the *Tribune* primarily supported protection because it was central to national economic development and independence, Greeley was also among those Whigs who after the 1837 Depression framed it as a way to protect American labor from pauperized overseas competitors. To the *Tribune,* protection was perfectly consonant with its socialism and its broader prolabor political economy, and this was hardly unique. Henry Carey, the driving intellectual force of protectionism, argued that economic progress and growth depended on associated individuality, and especially an economy that rewarded producers rather than parasites— speculators and merchants—who profited from exchange. In effect, Carey made claims that were similar to those of the Associationists who also supported a regional economy on a township model, but the former made the case primarily from the perspective of utility and efficiency.

Protectionist arguments had long resonated with American workers who resented free trade treatises that suggested that labor was a commodity like any other and ought to be exchanged according to the same laws of political economy—like, in fact, slaves.[55] Protectionism's critics likewise linked free trade to organized labor's efforts to tamper with the free operation of labor markets. Liberal reformer Edward Atkinson, for example, insisted that "wealth gained...by means of a protective tariff...[or] the leisure secured by eight and ten-hours laws" are "identical in principle" to communist "attempts to enforce an equitable distribution of our annual product."[56] Most of the leading Radical Republicans—Benjamin Butler, Thaddeus Stevens, Benjamin Wade, and Zachariah Chandler—were protectionists and inflationists, and thus the bitter enemies of Liberals. A prolabor cooperationist, a protectionist, but not a soft-money inflationist, Greeley was in many ways out of step with the ideological conflicts of the postwar era, occupying his own unique niche within what historian Michael Les Benedict describes as the "bitter struggle over financial and tariff policy" within the Republican Party.[57]

Protection and especially cooperation constituted the *Tribune*'s program for labor, and it was in some respects a modest one. There were occasional explorations of various forms of collective living. The *Tribune* closely followed the Earl of Shaftesbury's housing experiments. It also covered sympathetically efforts to establish consumer and producer cooperatives in England, Germany, Switzerland, Belgium, and France, as well as in American cities such as Pittsburgh, Chicago, Boston, and Cincinnati.[58] It even advocated a full-scale, quasi-Fourierist settlement founded in Colorado by Nathan Meeker, formerly an agricultural writer and editor at the *Tribune*. Meeker's settlement was called the Union Colony, and the town it was located in took the name of its inspiration: Greeley.[59] The Reconstruction revival of the women's movement inspired *Tribune* support for a "reform in household labors":

> When Woman is relieved from the never-ending round of work—of getting or of superintending three meals daily—a heavy load now pressing upon her will be removed. She will have time to take care of her children, and she will not so much care if she have children; she will be free to engage in more profitable industry, and mental culture will be more easily attained.[60]

On occasion it promoted cooperative households as a practical alternative for wives, who were forced either to become a "drudge" or an "unhappy" and "watchful overseer." Cooperative living—some twenty to fifty households connected by a central building, "easily approached"—could be a means to relieve some of the most labor-intensive household tasks: washing, ironing, food preparation, and "perhaps" a "nursery" for child care.[61] Even so, the paper took care to present cooperative living as little more than an inexpensive alternative to boardinghouses and hotels. "There is nothing speculative in the movement," it said. "All the old teaching theories are put at rest."[62] Compared to Fourierism, which inspired a seemingly endless series of explanatory and theoretical tracts, the cooperative scheme was relatively simple, and the key to its success was its moderation and the absence of attacks upon the "Social System," the "family relation," or conventional morality.[63]

Cooperation, born in the aftermath of Fourierism's failure, was a "system which makes every workman a partner in the concern," not unlike the "Yankee whale-ship, fitted out on a 'lay.'"[64] Throughout the fall and winter of 1869, the *Tribune* printed letters and reports on cooperative stores in England, France, and New England, cooperative banks in Italy and Germany, cooperative farms in France and England, cooperative lodging in France, and cooperative factories in such industries as iron, tanning, weaving, printing, baking, and shoemaking in both Europe and the United States. Starting in late 1869, it also began to advocate "industrial partnerships," modeled on the writings of George Jacob Holyoake, then the editor of the *Social Economist*. His system, suited to the practical mood of the times, was a top-down one, with manufacturers securing the loyalty and efficiency of their workers by granting company shares in exchange for work.[65]

Despite cooperation's similarities with its antebellum ancestor—the *Tribune*'s post-Fourierist socialism—it was, in a discursive context, radically repositioned. Before the war, the *Tribune*'s political economy was wielded against free-market Democrats and conservative Whigs, and both groups were profoundly suspicious of the paper's radicalism, its "isms." In this new ideological environment, the *Tribune* brandished cooperation as an alternative to the more confrontational tactics of the labor movement itself. As a result, despite the fact that its response to the "social question" had remained pretty consistent since Dana's series on Proudhon moved the paper toward a post-1848, scaled-down version of Association, the paper increasingly seemed like a mournful spectator rather than a leader or even participant in labor reform. During the 1840s and 1850s, Fourierism and cooperation were both advocated as practical measures, but they were also vehicles to critique the injustices of capitalism, competitive global markets, and class. During Reconstruction, cooperation remained a practical reform. But even though it was embraced by mainstream labor organizations such as the National Labor Union, in the *Tribune*'s hands the idea was more often raised to condemn strikes and class conflict.

The Reconstruction Labor Movement and the Eight-Hour Day

Though the *Tribune*'s positions on cooperation, protection, labor, and the market were consistent with what it had advocated during the antebellum era, the economic and social context that workers faced had changed radically. During the war, labor conflicts had a muted character, and that was reflected in the *Tribune,* which suspended much of its reform speculation, for the most part ceasing its agitation on the labor question. From the *Tribune*'s perspective, the Republican economic program of homesteads, railroad subsidies, tariffs, land grant colleges, and a national financial and revenue infrastructure was a boon for American workers, a class they regarded as aspiring small capitalists. It did engage in political controversy on political economy, but mostly within the context of wartime nationalism. And truth be told, the Civil War was largely good for American labor. Enlistments and military demand eradicated much of the unemployment left over from the 1857 depression. By the second year of the war, the United States reached something like full employment. Still, two results of the competitive wartime labor market, mechanization and the feminization of the workforce, held wages down, particularly when viewed against staggering wartime inflation. During the last two years of the war, workers resorted to strikes to force employers to address the decline in real wages. The combination of labor shortages and the resentment of workers who did not benefit equally from the prosperity of the war economy carried over into the postwar era.

During the Civil War, working-class discontent took a mostly local form, but in 1866 various local and trade unions formed the National Labor Union (NLU) under William Sylvis. When some sixty-five delegates from more than thirty trade unions or societies met in Baltimore in August 1866, the *Tribune* proclaimed that it marked a new "era in our history."[66] The movement's long-term goal was, not unlike Greeley's, to emancipate workers from the wage system altogether through a program of worker cooperation. In the meantime, however, the "moderate and wise deliberations of the National Labor Congress" resulted in a series of resolves that summarized the labor movement's agenda as it faced an uncertain future. They included planks on prison labor and the disposal of public lands. But the overriding issue at the Congress and for the subsequent Reconstruction labor movement was the eight-hour day. From the perspective of the present, where we take labor regulations as a matter of course, the eight-hour movement seems innocent, even naive. Yet because the initiative, in at least one of its forms, seemed to interfere with private, individual contracts between workers and capitalists, it cut to the very core of liberal political economy. Threatening the sanctity of private property in much the same way that Association had a generation ago, the eight-hour day was a divisive measure that tested the limits of the Republican Party's vision of free labor.[67]

The eight-hour day had long been one of labor's demands. Hours legislation was part of the platform of the antebellum Industrial Congress, an organization that Greeley helped lead. The issue galvanized the Workingmen's Union, the Congress's putative successor, which in May 1865 held a two-day "eight-hour picnic" to push the topic to the front of the postwar political agenda. It was attended by some fifty thousand workers.[68] The *Tribune's* initial response to the call for an eight-hour day was favorable, and would remain so over the next half decade. "As to the Hours of Labor," the *Tribune* proclaimed, "the reform proposed...must encounter strenuous opposition; yet we believe it will ultimately be carried, and *ought* to be." The *Tribune* argued that the rise in the overall productivity of labor demanded it. From there, however, the *Tribune* and the labor movement parted ways somewhat.

The eight-hour principle raised surprisingly complex questions about political economy, and philosophical divisions emerged between the *Tribune* and more radical voices in the labor movement over how the eight-hour day ought to be implemented. The *Tribune* agreed with the labor movement that an eight-hour day was ideal, and it had a long record of support for a reduction in the length of the workday.[69] But the *Tribune* was only partly reconciled to the NLU position on the subject and it was not alone. Inside and outside the labor movement, divisions emerged on hours legislation when employers, workers, and state and federal governments actually tried to implement it. The main issues were whether wages ought to be reduced along with the number of hours that wage laborers worked; whether workers should strike to achieve an eight-hour day; and whether state and federal governments should impose the eight-hour day by law. On all of these issues, the *Tribune* remained somewhat more moderate than most in the labor movement. But these philosophical divisions over the implementation of the eight-hour principle did not separate "reformers" from "workers" alone. Workers, too, were divided among themselves.

Within the Workingmen's Union, some believed that workers should petition the state or federal government for protective legislation. Others thought that labor should attempt to achieve the reform on their own through collective bargaining. The platform that the NLU produced at its 1866 Baltimore meeting, which set a Reconstruction agenda for the labor movement, included a series of contradictory statements. Their ambiguity reflected the uncertainty of labor activists and reformers as they grappled with how forcefully to intervene in the labor market on behalf of workers within the context of a society organized around the broad principle of free labor. It was an ambivalence that Greeley quite naturally shared.

Even though in April, four months before the National Labor Congress, Greeley spoke in support of the eight-hour day at a Union Square mass meeting, in response to the Baltimore congress the *Tribune* contended that the "Eight-Hour rule" as a "means of revolutionizing the relations of Capital and Labor—of obtaining more pay for less work" can "not succeed."[70]

Throughout the year, and the period more generally, Greeley supported hours limitations, but with qualifications. Much like his tactical opposition to strikes, Greeley never claimed that hours legislation was wrong in principle or, as others would, that it interfered with the inviolability of contracts between labor and capital. Rather, Greeley maintained that hours legislation, like strikes, was incapable of altering, substantively, the imbalance of power between capital and labor. Wage levels, Greeley came to believe, represented labor's natural price, and any effort to raise them by striking was inevitably temporary.[71] The eight-hour day, established by law, was likewise ineffective. Though he modified this view somewhat when some practical experiments suggested that workers were equally productive with a shorter workday (this "fact," he wrote, was "worth more to the cause of Short Hours than three balloons-full of denunciation of greedy capitalists and whining over the miseries of the Laboring Class"), Greeley would term superficial any reform that did not lift workers out of the class of wage earners entirely.[72]

The *Tribune's* series of prolabor dissents on the eight-hour question eventually opened a friendly public correspondence with Ira Steward, a New England machinist who became the acknowledged leader of the eight-hour movement and was among the most important labor leaders of the nineteenth century. Steward addressed the *Tribune* as an ally, praising the paper for supporting the movement, and he hoped that Greeley could play the same role in the eight-hour movement that he had with land reform. "If Horace Greeley should announce himself" in favor of the entirety of the movement's claims, Steward flattered the editor, "that single fact would constitute an epoch in the movement." Steward's main theoretical contention was that industry would be even more productive with a shorter workday, thus justifying steady wage levels despite reduced hours. He believed, most importantly, that a shorter workday would reduce the number of workers competing for employment and augment the portion of a commodity's value that accrued to labor. More Whiggishly, and more in line with Greeley's optimistic sensibility, Steward thought hours reduction would also stimulate consumption and technological innovation. But despite his flattering overtures, the *Tribune* could only go so far with Steward. Though hostile to monopoly and extremes of wealth and poverty, Greeley maintained faith that the main route to capital accumulation was industriousness and self-denial. More important, over the course of the late 1840s and 1850s Greeley had come to believe, however reluctantly, that the supply of labor determines its price, if not its value. For more than thirty years, Greeley had been casting about for a method of reform that would bring the price of labor into line with its value, or with what it produced in real terms. He hoped, to reiterate, to make every worker a capitalist. Steward, on the other hand, held that wages were determined socially, and that with the help of either the state or through collective action, workers could raise their wages simply by demanding justice. So, unlike Steward, the *Tribune* refused to endorse mandatory legislation on hours and even opposed establishing the eight-hour day for government workers.[73] Greeley's differences with Steward had practical manifestations and symbolized the divide within the Republican Party over labor legislation during the "free labor era."

The *Tribune*'s dialogue with Steward on the surface seems like a scholastic exercise, a minor squabble within the reform community over slight differences in doctrine. But the debate over how to implement an eight-hour day raised questions that were basic to nineteenth-century political economy and reform. Could workers organize to protect their interests? What methods should they use to combat the organized power of capital? What role should government play in mediating conflicts between capital and labor? Were wages, in the end, like the price of any commodity, determined by the *natural* laws of supply and demand, or were they part of a *social* dynamic, determined by the distribution of political and economic power? On this last question, Steward propounded the social origin of wage levels, and his rise in influence was representative of the way the labor movement was evolving in a vaguely Marxist way.

Steward would not actually read Marx until the middle 1870s, but many of his ideas were in the radical spirit of Marxism. He held, contrary to prevailing economic thought, that workers' needs, and perceived needs, determined wages. Steward also challenged the traditional assumptions of the labor movement and its advocates. Greeley's conventional view was that the source of labor's exploitation was not in the wage relationship itself, but rather in the process of exchange. The interests of capital and labor were aligned, and were threatened by usurious interest rates, financial speculation, transportation costs, and market manipulation of prices. To combat these forces—to protect the interests of production against those of exchange— some labor-oriented Republicans such as Greeley became protectionists and others Greenbackers, proponents of an inflationary currency (which Greeley adamantly opposed). The labor question, for them, was a matter of social organization: how to ensure that producers are rewarded to the fullest degree with the full product of their labors. As Greeley proclaimed to a New York City eight-hour meeting, "We must first double and quadruple labor and decrease very much the distributors of it.... Why should not the shoemakers sell to the housebuilders directly?"[74] Steward and the most radical eight-hour reformers broke with this tradition.

Departing somewhat from the conventional reform and Radical Republican paradigm, Steward, along with close friend and ally George McNeil, argued ever more assertively over the course of the 1860s and 1870s that the primary locus of capitalist exploitation was hidden in the wage relationship and in the myth of "free" contract. In this view, he moved closer to Marx, both theoretically and organizationally. And Marx's allies in the United States, though largely disdaining the native-born American reform community, returned the favor by adopting the campaign for a state-enforced eight-hour day as their own.

During the early 1870s, Steward and McNeil became the American favorites of the German Marxist wing of the American International Workingmen's Association, which was locked in a struggle for power with the native-born Yankee wing of the organization. The leader of the former, Friedrich Sorge, a German-born disciple of Marx, reached out to Steward and gave him an early English translation of *Capital*.[75] In an effort to recruit American trade unions into the organization during the early 1870s, the American International Workingmen's Association gave itself over almost entirely to the eight-hour idea. To this small pocket of American Marxists, the eight-hour campaign was a way to wean American workers away from their provincial organizations and toward a higher and more comprehensive Marxist movement.[76] Their efforts failed, however, mostly because American trade unionists were repelled by the radicalism of both wings of the International; they feared that any association with it would bring discredit to the trade union movement. Much to the frustration of the Marxists, the American Left was never able to "move beyond" either the incremental materialism that would climax in Samuel Gompers's American Federation of Labor or the humanitarianism of such movements as abolitionism, vegetarianism, spiritualism, feminism, and Associationism. Steward remained within the grain of the former, hoping to restore the status of American workers through legislation, to raise their standard of living by reducing hours and raising wages.

Subtle distinctions in doctrine on a seemingly simple issue like hours legislation were bottomless in their implications. Among the various voices contesting the postwar fate of labor—Greeley, Steward, and the NLU, just to name a few—there were few points of consensus. All agreed that when it came to the organization of labor, property in human beings (slavery) was wrong and that self-employment and universal property ownership was right. But beyond that, there was genuine confusion over whether an economy with a permanent wage-earning class could ever be a just one; divisions over how to implement the eight-hour reform reflected this ambivalence. Was labor a form of property that ought to be subject to public protection or was the wage relationship simply a private act with which the state or society had no compelling interest?

These theoretical questions came to a political head in Connecticut, where the eight-hour movement had its first major postbellum trial. That it would take place there was important for a variety of reasons. Connecticut is a state where New York slowly transitions into New England, so regionally it was important to two of the centers of the American labor movement, New York and Boston. Connecticut also was a state that was closely contested politically, so it would serve as a key barometer of how the eight-hour day and the labor question generally would play out within the political environment that had been transformed by sectional reconfiguration and the Civil War. The struggle for the eight-hour day in Connecticut would test how the Northern Republican Party understood the meaning of equality and the freedom of labor after slavery. Already, within a Southern context, Republicans were confronted with various forms of quasi slavery in the Black Codes, in racial violence, in racially discriminatory political disabilities, and the basic struggle by former slaves for an independent economic existence in an environment in which former masters monopolized most of the region's productive resources apart from black labor. All suggested, after a fashion, that "not slavery" was not precisely the same thing as freedom. Middle-class antislavery Republicans recognized the connection between the Southern and Northern struggle for a more expansive conception of freedom by endorsing the eight-hour day. As the antislavery reformer John Sargent put it, abolition was "only an argument, in another form, for the rights of labor at the South: essentially the same question as is now engaging and concerning us here at the North."[77] Connecticut was an important initial test, not only to see how the labor question would unfold within a new political context where war-made partisan loyalties were still very fragile and uncertain, but also because it raised the question of how eight-hour laws would be enforced. What role could the state play in regulating contracts between workers and capitalists?

Radical Republicans throughout the country were of a divided mind about the eight-hour reform. In Massachusetts, two Republican labor commissions weighed in on the question. The first, the 1865 Griffin Committee, which was dominated by Radicals, recommended an eight-hour day, and it was backed up by an 1866 endorsement at the Republican state convention. The following year, another group of Radicals, organized into a commission by Governor John Andrew, expressed sympathy with the plight of overworked wage workers. But in line with the increasingly influential sentiments of laissez-faire Liberal Republicans such as E. L. Godkin and Edward Atkinson, it endorsed an eight-hour program that was voluntary and did not intrude upon "the bargain between [the worker] and the capitalist." State regulation of this sort would destroy the "right of individual property" and all but bring "communism" to the state. Its proposals, more in the spirit of those of the *Tribune,* endorsed state regulation solely for minors, and counseled public education, progressive taxation, and cooperative labor.[78] Eventually the issue so divided Massachusetts Republicans that, in sections of the state with large working-class populations, the party and even the Radical faction split in two; the split was between, as historian David Montgomery so deftly phrases it, those Republicans who were "truly radical" and those who were "radical only for Louisiana."[79] In Massachusetts's 1866 election, Bay State voters, in a clear mandate, prioritized the fate of the South, voting overwhelmingly for the Republican slate, regardless of the candidates' positions on the eight-hour questions. The political situation was more complicated in Connecticut, though, a state with a stronger Democratic Party.

Given its investment in the labor question and the Republican Party, the *Tribune* monitored the spring elections in Connecticut closely. The election was one "of more than usual importance" for a number of reasons. Like Massachusetts, Connecticut had been a Republican state ever since the party began fielding statewide candidates. But in the immediate aftermath of the war, the party's large majorities evaporated almost overnight. In 1864, Lincoln won with a majority of only 2,500. In 1865, the party surged to a majority of 11,000 votes. In 1866, that margin fell to just 541.[80] There was much disagreement about why the Republicans were losing ground. The *Tribune* claimed that the only real "issues in this canvass are such as grew out of the war—the old issue between the Copperheads and the Union men." The Democratic effort to campaign on the eight-hour issue was, in the *Tribune's* view, a "fraud," an attempt "to substitute for the real issue an imaginary Labor question."[81] Although Connecticut's Republicans were not explicitly hostile to hours legislation, they hoped to let the issue die through inaction. In 1867, the Democratic opposition would not let them. Abandoning overtly racist appeals the Democrats crafted a platform that combined constitutional conservatism (a restrained Reconstruction policy in line with President Johnson's) with an explicit populist commitment to the eight-hour day. They hoped that the latter position would peel off the labor movement from the Republican Party. The Republicans ran incumbent Joseph Hawley who pledged in 1866 that he would never veto an eight-hour bill knowing that one would never reach his desk. The Democrats ran popular Congressman James English, a moderate on the race question who pledged to uphold the Democratic platform on the eight-hour day, which mirrored the one written at the nonpartisan State Convention of Connecticut Workingmen. English's moderation on Southern issues (he was one of sixteen Democratic congress-men to vote for the Thirteenth Amendment) placed the *Tribune* in a difficult position. English dampened his party's racial hysteria and took a position on the eight-hour reform more progressive than that of many reformers in the Republican Party. As a result, the *Tribune* took the low road, printing racially inflammatory material from previous Democratic campaigns. It also resorted to personal attacks, noting that English was one of the "wealthiest men in the State" and suggesting that he owned several mills that ran according to the "12 hour method."[82]

Despite last-minute efforts to recast Hawley as labor's candidate, the Dem-ocrats all but swept the election. Turnout increased by just under 10 percent, and more than two-thirds of those new voters went for English. Labor read English's victory as a triumph for the eight-hour day. As it had before the election, the *Tribune* naturally dismissed the eight-hour question as a diver-sion, continuing to insist that the more basic issue facing the party and the country stemmed from the war. Though the "aristocracy of the south has been destroyed," there was still "work to be done." The real issue was whether the war would mean "freedom to black man and white," and whether "he who digs may govern, that the hand which holds the hoe is not unworthy of the ballot." To an extent, its interpretation of the election was corroborated when the *Times,* a paper allied with President Johnson's more conservative form of Reconstruction, suggested that the Democrats' triumph repudiated Radical efforts to extend the right of suffrage "regardless of caste, race, and color." It was further validated when Jefferson Davis announced that the Connecticut Democratic Party's victory was a "turning point" and a victory for the South. But the *Tribune's* effort to cast the Connecticut election as a referendum on the South rather than on the conditions of labor in the North was undermined when, in 1868, voters split their ballots, reelecting English and sending Ulysses S. Grant to the White House. Connecticut voters, it seemed, opted for Radical Reconstruction both at home and abroad. Within two months of the election, an eight-hour bill became law, with the support of both parties.[83]

The eight-hour law's win in Connecticut was followed by similar suc-cesses in New York, Pennsylvania, Wisconsin, Missouri, Illinois, and Califor-nia. Congress, in 1867, also considered a bill introduced by Senator George Julian that would have mandated an eight-hour day for federal workers. But as the *Tribune's* initial debate with Steward augured, labor's triumphs were less than they seemed because of the struggle over implementation. Over and over again, legislatures approved hours legislation but shied away from making it mandatory. The result was that labor's legislative victories in the end amounted to little more than a nonbinding resolution. Proto-Liberal Republican journals such as *Harper's Weekly* rejoiced in labor's Pyrrhic victories. It mocked that all the eight-hour legislation meant was that once "the employer and the workingman agree that only eight hours shall be a working-day" the eight-hour day will be a reality; no "law of the Legislature," it concluded, "can outwit... the law of supply and demand."[84] The *Tribune* was inclined to agree, but with an important caveat. Ever since the collapse of the Fourierist communities, the *Tribune* for the most part had abandoned reform measures predicated on the idea that market mechanisms could be replaced by an alternative ethic based on Christian or fraternal values. "We cannot... legislate the golden rule of equality, excellent as it may be," the *Tribune* wrote. "Christian martyrs spend lives of toil and privation to exemplify it, but it is contrary to the nature of society to make a martyr of itself."[85]

Despite the fact that the *Tribune* was not willing to assault the principle of free contract, it had not become an opponent of labor by any means. In truth, the labor movement itself was divided on the issue of whether the law should mandate an eight-hour day. The Workingmen's Union in New York attempted to make the state's law enforceable, but other prominent figures and journals in the movement such as the anarchist Ezra Heywood, the Boston *Voice,* and even William Sylvis, founder of the NLU, advised that the law was more likely to prevail legislatively and in practice if it did not attack the principle of freedom of contract.[86] This ambiguity in the law—and the ambivalence of its supporters—made it possible for employers to evade the state and federal laws passed during the late 1860s. Typical was the fate of Congress's eight-hour mandate for all government employees; contractors ignored it, and when workers sued for back pay, the Supreme Court dismissed the suit and the law, ruling that the legislation was written in the spirit of sentimental "philanthropy" and was nullified "by the inexorable laws of business," which set the rate of wages.[87]

Defeated by the vagaries of politics and the law, the labor movement was forced, ultimately, to take the law into its own hands. The struggle for an eight-hour day, then, would not only call forth a general theoretical discussion of the role of the state, the dimensions of free labor, and the nature of market relationships, but also lead to class conflict as workers, capitalists, and local, state, and national governments battled over implementation. And once again, as in 1848, American labor reform unfolded within an international framework; events in France would for a second time play a decisive role in shaping American attitudes toward socialism, worker radicalism, and the larger collective effort to cope with the spread of the wage economy. Into the 1870s, Greeley and the *Tribune* continued to push the idea of property and cooperation as the linchpin of labor's emancipation, but increasingly they were challenged by both the Right and the Left. From the Right came an emerging generation of laissez-faire Liberals who would conclude that the wage system, the labor market, and even a permanent hierarchy of classes were the legitimate outcomes of economic competition and natural economic laws. But from the Left, the challenge was even more pronounced and significant, and ironically it came from a former friend and ally: Karl Marx.

The Paris Commune and the Marxist International

Karl Marx wrote for the *Tribune* for a better part of a decade. The first English-language mention of Marx in an American newspaper was most likely in the *Tribune*. Nonetheless, while writing for the *Tribune,* Marx remained largely obscure and provoked little comment. That changed when, during the late 1860s and early 1870s, he and his ideas coalesced into an international movement. The formal center of Marxist activity at home and abroad was the International Workingmen's Association, an organization that was founded by a diverse assortment of European radicals in 1864. The IWA did not have a significant American presence until 1870, but its spirit reflected the postwar radicalization of many in the labor movement. The American wing of the International was dominated by two main constituencies that were, like the wider organization, divided by ideology and, to an extent, by nationality. The dominant wing in the United States was controlled by German émigrés who, allied with Karl Marx, eventually made the association over into a vehicle for Marxist orthodoxy. But in its early years, the IWA also attracted a wide-ranging variety of reformers; two "Yankee" sections, in particular, housed "theorists, philosophers, reformers, and others, who sprang from a school of reformers known as the New Democracy." They included Lewis Masquerier (a former National Reformer), Stephen Pearl Andrews, Wendell Phillips, Charles Sumner, and, reportedly, Greeley himself. Initially, the *Tribune* embraced the American International and its diverse mixture of immigrant German radicals, native workingmen's societies, and antebellum humanitarian reformers giving it a sympathetic and careful hearing. But it was not long before the American International's spirit of experimentation and ideological fluidity became a casualty of the era's social conflicts.[88]

When, in 1869, the *Tribune* first began to pay serious attention to the International, it celebrated the fact that European workingmen had managed to overcome national prejudices to advocate on behalf of their common interests. Detailed reports on its members and philosophy would not come until later, but even into the fall of 1870 the paper's correspondent praised the organizational and theoretical genius of the International's founder, Karl Marx, whose great achievement was fusing English and French social reform theory. The two central components of the International's "New Theory," as the *Tribune* understood it, were first that any "great change of production, consumption, [or] exchange" revolutionizes social relations and "society," and second, that the emergence of modern capitalism replaced the "independent master mechanic, able to produce a variety of merchandise . . . [with] a dependent slave, employed by a capitalist, who furnishes him with materials, tools and machinery, and realizes all the profits, [and] pays him with only a portion of his earnings, called wages." "This working man," the *Tribune* reported without comment, "is no longer independent, intelligent, self-reliant and an element of a free community, but a *proletaire.*" The *Tribune*'s correspondent focused on two other elements of the International's "New Theory." The International, the correspondent noted, rejected organization by region, nationality, or trade, claiming that capitalism's international character rendered such divisions irrelevant. Equally important, the International embraced "production on a large scale, being cheaper, more scientific and thorough, and economizing time, force, and capital." Labor had to respond in kind by organizing itself in such a way that reflected this "scientific" centralization of production and convert all "indispensable means of existence . . . [into] the *common property of all*" save "the product of labor, *one's own labor.*"[89]

The *Tribune* had long assented to Marx's notion that capitalism was tending toward monopoly, but it vigorously rejected the idea that labor should violently reject the protections of property or relinquish "production on a small scale." Class consciousness, collectivism, internationalism, and Marxism's tactical determination to forsake politics for violent social struggle would all directly test the *Tribune*'s democratic producerism, and it was the first major challenge to its views on political economy in its history that emerged from its left. Nonetheless, as in 1848, the *Tribune* was one of the few mainstream organs not to recoil in horror from the International's radical politics. The *Boston Evening Transcript* characterized the International as "agrarians, levelers, revolutionists, inciters of anarchy, and . . . promoters of indiscriminate pillage and murder." The *Philadelphia Inquirer* cautioned its readers that its principles were at war with all classes except those "too idle, vicious or improvident to be of any use to themselves or any public cause." Though the *Tribune* too thought the International's theories "extreme" and counter to its small-producer economic nationalism, the IWA received a fair and relatively sympathetic hearing in the paper. Furthermore, unlike other organs that reacted with overheated horror when the International began to gain strength in the United States, the *Tribune* refused to engage in red-baiting, carefully distinguishing the distinct "objects" of the "American Internationals" from the "European Association."[90] But the sympathetic spirit in which the *Tribune* welcomed the rise of the International came crashing down during the Paris Commune uprising, an event with which Marx's organization came to be associated.

The Paris Commune's rise and fall ushered in a new age of industrial conflict throughout the advanced economies of the West. But it was actually a multifaceted event: it was the product of an imperial war between France and Prussia, a civil war between metropolitan Paris and a conservative countryside, and a class war between radical working-class parties and a conservative alliance of peasants, clerics, and industrialists. The roots of the Paris Commune stretched back to 1848 when the city's working class suffered a humiliating defeat at the hands of a reaction that destroyed not only the revolution's social-democratic possibilities but even the basic republican aspirations of France's metropolitan regions. Smoldering Parisian resentments against the order of Napoleon III were fanned into an open flame when, in the summer of 1870, Otto von Bismarck, the architect of German national consolidation, declared war on France. Within a matter of months, he had defeated the French army, and Napoleon was taken prisoner. The speed of France's defeat left the country in chaos. After a bloodless revolution, French republicans quickly organized a provisional government, but the country had been broken into two by the German occupation. In February 1871, elections were held, and they returned a conservative assembly, which in turn elected Adolphe Thiers as "head of the executive power," a position somewhere between emperor and president. His government very clearly represented conservative interests, namely the peasantry (labor's bête noire in 1848) and the industrial bourgeoisie. One of his first acts was to negotiate a shameful peace with Bismarck, one that ceded Alsace-Lorraine and more than a million French citizens to Germany. Paris resisted and formed a government of its own that was led by radical workers, many of whom were still armed, enrolled in the National Guard, and committed to a more vibrant nationalist resistance. In the middle of March, Paris's working classes proclaimed the Commune and elected their own assembly, a full third of which were members of the International. France's conservative provisional government, in turn, launched an attack on the city whose fury dwarfed the army's effort against Bismarck's Germany. Within a week, Paris was covered in blood. Thiers even ordered the use of combustible shells—he, in effect, ordered the firebombing of his own people. Some twenty-five thousand Parisians perished, and another twenty-five thousand were either jailed or exiled. Parisian Communards matched this fury, burning public buildings and murdering hostages, including the archbishop of Paris. Paris became the backdrop against which elites in countries across the West projected their own fears of violent workers movements, and this was particularly true in the United States and especially in New York, where the memory of the Civil War draft riots still smoldered. After a half decade of intermittent labor conflicts, many New Yorkers wondered whether their city would be the next Paris.[91]

There were a few Americans who sympathized with the Communards. W. J. Linton, a former Chartist, defended the uprising in his letters to the *National Anti-Slavery Standard*, a publication that was among the first to publish laudatory accounts of the International as well. Wendell Phillips, Benjamin Butler, and Moncure Conway saw the disturbance as part of labor's worldwide struggle against oppression and tyranny. From Brussels, George Wilkes wrote pro-Communard dispatches for the *New York Herald* and *The Spirit of the Times,* and later published them in pamphlet form along with a justification of the International.[92] The Commune inspired Victoria Woodhull and Tennessee Claflin—abolitionists, spiritualists, and feminists—to help organize one of the two Yankee sections of the International. Former *Tribune* managing editor John Russell Young also identified with the cause of the Commune, termed it the legitimate government of Paris, and condemned the brutality of the reaction.[93] Later on, the event prompted thoughtful reconsiderations by reformers such as Theodore Tilton, and inspired new interest in the International among American radicals. Marxism colored radical and conservative accounts of the Commune, but when Tilton took a closer look, he discovered that what the Communards demanded (republican government, the peaceful arbitration of international disputes, the eradication of standing armies and economic monopolies) was in the mainstream of American reform traditions. Young reported likewise that "rarely a red flag was seen."[94] Though some recent French historians have raised similar objections, arguing that the Commune's communism was part of a shared mythology, constructed by both Marxists and their reactionary critics, mainstream American opinion was quickly convinced that Paris was the work of a radical conspiracy and that domestic labor conflicts foreboded something similar.

Ultimately, the Paris violence unleashed and legitimized a brand of venomous and austere bourgeois Liberal Republicanism in the United States that, although not unknown before 1870, had mostly lurked beneath more mainstream celebrations of American social mobility. The *Times* declared that "communist leaders and 'philosophers' and reformers" threatened to goad the "seething, ignorant, passionate, half-criminal class" into a bloody conflict with decent society. Newspapers of both parties depicted the Paris insurgency as a "wild reckless, irresponsible, murderous mobocracy." Charles

Loring Brace published the *Dangerous Classes,* an exposé that expressed the Liberal reformers' common fears of Paris-like proletarian disorder. What the Commune signaled most dangerously, beyond the temporary violence, was the prospect of class-based politics—that a working class, on its way to becoming a permanent class and a majority, would use the democratic process to advance its own interests. During the 1840s, the National Reformers campaigned on the premise "Vote Yourself a Farm"; during Reconstruction, a worker's democracy threatened the abolition of private property and state regulation of private contracts. As one recent historian suggested, the Paris Commune became a metaphor for the struggle of labor against property on all fronts—the self-interested politics of the rabble against the disinterested political virtue of the better classes. It prompted Northern conservatives in the Republican Party to even take a second look at Reconstruction. They began to see parallels between their own fears of industrial class war with the struggle of Southern conservatives to subordinate their own labor force. After the Commune, it seemed that the prewar warnings of proslavery ideologues were coming to fruition; perhaps the politics of abolition actually had been a prelude to a more general war against property.[95]

The prominent role that communists aligned with the International played during the Paris Commune raised the specter of class conflict and revolution in New York and made many New Yorkers wonder about the organization's activities in their city. In this climate of ideological paranoia and fear, the *Tribune* broke with its own traditions and joined the Commune's conservative critics. The *Tribune's* correspondent in Paris, William Huntington, was relatively new to the paper. Hired by Whitelaw Reid, the *Tribune's* new managing editor, Huntington came by his conservative instincts honestly. Reid's predecessor was John Russell Young who, more in tune with the reform traditions of the paper, was one of the few American voices who was sympathetic to the Commune. Reid, on the other hand, was more disposed to modern Liberalism and would eventually guide the *Tribune* out of the turbulent waters of socialist reformism toward the professional "objectivity" and the thoughtful gentility that would define it for the remainder of its history. Under Reid, the *Tribune's* coverage of French radical movements was notably different than it had been in 1848. It featured more correspondents but fewer viewpoints. Huntington was the main correspondent, but he could hardly be considered responsible for the *Tribune's* editorial position on the revolution. His reports were unsigned, and the *Tribune* had other friends in the city sending it correspondence. More than likely, much of the material that made it to America first passed through the filter of George Smalley, whom Young had sent to London in 1866 to serve in a position that approximated the paper's "managing editor" for Europe.[96] Nearly everything the *Tribune* published on the Commune episode condemned the resistance. Gone were the days of Heinrich Börnstein.

The *Tribune* had been a critic of the empire and the Bonaparte regime. The only reason most Frenchmen submitted to it, the paper remarked, was because it was "their only practical defense against the Red Specter of Socialist Democracy." Like most Americans, including the American minister in Paris, Elihu Washburne, it welcomed the Second Empire's fall without regret: "Having detested and denounced it from the first, we heartily rejoice in the providence which has kept alive the high-priest of this baleful and bloody imposture to be a witness of its shameful collapse and dissolution." Initially, the paper sympathized with the provisional government that formed in the aftermath of Napoleon's surrender at Sedan, in no small part because many of its key actors were prominent "Forty-Eighters," including Jules Favre, the interior minister in the 1848 government. But when Favre and the republicans suffered a "disappointing" defeat in the February elections to a coalition of conservatives and monarchists, it hardly pushed the paper to the left. Given the paper's stance in 1848, one might have suspected that the paper would have hailed the Paris rebellion, but instead its response to the Commune was almost unremittingly hostile.[97]

The *Tribune* headlined the first signs of popular working-class resistance to the Thiers government as a "new reign of terror." Though it blamed the empire for retarding civic virtue, it also noted contemptuously that "civil disorder always brings to the surface a turbulent and reckless mob which has little to gain by peace and nothing, except worthless lives, to lose by a revolution." The *Tribune*'s portrait of the revolutionaries echoed the *Courier and Enquirer* and the other conservative journals during 1848. It described them as "devils" and butchers "who are exhibiting all the tigerish instincts of 'the untaught, savage mind.'" It called the municipal elections that followed the initial revolt as nothing but a sham designed to "endow with a species of sanction" a movement founded in anarchy and foreordained to set, illegitimately, "the Communists of Montmartre and Belleville above the Republicans of the whole nation." "There appear to be but two ways of ending the insufferable situation," the *Tribune* concluded, "one is by civil war, the slaughter of citizens by each other; and the alternative is the reoccupation of the city by the Prussian forces." By April, the *Tribune* had joined traditionally conservative journals in connecting the Paris Commune to mob rule in New York. In the Commune, "banks and churches are sacked; the assets of corporations are confiscated, tenants are to pay no rent, and property is declared to be theft." In New York, the "mob" presents the "same evils":

> The mob that has controlled this city for so many years and has all but secured control of the State, is recruited, like the mob of Paris, from the slums, and gutters, and drinking shops. It has nothing to lose by taxation, for it has no property to be taxed. It has no desire for an honest government, because government is its natural enemy. It has already nullified the ballot, and taken possession of a Legislature in which its representatives are really but a small minority. It has practiced confiscation, under one form or another.... Two-thirds of the money which it takes from the better class of citizens under the name of taxations is nothing but sheer robbery.

Such remarks were a far cry from the social democratic sentiments one had come to expect from the *Tribune*.[98]

Recent histories of Reconstruction have been quick to point out the way that American commentators connected the Commune experience to social and economic conflicts at home. But the Commune was also interpreted politically, and not a few Republicans saw disturbing parallels between the Commune and the spirit of secession that remained alive in the resistance of the South, and the Democratic Party, to national authority at the height of Reconstruction. To the *Tribune,* the spirit of the Commune was in many respects hostile to majoritarian democracy. Though it was perhaps too quick to credit the legitimacy of Thiers's government, it was the result of an election. The "Latin mob" that proclaimed the emancipation of Paris from the country was "self-appointed" and dispensed with basic democratic values such as "universal suffrage" and "parliament[s]." In France, the *Tribune* confronted a republican conundrum. French republicans, the paper concluded, were a minority and confined to the cities. They "assumed...a right to lead" but they were outnumbered. Republican logic insists on "the right of the people to choose their form of government" even if, the *Tribune* supposed, the people choose "a hereditary chief," an unrepublican form of government. The *Tribune* admitted that the "Working Men (*ouvriers*) of Paris are unquestionably more intelligent and politically more capable than the rural peasantry, who constitute a majority of the French people; but this fact gives them 'no right to rule.'" In the end, "he who does not realize that diverse forms of government are adapted to different stages of human development is a blockhead." The "revolt of the Commune," the *Tribune* finished, "was an attempt of Two Millions of people to dictate a form of government to

Thirty-four Millions, who naturally hold that they have some rights which the Two Millions are bound to respect." The Communards' rebellion against a constitutionally elected government not only recalled Southern secession but the racist mobs of the New York City draft riots. During the war, prominent city Democrats had sanctioned violent resistance to the draft, emancipation, and black equality; the *Tribune* building and Greeley were among its main targets. Now, many of these same Democrats defended the Commune, too, which they thought paralleled the efforts of their own working-class Irish constituency to resist moves by middle-class New York Republicans to wrest control of the city and its institutions from immigrant political machines.[99] Linking Communards to the persistent spirit of secessionism, the *Tribune* could not help but note the contrast between the "unconsciousness" with which France's government inflicted so "bloody a vengeance" on its anti-democratic rebellion, and "the insolent attitude...displayed by our beaten and convicted traitors" in resisting the full implementation of Reconstruction.[100] For many Republicans, including the *Tribune,* the Commune was hardly a symbol of progress and reform in the spirit of 1848, but was rather more akin to the reactionary populism that plagued abolitionists and other reformers throughout the antebellum, Civil War, and Reconstruction eras.

Despite the *Tribune's* efforts to link its opposition to the Commune to ongoing Republican efforts to impose a progressive, national order on the South, the paper's move to the right on the social question was marked. After the Commune, the *Tribune* broke, in a more public and passionate way, with the Republican Party's most vigorous advocates for labor—and the Commune—Wendell Phillips and Benjamin Butler. Butler and Phillips considered the Commune an extension of American labor's struggle against capital. Butler termed the Commune simply a struggle for "town government such as we have here." The *Tribune* labeled him a communist, and Butler rather oddly found himself aligned once again with Democrats who made similar arguments.[101] Democratic papers such as the *New York World* and the *New Orleans Picayune* joined Butler's and Phillips's defense of the Commune, but less on class grounds than as an extension of "local rule" arguments that derived from the Civil War era and before. The latter, in particular, disavowed any association with communist radicalism. To the *Picayune,* what bound the Commune to the Confederacy was that its size, sustained character, and unanimity made it less an insurrection than a legitimate political expression of the popular will against nationalism's despotic power. Its suppression was tyranny.[102] Divided reactions to the Commune reflected the extent to which the labor question resulted in ideological divisions within the Republican Party and across the political spectrum.

At the other extreme from Butler and Phillips were Liberal Republicans such as E. L. Godkin who viewed Parisian working-class self-government with the same suspicion that they regarded New York City's Democratic municipal government. In New York and other cities, young college-educated professionals like Godwin organized themselves into Social Science societies that advocated free trade, social Darwinism, and market principles. Politically, they backed civic renewal led by meritocratic elites, and looked to ensure government by the "best men" through such means as "cumulative voting," which, in a proto-Progressive fashion, reduced the power and influence of neighborhood-based politicians in favor of a more bureaucratic and faceless form of government that emphasized efficiency and expertise.[103] In this Liberal spirit, *Scribner's Monthly* wrote, "there is not enough . . . intelligence, principle, and virtue in France to sustain a republic." *Harper's Weekly* contended that France lacked the discipline to sustain republican values. With them, the *Tribune* vented that perhaps not every culture and people are at a stage where they are capable of self-government.[104] Breaking faith with plebian democracy in Paris and New York, it was only a short ideological leap to a renunciation of the black Republican governments of the South. It was, in some respects, the story of how the blacks became Irish (or French).

For the *Tribune,* the Commune was, then, a key ideological breaking point. Increasingly, the *Tribune* was coming under the control of a new generation of Liberals, who rejected the very idea of social and economic rights. Greeley's traditional brand of reform Whiggery was now positioned hopelessly between two ever more unbridgeable ideological visions, one that regarded the market's iron laws as immutable and another that was reconciled to permanent class warfare. The social-democratic free-labor model avowed that property and autonomy would emancipate slaves and that free workers would replace the authority and discipline of starvation and the lash with the internalized lure of incentive and mobility. The pessimism that was slowly emerging in the *Tribune's* accounts of Reconstruction labor movements, the Paris Commune, and the prospects of free labor in the post-emancipation South anticipated the outright break that the *Tribune* would make from its humanitarian traditions as a result of the 1872 New York City general strike.

The 1872 General Strike and the New Liberalism

The 1872 general strike was the culmination of a series of labor conflicts and it brought the era's reconsideration of the free-labor model to a dark conclusion. Reconstruction New York had been the scene of almost continual class and ethnic conflict. In 1866, shipyard workers went on strike on behalf of the eight-hour day. In 1867, New York's carpenters struck for a fifty-cent increase in their daily wages. In 1868, the city's bricklayers struck for an eight-hour day and to maintain control over their work rules. The summers of 1870 and 1871 witnessed repeated clashes between Protestants and Catholics that in July 1871 exploded into nearly unprecedented violence. That same year also witnessed the culmination of a nearly half-decade-long proto-Progressive campaign against Boss William Tweed. The last was both an ethnic struggle against Irish rule and, more ambiguously, a class struggle by middle-class reformers against a political organization with populist pretensions that attempted, at the expense of "good government," to use public works, graft, and patronage to build a ruling coalition that united large capitalists and the immigrant working class. The 1872 strike, in many respects, dwarfed them all.[105]

Like previous worker revolts, the 1872 strike was focused around the Reconstruction labor movement's central demand: the eight-hour day. Before the strike, New York City's workers had done everything they could to avoid a climactic struggle with the political and economic powers that ruled the city and state. They hoped to avoid what had occurred five years earlier in Chicago, when the workers who had called for a general strike on behalf of an eight-hour day were put down by a hostile press and a conservative mayor who used the police and a local militia to crush both the strike and the labor movement as a whole. Learning from the Chicago episode, New York's labor movement tried to work patiently and within the system. They first petitioned Governor Reuben Fenton, a Radical, to enforce the eight-hour law, and then petitioned the legislature to strengthen its language. Still, close to five years had elapsed since its passage in 1867 and it was still regularly ignored. As David Montgomery has pointed out, the issue that confronted the eight-hour movement "was one not of legislation but of execution"; "statute[s]" would not "change anything unless some administrative agency compelled citizens to comply with the laws' provisions."[106] Unfortunately for the workmen, few Radicals in power, including Fenton, embraced the idea of comprehensive state intervention in the economy. He argued that all laws should be assumed to be compulsory and should not require special officers to make certain that they are carried out, an evasion that meant that workers' groups themselves would have to realize the full meaning of the law. By the fall of 1871, their patience had worn thin. After the stonecutters' union went on strike for an eight-hour day, the stonecutters were subsequently joined by eight thousand workers in the building trades who walked off the job in sympathy. By the spring of 1872, worker frustration had peaked. Leaders from the Workingmen's Union, the NLU, the IWA, and Steward's Eight Hour League cooperated to harness that anger and managed to organize a general strike in New York City.[107]

During the initial stages of the strike, labor was in a strong position. Though the state and local government had all but abdicated its place as the arbiter of social conflicts, the manufacturing classes were divided, and not a few small capitalists were sympathetic to labor's demand for input into the hours, wages, and conditions of work. Elite division ensured that the state's police power, at least initially, was not brought to bear for or against the workers. Labor's claims, too, were largely conservative. Workers only called for the enforcement of the law, a request given added legitimacy when President Grant, eyeing a fall reelection campaign, issued an executive proclamation ordering the city's builders, under contract to construct a new post office, to comply with George Julian's 1867 federal statute mandating an eight-hour day for all federal workers.[108]

The first major move in the conflict was when the Workingmen's Union launched a strike in April. They hoped that it would realize a comprehensive labor agenda that included independent political organization and worker cooperation. The April strike started an avalanche of labor protest, which unfolded in stages but eventually engulfed an estimated one hundred thousand workers. It had ballooned into a classwide action when the Building Trades' League, inspired in part by Grant's recent order, convinced its associated unions to strike on behalf of an eight-hour workday. The building trades strike was a remarkable success. Though some of the member trades already enforced an eight-hour day on their own, masters in most of the other trades acceded to the demand in just weeks. Their success had less to do with their tactics than with the simple fact that the building trades maintained, in an almost antebellum way, independent journeymen and small masters, gradations between large capitalists and unskilled wage workers. The strike succeeded because small-scale master carpenters made up the bulk of the Master Carpenters' Association and it was in their interest to break with their large-scale, heavily capitalized brethren.[109]

The contagion of worker resistance then spread to other industries and other workers' organizations and reform groups, including Steward's Eight Hour League, the Furniture Workers' League, and the Iron and Metal Workers' League. The city's woodworkers went out the very day that the strike in the building trades came to a successful climax. These workers were well organized in the Furniture Workers' League, but so were their bosses, and both classes were radicalized and prepared for the confrontation. The woodworkers organized boycotts of shops that did not demonstrate their support for labor in their windows, and called for a colossal march in the city for June 10 to rally fellow workers to their cause across the boundaries of craft and trade. They took a more coercive approach than the construction trades, and organized a series of intimidating public assemblies. The bosses responded in kind, complaining to city authorities that the workers threatened violence. The city answered their complaints by assembling a sizable police presence near targeted factories. All in all it was a recipe for bloodshed, and it would get worse. Five days before the citywide demonstration, Theodore Banks, a member of the Workingmen's Union and a non-Marxist section of the International, disseminated a public call for a violent campaign against property. On the same day, the *Tribune* also reported that one striker attempted to kill another for trying to work a ten-hour day. Though all the workers' organizations disavowed Banks and his incendiary message, the Furniture Workers did not back down. Strikers carried a banner that read, "Eight Hours—Peaceably If We Can, Forcibly If We Must," which in many ways captured in a nutshell the tension within the free-labor tradition on how best to achieve a more socially democratic order.[110]

It was at this inopportune moment that New York's metal workers also decided to strike. Some of the city's metal workers had already demonstrated in sympathy with their brethren in other trades, but they were weaker organizationally, divided ideologically, and they faced stiffer opposition. On June 18, a committee of manufacturers, four hundred strong and led by the Board of Iron Founders, met to coordinate a cross-industry response to the strikes. The meeting included masters from the building and woodworking industries, and many of the former were already working under the eight-hour rule. Nonetheless, the manufacturers resolved that the eight-hour regulation was not "mandatory," that they had no intention of paying workers any way other than by the hour, and that they were adamantly opposed to any "arbitrary establishment of relations between employer and employed." By the end of June, capital's resolve was clear, and the large industrialists in particular were increasingly strident in their demand that the authority of property, individual contract, and the market determine the conditions of labor. The unity of capital prevailed and the strike was crushed. Among the casualties was the formerly broad appeal of the eight-hour movement, now discredited among small masters, middle-class reformers, and other groups once sympathetic to the workmen. By the end of July, some trades were even further from the eight-hour day than they had been in the spring, and many of the alliances that had been built, namely that between the trades and the International, had been broken.[111]

The more aggressive spirit of the 1872 strike's latter stages precipitated a drive in the mainstream papers to discredit the labor movement entirely. In the midst of the worst moments of the strike, the *Tribune,* which comparatively was a voice of reason, tried to stake out its traditional middle position.

Its Whiggish inclination toward social harmony would separate it from the most "advanced" elements of the Republican Party who saw it as the duty of the party, in Benjamin Butler's words, to take up and establish the "rights of labor as against capital." Though Butler held, like the *Tribune,* that capital is merely accumulated labor, the latter, he argued, "perishes in the using... [and] cannot be hoarded, accumulated, or put at interest, and is wholly lost if not employed day by day." As such, government has a duty to protect labor from the excesses of capital by enforcing such measures as the eight-hour day. In this, Butler and other radicals tilted left a little further than the *Tribune* ideologically, and it was a distinction that made all the difference practically.[112] The *Tribune's* former middle position, which rejected class conflict, strikes, and government interference in private contracts, on the one hand, and amoral utilitarianism, globalization, and the idea of a permanent wage class, on the other, became close to impossible to sustain in this era of violent social conflicts.

The 1872 workers' movement was launched to force the state to enforce the eight-hour law. In the aftermath, debate centered on the viability of strikes. Both statute and strike represented efforts to intervene in the wage economy, and even though the *Tribune* lamented the commodification of labor, it would never fully embrace more radical methods of resisting it. The *Tribune's* opposition to strikes had never been moral, and that remained the case in 1872, despite the fact that conflicts between labor and capital had grown increasingly violent. In its various postmortems on the 1872 strike in New York City, it termed the "great strike" untimely, "inopportune," and "disastrous," both for the "workingmen" and for their organizations. Even so, it maintained, as it had for decades, that strikes fail for the very reason that they are necessary: "The greatest sufferers from the conflict are almost invariably the strikers, who from the very nature of the case, cope with the capitalist on very unequal terms." It opposed strikes, in short, on precisely the same theoretical ground that Butler staked out when arguing that labor required protection from the inherently superior power of capital. Workers resort to strikes, and capitalists prevail over them, because the former are driven to them out of desperation whereas the latter can survive them because of strength. Capital fears two things, the *Tribune* argued after a strike by the Fall River, Massachusetts, textile workers: "commercial revulsion" and "a glut." Strikes are the "strongest possible safeguard against a glut" and "boss shoemakers as a class would like nothing better than to stop all shoemaking for the next two months."[113]

In some respects, the *Tribune's* logic was difficult to dispute. In 1872, strikers in most trades returned to work under terms worse than those that they had labored under before the strike.[114] And yet despite these professions of understanding and sympathy, the *Tribune*'s tactical opposition to particular strikes was undergirded by a philosophical opposition that stretched back some thirty years. To describe a particular strike as inopportune belies the fact that the *Tribune* almost never offered its support to a strike and almost always counseled labor to pursue other options. Typically, the *Tribune* framed the issue of strikes in the following manner:

> We hear that a pretty general strike for higher wages is contemplated by the journeymen mechanics of this and the adjacent cities. Some will require more pay; others less work for their present pay; but all expect to get more money or work fewer hours. We do not believe such results, if achieved, can be maintained at a time when lower prices are the rule and higher the rare exception. But every man has a right to set his own price on his services and refuses to give them for less; and those who have a common interest have a right to combine for protection. If they mistake in so doing, it is their own affair. Formerly, strikes were frowned upon by law, as at war with the public good; but if sellers of Coal, Butter, Pork, &c., are allowed to combine to enhance the prices of their respective commodities, we insist that laborers must be allowed to do the same.[115]

Though Greeley and the *Tribune* did not think a labor organization should be able to prevent an individual from signing a labor contract on his or her own, strikes, in sum, were both legal and moral, and unions, moreover, reflected the larger collective drift of the economy.[116] Still, in the long term strikes were ineffective because they tried to boost wages above their "natural," supply-driven rate. Only cooperation, the *Tribune* continued to contend in the face of ebbing worker interest, offered a real alternative to the wage system itself: "If Labor can accumulate funds whereby to support Strikes, it may accumulate them also for wiser, more beneficent ends. . . . We are trying to incite Labor to strike not *against* Capital but *for* Capital—that is, for the possession and direction of adequate capital, which shall be wholly its own."[117] "Our difference with the Trades Unionists," the *Tribune* asserted, is that "they mediate mitigations of the evils attendant upon the Wages system; we would gradually supersede and permanently replace that system by a better."[118]

Sadly, the *Tribune*'s struggle to carve out a viable position between laissez-faire liberalism and a more coercive brand of socialism was of little avail in the ever more polarized ideological atmosphere. At the outset of the 1872 general strike, the paper distinguished between "clear-headed artisans" and "their more reckless fellows," and praised the strike for its lack of violence and incendiary language: "There has been no bitter denunciation of the employers as the natural enemy of the employed; and happily, there has been heard nothing of the old cant or drivel about the antagonism of Labor and Capital." Even after Theodore Banks called for a war against property, the *Tribune* insisted that "the excitement over the labor movement is chiefly in the newspapers" and that "there is not the slightest reason to be apprehensive of riot or bloodshed," that is unless the "excited police" continue to "incite the strikers to hasty action." Despite this surface balance, the *Tribune* was moving to the right in a more subtle way. In the past, the *Tribune* had served as labor's unofficial organ within the "neutral" public of readers. Other "neutral" papers often called upon the *Tribune* to explain and defend labor's actions. Such was no longer the case. Now, there were few distinctions between the *Tribune* and the *Times;* as David Montgomery put it, both, "which up to this point had been remarkably dispassionate in reporting the strikes, began to see Communists as 'inciting trouble.'"[119]

The 1872 strike along with the larger struggle for an eight-hour day raised a number of fundamental questions that marked out competing visions of free labor. Could the state mandate the hours of work and regulate the conditions of labor? Would state regulation undermine private property and freedom of contract? Would workers use the power of the ballot to threaten private property? When the eight-hour issue materialized as the Reconstruction labor movement's central economic demand, even a bourgeois Liberal of E. L. Godkin's sort was of a divided mind. He recognized that a shorter workday could elevate the intellectual character of workmen and yet he viewed the privacy of contract as a sacred trust. But over the course of the late 1860s and 1870s, labor's increasingly assertive class politics and consciousness, along with its ever more alien and foreign character, had turned Godkin against the eight-hour principle to the extent that he came close to repudiating mass democracy entirely.[120]

The year 1872 marked, then, the emergence of an entirely new set of political and social alignments, and they would provide little space for the small-producer democratic capitalism that Greeley had been advocating since the launch of the *Tribune.* In many trades before the war, there was still some "reasonable expectation of attaining 'independence' as a small master" and, as Iver Bernstein put it, journeyman still exercised a degree of power and control. The movement between various classes did not "secure [a] new identity" but rather the gradation between small bosses and journeymen was something like a "revolving door." There were strikes throughout the antebellum era, of course, but small capitalists and journeymen also frequently cooperated politically and against outsider groups such as lenders and speculators.[121] But the postwar economic environment forced even Greeley to recognize that the idea of class harmony was becoming an unrealizable ideal. "Let us not deceive ourselves," the *Tribune* finally admitted, under the current system "there is a well-defined and absolute antagonism between the producing and employing classes of all nations. It is a necessity of their relative social positions."[122]

Given the shifting character of the economic environment, the party system had become necessarily ideologically incoherent. Within each party there were factions for inflation and others for hard currency, some for protection and others for free trade. Both parties' class alignments were also hopelessly muddled between large industrialists, master artisans, and journeymen, as well as by race and ethnicity. Sectional politics and the memory of the war scrambled the social and ideological basis of the parties even further. But 1872 was a turning point. After 1872, the North's social and ideological conflicts, so molten and unstable for more than a decade, solidified into the conflict between capital and labor. Equally important, this conflict would only rarely take political form. Partisans of both capital and labor now concluded that their conflicts transcended politics. Nascent industrialists and manufacturers who had once conceived of a valued partnership between economic activity and the state during the antebellum period were now increasingly drawn to the laissez-faire vision of the new Liberalism. Most worker organizations, typified by the IWA, also concluded that the party apparatus, formerly seen as a way to build cooperative consensus between various interests, was hopelessly corrupt. Even within worker organizations, the boundaries between classes and ideologies hardened, symbolized by the 1871 divorce of the German-dominated orthodox Marxist sections of the IWA from their American brethren; the latter sections included a diverse range of reform traditions and welcomed a bohemian middle-class element to its membership whereas the former hoped to exclude all but wage laborers from the movement.[123] All of the changes of the postwar years had created a chasm between liberalism and socialism, which itself resembled the growing distance between the middle class and the working class. Ideologically, the *Tribune's* social-democratic third way had been a reflection of its artisanal base, which occupied an indeterminate and fluid class position—a middle/working class hybrid. But in this new context, the *Tribune's* ongoing support for property, self-reliance, and social mobility became almost indistinguishable from the individualistic values that defined the emerging bourgeois industrial order. Out of place in this new environment, Greeley improbably became attached to an emerging form of Liberalism that, if looked at in its pure form, violated everything that he had ever stood for.

CHAPTER 7

Liberal Ambiguities

> History cannot show a nobler picture. Four mil-
> lion... human creatures are, by the lightning stroke of
> an inspired pen, invested with the highest right a citi-
> zen can claim... and yet no violent assertion of these
> new-born rights; no outbreak of misled ignorance;
> not the first instance... in three years of even an
> attempt to usurp power or place; standing face to face
> as their political equals with the men who bought and
> sold and whipped and branded them.... When the
> historian of the coming century writes up the record
> of these six years, he will wonder alike at the infamy
> of the provocations... and the noble forbearance with
> which these heroic people met the assaults of their
> unscrupulous enemies.
>
> *New-York Daily Tribune,* March 21, 1868

In May 1872, a diverse collection of reformers,
journalists, and disaffected Republicans met in Cincinnati to consolidate the
various local and state efforts to overturn the rule of the regular Republican
Party and to defeat "Grantism," the pejorative label dissatisfied reformers
used to describe the corrupt, patronage-ridden administration of Ulysses S.
Grant. After six ballots, the Liberal Republican convention, improbably, nominated Horace Greeley for the presidency. What followed was even more
implausible. In July, the regular Democratic Party gathered in Baltimore to
select a candidate for the presidency. They decided to link their fate to the
Liberal Republicans, nominating Greeley to head a fusion ticket—the very
same Greeley who once characterized their party as a collection of "murder-
ers, adulterers, drunkards, cowards, liars, [and] thieves."[1]

Greeley's nomination has always been something of a curiosity, and even
dumbfounded the architects of the Liberal Republican movement. As the
editor of the North's paper of record, he had popular appeal, deep roots in the
reform community, and grudging respect from intellectuals, not for his mind
necessarily, but rather for his long service as the reform community's conduit
to mass democracy; and yet he was also clearly an unacceptable candidate.

Greeley nauseated many of the originators of the Liberal movement—
E. L. Godkin, William Cullen Bryant, Edward Atkinson. Most either refused
to endorse Greeley or only submitted to it after begging him to withdraw
his name. Godkin complained that Greeley's "sincerity" did not outweigh
his "general knowledge [which] was deplorably small" or "his prejudice and
self-conceit [which] made him ridiculous."[2] James Garfield considered him
"weak," and August Belmont called the nomination "one of those stupen-
dous mistakes which it is difficult even to comprehend." Stalwart Republicans
and Grant loyalists, of course, who counted among their number many who
had questioned Greeley's reliability for more than two decades, were even
more repulsed. As Benjamin Butler, the apotheosis of everything the Liberal
Republicans despised about popular partisan politics, put it: "Go vote to burn
school houses, desecrate churches and violate women, or vote for Horace
Greeley, which means the same thing."[3]

Historical characterizations of Greeley's Liberal Republican run for the
presidency have ranged from accident to farce, but most agree that it had
serious consequences. The early historiography of the Liberal Republican
insurgency was dominated by disappointed participants, not surprisingly
given that the movement was the work of historians and journalists such as
Henry Adams, E. L. Godkin, Henry Demarest Lloyd, Samuel Bowles, Murat
Halstead, and Horace White. In early accounts of the rise and fall of Liberal
Republicans, these self-described "purists" depicted Greeley's nomination as
the effort of conniving political professionals who usurped the leadership of
the Cincinnati convention and corrupted its ends.[4] This interpretation held
for the most part into the 1950s and 1960s when political historians, shaped
by the broker-state values of the New Deal, questioned the motives of the
Liberal reformers and considered their platform of "good government," civil
service reform, local rule, and limited government misguided and naive. Since
the blossoming of the neo-abolitionist historiography of the civil rights era,
however, the historical literature on 1872 has moved from farce to tragedy.
To recent scholars, the Liberals' 1872 campaign was significant because, even
though it was unsuccessful politically, it generated a bipartisan consensus
against the continuation of Reconstruction. The Liberal Republican movement represented a counterrevolution, the conservative turn of a war-weary
North and its failure to sustain its commitment to racial justice. Because
Liberalism was in many respects an editors' revolt, their repudiation of the
postwar political experiment made it next to impossible for Southern black
and Republican voices to be heard in the North.[5] Thus it is implicated as
one of the key villains in the tragic history of American race relations. Worst
of all, Liberalism's racism, undergirded by its social Darwinist free-market

ideology, seemed to anticipate, to put it bluntly, modern conservative rhetoric about "welfare queens in their Cadillacs." In short, by ideologically discrediting the drive of both black agrarians in the South and white workers in the North for a more expansive and inclusive form of economic freedom, Liberal Republicanism represented the purest expression of the emerging modern Republican Party's free-market ideology.[6]

Greeley's presence at the top of the Liberal Republican ticket was, in the larger scheme of things, a smaller mystery in the midst of a larger one. The larger mystery of the Liberal movement was that it included many if not most of the Republican Party's humanitarian reformers, its most idealistic members. Many had been "Radicals," Republicans who had been their party's "antislavery vanguard" and had demonstrated, during the early years of Reconstruction, the fiercest commitment to meaningful racial change in the South. The Liberal Republicans nonetheless pledged to bring Reconstruction and sectional conflict to a quick conclusion, despite ongoing violence against blacks in the South. Why, on the question of Reconstruction and race, so many of the Republican Party's most committed reformers swung from the Left to the Right remains an enigma. Equally so was Greeley's participation in the split. Greeley was also identified with the Radicals, but he also was either largely indifferent toward or opposed to most of the Liberal program. Though Greeley did in fact move closer to Liberalism's brand of bourgeois liberal individualism on a number of issues, it also represented an ideology with which he had long battled. Clearly, the Liberals, who proclaimed the sanctity of property and contract, the virtues of limited government, and the dangers of a labor-inflected participatory democracy, undermined the drive for social democracy in both the North and the South. In the case of the South, Liberal antigovernment rhetoric facilitated the triumph of reactionary governments designed to serve the economic prerogatives of large landholders (hardly a class with which Greeley had ever sympathized) and the social prerogatives of whites more generally. Sadly, when Greeley's name appears in American history textbooks he usually appears in the guise of a free-market Liberal Republican who helped close the door on Radical Reconstruction. In John Faragher's *Out of Many*, Greeley's harsh advice to the freedmen—"Root, Hog, or Die"—is cited to symbolize the relationship between the waning idealism of Republican Reconstruction and the core values of the Liberal Republicans: "classical economics," "supply and demand," "free trade," "property rights," "limited government," and "individualism."[7]

Ultimately, Greeley's role in the Liberal revolt has produced two somewhat contradictory interpretations. In general surveys of the period, Greeley is depicted as a representative Liberal, and this view does have some merit. Greeley had been moving toward the Liberal view on the labor question throughout Reconstruction—and the labor movement had been moving away from him—and this conservative turn made him less open to the demands of freedmen for social democracy in the South. Liberal memoirists and historians, on the other hand, represent Greeley's candidacy as some combination of a tragic accident and a political conspiracy, orchestrated by seasoned political operatives who easily outmaneuvered the less politically savvy Liberal reformers at the Cincinnati convention. But beyond these partial truths lies a larger reality. The reformers who initiated the Cincinnati movement dreamed of a party that stood for something beyond victory and "the spoils," yet they were not able to overcome the inertia of American politics. In the end, the effort to create a national political movement overwhelmed its idealism, and Liberal Republicanism became something like a catch-all that absorbed everyone who was "on the outs" with the partisans who inherited the Republican Party after the war.

That pure, orthodox Liberals were never able to control the direction of their own insurrection ultimately reflects the ideological confusion and diversity of Civil War–era Republican politics. The free-labor tradition that was the foundation of the Republican Party proved unsustainable in the latter half of the century, and its fractures reflected the ambivalence at the heart of liberalism in an age of industrialization. Unlike the regular Republican Party's broad and fuzzy commitment to free labor, the Liberal Republicans did have an ideology in a pure form—an orthodoxy—but they also operated in a larger, and highly unstable, political context. During the middle of the nineteenth century, small-producer capitalism was giving way to a highly consolidated industrial form. American politics, however, remained organized primarily by sectional loyalties. The combination did not lend itself to ideological coherence. Although it was a failure in practical terms, orthodox Liberalism was an intellectual success, nudging the Republican Party away from its powerful reform roots so that, by the last quarter of the nineteenth century, it would become firmly entrenched as the party of business. On a variety of levels, then, 1872 was a breaking point. It represented a kind of ideological estuary, the meeting of the old and new Republicanism, where the party's former boundless eclecticism gave way to the modern party's consolidated classically liberal form; where the complexities of Reconstruction not only pierced the ambiguity of the antebellum Republican Party's free-labor ideology but exposed inherent tensions within the liberal tradition itself.

The New Liberalism and the Professionalization of the Tribune

On the *Tribune,* no figure symbolized the transition from the antebellum reform tradition to Liberalism's more austere free market ideology than Whitelaw Reid. Reid, who with the help of railroad magnate Jay Gould eventually would acquire an ownership stake in the paper, would steer the *Tribune* toward the brand of Liberal reform associated with E. L. Godkin's *Nation* magazine.[8] In fact, Reid was actually offered the editorship of the *Nation,* after George William Curtis and before Godkin, but he turned it down because he was not comfortable with the "come-outer," "Brahminical caste which took the paper under its special protection." Though the sober-minded, calculating, Ohio-born Reid would come to share many of Godkin's views, he was never comfortable with crusading ideologues of any stripe. Before becoming an owner of the paper, Reid became the last of Greeley's managing editors. More than most, Reid's sensibility clashed with the paper's founder. The one saving grace was that in spite of his "high colored speech," Reid thought Greeley maintained a "fund of practicality...despite the old Fourierite symposia which had graced the columns of The Tribune in the forties."[9]

Like his two predecessors, Reid struggled to modernize the paper and to rescue it from economic oblivion. After the paper was scapegoated for goading the Union army on to defeat in its "On to Richmond" editorials in 1861, the *Tribune's* circulation had dropped precipitously. The number of subscribers to the weekly fell from 215,000 to 189,000. Rivals such as the *Herald* prospered. With annual expenses at more than a half a million dollars throughout the 1860s, any dip in circulation threatened the paper's survival.[10] The wartime transition toward politically neutral, information-driven journalism, though completed by Reid, was actually launched by two earlier managing editors, Sydney Howard Gay, who held the position during most of the war, and John Russell Young, who held it afterward. Though quite distinct, all three, in their own way, labored against the perceived excesses of the *Tribune's* spirit of engagement and reform.

Before the war, Dana and Greeley had worked hand in hand, and, if anything, as a reformer Dana was even more radical than Greeley. But Dana's departure meant that the most powerful position on the paper—Greeley's proxy—would no longer be occupied by a fellow antebellum reformer with deep roots in the communitarianism of the 1840s and the cooperative enterprises of the 1850s. The *Tribune* would now be managed by professionals. Gay, the first of the three, was similar in age to Greeley, and had been an editorial writer on the paper for some five years. During the 1840s, Gay had been a lecturer for the American Antislavery Society and the editor of the *Anti-Slavery Standard,* so his personal history was in tune with the paper's humanitarianism, but few signs of it made their way into the paper in a period when war coverage was an overwhelming priority. Despite his antislavery background, Gay worked to make the *Tribune* a little more like the *Herald* in everything but its obscenity. Gay even placed the Washington department, over Greeley's objections, under the command of Adams Sherman Hill, a delicate but determined minister's son and Harvard graduate who was, in the manner of the *Herald's* managing editor Frederic Hudson, indifferent to politics and reform. "I think that the *Tribune* gains by giving all sides a hearing," he once wrote on behalf of publishing a government document that might embarrass Radicalism, "and this is no side but an apparently impartial statement of facts. Above all, it is *news.*" Hill became Gay's principal confidant. During the war, Gay practically lived at the paper's offices, and the pace of Civil War news gathering nearly destroyed him. In 1866, he left the paper under murky circumstances.[11]

After Gay's departure, the *Tribune* became even more "professional," and thus even more distant from its reform origins. As one historian of the post–Civil War *Tribune* put it, the mid-'60s "marked the end of the *Tribune's* function as the evangel of abolition and the personal organ of Horace Greeley, and its real beginnings as a modern newspaper." John Russell Young, who replaced Gay, recalled that "the press is no longer the expression of personal power as when these illustrious men were reigning.... Then the newspaper was a teacher, the voice of one thinker, one leader. Now it is a University."[12] Young, a former bond agent for Jay Cooke, embodied the intellectual and generational shift on the paper. By the end of 1867, men under thirty, like Young, occupied almost all of the important positions on the paper. The new generation of writers labored to duplicate the paper's "trim severity." The cost of telegraph reports and the new professionalized ethos of the paper demanded the oracular style of the "Grocer's Bill": "barren" of all but facts.[13] Young respected Greeley but did not sympathize with the paper's traditional reform absolutism. He said of Greeley that his "moral aims were high" but they were mixed with a naiveté that trusted that the world's evils could "be converted...through the spirit of daily reproof and objurgation." He described the writers who gathered around Greeley in the early days as "resolute, brilliant, capable, irresponsible," but most of all "intolerant."[14] Young's ambition, though, proved to be his undoing. In the gilded spirit of the times, Young made Associated Press articles available to one of the two Philadelphia newspapers in which he had invested, in violation of the consortium's rules.

He also used the *Tribune* to promote the careers of political friends in Pennsylvania who, in turn, invested generously in Young's Philadelphia papers. Two of the men on the bitter end of the *Tribune*'s snubs in the past—Charles Dana and Amos Cummings—exposed the corruption in the New York *Sun,* and Young was forced to leave the *Tribune* in 1869.[15]

Young was replaced by Whitelaw Reid. Just four when Greeley launched the *Tribune,* Reid was college educated and had made his name as a war correspondent for the Cincinnati *Gazette.* He was initially a Radical Republican, and was among that crowded field of Northern observers who rushed into the South during Reconstruction to observe the aftermath of war. Reid ended up making three trips to the South. The first was a tour of the South's more lavish and cosmopolitan coastal cities as the invited guest of Salmon Chase. His latter trips were prompted primarily by his own speculation in the cotton crop, and brought him to the South's interior where he was a witness to both black and white squalor. As a cotton speculator, Reid, like the former masters, struggled to make sense of the region's conversion to free labor, and personally experienced black resistance to their continued subordination.

The published result of Reid's Southern sojourns was *After the War: A Tour of the Southern States, 1865–1866.* It became among the most influential accounts of postwar Southern society and helped provide the context for congressional Reconstruction policy. He was a Republican partisan, but lacked the idealism of his older colleagues. Most important, Reid was a moderate on the race question, but his politics stemmed as much from personal relationships as from ideology. Identified with the Lincoln wing of the party on race, he was antislavery, but had doubts about the economic, moral, and intellectual capacity of blacks and was ambivalent about the prospects of racial integration or biracial democracy. In *After the War,* his free-labor optimism that emancipation would unleash Southern agriculture was undercut by his racial doubts; whether it was slavery or something inherent in their race, blacks were stupid, lazy, careless, and immoral. The freedmen, he wrote, were not the sort of "material as, under ordinary circumstances, one would now choose for the duties of American citizenship." Matters were not helped by the fact that Reid, while in the South, invested much of his wealth in the 1866 and 1867 cotton crops. He failed miserably, and the experience eroded his faith that much more in the freedmen. Not long afterward, he would confess privately, despite public proclamations of the opposite, that he could no longer support black suffrage with unmixed enthusiasm. Though Reid recognized intuitively that all conclusions about the fate of black labor and the Southern economy were inherently political, his firsthand financial speculations in the South contradicted optimistic Republican visions of the South's free-labor transformation. Reid was among the first Northern Republicans who broke with the then conventional view that with reliable wages, the former slaves would work even harder than free white labor. Increasingly, he sympathized with fellow planters who experienced the transition to free labor and were convinced that free black labor would yield only half of what slavery did; ultimately, and even though he scarcely admitted it to himself, Reid did not believe that the former slaves were truly ready to become fully free laborers. Instead, he would acknowledge only that blacks worked hard—harder than most Southern whites—but not rationally, regularly, or without close supervision.[16] On race, then, at this early point in Reconstruction Reid was more conservative than Greeley, but they intuitively shared the implicit assumption that true free labor was self-directed and autonomous. The faintly conservative turn Reid made in 1866 and 1867 would become even more pronounced by the time he joined the *Tribune* in 1868, and become even stronger by the spring of 1869 when he became the de facto managing editor.[17] And Greeley was on the cusp of joining him.

By 1870, Greeley, whose voice once resonated equally in political, reform, and labor circles, was rapidly becoming an anachronism, along with his antebellum small-producer faith in the moral, political, and social benefits of the democratization of property. Even Greeley's own faith in that dream was losing its resolve. Greeley had always advocated ascetic self-discipline—a "Protestant ethic"—that linked the denial of the appetites to upward mobility and moral self-improvement, but he rarely wielded it in a negative way. Increasingly, though, hostility began creeping into *Tribune* accounts of the labor movement. As late as 1868, in response to the resolutions of the Boston eight-hour league, the *Tribune* noted that a "melancholy feature" of the movement was its seeming "acceptance of the Wages system as perfect and final" when "we regard it as a step in advance of slavery." But after the Commune, the *Tribune* began conceding ground to the idea of a wage-based economy. "We believe that those who work for wages are as fairly and fully recompensed as those who work for themselves," the *Tribune* concluded. It suggested further that worker dissipation was the main factor that prevented them from ascending into the class of capitalists. In a May address to the New England Labor Reform League, Greeley said that the poor "have spent for liquors and tobacco money enough to have given them half the property in the city," and quoted approvingly his friend Gerrit Smith's identical message to the Virginia freedmen.[18] In mirror accounts of former slaves and Northern workers, Reid, Greeley, and the Republican Party more generally were, in essence, repudiating the progressive promise of free labor for both whites and blacks. This evolution became complete in 1872 with Greeley's run for the presidency.

Liberal Republicanism and the Revival of Whiggery

Understanding Greeley's role in the 1872 Liberal revolt, given the delicate balance of conservatism and radicalism in his thought, is a complicated proposition. It has always been one of the mysteries of 1872 that so many of the most aggressive advocates of comprehensive citizenship for the freedmen—George Julian, Lyman Trumball, and Charles Sumner—ended up joining a movement ostensibly devoted to the opposite. That said, Greeley's fusion of conservatism and radicalism was characteristic of Liberal thought in a general sense. Like most of the Liberals, he could never long stomach social conflict, to say nothing of an extended war against property. His well-established faith in education, civility, self-reliance, public honesty, and rational reform all suggest that his Liberalism had a long foreground. At times, however, his moralistic language and his tendency to sacralize the virtues of work and self-reliance could be confused with the more austere bourgeois individualism of the Liberals. His oft-noted notorious command to the freedmen—"Root, Hog, or Die"—seems, on the surface, the embodiment of Liberal faith in market outcomes. Yet Greeley applied the phrase as often to the planters as to the freedmen when the former begged for "public money" in the form of "tax remissions, loans, gratuities."[19] But it was hardly the Liberal insistence on market individualism that attracted Greeley to the movement.

Temperamentally and ideologically, Greeley was ill-equipped to cope with the crisis of the war and its aftermath. He had never been comfortable with the idea of near-permanent subjugation of the South. Unlike the most extreme voices in the Radical wing of the party, Greeley could never abide the sort occupation envisioned by someone like Wendell Phillips who proclaimed that Southern elites must either be "hung" or "exiled," or "*the Government must hold that territory by the iron arm of military despotism for some years to come.*" The *Tribune,* on the other hand, held out the reflexively Whiggish hope that despite foreboding reports to the contrary, the freedmen could cooperate with the "better portion of the Whites" to create a ruling coalition sympathetic to Republican values.[20] In the faith that a new order could be achieved in the South without force or violence, the *Tribune* proclaimed, once again, the existence of a latent free-labor Republican majority that, if emancipated from the domination of a small elite, would on its own create a new South in the political image of the North. In a new context, it was a revival of the Republican "slave power thesis," which allowed the *Tribune* to sketch a vision for Reconstruction that was both voluntary and resulted in a political and economic order aligned with Republican values.[21] The ongoing belief in a slave-power minority kept alive the desire "to win the South to the Union by a magnanimous pardon, rather than to bind it by chains of fear."[22]

Though it was often in tension with his post-1848 political and economic realism, there remained deep within Greeley a reservoir of Whig values that held that individuals, communities, economies, and nations are, in an ideal sense, organic. Individuals may have different organs, passions, and capacities; economies may have separate orders, ranks, classes, and sectors; and communities and nations may have diverse regions, geographies, ethnicities, and characters; but the role of reform, religion, culture, education, and law was to instill, maintain, and restore the innate harmonies that exist in the self, ·nature, and society. This Whig sensibility recoiled in horror from violence, passion, conflict, crime, and especially insurrection and war—all represented a breakdown of discipline and reason. During periods of crisis and conflict, throughout Greeley and the *Tribune*'s "post-Whig" existence, its core Whig values would continually reassert themselves.

Perhaps the most dramatic example of the postwar revival of Greeley's Whiggery was his role in securing the release of Jefferson Davis from jail. Greeley's gesture to Davis reflected his fervent hope that the "better classes" of the North and the South could be reconciled. It was a view that would eventually be widely shared by the Liberal Republicans. But Davis's release was achieved in the spring of 1867, when few were calling for an end to Reconstruction and the paper itself was packed with reports of Southern racism and violence. This combination of seemingly contradictory impulses lays open the disordered nature of his political instincts and his thought, but also, in a broader sense, it is one more eruption of his intrinsic Whiggery, his faith that all conflicts, social and sectional, could be reasonably harmonized. In the context of Reconstruction, it illustrates the paradoxical way that Greeley cultivated political controversy while avoiding hard political choices. Never a dialectical thinker, Greeley perceived little contradiction between leniency toward the South's Confederate elite and the political, social, and economic aspirations of the former slaves. Through Davis, Greeley thought he could demonstrate the *Tribune*'s Reconstruction-long commitment to the dual policy of "impartial suffrage" and "universal amnesty," and literally enact the theme of his later 1872 anti-Reconstruction campaign rhetoric: "Let us clasp hands across the bloody chasm." Greeley's embrace of Davis drew its share of radical condemnation. Wendell Phillips called it "treason made easy and respectable."[23] But in 1867, as in 1872, Greeley's ambivalence about a punitive Reconstruction stemmed less from latent racism than from a desire for social reconciliation and harmony that was deeply embedded in his Whiggery, even if it often ran counter to the element of his thought that demanded meaningful social reform.

Two interconnected principles ultimately defined the 1872 Liberal revolt. First, the Liberals were made uneasy by class politics and the prospect of democratic majorities launching a war against property through lawful means. The Liberals, whose opposition to plebeian democracy was nurtured by years of contempt for the corruption and cronyism of the Northern urban Democratic Party, recoiled from its black Southern Republican counterpart where racial divisions made politics a thin substitute for social warfare. Second, Liberal opposition to class politics was underwritten philosophically by its shared commitment to orthodox political economy, a brand of economic individualism opposed to state intervention in the market. Both doctrines, but especially the latter, were profoundly alien to nearly everything for which Greeley had ever stood. Despite areas of intellectual overlap that I detailed above, his participation in the Liberal crusade also represents a profound ideological conversion. Even conceding that Greeley's ingrained Whiggish instincts could be deeply conservative, his abrupt ideological turn on race and Reconstruction was disorienting and close to inexplicable. What registered the swiftness of his and the *Tribune*'s Liberal transformation most clearly and definitively was the sea change in the paper's coverage of the ongoing turmoil in Reconstruction South Carolina.

South Carolina as Liberal Laboratory

South Carolina, of course, was explosive terrain both politically and symbolically. The state had been the cradle of the Confederacy. It had a small black majority but was ruled historically by a single-party white ruling-class aristocracy. All of these factors made it a natural testing ground for the meaning and limits of Reconstruction. During the years surrounding the 1872 presidential campaign, South Carolina was home to the sorts of events that defined the politics of the Reconstruction era. In 1870–71, it was plagued by Klan terror, which had several purposes and took a variety of forms: voter intimidation, assassination, and the basic enforcement of an economic and social order that kept blacks on the bottom. Klan terror tested the political will of Washington Republicans as well as the endurance of Northern voters who sustained their offices. In the spring of 1871, ironically just as Klan activity in the state was beginning to ebb, South Carolina witnessed what would sadly be the last major national Republican effort to defend forcefully their fledgling Southern state-level allies when Congress passed a series of three Enforcement Acts, which allowed President Grant to suspend habeas corpus and to use the military to defend civil rights. Grant exercised that right, ordering the newly created Department of Justice and the 7th Cavalry to bring the Klan to its knees. The effort resulted in a number of arrests, but the size of the Klan overtaxed the army and the court system's capacity to deal with them. The endeavor was also handicapped by an increasing number of calls within the Republican Party for an end to federal intervention in the South. The rising tide of retrenchment was an impulse that not only motivated the Liberal revolt that was just around the corner but was also taking hold within the Grant administration itself, which in the end resisted entreaties for adequate military and judicial resources to cope with the scale of the problem. Within this context of the polarized extremes of Reconstruction politics—namely occupation, white terror, and black political self-assertion—sat a conservative alternative that took shape in the early 1870s that was distinct from the Klan's racial reign of terror, but driven by a similar goal: the restoration of local rule and white supremacy.[24]

Violence, of course, was ever present during Reconstruction, and it would always undergird Southern resistance to Northern rule and racial equality, but it had also become obvious to many South Carolina conservatives that violence could often bring with it a counterproductive Northern reaction. Starting in the early 1870s, South Carolina political elites added a new weapon to their arsenal. Rather than attacking Republican rule solely with racism and violence, they changed course somewhat and worked to discredit Southern Republican governments ideologically, using the more impersonal language of limited government, corruption, and the market. The strategy proved more effective because it divided the Southern Republican party on racial grounds, and it attracted the sympathy of Northern Republicans who for some time had been carrying out a similar struggle against municipal governments in their midst. Honest government and limited government had been rallying points for proto-Liberal Republicans in factional struggles between various wings of the Republican Party for years; starting in the early 1870s, it also became their Reconstruction exit strategy. In South Carolina, a systematic propaganda war on the size, scope, and honesty of black Republican governments divorced white conservative assaults on the government from more overt racial violence. Styled nationally as the "New Departure," this new, "good government" critique of black Republicanism coalesced in South Carolina as the Citizen's Party, Union Reform, and various Taxpayer' Unions. They chipped away at the Republican Party's biracial coalition by fusing Republicans worried about corruption to moderate Democrats looking for ways to unsettle the new political order.[25] Through the "neutral" idiom of the free market and honest government, the Liberals, allied with the

South's "best men," could attack black Republican rule without appealing to violence or overt racism. Good government and white government were one and the same.

In the *Tribune,* South Carolina became a focus of attention through the writings of James Pike, who wrote intermittently for the paper for the better part of two decades. Pike's transformation from antebellum radicalism to Reconstruction conservatism was even more severe than Greeley's. Pike was a Maine abolitionist who first started writing for the *Tribune* in 1850. His previous employer, Boston's conservative Whig *Courier,* had fired him because his antislavery politics were too zealous, and throughout the 1850s his Washington letters to the *Tribune* were so fiery and controversial that even Greeley was somewhat uncomfortable with them. Nonetheless, his Reconstruction reports from South Carolina would help dismantle Radical Republicanism both on the paper and in the North more generally.[26]

Pike actually had two careers with the *Tribune,* split by several years of service abroad as Lincoln's minister to the Netherlands. When he returned to New York in 1866, the city repelled him. He was horrified by its "stink" and its polyglot populace; those "who are not German are Irish," he remarked, and "those who are not Irish are Chinese, & those who are not Chinese are nigger."[27] It was a sign of what was to come. Though he generally followed the paper's political line on Reconstruction, he, unlike Greeley, held profound though largely private doubts about black suffrage and the ability of the former slaves to act as responsible citizens. Pike reacted viscerally against their lack of education. When Pike started to report on what would later be recognized as Reconstruction's 1872 climax in South Carolina, he symbolized Greeley and the *Tribune's* conservative turn, its shift from Radicalism to Liberal reform. It was a conservative turn, however, dressed up as rational moderation.[28]

In March 1872, Pike wrote an extended piece on South Carolina titled "A State in Ruins" that not only evidenced the paper's sea change on Reconstruction but also played a decisive role throughout the North in discrediting biracial democracy and the ongoing occupation of the South.[29] Pike had long vented privately that the "nigger is a porcupine" that "fills with quills everybody who undertakes to hug him," and that "there is nothing more absurd than that we in America should allow the [ballot] to ignorant tribes of Irishmen." He also contended that the Radical Republicans and their carpetbagger allies had brought Klan violence upon themselves. Like not a few Republicans, Pike's antislavery views had been shaped in large part by his racism. He hoped, in short, that "black, mixed, degraded and ignorant, or inferior races" could be confined to the Gulf States.[30]

In "A State in Ruins," Pike took his critique of popular democracy to
a public forum and rallied the forces of Liberalism. In just a column and a
half, Pike struck notes that would resonate in the conservative historiography
of Reconstruction for the better part of a century. All of the characters
that would litter Dunning school histories of the era were present.[31] Its villains were rogue carpetbaggers and ignorant, minstrelized blacks. Its tragic
heroes were virtuous former aristocrats, humbled by the war and appre-
ciative of its result, who patiently awaited good government and justice.
His indictment of Southern Republicanism was comprehensive. His most
basic complaint was the "deplorable" condition of the state itself, for which
Pike held black misrule entirely responsible. "The men who lead and manage . . . the State Government are thieves and miscreants," he wrote, "ignorant
and corrupt." Black legislators are "bought and sold," and the "negro himself
is hardly conscious of criminality": "He considers his vote just as much a
part of his personal property as his mule and his chicken." Official corruption, in Pike's view, paralyzed the state. Black and carpetbagger rule placed
"unprincipled adventurers" and "pauper blacks, fresh from a state of slavery
and ignorance" above the "tax-paying" classes of the state. The onerous and
"grinding" taxation that resulted was simply a direct transfer of wealth, a
form of "virtual confiscation." As a result, mobile capital fled the state and its
landholding classes were soon to follow, whatever the consequences. In light
of South Carolina's basic political arithmetic, which placed a black majority
over a white minority, the only solution, which Pike not so subtly expresses
through the voice of a "Boston man who was lately traveling through the
state," was "rebel[lion]": "'This time you would have a reason.'"[32]

Earlier *Tribune* reporting from the Carolinas displayed signs of the paper's
Liberal transformation but had also tried to strike a balance between viewpoints. An 1871 report, "Through the South," for example, argued much like
Pike the following year that the "chief reason" that "negroes do not accumulate property is . . . because they are ignorant and unthrifty": "Happy is the
darkey who has a cabin, a boat, a corn-field, and a garden-patch." But it also
noted structural factors that frustrated social mobility in the South; namely,
it cited the damaging legacy of "absolute dependence" and the fact that
the "prevailing system of working the land does not conduce to economy."
The report also admitted that the "failure" of the South's experiment in free
labor was largely confined to rural areas: "The colored men of the towns
who work at trades, and are much more intelligent and self-reliant."[33] More
remarkably, the earlier report actually quoted black South Carolinians.

What makes Pike's "A State in Ruins" all the more astounding was
that he had written it without having visited the state. Its byline was from

Washington, D.C., and it was based primarily on interviews done there with wealthy U.S. Senator William Sprague of Rhode Island, who had invested heavily in the state. More important, it relied on the testimony of Senator Wade Hampton, a conservative South Carolina obstructionist who clung to white supremacy and devoted his postwar political career to redeeming the Palmetto State from Republican rule by restoring its "natural" racial order.[34] In the end, though, visiting the state made little difference. When Pike actually visited South Carolina the following year, he would make identical points about the state, though in a more prolonged form. Convinced that Reconstruction was a grotesque political monstrosity, he went to South Carolina with "his basic indictment" of the region already established, as one historian put it, and "all he really wanted was material to give his story local color."[35] The public and private record suggests that he only formally interviewed one African American.[36] Naturally, Pike described South Carolina's biracial government as "the most ignorant democracy that mankind ever saw, invested with the functions of government." He characterized the white conservative opposition as the victims of historical developments that tragically inverted society's natural order:

> Here, then, is the outcome, the ripe, perfected fruit of the boasted civilization of the South, after two hundred years of experience. A white community, that had gradually risen from small beginnings, till it grew into wealth, culture, and refinement, and became accomplished in all the arts of civilization; that successfully asserted its resistance to a foreign tyranny by deeds of conspicuous valor, which achieved liberty and independence through the fire and tempest of civil war, and illustrated itself in the councils of the nation by orators and statesman worthy of any age or nation—such a community is then reduced to this. It lies prostrate in the dust, ruled over by this strange conglomerate, gathered from the ranks of its own servile population. It is the spectacle of a society suddenly turned bottom-side up.[37]

This later series of newspaper reports eventually took book form in late 1873 as *The Prostrate State,* which helped coalesce bipartisan opposition to Reconstruction and black political participation. Claude Bowers, a Democratic politician and Dunning school historian of the South, called it "the 'Uncle Tom's Cabin' of . . . redemption."[38]

Though singular in influence—the *Prostrate State* was cited on the House floor after racial violence erupted in Hamburg, South Carolina, in the summer of 1876—Pike's dispatches gained credibility because they mirrored so many other newspapers' Southern correspondence.[39] Pike was among a second wave

of Northern correspondents sent to the South to report on political conditions there. Unlike the diversity of the first wave of postwar reporting, which
occurred in the immediate aftermath of the war and included correspondents
such as Sidney Andrews and Whitelaw Reid, the second wave of reporting was clearly determined to bring discredit on the Radical project. Pike,
along with later correspondents, the New *York Herald*'s Charles Nordhoff,
the Cincinnati *Commercial*'s H. V. Redfield, and the *Tribune*'s own Zebulon
White, forged the narrative that would be ideological basis of Redemption.
They managed to depict Reconstruction as an unnatural and corrupt process,
overstating the extent of "negro rule" and the ignorance of "negro rulers."
They also exaggerated the influence and the illegitimacy of the carpetbaggers,
a class of whites that were among the few allies of the black Republicans.
Overall, their portrait of the Southern Republican governments' profligacy
and dishonesty became part of a larger attempt to highlight the corruption of
the national Republican Party, which had become, in their view, a vehicle for
patronage and cronyism. Their efforts sowed the seeds of the 1872 revolt.[40]

Ironically, Pike would initially press Greeley to remain loyal to the regular Republican Party in 1872 before following him into the movement for
which his own work had ideologically cleared space.[41] Despite different
starting points, Greeley and Pike's Reconstruction politics began to converge
in the early 1870s. In the spring of 1871, Greeley went on a much ballyhooed
tour of the South. It was there, and in the aftermath of the trip, that Greeley's modified theory of Reconstruction emerged fully articulated. He proclaimed, once and for all, that if the old Whig, "conservative" element of the
region could seize the political reins of the South, they would steer a course
between Klan violence and black "ignorance." Greeley began promoting
"New Departure" and vaguely "New South" initiatives such as former Confederate H. D. Caper's proposal for an industrial exposition in Georgia. Giving speeches in Gulf state and Mississippi port cities such as New Orleans,
Galveston, and Vicksburg, his message was becoming increasingly consistent
with the emerging Liberal movement. In his Vicksburg lecture, he blamed
Klan violence and Republican misrule equally for the ongoing turmoil in the
South and expressed hope that there would come a "time" when "we of the
North would...feel a just pride in the soldierly achievements and military
character of Lee and Stonewall Jackson" and "late confederates would learn
to feel a patriotic pride in the achievements of Grant and Sherman."[42] His
address to the "Farmers of Texas" reprised nearly all of the old Whig pieties:
farmers ought to embrace progress and technology, become careful stew-
ards of the land, practice patience, thrift, and self-denial, and work toward
a diverse economy independent of the vagaries of the world market.[43]

When Greeley returned from the South, he delivered a major speech at the Lincoln Club-Rooms at Union Square, before a painted portrait, a marble bust, and assorted photographs of his own image. In it, he continued to insist that racial equality and sectional reunion were not irreconcilable, and that only false political obstacles stood in the way of perfect justice. He claimed that "if there had been Universal Amnesty four years ago, there would have been no Ku-Klux in 1871"; that if the South were permitted to vote for their "best men," the "Republican party would have been a great deal stronger and Reconstruction very much further advanced and more certain than it is to-day."[44] Like Pike, Greeley positioned himself as a centrist, between the Klan and the "corrupt" Republican parties now in power in some Southern states. He regarded the Klan with "profound disgust," wholeheartedly supported the "Ku-Klux act," and said "our Government is no Government, but a sham" if it is unable to protect "citizens in their fundamental rights." But Greeley thought that "thieving carpetbaggers" posed a greater danger to the country and to the Republican Party. Not those who went south as educational missionaries, but rather Northerners who "ingratiated themselves" with the "simple, credulous, ignorant...Blacks" in order to profit when the region's "most urgent and special necessity [was] for rigid economy."[45] Clearly, Greeley was positioning himself to run for high office, most likely against Ulysses S. Grant.

Greeley's Liberal Turn

Greeley's support for Grant had always been lukewarm. In 1868, he hoped that a committed Republican such as Salmon Chase would be the party's standard bearer. "If we want to talk about horses or tobacco," the *Tribune* then editorialized, Grant is perfectly well qualified, but he has not offered "[us] one word on" the fate of the Reconstruction South, "the question that racks the heart of the country!"[46] Nonetheless, after his election, the paper quickly reconciled itself to Grant's presidency, pronouncing it as late as 1870 a "very safe and substantial success."[47] In the summer of 1871, though, Greeley began to hedge once again. He wrote under his own name that he would support Grant if the Republicans renominated him because he held "his election infinitely preferable to that of any candidate whom the Democrats may nominate," yet he also acknowledged that he "favors the One-Term principle, and believes that another Republican candidate...[would] encounter less opposition."[48] Not long after, the *Tribune* began venting openly the idea of a third-party fusion movement and covering the administration with a negative slant.[49] Greeley started making moves to challenge Grant in 1872, and the paper began to ramp up its coverage of the Republican dissidents.[50]

FIGURE 7.   Thomas Nast's cartoon of Greeley and Carl Schurz pillories the 1872 Liberal Republican revolt. The cartoon appeared in *Harper's Weekly* 16, no. 817 (August 24, 1872), 652. Courtesy of the Library of Congress, Prints and Photographs Division, LC-USZ62-97505.

Initially, Greeley viewed the Liberal Republican movement with unease, despite the fact that he, like many Liberals, was all but frozen out of the regular organization in his home state. Greeley counted few long-standing allies in the Liberal movement, though. He had long battled William Cullen Bryant, publicly opposed Missouri Liberals Carl Schurz and B. Gratz Brown, and would not publicly renounce his ties to the regular Republican Party until March 1872. Nonetheless, he shared the Liberals' distaste for the "shift within the Republican party from an ideological to an organizational mode of politics," the way "state parties fell under the control of powerful Senators who saw government less as an instrument of reform than as a means of obtaining office and mediating the rival claims of the diverse economic and ethnic groups that made up Northern society."[51] More opportunistically, he began to mimic Liberal sentiments on Southern blacks. An April *Tribune* editorial alleged that if the freedmen were suffering economically, they were responsible for their own condition: "Had they saved the money they have since 1865 spent in drink, tobacco, balls, gaming, and other dissipation, they might have bought therewith at least Ten Million acres of the soil of their respective States which would have given each family an average of ten acres of mother earth; and the free and clear owner of ten acres need never stand idle or accept half wages."[52] So when the call went out for a Liberal

Figure 8. Whitelaw Reid joined the *Tribune* in 1868 and symbolized the paper's Reconstruction-era generational and ideological shift. Courtesy of the Library of Congress, Prints and Photographs Division, LC-BH826-1459.

Republican convention in Cincinnati, Greeley was sympathetic but also cautious, uncertain whether he could commit in advance to a movement that might become avowedly free trade.[53]

When Greeley became the Liberal Republican nominee, the result was only partly unexpected. Before the Cincinnati convention, Carl Schurz came to New York to solicit support for the movement at a public rally. When Greeley was called to the front of the platform to conclude the meeting, his words were drowned out with applause. At Cincinnati, Whitelaw Reid managed Greeley's candidacy. He was uniquely positioned to do so. Unlike Greeley, Reid opposed Grant from the outset of his administration, and shared generational ties with the editors and intellectuals who were Liberalism's main pillars of support. Reid's efforts had to be Herculean, though, because

Greeley was hardly the first choice of the movement's original movers. That designation belonged to Charles Francis Adams, who all but disdained the honor. Greeley was nominated after six ballots, but Adams led on all but the second and the last votes.[54]

Not a few original Liberals were disgusted by Greeley's convention triumph and opposed the nomination publicly. Some, such as Carl Schurz, only reluctantly supported it, and others drifted away in apathetic despair. Making Greeley's marriage to Liberalism particularly difficult was his record on protection. In 1870, only two years before his nomination, Greeley had published a pamphlet on political economy in which protection was a central component. Protection was the cross-class cornerstone of Greeley's impulse to insulate both labor and manufactures from the grinding effects of foreign competition. To most Liberals, though, protection intervened, "artificially," in the free play of the market and was a major contributor to political corruption. Godkin called it the "cancer of popular government."[55] The Liberal platform eventually evaded the issue altogether: "Recognizing that there are in our midst honest but irreconcilable differences of opinion with regard to the respective systems of Protection and Free Trade, we remit the discussion of the subject to the people...wholly free of Executive interference or dictation." Liberal purists naturally found the party's vacillation on the issue distasteful. Even so, many orthodox free-trade Liberals eventually supported Greeley because they concluded that Reconstruction remained the central question of the day and they hoped that a Greeley victory would shatter the party system, leaving the Liberals to pick up the pieces.[56] But because of the protection issue, Greeley and his allies had to ward off a second "bolt" by disappointed "Free-Trade" Liberals led by William Cullen Bryant, Edward Atkinson, and David Wells. The "bolters" even went so far as to organize an anti-Greeley meeting in New York City. There Atkinson called him a "malign influence" and David Wells remarked that "Greeley meant disorganization."[57]

Greeley's alliance with the Liberals was indeed an odd fit. As the *Tribune* admitted, 1872 witnessed a "Protectionist...supported by Free-Traders," a "Republican...accepted by Democrats," and the "leading Emancipationist of the age...the candidate of men whose slaves he labored long and successfully to liberate."[58] Two weeks after his nomination, Greeley wrote a lengthy public letter of acceptance citing his obedience to the Liberal platform and pledging fealty to its call for an end to Reconstruction and a restoration of Southern home rule. He remarked that he, like "the masses of our countrymen, North and South," was "eager to clasp hands across the bloody chasm."[59] In a major speech to Poughkeepsie, New York's African American community, Greeley echoed Liberal themes on race, individualism, and the market. He advised the black community to avoid politics, to cultivate "self-trust," and to eschew "outside" aid and the "spirit of beggary." He also professed the reality of racial differences and predicted that "the colored people... will naturally gravitate toward... the tropics." Most of all, he derided the post-emancipation expectation that government would address the economic disabilities that were the legacy of slavery by redistributing land. In all, he repudiated more clearly and emphatically than ever the social democratic doctrines he had advocated most of is life.[60]

Unlike traditional contenders for the presidency, Greeley campaigned actively for the job, so hard that he was forced to excuse "himself on account of his extreme weariness" during a late September swing through western Pennsylvania.[61] Nonetheless, within the space of a week, Greeley gave major speeches in Pittsburgh, Cincinnati, Louisville, Indianapolis, Cleveland, and an untold number of smaller towns all along the way.[62] Throughout, the *Tribune* worked to align itself with conservative opinion on racial questions. It praised the House for blocking the Senate's effort to extend the Ku Klux Klan Act and Grant's power to suspend habeas corpus in the South.[63] Later that summer it started to refer to Klan violence as the "outrages... [of] a few scattered ruffians" that were publicized "for political effect." It declared, further, that the organization's "disappearance" was testament to the degree to which "the white people of the Southern States and the more intelligent among the blacks are more faithfully devoted to a restoration of peace, law, and honest legislation."[64] The above only reaffirmed the instinct of many former abolitionists to oppose their former ally. Gerrit Smith condemned the campaign's association with the "negro-bating, negro-whipping, negro-hanging Democrats," and Frederick Douglass wrote a public letter to the country's African American voters calling upon them to stick with Grant.[65]

Greeley also carefully aligned his beliefs with more orthodox Liberals in the realm of political reform. One of the elements that galvanized the Liberals was their fear of mass democracy and class legislation. Francis Lieber argued that "truth is not settled by majorities" and Henry Adams once remarked that "the great problem of every system of Government has been to place administration and legislation in the hands of the best men."[66] Unlike the Liberals, Greeley had never been an elitist and he did not share their ambivalence about democracy. He did, though, embrace their commitment to "good government." He long favored economy in government and technocratic approaches to social problems, yet he never really made vulnerable social groups—immigrant Irish Catholics or later blacks—the scapegoats for corruption. Even as late as 1871 and 1872, when Greeley and the *Tribune* were turning in a more conservative or Liberal direction, its relentless coverage of the scandals plaguing the Tammany political machine almost never descended into nativism. There was also hardly any mention of Southern corruption. Mostly, the *Tribune* focused on the way in which corrupt party machines and their gaggle of opportunists had seized a political reform movement from its idealistic progenitors. Greeley and the *Tribune*'s "corruption narratives" were as likely to be top down as to be bottom up. Still, it came as no surprise that Greeley endorsed the Liberal platform advocating civil service reform.

The spirit of nonpartisan political reform pervaded New York in the early 1870s. In 1871, Greeley battled with Roscoe Conkling for control of the New York City Republican Committee and the soul of the party itself. Throughout 1871 and 1872, the *Tribune* leveled charges of corruption against Conkling's "custom house" faction of the party and was particularly critical of Thomas Murphy, a Conkling ally and New York's collector of the port. In New York, though, "good government" was not simply a code for elite rule. Among the reasons Greeley turned against Conkling during the late 1860s was because he, with the help of Ulysses Grant, reorganized the party in the state and placed it on a foundation of patronage and "business backing," forsaking black suffrage and other allied reforms. Nationally, Grant may have been the "negro's friend," but in New York State he was represented by forces that stood in the way of the party's progressive wing.[67] Battling Conkling in his own party and the even more egregious Boss Tweed Democrats outside it, Greeley came by his support for "examination[s]" and "promotion...by merit" honestly.[68]

For pure Liberals, political reform was an end in itself, but it was also part of a larger opposition to class politics. At bottom, the Liberals shared a faith in social science, that economic behavior in particular was governed by discoverable natural laws. These were not new ideas necessarily—the Associationists also had a social science mind-set—but the Liberals applied them with the full force of their being and with individualistic implications. In the realm of political economy, the basic Liberal unit was the self-interested individual who maximized his happiness and whose exertions were rewarded by the market according to both his talents and his efforts. Any effort to intervene in the economic realm by the state or by workers acting collectively perverted natural laws and marred the public good. The basis of the Liberal movement, and what held it together intellectually, was laissez-faire, pure and simple.[69] E. L. Godkin was representative, castigating the North's "Eight-Hour Movement" because it threatened to disrupt artificially "the market price [of labor], which is settled by competition or by the natural operation of the law of supply and demand." He was even more outraged by

Southern efforts to redress social inequality. Government land programs, he wrote, would stupefy the freedmen, and "render all labor irksome to him, all gains slowly acquired seem not worth having, and patience and scrupulousness seem marks of imbecility." The South's Reconstruction governments, more generally, sponsored a form of "socialism," a "queer aristocracy of color with the rich Congo chief on top and the degraded Anglo-Saxon at the bottom."[70] To the Liberals, the freedmen's salvation should rest only on their own frugality, hard work, patience, and self-discipline.

Ironically, Greeley's differences with the Liberals on the fundamentals of political economy resurrected the very same debates that he had carried on during the 1840s with conservative Whigs, notably Henry Raymond. What popular political economists such as Greeley, Raymond, and Godkin were attempting to work out were answers to a number of fundamental questions raised by the emergence of the free-labor paradigm: What forces would sustain a society constructed on free contract and mutual self-interest, and in such a society, who, as one historian recently phrased it, would do the "world's dirty work"? Many, if not most, Northerners rejected the outright violence of slavery, but disagreed about what would serve as a coercive substitute. During the decades surrounding the Civil War, Republicans would answer these questions in two main ways. One, Lincolnian and optimistic, would emphasize incentive, mobility, and the right to rise; their America was one of Algeresque opportunity. Increasingly prevalent in the postwar period was the more pessimistic discourse of dissident Republicans such as Godkin and William Graham Sumner who stressed the pull of necessity, eventually articulated as social Darwinism, which frowned on any sort of intervention in the economy as interference in its natural laws. Along with voices in organized labor, Greeley had offered a third answer, which contended that the market's "differential rewards" were to an extent the product of incentive and talent, but also recognized that industrialization rendered individuals interdependent and acknowledged that inequality was the result of unfair consolidations of power. By democratizing property, Greeley hoped that society could reward real virtue, punish sloth, and more generally diminish the extent of social conflict; the moralism inherent in his vision was both distinct from, and overlapped with, Liberal social Darwinism. Frugality, mobility, work, and self-reliance had always been a part of that vision, but it had always been married to the more progressive view that the unimpaired operation of market principles created unwitting victims and that the distinct challenge of reform was to organize society in such a way that meaningful work would be available to all and that the rewards of work would accrue to the laborer. Although Greeley was, like Godkin, uncomfortable with punitive policies such as confiscation, he had also always acknowledged "propertylessness" as an unrepublican problem and would rarely if ever resort to Algeresque pieties that implied that the poor were responsible for their own poverty. Greeley acknowledged that the impersonal mechanisms so prized by later Liberals had to be reckoned with, yet the duty of reform was not to facilitate the free flow of commodities, but to organize the economy in such a way that labor would become its own master. So in nearly every way, Greeley had opposed many if not most of Liberalism's core ideological principles before the 1870s and in some cases even after.[71]

The Legacy of Liberal Republicanism

In 1872, Liberal Republicanism was, in a narrow historical sense, a colossal failure. Greeley's candidacy faced a torrent of abuse, and he won just 43 percent of the vote and six states. Thomas Nast's political cartoons savaged him. Apathy plagued the Southern electorate, which stayed home in droves. The previous Democratic nominee, Horatio Seymour, ran the most rabidly white supremacist campaign in American history and he, nonetheless, polled 3 percentage points better than Greeley in the popular vote and he won fourteen more Electoral College votes. Throughout the country, Greeley ran behind down ballot Democrats and Liberal Republicans.[72] Humiliated, Greeley died just a few weeks after the close of the campaign, on November 29, 1872. Ultimately, the movement's effort to combine so many disparate elements—"free traders and protectionists, conservative New England patricians and agrarian radicals, civil service reformers and unvarnished spoilsmen, advocates of Negro rights and Southern redeemers"—doomed it to political disappointment.[73] Whitelaw Reid's biographer described the movement as "too heterogeneous to be effectively united with the cement of mere discontent."[74] In the long term, however, Liberal Republicanism played an important role in sifting out the larger party ideologically.

After 1872, the Liberal ideal of limited government became the rule in both parties. For the Democrats, this was part of their rural, Southern, Jacksonian inheritance, but for the Republicans it was attached to a more modern, procapitalist vision of laissez-faire. Elections became solely the contest of parties that were virtually stripped of meaningful ideological divisions. "Politicians," as historian James Mohr put it, "were no longer prepared to stake their political careers...[on] sharply defined alternative programs to deal with large-scale industrialization and urbanization."[75] The presidential election that followed the 1872 revolt was among the most vigorously contested in American history, despite the fact that both candidates—Rutherford B. Hayes and Samuel Tilden—were Liberals in one fashion or another. Hayes supported retrenchment, hard money, and reconciliation with the South; Hayes's Republican Party would repeal the 1866 Southern Homestead Act to make reserves of public land available to lumber and mining interests. The Democrat Tilden, a wealthy railroad financier who emerged from the struggles in New York State against bossism, was an ally of the moneyed classes, railed against political corruption and misrule, and was devoted even more firmly to the return of local self-rule to the South.[76]

Within this much larger ideological transition, Greeley played, fundamentally, a small role. To many historians, he is virtually indistinguishable from the Liberals with which he allied in 1872 and the Liberal ideological consensus that seized the entirety of electoral politics thereafter. But truth be told, by the 1870s Greeley was an anachronism. His vision of small-producer capitalism made him equally plausible as a friend to labor and to business interests in both the Whig and Republican parties. But within a postwar political environment ever more divided by race and class, Greeley's brand of conservative radicalism was no longer sustainable. That his rhetoric managed to parallel the language of both Reconstruction labor and Liberal movements says something profound about how capacious the free-labor tradition turned out to be. Within the context of sectional and national struggle between two radically different social systems, the concept of free labor was flexible enough to organize the North's political culture, but with the return to "normalcy" in the 1870s its ambiguity made it less plausible. Reconstruction in the North and the South exposed the free-labor tradition and liberalism's many and often contradictory meanings, rendering obsolete the prewar Republican political coalition. Its breakdown, though, was part of a much larger dialogue within liberalism between social democrats and bourgeois individualists who conceptualized the nature of the market in radically different ways. This division within the liberal tradition remains with us today.

Horace Greeley's Lost Book

In September 1860, on the eve of the presidential election that would propel the country toward civil war, proslavery ideologue George Fitzhugh published "Horace Greeley and His Lost Book," an essay that argued that the ideological roots of Abraham Lincoln's Republican Party could be found in the 1846 debate between Horace Greeley and Henry Raymond. Though Raymond and Greeley were prominent national figures even in 1846, from the perspective of 1860 this discussion of socialism by the two editors seemed, in one respect, remote and rather sectarian: a "Lost Book" as Fitzhugh referred to it in his title. Yet for Fitzhugh, Greeley's vociferous 1846 defense of a socialist future also unlocked many of the political and social dilemmas of the period. To Fitzhugh and other apologists for Southern slavery, the issues raised by Northern socialists such as Greeley were at the heart of the conflict between the North and the South, and at times the basis of their own critique of Northern individualism. Fitzhugh even admitted a certain kinship with socialism. "We were much interested in" socialism, Fitzhugh remembered, and we "set about studying the subject seriously and profoundly and came to the conclusion that Mr. Greely [sic] was right—that society, such as surrounded him, was a failure . . . [and] that association of labor is the only remedy." But like many Southern firebrands, Fitzhugh also tried to link Republicanism with socialism and various other "agrarian, communistic, free-love, anarchical and leveling doctrines" in order to discredit it. Radical socialism, as Fitzhugh put it, was the foundation of "that Fire-Ship, the Chicago [1860 Republican] Platform," and "the great Republican Party" itself. To modern readers, Republicanism and socialism may very well make for an odd coupling. To most students of the nineteenth century, the rise of the Republican Party was intimately linked to the spread of free-market individualism and helped usher modern American industrial capitalism into existence. Yet Horace Greeley, who well before 1860 had established himself as antebellum America's most influential opponent of Northern individualism and unrestrained competitive capitalism, was also, in Fitzhugh's eyes and others, "the parent and originator of this great party."[77]

The formation of the Republican Party shifted the ground of American politics and political culture in any number of ways. The party was, in effect, like the *Tribune*: both conservative and radical. It was radical in the sense that it rejected compromise and viewed democratic politics as a thinly veiled struggle for power—a clash of civilizations. Its rise coincided with and was linked to the explosion of violence in Kansas and it operated within a political environment where the give-and-take of democratic politics had given way to a naked struggle for supremacy. The Republican Party also challenged, subtly but no less radically, absolutist conceptions of property rights—both in slaves and land—and, more broadly, committed the federal government to becoming, at least minimally, an agent of social welfare.[78] At the same time, the party had both implicit and explicit conservative elements. In an effort to forge a national majority, it was forced to reach beyond the reform elements—nativists, conservative business interests, and border state and Southern Whigs—of the existing parties. The constitutional structure of politics in the United States funnels political factions into broad partisan coalitions, and this impulse became even more exaggerated during the Civil

War era when the parties became explicitly sectional. So given its diverse origins, constituency, and motives, the Civil War–era Republican Party lacked a precise or unified ideology.[79]

The Civil War was rooted in a fundamental conflict between slavery and freedom; at bottom it was a struggle over the "organization of labor," to borrow the language of nineteenth-century socialists. Before the war, though, there was very little consensus in the North about what "free labor" actually meant. And once the war turned into a protracted and bloody struggle, the national question—the issues of secession, war, and reconstruction—became ever more immediate, and overwhelmed in the near term significant cleavages within the Republican Party on political economy and the nature of economic liberty. When the war ended, sectional pride and the larger constitutional issues surrounding Reconstruction remained potent forces in American politics, but the labor question also returned to the fore. Moreover, the death of slavery made it possible for the first time for Northerners to assess the consequences of the market revolution directly. At the heart of these battles in some cases was profound disagreement about the nature of the market, and it was a moving target.

The twentieth-century liberal achievement of the New Deal and the Great Society has inspired political and ideological genealogies that make the Democratic Party the central reservoir of popular resistance to the onset of market relationships.[80] There is little doubt on one level, particularly in the early stages of its formation, that the Democratic Party's denunciation of a "money power" was the basis of its appeal to Western farmers and urban workers whose lives were being unmoored by anonymous forces that threatened their propertied independence. But what is all too easy to ignore is that the form Jacksonian political resistance to the market took was nearly identical to the one taken up by conservative, postwar Republicans to defend capitalism against the organized opposition of labor. The Jacksonian answer to the market was a classically liberal vision of a virtually stateless society. Greeley would condemn this sentiment as the Democratic Party's penchant for "the negative, let-alone, do-nothing axioms of Free Trade Economists."[81]

Whig and Republican opposition to elements of the emerging market culture, in contrast, has been obscured by both the subsequent history of the latter party and by the ever shifting social and economic context.[82] The *Tribune*'s democratic producerism, for example, remained plausible in the 1850s, but by the 1870s the scale of the consolidated industrial economy made propertied self-reliance anachronistic. In a postbellum context, the sort of social mobility that Lincoln celebrated became primarily an ideological weapon, legitimating increasingly permanent forms of inequality. But in many respects what obscures the Republican Party's Civil War–era progressive achievement the most was the nebulousness and ideological fluidity of its own free-labor rhetoric.

Conventionally, "free labor" is associated narrowly with the ideology of the Republican Party, and broadly with the socioeconomic revolution that unfolded in the United States across the nineteenth century. Free-labor ideology was a partisan discourse, the unifying element behind both the Republican Party's and the North's resistance to Southern slavery and Southern rule. The original Republican campaign mantra, of course, was "free soil, free speech, free labor, and free men." But free labor also points to something larger that transcends political discourse. The rise of a free-labor social system was what brought about sectional divergence; it describes the rise in the North of a potent, market-based economy, with which liberalism has traditionally been associated.[83] Historians have rightly emphasized the importance of free-labor ideology because, along with the preservation of the union, it was what Northern soldiers principally fought and died for during the Civil War. But it has always been difficult to define what exactly Northerners and Republicans meant by "free labor." Historians' use of the concept has been as broad as its use by the original Republicans. The most important historical expositor of free-labor ideology, Eric Foner, wavers between a post-progressive conception of ideology as a "social outlook" or worldview, one drawn from cultural history and anthropology, and a more traditional understanding of ideology that emphasizes the way a set of ideas, social arrangements, laws, and predilections served particular economic interests. As a consequence, free-labor ideology becomes something that both organized the worldview of the entire North and legitimated the interests and values of a particular class within the North—namely the middle class, by naturalizing self-interest and the outcomes of market competition.[84] But what the history of the *Tribune* reveals is that this laissez-faire, purely contractual understanding of free labor had both its champions and its critics in the North and the South.

To many nineteenth-century Americans—proslavery ideologues, labor activists, and sentimental writers, to name a few—free labor's reliance on a set of temporary, specialized, and disposable relationships represented something radically new and dangerous. To others, the emergence of markets and even a labor marketplace was hardly revolutionary; instead, it seemed to be but a reflection of a "natural" order. The market rewarded hard work and facilitated individual self-improvement. The market's losers—the poor—were responsible for their own poverty. Any statist or collective response to social ills interfered illegitimately in the laws of the economy. Between these two poles were likely the vast majority of Americans who, not unlike the

Tribune, embraced social mobility and property, but defined the free-labor ideal, most importantly, as an economy in which every man could call himself his own master.

The free-labor idea, then, was capacious enough to account for nearly the entire range of Northern opinion on political economy; in the crisis atmosphere of the Civil War era, its ambiguity and its variety of meanings was a source of its political strength.[85] Free labor could mean, conservatively, the individual freedom to negotiate a contract for wages and, more radically, the emancipation of labor from the thralldom of wages. Emancipated or "free" labor could also legitimate labor-oriented reforms, such as free land, unions, cooperative organization, or other varieties of statist or nonstatist interventions in the economy and market relationships. That historians have elusively applied free-labor ideology simultaneously as both a regional and a class worldview is in the end remarkably apt.[86] It is a reflection of the concept's adaptability and, frankly, its amorphousness. But the crisis of Reconstruction brought the age of free labor to a close. Once Republicans seized control of state and national governments, they had to consider the meaning of freedom, equality, and citizenship, and there was robust disagreement even within the Radical wing of the party about the nature of work, property, and the market.[87]

Despite the Republican Party's reform origins, ultimately during the Civil War and after it faced an ideological dilemma that was almost circular. In its earliest days, Republicanism united the progressive factions of the existing parties, factions that were, in antebellum terms, antiracist and sympathetic to the problems of labor and social democracy. The Republicans were initially a reform party, and, not surprisingly, New York City's merchant elite backed either the Democrats or the alliance of conservative Whigs and Know-Nothings. Charles Dana's complaint—that "the rich men here, who used to give to the Whigs, are now for Fillmore and Buchanan"[88]—is suggestive of what Greeley termed the party's "progressive" nature. But the failure of the *Tribune* and the Republican Party to sustain its reform promise has a deeper historical cause. Though defenders of propertied individualism, reform Republicans were also firm believers in the labor theory of value and sought out a variety of positive liberal initiatives to foster upward mobility and propertied self-reliance.[89] As a socialist, Greeley went further than most. Nonetheless, the central dilemma that he and other public intellectuals who thought about the fate of workers under capitalism faced—just "how free" was wage labor and free contract in an age of increasing economic complexity?—became ever more pressing in the "new America" of the Gilded Age when American liberalism witnessed "the transformation of the majority of the citizenry into wage earners, the rise of the corporation as a new type of property, [and] the devastating fluctuations of the international market economy." On all of these questions, the *Tribune's* antebellum democratic producerism was found wanting. Greeley and like-minded reformers were never able to come up with a workable way to ensure the democratic extension of property and independence, or a satisfactory democratic alternative to traditional forms of economic autonomy.[90]

In the end, the *Tribune's* vision of free labor, its social democratic liberalism, and its search for harmonious solutions to profound social conflicts would amount to a linguistic and intellectual revolution, but it was one that would secure few practical achievements. Nevertheless, Greeley's critique of the reign of market values along with his sometimes modest solutions to them represented liberalism's midcentury movement toward one of its modern forms. Antebellum liberal socialists were among the most forceful voices proclaiming the hazards of the free market and the necessity of collective responses, be they state or cooperative, and they had their successors. Henry George, the Knights of Labor, and the farmers' alliances, although surrounded by communists and anarchists to their extreme left and orthodox, classical liberals to their right, sustained Greeley's vision of a capitalism dominated by self-governing producers. Even amid the more polarized ideological climate of the United States in the age of capital, they held fast to "ideals of economic independence and meaningful republican citizenship...[and] developed the cooperative and egalitarian ideals implicit in the antebellum vision of an equitable and harmonious market society and a republic of equal citizens, devoted to the public good."[91] Together with their antebellum predecessors, their critique of the inequities of capitalist disorganization laid the ground-work for later reformers who would call for state regulation of the market and for public works to ensure basic living standards. Despite his political and ideological failures, then, Greeley did advance what was a profound revolution. In the course of fighting for emancipation and the rights of labor, Greeley became a social democratic pioneer, calling forth a new kind of equality. It was a conceptual revolution to be sure, but it was one that challenged conventional understandings of America's most sacred vocabulary: liberty, equality, democracy, and property.

NOTES

Preface

1. Greeley has never really had what historian Daniel Walker Howe, in his seminal study of Whig political culture and thought, called a "satisfactory intellectual portrait." Though succinct, Howe's portrait of Greeley, more than any, does his complexity justice. Any study of Whig ideology and culture begins with his work. See Daniel Walker Howe, *The Political Culture of the American Whigs* (Chicago, 1979), 184–98. Greeley has been the subject of four major biographies, but all but one were published in the late 1940s and early 1950s. Biographical and institutional studies include William Harlan Hale, *Horace Greeley: Voice of the People* (New York, 1950); Glyndon G. Van Deusen, *Horace Greeley: Nineteenth-Century Crusader* (Philadelphia, 1953); Jeter Allen Isley, *Horace Greeley and the Republican Party, 1853–1861: A Study of the* New York Tribune (Princeton, 1947); Robert C. Williams, *Horace Greeley: Champion of Freedom* (New York, 2006); Richard Kluger, *The Paper: The Life and Death of the* New York Herald Tribune (New York, 1986). Interest in literary professionalism and the history of authorship has produced two magnificent works that make Greeley a central actor: Steven Fink, *Prophet in the Marketplace: Thoreau's Development as a Professional Writer* (Princeton, 1992); and Richard F. Teichgraeber, *Sublime Thoughts/Penny Wisdom: Situating Emerson and Thoreau in the American Market* (Baltimore, 1995). The recent profusion of books on Reconstruction and its failures have largely rendered Greeley as a conservative ideological villain by focusing entirely on his role in the 1872 Liberal Republican revolt. Examples include Heather Cox Richardson, *The Death of Reconstruction: Race, Labor, and Politics in the Post–Civil War North, 1865–1861* (Cambridge, Mass., 2001), 93–104; Eric Foner, *Reconstruction: America's Unfinished Revolution, 1863–1877* (New York, 1988), 488–511. Jonathan A. Glickstein, *American Exceptionalism, American Anxiety: Wages, Competition, and Degraded Labor in the Antebellum United States* (Charlottesville, 2002), 33–34, 97–114, grounds Greeley's perspective against wide-ranging antebellum political-economic discourse. My interpretation of Greeley is in sympathy with both Glickstein and John R. Commons, "Horace Greeley and the Working-Class Origins of the Republican Party," *Political Science Quarterly* 24 (1909): 468–88. They both claim that sizable portions of the major anti-Democratic parties, the Whigs and the Republicans, expressed profound reservations about elements of capitalist culture.

2. James Parton, *Life of Horace Greeley* (Boston, 1872), 169.

3. Hale, *Horace Greeley*, 91, see 91–107; William Harlan Hale, "When Karl Marx Worked for Horace Greeley," *American Heritage* 8 (April 1957): 20–25. See also Morten Borden, "Some Notes on Horace Greeley, Charles Dana, and Karl Marx," *Journalism Quarterly* 34 (Fall 1957): 457–65. In 1959, Borden also edited and published some of

the correspondence between Dana and Marx in Morten Borden, ed., "Five Letters of Charles A. Dana to Karl Marx," *Journalism Quarterly* 36 (Summer 1959): 314–16. See Henry Christman, ed., *The American Journalism of Marx and Engels: A Selection from the* New York Daily Tribune (New York, 1966), xx.

4. Sean Wilentz, *The Rise of American Democracy: Jefferson to Lincoln* (New York, 2005).

5. Michael F. Holt, *The Rise and Fall of the American Whig Party: Jacksonian Politics and the Onset of the Civil War* (New York, 1999).

6. *New-York Daily Tribune,* June 20, 1845; quoted in Bernard Mandel, *Labor, Free and Slave: Workingmen and the Anti-Slavery Movement in the United States* (New York, 1955), 87.

7. Adam-Max Tuchinsky, "'The Bourgeoisie Will Fall and Fall Forever': The *New-York Tribune,* the 1848 French Revolution, and the Evolution of Social Democratic Discourse in the United States," *Journal of American History* 92 (September 2005): 470–97; Copyright © Organization of American Historians; all rights reserved; reprinted with permission. Adam-Max Tuchinsky, "'Her Cause against Herself': Margaret Fuller, Emersonian Democracy, and the Nineteenth-Century Public Intellectual," *American Nineteenth Century History* 5 (Spring 2004): 66–99; reproduced with the permission of *American Nineteenth Century History* and Taylor & Francis, http://www.informaworld.com.

A People's Newspaper

1. W. E. B. Du Bois, *The Souls of Black Folk* (Boston, 1997), 45.

2. Edwin Lawrence Godkin, *Life and Letters of Edwin Lawrence Godkin,* vol. 2, ed. Rollo Ogden (New York, 1907), 167; James Ford Rhodes, "Newspapers as Historical Sources," *Atlantic Monthly* 103 (May 1909), 650; quoted in Isley, *Horace Greeley and the Republican Party,* 1, see 337–38 for the *Tribune's* circulation.

3. Robert Darnton, "The Great Book Massacre," *New York Review of Books* 48 (April 26, 2001), 18. For the centrality of newspapers to early nineteenth-century political culture, see Jeffrey L. Pasley, *"The Tyranny of Printers": Newspaper Politics in the Early American Republic* (Charlottesville, 2001).

4. For Greeley's early life, see Horace Greeley, *Autobiography: Recollections of a Busy Life* (New York, 1872), 17–82; Parton, *Life of Horace Greeley,* 1–83; Van Deusen, *Horace Greeley,* 1–14; Hale, *Horace Greeley,* 1–14.

5. Van Deusen, *Horace Greeley,* 26.

6. Greeley, *Recollections of a Busy Life,* 146–47.

7. Edwin G. Burrows and Mike Wallace, *Gotham: A History of New York City to 1898* (New York, 1999), 603–18.

8. Allan Nevins and Milton H. Thomas, eds., *The Diary of George Templeton Strong: Young Man in New York, 1835–1849,* vol. 1 (New York, 1952), 55–65; quoted in Charles Sellers, *The Market Revolution: Jacksonian America, 1815–1846* (New York, 1991), 355.

9. Van Deusen, *Horace Greeley,* 25–34.

10. Lee Benson, *The Concept of Jacksonian Democracy: New York as a Test Case* (Princeton, 1961), 11–46.

11. Greeley to Weed, February 19, 1841, *Passages From the Correspondence and Other Papers of Rufus W. Griswold* (Cambridge, Mass., 1898), 54.

12. For a coherent summary of these changes, see William L. Barney, *The Passage of the Republic: An Interdisciplinary History of Nineteenth-Century America* (Lexington, Mass.: D.C. Heath, 1987), 9–54. The idea of a "market revolution" as a way to understand nineteenth-century America became increasingly influential with the publication of Charles Sellers, *The Market Revolution*. See also Harry L. Watson, *Liberty and Power: The Politics of the Jacksonian Era* (New York, 1991); Sean Wilentz, "Society, Politics, and the Market Revolution," in *The New American History*, ed. Eric Foner (Philadelphia, 1990); Wilentz, *The Rise of American Democracy: Jefferson to Lincoln* (New York, 2005). For thoughtful considerations of the market's strengths and weaknesses as an explanatory paradigm, see Melvin Stokes and Stephen Conway, eds., *The Market Revolution in America* (Charlottesville, 1996). Daniel Walker Howe's recent synthesis decouples the "communication" and "market revolutions," denying that any substantive rupture occurred during the first half of the nineteenth century. Nonetheless, his work describes the dramatic changes that did take place in the antebellum period in the realms of family, work, social relationships, and self. See Howe, *What God Wrought: The Transformation of America* (New York, 2007), 5.

13. Most economic historians reject the notion of a market revolution entirely. They argue that markets, and market orientation, long preceded the nineteenth century. Some do concede, however, that the market's "development" and "growth," while not "revolutionary," did cross a threshold by the second quarter of the nineteenth century that might be termed "modern." See Stanley L. Engerman and Robert E. Gallman, "The Emergence of a Market Economy before 1860," in *A Companion to 19th Century America,* ed. William L. Barney (Malden, Mass., 2001), 121–38; Paul A. Gilje, "The Rise of Capitalism in the Early Republic," *Journal of the Early Republic* 16 (1996): 159–82.

14. I refer here to Benedict Anderson, *Imagined Communities: Reflections on the Spread of Nationalism* (New York, 1991), 61–65, which makes newspapers and more broadly print culture one of the foundations of national identity. For the movement of ideas, see Allan R. Pred, *Urban Growth and the Circulation of Information: The United States System of Cities, 1790–1840* (Cambridge, Mass., 1973), 20–77.

15. Van Deusen, *Horace Greeley,* 51.

16. Most recent (and not so recent) cultural history has tended to assume that high culture and antebellum reform were hostile to democratization, and that such hostility was a merely veiled attempt to reestablish the privilege and legitimacy of a ministerial intelligentsia displaced by the rise of a popular reading market. See Michael Denning, *Mechanic Accents: Dime Novels and Working-Class Culture in America* (London, 1987); David Reynolds, *Beneath the American Renaissance: The Subversive Imagination in the Age of Emerson and Melville* (New York, 1988). On "disconnected" intellectuals, see traditional studies such as Stanley M. Elkins, *Slavery: A Problem in American Institutional and Intellectual Life* (Chicago, 1959); Aileen S. Kraditor, *Means and Ends in American Abolitionism: Garrison and His Critics on Strategy and Tactics, 1834–1850* (New York, 1967); Arthur M. Schlesinger Jr., *The Age of Jackson* (Boston, 1945). On the politics of cultural hierarchy, see Peter Buckley, "To the Opera House: Culture and Society in New York City, 1820–1860," (PhD diss., State University of New

York at Stony Brook, 1984); Nathan Hatch, *The Democratization of American Christianity* (New Haven, 1989); John Kasson, *Rudeness and Civility: Manners in Nineteenth-Century Urban America* (New York, 1990); Lawrence Levine, *Highbrow/Lowbrow: The Emergence of Cultural Hierarchy in America* (Cambridge, Mass., 1988).

17. Since Carl Guarneri's grand study of American Fourierist socialism appeared in 1991, it should be difficult for historical accounts of the antebellum period not to address socialism's significance both as a theory and as a mass movement. Guarneri, though, ultimately concludes that despite Fourierism's radical promise as a social movement, it was too rooted in the liberal capitalist status quo to transform the society in any fundamental way. Its comprehensive critique of capitalist social relations during the 1840s was supplanted by the conservative limits of an antislavery crusade that implicitly defended a constellation of capitalist values: free contract, property, social mobility, and laissez-faire individualism. Carl J. Guarneri, *The Utopian Alternative: Fourierism in Nineteenth-Century America* (Ithaca, 1991). In a more recent essay, Guarneri argues more vehemently than in his original book-length treatment of Fourierism that the movement fell prey to the deepest strain of America's Utopian or perfectionist nationalism, which made socialism less an "alternative *to* them [conventional liberal defenses of private property and competitive individualism] than an alternative version *of* them" (emphasis in original). See Carl J. Guarneri, "Brook Farm, Fourierism, and the Nationalist Dilemma in American Utopianism," in *Transient and Permanent: The Transcendentalist Movement and Its Contexts,* ed. Charles Capper and Conrad Edick Wright (Boston, 1999), 461. Guarneri is hardly alone in the view that the antislavery movement, which crested in the 1850s, helped legitimate the triumph of capitalist liberalism. See also John Higham, *From Boundlessness to Consolidation: The Transformation of American Culture, 1848–1860* (Ann Arbor, 1969), 15–16, 17. For the relationship between antislavery, capitalist values, and antebellum labor movements, see Thomas Bender, ed., *The Antislavery Debate: Capitalism and Abolitionism as a Problem in Historical Interpretation* (Berkeley, 1992), 19; David Brion Davis, *Slavery and Human Progress* (New York, 1984), 109; Davis, *The Problem of Slavery in the Age of Revolution, 1770–1823* (Ithaca, 1975); Mandel, *Labor: Free and Slave;* Daniel J. McInerney, *The Fortunate Heirs of Freedom: Abolition and Republican Thought* (Lincoln, Nebr., 1994), 107–25; James L. Huston, *Calculating the Value of the Union: Slavery, Property Rights, and the Economic Origins of the Civil War* (Chapel Hill, 2003); Kraditor, *Means and Ends in American Abolitionism,* 235–73; Erie Foner, *Free Soil, Free Labor, Free Men: The Ideology of the Republican Party before the Civil War* (New York, 1970).

18. Karl Marx and Friedrich Engels, *The Communist Manifesto* (New York, 1967), 114–17; Marx to Engels, June 14, 1853, in *Collected Works* 39 (49 vols., New York, 1975–), 346.

19. Thomas Wentworth Higginson, *Margaret Fuller Ossoli* (Boston, 1884), 205.

20. See Sean Wilentz, *Chants Democratic: New York City and the Rise of the American Working Class* (New York, 1984); Leon Fink, *Workingmen's Democracy: The Knights of Labor and American Politics* (Urbana, 1983); David Montgomery, *Beyond Equality: Labor and the Radical Republicans, 1862–1872* (New York, 1967).

21. The most recent example of this perspective is Sean Wilentz's *Rise of American Democracy,* which in many respects reflects the classic account of the period, Arthur Schlesinger Jr., *Age of Jackson.*

22. Heather Cox Richardson, *The Greatest Nation of the Earth: Republican Economic Policies during the Civil War* (Cambridge, Mass., 1997).

23. Foner, *Free Soil Free Labor, Free Men*. Most of the major modern works that first argued for the existence of a "market revolution," defined primarily by the transformation of social relationships, argue further that it was resisted by the Jacksonian Democratic Party and welcomed by the Whigs and later by the Republicans. See Sellers, *Market Revolution;* Watson, *Liberty and Power;* Wilentz, *Rise of American Democracy.* Some more recent work has questioned this assumption. See Glickstein, *American Exceptionalism;* John Majewski, "A Revolution Too Many?" *Journal of Economic History* 57 (1997), 476–80; Stewart Winger, *Lincoln, Religion, and Romantic Cultural Politics* (De Kalb, Ill., 2003); Daniel Walker Howe, *Making the American Self: Jonathan Edwards to Abraham Lincoln* (Cambridge, Mass., 1997).

24. Roy P. Basler, ed., *The Collected Works of Abraham Lincoln,* vol. 3 (New Brunswick: Rutgers University Press, 1953), 478, 479.

25. The contemporary disconnect between conservative politicians and left-leaning academics on the meaning of liberalism stems from its historically dynamic character, especially within the context of the market revolution; see James T. Kloppenberg, *The Virtues of Liberalism* (New York, 1998), 8. For liberalism and individualism more generally, see C. B. Macpherson, *The Political Theory of Possessive Individualism: Hobbes to Locke* (New York, 1964); Nancy Cohen, *The Reconstruction of American Liberalism, 1865–1914* (Chapel Hill, 2002); and "Liberal Cultures and Their Critics: The Trials of Transatlantic Discourse," special issue of the *Intellectual History Newsletter* 24 (2002), 1–83.

26. See Adam-Max Tuchinsky, "'The Bourgeoisie Will Fall and Fall Forever': The *New-York Tribune,* the 1848 French Revolution, and the Evolution of Social Democratic Discourse in the United States," *Journal of American History* 92 (September 2005): 470–97. The classic historical portraits of "liberal America" are Louis Hartz, *The Liberal Tradition in America: An Interpretation of American Political Thought since the Revolution* (New York, 1955), and Carl Degler, *Out of Our Past: The Forces That Shaped Modern America* (New York, 1959). See Wilentz, *Chants Democratic,* 101, in which Wilentz paraphrases Degler's claim that "capitalism came in the first ships." See Degler, *Out of Our Past,* 1.

27. See the *New-York Weekly Tribune,* March 26, April 16, 30, 1842.

28. John Dewey, *Liberalism and Social Action* (New York, 2000). Most studies that posit an "evolving" liberal tradition in the United States consider the Gilded Age and the Progressive Era more central and emphasize to a greater degree technocratic reforms and statism. Though earlier social democrats, steeped as they were in the Whig tradition, imagined a role for the state in such areas as land policy, education, protection from foreign competition, and banking, few imagined anything so elaborate as a full-blown welfare state. See Cohen, *Reconstruction of American Liberalism;* R. Jeffery Lustig, *Corporate Liberalism: The Origins of Modern American Political Theory, 1890–1920* (Berkeley, 1982); Gillis J. Harp, *Positivist Republic: Auguste Comte and the Reconstruction of American Liberalism, 1865–1920* (University Park, Penn., 1995); Elizabeth Sanders, *Roots of Reform: Farmers, Workers, and the American State, 1877–1917* (Chicago, 1999); Martin J. Sklar, *The Corporate Reconstruction of American Capitalism, 1890–1916* (New York, 1988); Richard Schneirov, *Labor and Urban Politics: Class Conflict and the Origins of Modern Liberalism in Chicago, 1864–1897* (Urbana, 1998).

29. Kloppenberg, *Virtues of Liberalism,* 8. In many respects, this should not be surprising. Liberalism by definition is open, elastic, pragmatic, and resists precise classification; it, ideally, evades "ideology" as Daniel Bell understood the term: it rejects orthodoxy and fanaticism.

30. Ruth H. Bloch, "Utopianism, Sentimentalism, and Liberal Culture in America," *Intellectual History Newsletter* 24 (2002): 47.

31. Major works include Bernard Bailyn, *The Ideological Origins of the American Revolution* (Cambridge, Mass., 1967); Gordon S. Wood, *The Creation of the American Republic, 1776–1787* (New York, 1969); J. G. A. Pocock, *The Machiavellian Moment: Florentine Political Thought and the Atlantic Republican Tradition* (Princeton, 1975); Robert E. Shalhope, "Toward a Republican Synthesis: The Emergence of an Understanding of Republicanism in American Historiography," *William and Mary Quarterly* 29 (1972): 49–80.

32. Examples include Lance Banning, *The Jeffersonian Persuasion: Evolution of a Party Ideology* (Ithaca, 1978); Watson, *Liberty and Power;* Wilentz, *Chants Democratic;* Fink, *Workingmen's Democracy;* Joyce O. Appleby, *Capitalism and a New Social Order: The Republican Vision of the 1790s* (New York, 1984); Appleby, *Liberalism and Republicanism in the Historical Imagination* (Cambridge, Mass., 1992); and especially Daniel T. Rodgers, "Republicanism: The Career of a Concept," *Journal of American History* 79 (1992): 11–38. Other recent and important contributions to the history of liberalism are Howe, *Making the American Self;* Dorothy Ross, "Liberalism," in *Encyclopedia of American Political History: Studies of the Principal Movements and Ideas,* vol. 2, ed. Jack P. Greene (New York: Charles Scribner's Sons, 1984): 750–62; Ross, "Liberalism," in *A Companion to American Thought,* ed. Richard Wightman Fox and James T. Kloppenberg (Cambridge, Mass., 1995): 397–400; William J. Novak, *The People's Welfare: Law and Regulation in Nineteenth-Century America* (Chapel Hill, 1996); Howe, *Making the American Self,* 10–17.

33. Rodgers, "Republicanism," 11.

34. Bloch, "Utopianism, Sentimentalism, and Liberal Culture in America," 47; Dorothy Ross, "Liberalism and American Exceptionalism," *Intellectual History Newsletter* 24 (2002): 72–83. James Kloppenberg uses a much more precise definition of social democracy that distinguishes it from progressivism and frames it as a turn-of-the-century fusion and transformation of a diverse variety of Utopian, Marxist, and Christian socialist theory that repudiated ideology and revolution and devoted itself to the implementation of the welfare state. His focus on formal thought, a later period, and on Europe, where explicitly social democratic political parties appeared, are some of the factors that allow him to do so. Even so, he still describes it as "chameleonic," "eclectic," and with "obscure origins" and a "genetic proclivity to adaptation." See Kloppenberg, *Uncertain Victory,* 3–11. See also Eric Foner, *The Story of American Freedom* (New York, 1998), 3–28.

35. Benson, *Concept of Jacksonian Democracy,* see esp. 86–109, 329–38.

1. The Emancipation of Labor

1. Horace Greeley, *Hints Toward Reforms* (New York, 1850), 8.

2. For the above paragraphs on Fourier, see esp. Carl J. Guarneri, *Utopian Alternative;* Jonathan Beecher, *Charles Fourier: The Visionary and His World* (Berkeley, 1986);

Beecher, *Victor Considerant and the Rise and Fall of French Romantic Socialism* (Berkeley, 2001).

3. Walt Whitman, "New York Dissected, V. Street Yarn," in *New York Dissected,* ed. Emory Holloway and Ralph Adimari (New York, 1936), 129, quoted in Guarneri, *Utopian Alternative,* 25.

4. Guarneri, *Utopian Alternative,* 21–25; Robert B. Carlisle, *The Proffered Crown: Saint-Simonianism and the Doctrine of Hope* (Baltimore, 1987); Frank Manuel, *The New World of Henri Saint-Simon* (Cambridge, Mass., 1956).

5. Victor Considerant to Charles Fourier, January 5, 1832, quoted in Beecher, *Victor Considerant,* 45; see also 44–52.

6. Arthur Bestor, "Albert Brisbane—Propagandist for Socialism in the 1840s," *New York History* 28 (April 1947): 139.

7. See Redelia Brisbane, *Albert Brisbane: A Mental Biography* (Boston, 1893), 199–200; Guarneri, *Utopian Alternative,* 20–34.

8. See Bestor, "Albert Brisbane," 150–54.

9. *New-Yorker* 10 (October 17, 1840), 78; *New-Yorker* 10 (January 2, 1841), 250; *New-Yorker* 10 (January 16, 1841), 281.

10. Brisbane, *Mental Biography,* 206.

11. Guarneri, *Utopian Alternative,* 33.

12. The *Tribune's* direct impact on Fourierism's success in the United States is, of course, impossible to assess. The rapidity of socialism's spread is suggestively rendered in Bestor, "Albert Brisbane," 128–30. My information on Brisbane derives primarily from the above article, Guarneri's *The Utopian Alternative,* 25–34, and Brisbane's occasionally unreliable autobiography, *Mental Biography.* Other general histories of pre-Marxist secular socialism in America include Arthur Bestor, *Backwoods Utopias: The Sectarian Origins and the Owenite Phase of Communitarian Socialism in America: 1663–1829* (Philadelphia, 1970); T. D. Seymour Bassett, "The Secular Utopian Socialists," in *Socialism and American Life,* vol. 1, ed. Donald Drew Egbert and Stow Persons (Princeton, 1952), 155–211; Michael Fellman, *The Unbounded Frame: Freedom and Community in Nineteenth-Century American Utopianism* (Westport, Conn., 1973); and Charles Sotheran, *Horace Greeley and Other Pioneers of American Socialism* (New York, 1915).

13. Guarneri, *Utopian Alternative,* 60.

14. Guarneri, *Utopian Alternative,* 4–11.

15. Their goal was to "adapt" Fourierist theory to "popular understanding in as great a degree as possible," *New-York Weekly Tribune,* April 15, 1843.

16. See Brisbane, *Albert Brisbane: A Mental Biography,* 194–95; Parke Godwin, *A Popular View of the Doctrines of Charles Fourier* (New York, 1844; reprint, Philadelphia, 1972), 74; and Godwin to Dana, September 17, 1844, Bryant-Godwin Papers, NYPL. For an overview, see Guarneri, *Utopian Alternative,* 93–98.

17. See *New-York Weekly Tribune,* April 16, 1842; Albert Brisbane, *Association; or, A Concise Exposition of the Practical Part of Fourier's Social Science* (New York, 1843), 7, 12–14. For Greeley's environmentalism, see Greeley, *Recollections,* 299–301.

18. Emerson argued both that socialism was *over*-theorized, ignorant of the basic constraints of human nature, and *under*-radicalized, merely an account of economy and society's movement toward greater degrees of collectivity. He wrote in the *Dial,* for example, that Fourier "skipped no fact but one, namely life." Ralph Waldo Emerson, "Fourier and the Socialists," *Dial* 3 (July 1842): 88–89; see also *Journals and*

Miscellaneous Notebooks of Ralph Waldo Emerson, vol. 9, ed. William Gilman et al., November 12, 1843, 54–55. See also Emerson, "Historic Notes of Life and Letters in New England," *The Works of Ralph Waldo Emerson: Lectures and Biographical Sketches,* vol. 10 (Boston, 1883), 327–47. Carl J. Guarneri, especially in his article "Brook Farm, Fourierism, and the Nationalist Dilemma in American Utopianism," in *Transient and Permanent: The Transcendentalist Movement and Its Contexts,* ed. Charles Capper and Conrad Edick Wright (Boston, 1999), 447–70, takes this view, repudiating to some extent his assertion in the *Utopian Alternative* that Fourierist socialism was the political-economic "road-not-taken."

19. *New-York Weekly Tribune,* June 18, 1842.

20. Ibid., June 24, 1843. See also January 29, 1842, for a sympathetic account of Orestes Brownson's Clinton Hall lecture on the "influence of Property on Civilization"; Brisbane, *Association,* 30–38; Parke Godwin, *Democracy, Constructive and Pacific* (New York, 1844), 20.

21. *New-York Weekly Tribune,* July 9, 1842.

22. Ibid., March 26, 1842.

23. Ibid., May 14, July 2, May 7, 1842; see also April 9, June 25, 1842.

24. *New-York Daily Tribune,* October 14, 1845.

25. Brisbane, *Association,* 4. See *New-York Weekly Tribune,* March 26, 1842.

26. *New-York Weekly Tribune,* March 5, 1842.

27. Brisbane, *Association,* 6.

28. *New-York Weekly Tribune,* April 12, 1845. On Association and class, see also April 2, May 7, June 11, August 30, 1842; Brisbane, *Association,* 28.

29. To James Huston, the Associationists were the pinnacle of radical political economy in the nineteenth century: "Not only did they reject almost every philosophical argument of classical economics, but they also attacked many of the economic tenets of republicanism, the American proclivity to explain all events in political terms." See James L. Huston, *Securing the Fruits of Labor: The American Concept of Wealth Distribution, 1765–1900* (Baton Rouge, 1998), 273, 278, on socialism generally, 272–78. For older works that emphasize the conservatism of Association, see Whitney R. Cross, *The Burned-Over District: The Social and Intellectual History of Enthusiastic Religion in Western New York, 1800–1850* (Ithaca, 1950); Schlesinger, *Age of Jackson;* Norman Ware, *The Industrial Worker, 1840–1860: The Reaction of American Industrial Society to the Advance of the Industrial Revolution* (Boston, 1924; reprint, Chicago, 1964); and to some extent, Henry E. Hoagland, "Humanitarianism," in *History of Labour in the United States,* vol. 1 (New York, 1921), 496–506.

30. Brisbane, *Association,* 3.

31. *New-York Weekly Tribune,* February 1, 1845; see also April 23, 1842.

32. Brisbane, *Association,* 7. On the national question, see also *New-York Weekly Tribune,* April 23, May 7, June 11, 1842; Guarneri, *Utopian Alternative,* 98–99; Sacvan Bercovitch, *The American Jeremiad* (Madison, 1978); Bercovitch, *The Rites of Assent: Transformations in the Symbolic Construction of America* (New York, 1993).

33. Horace Greeley, "Emancipation of Labor," in *Hints Toward Reforms,* 42.

34. Brisbane, *Mental Biography,* 71, 67–68, 190–91, 205.

35. *New-York Weekly Tribune,* April 23, 1842.

36. Association's antipolitical rhetoric was also hardly idiosyncratic. See Ronald P. Formisano, "The 'Party Period' Revisited," and Mark Voss-Hubbard, "The 'Third

Party Tradition' Reconsidered: Third Parties and American Public Life, 1830–1900,"
Journal of American History 86 (June 1999): 93–120, 121–50; Stephen Skowronek,
Building a New American State: The Expansion of National Administrative Capacities,
1877–1920 (New York, 1982), 24–52; John Ashworth, *"Agrarians" & Aristocrats":*
Party Ideology in the United States, 1837–1846 (London, 1983), 205–14. On Whig
antipolitics, see Howe, *Political Culture of American Whigs* (Chicago, 1979), 52–54,
157–59; Richard P. McCormick, *The Second American Party System: Party Formation*
in the Jacksonian Era (Chapel Hill, 1966), 282–93; Holt, *Rise and Fall of the American*
Whig Party, 30–32.

37. *New-York Weekly Tribune,* April 30, 1842.

38. *New-York Daily Tribune,* July 28, 1845.

39. John Ashworth is typical in claiming that Greeley's "ideology and politics
were out of alignment." Sympathetic to the "need for fundamental reforms," he
was never able to completely harmonize his indictment of industrial equality to his
"Whiggery." "The result," Ashworth concludes, "was not so much a synthesis as an
amalgam of opinions, and one which belonged to Greeley alone." See Ashworth,
"Agrarians & Aristocrats," 159, 156, and 151–70. See also Guarneri, *Utopian Alterna-*
tive, 93–120.

40. See Schlesinger, *Age of Jackson,* 361, 363, 364, and generally 361–68; Ashworth, *"Agrarians & Aristocrats,"* 157, 154–60; Watson, *Liberty and Power;* Wilentz, *Rise*
of American Democracy; Lawrence Frederick Kohl, *The Politics of Individualism: Parties*
and the American Character in the Jacksonian Era (New York, 1989); Sellers, *Market*
Revolution; and Huston, *Securing the Fruits,* 219–58.

41. Godwin, *Democracy,* 24.

42. Howe, *Political Culture of the American Whigs;* Benson, *The Concept of Jacksonian*
Democracy, 86–109; Gerald N. Izenberg, *Impossible Individuality: Romanticism, Revolu-*
tion, and the Origins of Modern Selfhood, 1787–1802 (Princeton, 1992).

43. *New-York Weekly Tribune,* October 22, 1842.

44. Beecher, *Victor Considerant,* 2.

45. Huston, *Securing the Fruits of Labor,* 23, see also 69–75; David Joseph Voelker,
"Orestes Brownson and the Search for Authority in Democratic America" (PhD
diss., University of North Carolina, Chapel Hill, 2003).

46. Greeley hailed him as "the keenest observer and among the deepest thinkers
of our time." Greeley to O. A. Bowe, May 16, 1843, Horace Greeley Papers, New
York Public Library; quoted Van Deusen, *Horace Greeley,* 61. *New-York Daily Tribune,*
May 12, 16, 1843, December 16, 1847.

47. Raymond Williams discusses the transformation of the Western social vocabulary in *Culture and Society, 1780–1950* (New York, 1983), xiii–xx.

48. Albert Brisbane, *Social Destiny of Man; or, Association and Reorganization of*
Industry (Philadelphia, 1840); see also, Guarneri, *Utopian Alternative,* 99, 104; Yehoshua
Arieli, *Individualism and Nationalism in American Ideology* (Cambridge, Mass, 1964),
183–245; Kohl, *Politics of Individualism;* Izenberg, *Impossible Individuality.*

49. *New-York Weekly Tribune,* May 7, 1842.

50. Howe, *Political Culture,* 3.

51. Howe, *Political Culture,* 29.

52. William Ellery Channing, *Works,* vol. 2 (Boston, 1849), 368.

53. *Log Cabin,* May 9, 16, 23, 30; cited in Howe, *Political Culture,* 187.

54. Channing, "Lectures on the Elevation of the Laboring Portion of the Community," *Works* 5, 154, 157. For an account that questions the sincerity of reform Whigs, see Wilentz, *Rise of American Democracy,* 482–518.

55. Channing, "Lectures," 160.

56. Greeley, "Relations of Learning to Labor," *Hints Toward Reforms,* 114, 116.

57. On work and its rewards in the nineteenth century, see Glickstein, *American Exceptionalism, American Anxiety,* 31–59.

58. On Raymond, see Paul K. Conkin, *Prophets of Prosperity: America's First Political Economists* (Bloomington, 1980), 77–107; Charles Patrick Neill, "Daniel Raymond: An Early Chapter in the History of Economic Thought," *Johns Hopkins Studies in Historical and Political Science,* series 15, no. 6 (Baltimore, 1897): 218–73; Joseph Dorfman, *The Economic Mind in American Civilization,* vol. 2 (New York, 1966), 566–74, 771–74; Allen Kaufman, *Capitalism, Slavery, and Republican Values: Antebellum Political Economists, 1819–1848* (Austin, 1982), 37–81.

59. *Harbinger* 6 (January 26, 1848), 100; see also January 15, 1848. For Carey, see Conkin, *Prophets of Prosperity,* 261–307; Wilentz, *Rise of American Democracy,* 488–90; Howe, *Political Culture,* 108–22.

60. Guarneri, *Utopian Alternative,* 37, for Greeley's Whig Associationism, see 36–39.

61. For surveys of American political economy from the Early Republic through the Age of Jackson, see Conkin, *Prophets of Prosperity;* Drew R. McCoy, *The Elusive Republic: Political Economy in Jeffersonian America* (New York, 1980); Dorfman, *Economic Mind in American Civilization,* vol. 2; Huston, *Securing the Fruits of Labor;* Stanley Elkins and Eric McKitrick, *Age of Federalism: The Early American Republic, 1788–1800* (New York, 1993), esp. 77–131, 257–302; Kaufman, *Capitalism, Slavery, and Republican Values.*

62. Commons, "Horace Greeley and the Working Class Origins of the Republican Party," 471.

63. See Huston, *Securing the Fruits of Labor:* on the political economy of aristocracy, see xiii–xiv, 29–58; on "Dissenters," see 259–95; Timothy Messer-Kruse, *The Yankee International: Marxism and the American Reform Tradition, 1848–1876* (Chapel Hill, 1998), 6–44.

64. See, for example, [Anonymous review], "Social Destiny of Man," *United States and Democratic Review* 8 (November 8, 1840), 448–49; "The Laboring Classes," *Boston Quarterly Review* 3 (July 1840): 358–95. Godwin, *A Popular View,* 3–12.

65. Griswold, *Passages From the Correspondence,* 54–55.

66. *New-York Weekly Tribune,* 1 January 1842.

67. Ibid., July 30, 1842.

68. The Anti-Rent rebellion and the land reform movement more generally are the subjects of chapter 5.

69. See Charles W. McCurdy, *The Anti-Rent Era in New York Law and Politics* (Chapel Hill, 2001).

70. See *New-York Daily Tribune,* August 6, 5, 1845; see also *New-York Weekly Tribune,* August 23, 30, 1845.

71. The "Loco Focos" were a New York City Democratic Party faction that broke with the regular party when it betrayed a promise to working-class radicals to block the proliferation of state banks. Whigs used the term "loco foco" as a blanket

term of aspersion for all Democrats, much as Democrats, during Reconstruction, would refer to all Republicans as "Radicals."

72. *New-York Daily Tribune,* August 5, September 5, 1845. See also "The Assaults of the New York Express," *Harbinger* 1 (August 30, 1845), 189–91; Greeley to Colfax, September 23, 1845, Horace Greeley Papers, New York Public Library; see also Greeley to Thurlow Weed, January 22, 1846, Horace Greeley Papers, New-York Historical Society.

73. Parton, *Life of Horace Greeley,* 171; Guarneri, *Utopian Alternative,* 276, see also 275–76; Glickstein, *American Exceptionalism, American Anxiety,* 33–34.

74. Holt, *Rise and Fall of the American Whig Party,* 238–43.

75. Greeley to O. A. Bowe, January 21, 1840, Horace Greeley Papers, New York Public Library.

76. See James L. Crouthamel, *James Watson Webb: A Biography* (Middletown, Conn., 1969), 3–109.

77. For the early years of the Greeley-Raymond relationship see Francis Brown, *Raymond of the Times* (New York, 1951), 13–42; some of the correspondence between Greeley, Raymond, and Rufus Griswold has been published in *Passages From the Correspondence and Other Papers of Rufus W. Griswold;* John J. Duffy, ed., *Coleridge's American Disciples: The Selected Correspondence of James Marsh* (Amherst, Mass., 1973), 244–48, 254–57; see also Henry J. Raymond Miscellaneous Manuscripts, New-York Historical Society; Henry J. Raymond Papers, New York Public Library; Horace Greeley Papers, New York Public Library; Horace Greeley Collection, Library of Congress.

78. Raymond to James Marsh, January 14, 1841, published in Duffy, *Coleridge's American Disciples,* 245.

79. "Ultra-Federalism," in Greeley to Griswold, January 15, 1841, Horace Greeley Collection, Library of Congress. Greeley believed that journals ought to be open to competing points of view, but also attached themselves to "some distinct interest, not noisily, but in such a manner as to secure its support," Greeley to Raymond, June 20, 1840, Raymond Papers, New York Public Library. "Infernally Tory" and "sympathies of the true democracy" quoted in Brown, *Raymond of the Times,* 24, 41, for Raymond's career up to the Civil War, see 3–198. See also Augustus Maverick's *Henry J. Raymond and the New York Press for Thirty Years: Progress of American Journalism From 1840–1870* (Hartford, Conn., 1870) for a biased but firsthand account of Raymond's life.

80. Brown, *Raymond of the Times,* 41; Crouthamel, *James Watson Webb,* 87.

81. *New-York Weekly Tribune,* October 21, 1843; *Courier,* December 16, 1843.

82. Guarneri, *Utopian Alternative,* 274–75; Godwin to Dana, August 12, 1846, Dana to Godwin, August 18, 1846, Bryant-Godwin Papers, New York Public Library. In view of the upcoming discussion between Greeley and Raymond, both Godwin and Dana worried that the *Tribune* editor "plays coward on this question of marriage." See also Godwin to Dana, undated, Bryant-Godwin Papers, New York Public Library.

83. Godwin to Dana, August 12, 1846, Bryant-Godwin Papers, New York Public Library.

84. *New-York Daily Tribune,* September 8, 10, 1846. For discussion of the terms of the debate, see the above and November, 12, 16, 18, 1846; *Courier,* September, 7, 9, November 10, 12, 14, 17, 1846.

85. *New-York Daily Tribune,* November 20, 1846.

86. On the antebellum debate over the sources of property rights, see Huston, *Calculating the Value of the Union.*

87. Niles and Barlow quoted in Jeffrey Sklansky, *The Soul's Economy: Market Society and Selfhood in American Thought, 1820–1920* (Chapel Hill, 2002), 26, 27, see also 22–31.

88. Conkin, *Prophets of Prosperity,* esp. 30–34.

89. *New-York Daily Tribune,* November 20, 1846.

90. Ibid., November 20, 1846; see also December 1, 1846.

91. Ibid., November 26, 1846.

92. *Courier,* November 23, 1846.

93. *Courier,* November 23, 1846.

94. *Courier,* November 30, 1846.

95. *New-York Daily Tribune,* December 8, 1846. See also December 16, 1846.

96. *Courier,* December 8, 1846.

97. *New-York Daily Tribune,* December 28, 1846.

98. Raymond here echoed the sentiments of his religious and philosophical mentor, James Marsh, of the University of Vermont. In 1841, Marsh wrote Raymond: "Every scheme of social existence that does not assume the principles of self-seeking, as giving law practically to the conduct of men in their intercourse with each other, and form its arrangements on that assumption, will and must fail. . . . Now it is the business of the Christian philanthropist to aim at ends which require men to overcome and rise above that principle, but he must provide for its being overcome. . . . These reformers, on the other hand, hope to redeem the world by a sort of dilettanti process, to purge off its grossness, to make a poetical paradise in which hard work shall become easy, dirty things clean, the selfish liberal, and the churl a churl no longer," Marsh to Raymond, March 1, 1841, published in Duffy, *Coleridge's American Disciples,* 255.

99. Greeley, on the other hand, participated in an environmentalist revolution in American reform that was a broad product of the Enlightenment and a signature element of 1830s labor movements. See Edward Pessen, *Most Uncommon Jacksonians: The Radical Leaders of the Early Labor Movement* (Albany, 1967), 103–44; Iver Bernstein, *The New York City Draft Riots: Their Significance for American Society and Politics in the Age of the Civil War* (New York, 1990), 162–90; Christine Stansell, *City of Women: Sex and Class in New York* (Urbana, 1987), 200, 202, 208, 215; Carroll Smith Rosenberg, *Religion and the Rise of the American City: The New York City Mission Movement, 1812–1870* (Ithaca, 1971); Paul S. Boyer, *Urban Masses and Moral Order in America, 1820–1920* (Cambridge, Mass., 1978).

100. Huston, *Calculating the Value.*

101. *Courier,* December 24, 1846. "Orthodox" Fourierists argued that "the Passions . . . are forces which cannot be suppressed or annihilated, but merely directed." Brisbane wrote in the *Tribune* that "either the Passions—those springs of action, those impelling powers within us—*are bad,* or the social mechanism *is false;* for evil prevails, and to a melancholy extent." "If the former be true," Brisbane continued, "then there is no hope for a better state of things; for every means of repression and constraint that human ingenuity could invent has been applied to regulate their action, but all in vain; they have remained unchanged. . . . If, however, the latter be true—that is, if the social mechanism be false—then there is a chance of a better future." *New-York Weekly*

Tribune, August 20, 1842. See also *New-York Weekly Tribune,* September 9, 1842. For a broader discussion of antebellum political economy and the question of incentive, see Glickstein, *American Exceptionalism, American Anxiety,* 31–96.

102. Ann C. Rose, *Transcendentalism as a Social Movement, 1830–1850* (New Haven, 1981), 142.

103. *Courier,* January 6, 1847.

104. *Courier,* February 10, 1847.

105. Raymond quoted from Brisbane's *Social Destiny of Man,* in which he argues that the care of infants and toddlers ought to be left to professional nurses. A warehouse filled with children, according to Brisbane, would inculcate social instincts, and its efficiency would release women to more "productive" and public labor. Brisbane imagined that even "the cradles are moved by a mechanical contrivance, so that twenty can be rocked at once." Brisbane, *Social Destiny of Man,* 398–99. *Courier,* January 6, 1847; see also January 20, 1847.

106. *Courier,* March 5, 1847. Raymond critiques the "moralities" of Association more comprehensively in his March 19, 1847, letter.

107. *Courier,* March 5, 1847.

108. *Courier,* April 16, 1847.

109. *New-York Daily Tribune,* March 12, 1847.

110. Ibid., March 26, 1847.

111. Brisbane, *Social Destiny,* 18. Norma Basch, *Framing American Divorce: From the Revolutionary Generation to the Victorians* (Berkeley, 1999), 80–90.

112. Association's mixture of passional theory and environmentalism makes socialism somewhat ambivalent on the "woman question." On the one hand, Associationists believed that aptitudes and talents were biological. On the other hand, Associationists also maintained that law, custom, and institutions—education, labor, and systems of labor—configured the attractions and shaped human personality. As a consequence, Associationists argued both that isolated households underdeveloped women's talents yet they were still confident about the essentiality of sexual types. See *New-York Weekly Tribune,* December 31, 1842.

113. *New-York Daily Tribune,* January 13, 1847.

114. Raymond accepted a stratified society as the natural result of complexity and merit: "We believe Social Equality to be as undesirable, as it is impossible,—holding, rather, with Plato and Aristotle, that a true Society requires a *union* of unequal interests, mutually sustaining and aiding each other, and not an aggregation of identical elements." See *Courier,* May 20, 1847 (82–83).

115. Parton, *Life of Horace Greeley,* 205.

2. Transcendental Cultural Democracy

1. Important interpretations and biographical treatments of Margaret Fuller include Margaret Fuller, *Woman in the Nineteenth Century: An Authoritative Text, Backgrounds, and Criticism,* ed. Larry J. Reynolds (New York, 1998); Larry Reynolds, "From *Dial* Essay to New York Book: The Making of *Woman in the Nineteenth Century,*" in *Periodical Literature in Nineteenth-Century America,* ed. Kenneth M. Price and Susan Belasco Smith (Charlottesville, 1995); Margaret V. Allen, "The Political and Social Criticism of Margaret Fuller," *South Atlantic Quarterly* 72 (Autumn 1973):

560–73; Bell Gale Chevigny, *The Woman and the Myth: Margaret Fuller's Life and Writings* (Boston, 1994); Paula Blanchard, *Margaret Fuller: From Transcendentalism to Revolution* (New York, 1978); Madeline B. Stern, *The Life of Margaret Fuller* (New York, 1942), 336–75; Julie Ellison, *Delicate Subjects: Romanticism, Gender, and the Ethics of Understanding* (Ithaca, 1990); Christina Zwarg, *Feminist Conversations: Fuller, Emerson, and the Play of Reading* (Ithaca, 1995), 189–220, 203–5; Howe, *Making the American Self,* 214–34; and esp. Charles Capper, *Margaret Fuller: An American Romantic Life, The Private Years* (New York, 1992); Capper, *Margaret Fuller: An American Romantic Life, the Public Years* (New York, 2007). Two fine editions of Fuller's *Tribune* writings have recently been published. Fuller's complete New York writings are collected in Judith Mattson Bean and Joel Myerson, eds., *Margaret Fuller, Critic: Writings from the New-York Tribune, 1844–1846* (New York, 2000). Fuller's European correspondence has been collected in Larry J. Reynolds and Susan Belasco Smith, eds., *"These Sad But Glorious Days": Dispatches from Europe, 1846–1850* (New Haven, 1991).

2. Greeley, *Hints Toward Reforms,* 86.

3. Teichgraeber, *Sublime Thoughts/Penny Wisdom,* 211, for Thoreau, see 255–60. See also Joel Myerson, *The New England Transcendentalists and the "Dial"* (Rutherford, N.J., 1980); Fink, *Prophet in the Marketplace.* For the relationship of *Tribune* publicity and criticism to the antebellum lyceum movement, see Robert A. Gross, "Printing, Politics, and the People," *Proceedings of the American Antiquarian Society* 99 (October 1989): 375–97; David Mead, *Yankee Eloquence in the Middle West: The Ohio Lyceum, 1850–1870* (East Lansing, Mich., 1951); Donald Scott, "The Popular Lecture and the Creation of a Public in Mid-Nineteenth-Century America," *Journal of American History* 66 (March 1980): 791–809; Donald Scott, "Print and the Public Lecture System," in *Printing and Society in Early America,* ed. William L. Joyce, David D. Hall, Richard D. Brown, and John Hench (Worcester, Mass., 1983), 278–99.

4. Greeley, *Recollections,* 176.

5. Capper, *Margaret Fuller,* 2:165–68; Fink, *Margaret Fuller,* 66; Ralph Waldo Emerson, W. H. Channing, and J. F. Clarke, eds., *Memoirs of Margaret Fuller Ossoli,* vol. 2 (Boston, 1851), 152; *Letters of Margaret Fuller,* 3:228, 230. On the Conversations, see Charles Capper, "Margaret Fuller as Cultural Reformer: The Conversations in Boston," *American Quarterly* 39 (Winter 1987): 509–28; Capper, *Margaret Fuller,* 290–306. Larry Reynolds, "From *Dial* Essay to New York Book," 25–30, pays close attention to Fuller's attempts to move between high and popular literary forms, and her more general efforts to come to terms with a mass audience.

6. *Letters of Margaret Fuller,* 4:40; *Letters of Margaret Fuller,* 3:196.

7. Joseph Slater, ed., *The Correspondence of Emerson and Carlyle* (New York, 1964), 498; William Gilman et al., eds., *Journals and Miscellaneous Notebooks of Ralph Waldo Emerson* (Cambridge, Mass., 1960–82), 7:76; Ralph L. Rusk and Eleanor Tilton, eds., *Letters of Ralph Waldo Emerson* (New York, 1939–), 7:618. See Robert Rutland, *The Newsmongers: Journalism in the Life of the Nation* (New York, 1973), 166.

8. *Letters of Margaret Fuller,* 3:196; *Letters of Margaret Fuller,* 4:39.

9. *Letters of Ralph Waldo Emerson,* 3:19–20.

10. *Passages From the Correspondence and Other Papers of Rufus W. Griswold* (Cambridge, Mass., 1898), 142, 163, 166, 204; Greeley, *Recollections,* 171.

11. *Letters of Margaret Fuller,* 3:256; *Letters of Margaret Fuller,* 4:40.

12. See *New-York Daily Tribune,* August 6, 5, 1845; *New-York Weekly Tribune,* February 4, 1843.

13. Peter S. Field, *Ralph Waldo Emerson: The Making of a Democratic Intellectual* (Lanham, Md., 2002), 29, see also 11–35.

14. [Theodore Parker], "Hollis Street Council," *Dial* 3, 215. A. W. Plumstead and Harrison Hayford, eds., *The Journals and Miscellaneous Notebooks of Ralph Waldo Emerson, 1838–1842,* vol. 7 (Cambridge, Mass., 1971), April 23, 1841, 434. See Ann Douglas, *The Feminization of American Culture* (New York, 1977); Peter S. Field, *The Crisis of the Standing Order: Clerical Intellectuals and Cultural Authority in Massachusetts, 1780–1833* (Amherst, Mass., 1998); Hatch, *Democratization of American Christianity*); William R. Hutchison, *The Transcendental Ministers: Church Reform in the New England Renaissance* (New Haven, 1959); Rose, *Transcendentalism as a Social Movement;* Darren Marcus Staloff, *The Making of an American Thinking Class: Intellectuals and Intelligentsia in Puritan Massachusetts* (New York, 1998); Gilman M. Ostrander, *Republic of Letters: The American Intellectual Community, 1776–1865* (Madison, 1999). The "conflict" between "orthodox" Unitarianism and its Transcendental critics involved more than the "narcissism of minor differences," but two major works demonstrate the way in which the Transcendental movement grew organically from its Unitarian ancestor: Daniel Walker Howe, *The Unitarian Conscience: Harvard Moral Philosophy, 1805–1861* (Cambridge, Mass., 1970); David Robinson, *Apostle of Culture: Emerson as Preacher and Lecturer* (Philadelphia, 1982). Two important histories of Transcendentalism have recently been published, Philip F. Gura, *American Transcendentalism: A History* (New York, 2007), and Barbara L. Packer, *The Transcendentalists* (Athens, Ga., 2007).

15. Ralph Waldo Emerson, "The Divinity School Address," *Selections from Ralph Waldo Emerson: An Organic Anthology,* ed. Stephen Whicher (Boston, 1957), 112.

16. Robert D. Richardson Jr., *Emerson: The Mind on Fire* (Berkeley, 1995), 265. See also Field, *Ralph Waldo Emerson,* 3–5, 209–27. For a definition of the concept, see Michael Walzer, *The Company of Critics: Social Criticism and Political Commitment in the Twentieth Century* (New York, 1988); Michael Walzer, *Interpretation and Social Criticism* (Cambridge, Mass., 1987); Leon Fink, Stephen T. Leonard, and Donald M. Reid, eds., *Intellectuals and Public Life: Between Radicalism and Reform* (Ithaca, 1996). See also Kenneth S. Sacks, *Understanding Emerson: The "American Scholar" and His Struggle for Self Reliance* (Princeton, 2003).

17. Ralph Waldo Emerson, "American Scholar," in *Collected Works of Ralph Waldo Emerson: Nature, Addresses, and Lectures,* ed. Robert E. Spiller and Alfred R. Ferguson (Cambridge, Mass., 1971), 1:62, 67, 63; Emerson, "Man the Reformer," *Collected Works,* 1, 150, 158–59. On Emerson's vocational crisis, see esp. Field, *Ralph Waldo Emerson,* 59–166.

18. Perry Miller, ed., *The Transcendentalists: An Anthology* (Cambridge, Mass., 1950), 464.

19. Ripley to Emerson, November 9, 1840, quoted in Octavius Brooks Frothingham, *George Ripley* (Boston, 1882), 307–8.

20. As Richard Francis points out, Transcendental studies have unwisely imposed a "false dichotomy" on the movement that unnaturally opposes "inward mysticism" to "utopian socialist" reform. Instead, the "central doctrine" of Transcendentalism, Francis points out, was the serial connectedness of spiritual and material matter, that natural facts are signs of spiritual facts. So even if Emerson and the Brook Farmers disagreed on means and method—Emerson said it seemed "circuitous... to put on your community the task of my emancipation which I ought to take on myself"—they shared similar ends. Richard Francis, *Transcendental Utopias: Individual*

and Community at Brook Farm, Fruitlands, and Walden (Ithaca, 1997), ix–xi, 42–43; *Letters of Ralph Waldo Emerson,* 2:369.

21. See Rose, *Transcendentalism as a Social Movement,* 130; Guarneri, *Utopian Alternative,* 46; Sterling F. Delano, *Brook Farm: The Dark Side of Utopia* (Cambridge, Mass., 2004); Adam-Max Tuchinsky, ' "Her Cause Against Herself": Margaret Fuller, Emersonian Democracy, and the Nineteenth-Century Public Intellectual," *American Nineteenth Century History* 5 (Spring 2004): 66–99. For Fuller's partial practical and ideological resistance to Brook Farm, see Capper, *Margaret Fuller,* 2:104–6.

22. Myerson, *The New England Transcendentalists and the* Dial; Reynolds, "From *Dial* Essay to New York Book," 19–22.

23. Capper, *Margaret Fuller,* 1:313; see also ix–xii, where Capper implicitly links Transcendentalism to later cultural avant-gardes, and ties the movement's emergence to that of the "intellectual as a cultural type."

24. Field, *Ralph Waldo Emerson,* 11–35, 117–18; Steven Fink, "Margaret Fuller: The Evolution of a Woman of Letters," in Fink's *Reciprocal Influences: Literary Production, Distribution, and Consumption in America* (Columbus, Ohio, 1999), 61–66.

25. *Dial* 1 (July 1840), 2; Myerson, *New England Transcendentalists and the* Dial, 29, 32. *Dial* 1 (July 1840), esp. Fuller, "A Short Essay on Critics," 7–8. As Steven Fink points out in his subtle reading of the *Dial* prospectuses, for Emerson the main end of the *Dial* and intellectual/critical work more generally was "provocation" and "expression." Fuller, on the other hand, valued "communication," "translation," and "mediation"—that literature, fundamentally, is a process of exchange. See Fink, *Prophet in the Marketplace,* 16–23.

26. See Capper, *Margaret Fuller,* 2:3–18; *Letters of Ralph Waldo Emerson,* 2:316; Myerson, *New England Transcendentalists and the* Dial, 23, 65; Field, *Ralph Waldo Emerson,* 131–66. The fate of the *Western Messenger,* a periodical that was in many ways the *Dial's* antecedent, should have been instructive. It too suffered less from the constraints of orthodoxy than from popular indifference. See Robert D. Habich, *Transcendentalism and the* Western Messenger: *A History of the Magazine and Its Contributors* (Rutherford, N. J., 1985), 41, see also 27, 70–81, 108.

27. *New-York Weekly Tribune,* January 27, 1841.

28. *Memoirs of Margaret Fuller Ossoli* (Boston, 1851), 2:152. See Greeley, *Autobiography,* 176. Teichgraeber, *Sublime Thoughts/Penny Wisdom,* 211–60. Myerson, *New England Transcendentalists and the* Dial; Fink, *Prophet in the Marketplace.*

29. *New-York Daily Tribune,* December 7, 1844.

30. Ibid., December 20, 7, 1844.

31. Fink, "Margaret Fuller"; William Charvat, *The Profession of Authorship in America: The Papers of William Charvat* (Columbus, Ohio, 1968), 55–7; Michael T. Gilmore, *American Romanticism and the Marketplace* (Chicago, 1985), 1–17; Ronald J. Zboray, *A Fictive People: Antebellum Economic Development and the American Reading Public* (New York, 1993).

32. *New-York Daily Tribune,* January 17, February 3, 1846, August 22, 1845; Fuller, "American Literature," in Chevigny, *The Woman and the Myth,* 195.

33. *New-York Daily Tribune,* January 25, June 17, November 18, December 10, 1845; *Letters of Margaret Fuller,* 3:58; Fuller in her journal quoted in Capper, *Margaret Fuller,* 341. See also Charvat, *Profession of Authorship in America,* 106–67. In his journal, Emerson praised the vernacular—the same vernacular that often worried him in

the newspapers—as a more vital and democratic alternative to the empty, desiccated safety of New England's official high culture: "I begin to feel the force of the double negative, though clean contrary to our grammar rules. And I confess to some pleasure from the stinging rhetoric of a rattling oath in the mouth of truckman & teamsters. How laconic & brisk it is by the side of a page of the North American Review. Cut these words & they would bleed; they are vascular & alive; they walk & run." *Journals and Miscellaneous Notebooks of Ralph Waldo Emerson,* 7:374.

34. See also David Leverenz, *Manhood and the American Renaissance* (Ithaca, 1989), 42–71; Douglas, *Feminization of American Culture.* Thoughtful explorations of the relationship between taste, class formation, democracy, and the emerging "high culture" include Kasson, *Rudeness and Civility;* Karen Halttunen, *Confidence Men and Painted Women: A Study of Middle-Class Culture in America, 1830–1870* (New Haven, 1982); Levine, *Highbrow/Lowbrow.*

35. Capper, *Margaret Fuller,* 295; *New-York Daily Tribune,* July 24, June 10, 1845. See also "Italy," *New-York Daily Tribune,* November 13, 1845.

36. Bell Gale Chevigny, "To the Edges of Ideology: Margaret Fuller's Centrifugal Evolution," *American Quarterly* 38 (Summer 1986), 182; *New-York Daily Tribune,* August 22, June 28, 1845.

37. Child argued, as Fuller would later, that prisons ought to use a "mode of discipline as is best calculated to reform the inmate, by stimulating and encouraging what remains good within them." Traditionalists attacked Child in the same way that they assailed Fuller and the *Tribune,* and Child even admitted that her less punitive solutions to social problems "will sound very sentimental" and strike many as a "new transcendental mode of curing crime by music and flowers." Child's column reprinted in the *New-York Daily Tribune,* December 20, 1844. On Child's biography with close attention to her New York writings, see Carolyn L. Karcher, *The First Woman in the Republic: A Cultural Biography of Lydia Maria Child* (Durham, N.C., 1994), 295–319.

38. *New-York Daily Tribune,* February 11, 1846.

39. Ibid., March 19, 1845.

40. Ibid., March 19, 1845. See Capper, *Margaret Fuller,* 2:173–77.

41. *New-York Daily Tribune,* May 31, 1845, March 11, 1846. See Burrows and Wallace, *Gotham,* 729–30, 717.

42. *New-York Daily Tribune,* December 28, 12, 1844.

43. Henry L. Golemba, *George Ripley* (Boston, 1977), 98–149; Guarneri, *Utopian Alternative,* 347, see also 345–47.

44. Douglas, *Feminization of American Culture,* 281.

45. Capper, *Margaret Fuller,* 2:276, see also 270–78.

3. The 1848 French Revolution and the Radicalization of the *Tribune*

1. John Higham, *From Boundlessness to Consolidation: The Transformation of American Culture, 1848–1860* (Ann Arbor, 1969), 15–16, 17.

2. *New-York Weekly Tribune,* June 17, 1848; May 6, 1848.

3. Ibid., March 25, 1848; *National Intelligencer,* March 21, 27, 1848. For the 1848 revolutions in Europe and France, see Beecher, *Victor Considerant;* E. J. Hobsbawm, *The Age of Revolution: Europe, 1789–1848* (London, 1977); Jonathan Sperber, *The*

European Revolutions, 1848–1851 (New York, 1994); Charles Breunig, *The Age of Revolution and Reaction, 1789–1850* (New York, 1977); and Roger Price, *The French Second Republic: A Social History* (Ithaca, 1972). For a general survey of the American response, see Timothy M. Roberts, "The American Response to the European Revolutions of 1848" (PhD diss., University of Oxford, 1998); Roberts, "'Revolutions Have Become the Bloody Toy of the Multitude': European Revolutions, the South, and the Crisis of 1850," *Journal of the Early Republic* 25 (Summer 2005): 259–283; Timothy M. Roberts and Daniel Walker Howe, "The United States and the Revolutions of 1848," in *The Revolution in Europe 1848–1849: From Reform to Reaction,* ed. R. J. W. Evans and Hartmut Pogge von Strandmann (New York, 2000); Paola Gemme, *Domesticating Foreign Struggles: The Italian Risorgimento and Antebellum American Identity* (Athens, 2005); Eugene N. Curtis, "American Opinion of the French Nineteenth-Century Revolutions," *American Historical Review* 29 (January 1924): 249–70; Merle Curti, "Impact of the Revolutions of 1848 on American Thought," *Proceedings of the American Philosophical Society* 93 (June 1949): 209–15; and Larry J. Reynolds, *European Revolutions and the American Literary Renaissance* (New Haven, 1988).

4. Fuller's letter is dated March 29, but it was not published in the *Weekly Tribune* until May 6, 1848. The *Advertiser* is quoted in the *Harbinger,* April 15, 1848, 187. *Courier and Enquirer,* April 8, 1848. On the conservative turn of American opinion, see *Courier and Enquirer,* March 22, 28, April 1, 14, 1848; Savannah *Republican,* April 4, 1848; Curtis, "American Opinion of the French Nineteenth-Century Revolutions," 258–9; Curti, "The Impact of the Revolutions of 1848 on American Thought," 211; *New-York Weekly Tribune,* May 13, 1848.

5. *New-York Weekly Tribune,* May 13, April 22, 1848. See the *Harbinger,* March 25, April 1, 8, 15, May 13, 27, July 22, 29, 1848.

6. *New-York Weekly Tribune,* April 29, 1848.

7. Ibid., November 4, 18, 1848.

8. Roger Magraw, *A History of the French Working Class,* vol. 2 (Cambridge, Mass., 1992), 40–43.

9. See William H. Sewell, *Work and Revolution: Language and Labor from the Old Regime to 1848* (New York, 1980).

10. Macgraw, *History of the French Working Class,* 57; see also 33–184.

11. Sewell, *Work and Revolution,* 202–3.

12. Magraw, *History of the French Working Class,* 72–73.

13. Louis Blanc, *The History of Ten Years,* vol. 1, Walter K. Kelly, trans. (Philadelphia, 1848), 50, 13, 14, 31, 46, 47. Sewell, *Work and Revolution,* 232–36.

14. *Harbinger* 6 (April 15, 1848), 187.

15. *New-York Weekly Tribune,* October 28, 1848.

16. Sewell, *Work and Revolution,* 222.

17. German reform was divided ideologically and by class. See Bruce Levine, *The Migration of Ideology and the Contested Meaning of Freedom: German Americans in the Mid-Nineteenth Century* (Washington, D.C., 1992); Levine, *The Spirit of 1848: German Immigrants, Labor Conflict, and the Coming of the Civil War* (Urbana, 1992).

18. *New-York Weekly Tribune,* April 29, 1848. Börnstein would leave Europe in 1849 and settle in Saint Louis where he and Karl Bernays started the Saint Louis German-language newspaper *Anzeiger des Westerns.* German "forty-eighters" became vital constituents of the Republican cause both before and during the Civil War in the key

battleground state of Missouri. Heinrich Börnstein, *Memoirs of a Nobody: The Missouri Years of an Austrian Radical, 1840–1866,* trans. and ed. Steven Rowan (St. Louis, 1997). Rowan translated the complete text of the second volume of Börnstein's memoir and summarized the first. The first volume is available only in German, Heinrich Börnstein, *Fünfundsiebzig Jahre in der Alten und Neuen Welt: Memoiren eines Unbedeutenden* (Memoirs of a Nobody), ed. with English introduction by Patricia Herminghouse (2 vols., New York, 1986). See also Carl Frederick Wittke, *Refugees of Revolution: The German Forty-Eighters in America* (Philadelphia, 1952); A. E. Zucker, ed., *The Forty-Eighters: Political Refugees of the German Revolution of 1848* (New York, 1967); and Levine, *Spirit of 1848.*

19. David McLellan, *Karl Marx: A Biography* (London, 1995), 69–87, 111–14; Fritz J. Raddatz, *Karl Marx: A Political Biography,* trans. Richard Barry (Boston, 1978), 50.

20. McLellan, *Karl Marx,* 87; Auguste Cornu, *Karl Marx et Friedrich Engels: Leur Vie et leur Oeuvre* (Karl Marx and Friedrich Engels: Their Life and Work), 3 vols. (Paris, 1954–1970), 3:7; quoted in Raddatz, *Karl Marx,* 58.

21. Engels to Marx, August 19, 1846, in *Collected Works,* 49 vols. (New York, 1975–), 38:55. See also Engels to Joseph Weydemeyer, February 27, 1852, *Collected Works,* 34:52. Wittke, *Refugees of Revolution,* 263, 265, 270–71. *New-York Daily Tribune,* January 6, 25, 27; August 5, 1845. Two fine editions of Fuller's *Tribune* writings have been published. Fuller's complete New York writings are collected in Judith Mattson Bean and Joel Myerson, eds., *Margaret Fuller, Critic: Writings from the* New-York *Tribune, 1844–1846* (New York, 2000). Fuller's European correspondence has been collected in Larry J. Reynolds and Susan Belasco Smith, eds., *"These Sad But Glorious Days": Dispatches from Europe, 1846–1850* (New Haven, 1991).

22. Börnstein, *Memoiren,* 1:383, 322–3. See James H. Wilson, *Life of Charles Dana* (New York, 1907), 36.

23. Börnstein, *Memoiren,* 1:383.

24. *New-York Weekly Tribune,* May 6, 13, June 3, 1848.

25. (New York) *Evening Express* (hereafter abbreviated as *Express*), May 23, 1848.

26. *New-York Weekly Tribune,* April 22, 1848; *New-York Daily Tribune,* August 5, 1845.

27. Karl Marx, *Selected Writings,* ed. David McLellan (New York, 1977), 124; *New-York Weekly Tribune,* July 1, 1848; see also June 24, 1848; McLellan, *Karl Marx,* 100–102.

28. *New-York Weekly Tribune,* July 1, 1848 [letter dated June 8, 1848].

29. *Express,* July 15, 1848; see also July 18, 1848. *Courier and Enquirer,* July 14, 24, 1848. The *Post's* laissez-faire sentiments mirrored those of the conservative Whig *Express,* both of which condemned the *Tribune's* support for ten-hour day legislation. "Everything must by *enacted by law,"* the *Express* critiqued. "There is a class of politicians, in this country, who are for regulating everything, and everybody by law" (January 28, 1848). Likewise, the *Post* warned that socialists were close to instituting a "government of terror," termed Ledru-Rollin's faction the *"coercive Republican party,"* and dismissed Louis Blanc's plans for the reorganization of labor and industry as "a system leading clearly and unequivocally to the interference of government in almost every branch of industry." *Evening Post,* May 8, 15, 17, June 2, July 18, 1848.

30. *New-York Weekly Tribune,* August 12, 1848.

31. There is no direct record of Dana's first meeting with Marx, and historians and biographers have speculated that either Ferdinand Freiligrath (the poet and future

occasional contributor to the *Tribune*) or Albert Brisbane (who was then also in Germany) made the introduction. See Borden, "Notes on Greeley, Dana, and Marx," 461–62; Franz Mehring, *Karl Marx: The Story of His Life,* trans. Edward Fitzgerald (London, 1936), 171. Apart from Janet Steele's *The Sun Shines for All: Journalism and Ideology in the Life of Charles A. Dana* (Syracuse: Syracuse University Press, 1993), very little recent work has been done on Charles Dana. Unfortunately, Dana did not leave an extensive collection of papers behind either, particularly for the pre–Civil War period. See Edward P. Mitchell, *Memoirs of an Editor: Fifty Years of American Journalism* (New York, 1924); Frank M. O'Brien, *The Story of the Sun* (New York, 1928); Charles J. Rosebault, *When Dana Was the Sun* (New York, 1931); Candace Stone, *Dana and the Sun* (New York, 1938); and Wilson, *Life of Charles Dana.* Wilson's *Life,* of the older works, is the most complete survey of Dana's young adulthood.

32. *New-York Weekly Tribune,* April 23, 1853.

33. Wilson, *Life,* 40; Steele, *Sun Shines for All,* 7.

34. Wilson, *Life,* 36.

35. Steele, *Sun Shines for All,* 22.

36. Wilson, *Life,* 63.

37. *New-York Weekly Tribune,* July 22, 1848 [letter dated June 29, 1848].

38. Börnstein's account of Dana's arrival is somewhat different. According to Börnstein, Dana arrived during the evening of the 22nd and immediately sent word to Börnstein to help him "see the beast" that was "republican France up close." It was late in the evening, though, and Dana was tired from his travels. He went to sleep that night and didn't wake up until mid-afternoon the next day. By then, the fighting had already started in earnest. The doors of Dana's hotel had been locked and the streets were shut down. Dana was trapped in the hotel "in an unwilling house arrest" deprived not only of a firsthand view of the conflict but of all newspapers and letters. When he finally reached Börnstein on the 27th Dana told him that, because of sheer boredom, they were the worst days of his entire life. See Börnstein, *Memoiren,* 433.

39. *New-York Weekly Tribune,* July 22, 1848.

40. Ibid., July 22, 1848.

41. Ibid., March 24, 1849, August 17, 1850.

42. When Proudhon was elected to the Assembly in June 1848, he was seated on the Committee of Finance, chaired by Adolphe Thiers. Thiers's committee oversaw, and shut down, the workshops. See K. Steven Vincent, *Pierre-Joseph Proudhon and the Rise of French Republican Socialism* (New York, 1984), 180–85.

43. *New-York Weekly Tribune,* August 26, 1848.

44. Ibid., September 2, 1848; October 7, 14, 1848.

45. Dana later (1849) expanded and revised the articles for William Henry Channing's weekly *The Spirit of the Age.* In 1896, Benjamin Tucker republished the articles to embarrass Dana whose politics had evolved in the half century since then. My citations, for convenience, Charles A. Dana, "Proudhon and His Bank of the People," republished in *Proudhon's Solution of the Social Problem,* ed. Henry Cohen (New York, 1927).

46. See Dana's *New-York Daily Tribune,* February 13, 1849, letter from Paris (dated January 2, 1849).

47. See Wilentz, *Chants Democratic,* 339, for Bray, and more generally, 326–43. On Ripley, Association, and cooperative reform, see Charles Crowe, *George Ripley: Transcendentalist and Utopian Socialist* (Athens, Ga., 1967), 207–8.

48. Vincent, *Proudhon,* 147, 170–74.

49. Cohen, *Proudhon's Solution of the Labor Problem,* 6, 11.

50. Vincent, *Proudhon,* 173.

51. See Vincent, *Proudhon,* 11–118.

52. Cohen, *Proudhon's Solution of the Labor Problem,* 13, 14.

53. Ibid., 18–19.

54. Ibid., 24.

55. Ibid., 25.

56. *New-York Weekly Tribune,* May 4, 1850.

57. Ibid., January 24, 1852.

58. Ibid., April 23, 1853.

59. Ibid., November 26, 1859.

60. See, for example, April 2, 1853.

61. *New-York Weekly Tribune,* January 5, 1850.

62. Ibid., May 4, 1850; see also May 4, 18, December 28, 1850; March 6, April 3, April 10, November 27, 1852.

63. Ibid., April 29, 1854. On the issue of strikes, the paper's views could vary widely. See April 16, 1859. See also April 23, 1853; March 3, 1860.

64. Ibid., August 17, February 9, 1850.

65. McLellan, *Karl Marx,* 255, 256.

66. *New-York Weekly Tribune,* Oct. 25, Nov. 6, 1851, Nov. 20, 1858.

67. Marx to Engels, June 14, 1853, in *Collected Works,* 34:346. When Marx reported to Engels that he had discovered that the *Tribune* was a protectionist organ, Engels responded the following day that the *Tribune's* protectionism "does no harm" and "by no means implies that they belong to the landed aristocracy" as was the case in England. Most important, Engels rightly concluded that the sharp theoretical distinctions, which would threaten their place at a European paper, would be lost on the Americans: "To the Yankees, this European politicising is mere dilettantism in which he who writes best and with the greatest *esprit* comes out on top." See Marx to Engels, August 5, 1852, *Collected Works,* 34:145–46; Engels to Marx, August 6, 1852, *Collected Works,* 34:147. Karl Marx, "The British Rule in India," *Collected Works,* 12:127, 126, 131, 132. See McLellan, *Karl Marx,* 285.

68. See Messer-Kruse, *Yankee International.*

69. For a published version of her writings, see Reynolds, ed., *"These Sad But Glorious Days."* See also Timothy Roberts, "Margaret Fuller's Rome and the Problem of Provincial American Democracy," *Patterns of Prejudice* 40, 45–60; Gemme, *Domesticating Foreign Struggles.*

70. *New-York Weekly Tribune,* January 12, 1850.

71. Guarneri, *Utopian Alternative,* 349, 368. For an interpretation of the continuity of American radicalism that accords to some extent with my own, see Messer-Kruse, *Yankee International.*

4. Marriage, Family, and the Socioeconomic Order

1. See Redelia Brisbane, *Albert Brisbane: A Mental Biography* (Boston, 1893), 194–95; Parke Godwin, *A Popular View of the Doctrines of Charles Fourier* (New York, 1844; reprint, Philadelphia, 1972), 74, and Godwin to Dana, September 17, 1844,

Bryant-Godwin Papers, New York Public Library. For an overview, see Guarneri, *Utopian Alternative,* 93–98.

2. He went on, "Before questions of Intellectual Training or Political Franchises for Women—not to speak of such a trifle as costume—do I place the question of enlarged Opportunities for Work—of a more extended and diversified field of Employment," Greeley to Paulina Davis, September 1, 1852. See also Greeley fragment, October 25, 1850, Thomas F. Madigan Collection, New York Public Library.

3. Stephen Pearl Andrews, Henry James, and Horace Greeley, *Love, Marriage, and Divorce, and the Sovereignty of the Individual* (New York, 1853; reprint, New York, 1972), 24.

4. See, in addition to numerous editorials in the *Tribune,* Greeley to Emma Newhall, undated, Horace Greeley Papers, Library of Congress; Greeley to Beman Brockaway, March 31, 1859, Horace Greeley Papers, New York Public Library. The literature on marriage and the family is vast. See Karen Lystra, *Searching the Heart: Women, Men, and Romantic Love in Nineteenth-Century America* (New York, 1989); John Spurlock, *Free Love: Marriage and Middle-Class Radicalism in America, 1825–1860* (New York, 1988), esp. 1–22; Halttunen, *Confidence Men and Painted Women;* William Leach, *True Love and Perfect Union: The Feminist Reform of Sex and Society* (Middletown, Conn., 1989); Mary P. Ryan, *Cradle of the Middle Class: The Family in Oneida County, New York, 1790–1865* (New York, 1981); Michael Grossberg, *Governing the Hearth: Law and the Family in Nineteenth-Century America* (Chapel Hill, 1985).

5. Mary Ryan's masterful study of New York's burned-over district, *Cradle of the Middle Class,* pays careful attention to both the changing demographics and ideology of middle-class family life. Seldom does any historical work capture, to this extent, the internal and external lives of its subject.

6. See esp. Lystra, *Searching the Heart;* Spurlock, *Free Love,* esp. 1–22; Halttunen, *Confidence Men and Painted Women;* Ryan, *Cradle of the Middle Class.* Timothy Messer-Kruse argues that out of the free love movement of the 1850s sprung the most vigorous faction of the postbellum American wing of the International Workingmen's Association. Messer-Kruse, *Yankee International,* 13.

7. Mrs. E. Oakes Smith, *Woman and Her Needs* (New York, 1851; reprint, New York, 1974), 34.

8. See Alfred Habegger, *The Father: A Life of Henry James, Sr.* (New York, 1994), 281.

9. See Rose, *Transcendentalism as a Social Movement,* 130–61.

10. See Arthur R. Schultz and Henry A. Pochmann, "George Ripley," *American Literature* 14 (March 1942), 1–19; Guarneri, *Utopian Alternative,* 344–47; Crowe, *George Ripley, Transcendentalist and Utopian Socialist;* Rose, *Transcendentalism as a Social Movement,* 49–52. For Ripley's post–Brook Farm career as a "man of letters," see Golemba, *George Ripley,* 98–149; Frothingham, *George Ripley,* 199–294; Crowe, *George Ripley,* 222–63.

11. Rose, *Transcendentalism as a Social Movement,* 135, 158–59; Frothingham, *Ripley,* 147.

12. Josiah Warren, *Equitable Commerce: A New Development of Principles as Substitutes for Laws and Governments, for the Harmonious Adjustment and Regulation of the Pecuniary, Intellectual, and Moral Intercourse of Mankind Proposed as Elements of New Society* (New York, 1852; reprint, New York, 1967), vi, x.

13. Quoted in Roger Wonderlich, *Low Living and High Thinking at Modern Times, New York* (Syracuse, 1992), 2, 30–31.

14. Josiah Warren, *Positions Defined* (Modern Times, 1853), quoted in Wonderlich, *Modern Times,* 76.

15. See Guarneri, *Utopian Alternative,* 353–63; Taylor Stoehr, *Free Love in America: A Documentary History* (New York, 1979); Sidney Ditzion, *Marriage, Morals, and Sex in America: A History of Ideas* (New York, 1969); Wonderlich, *Modern Times,* 53–90; Spurlock, *Free Love.*

16. See Giles Gunn, ed., *Henry James, Senior: A Selection of His Writings* (Chicago, 1974), 9, 12, 22–23.

17. Quoted in Habegger, *The Father,* 321; for James at the *Tribune,* see esp. 319–42.

18. Habegger, *The Father,* 322, 324.

19. *Love vs. Marriage* claimed inspiration from Emerson, Emanuel Swedenborg, Fourier, and even James himself, and its attack on marriage, whatever its intent, held back from making any sort of positive case for the reconstruction of sexual relationships on more libertarian lines. Lazarus offered the pretense that he hoped to "purify marriage," but he argued for erotic freedom and provided information about how to prevent pregnancy. Marx Edgeworth Lazarus, *Love vs. Marriage* (New York, 1852).

20. *New-York Daily Tribune,* September 18, 1852.

21. Ibid., September 18, 1852. See Habegger, *The Father,* 331–34.

22. Andrews, *Love, Marriage, and Divorce.*

23. [Samuel Irenaeus Prime], "The 'Tribune' on Marriage," *New York Observer* 30 (September 30, 1852), 318.

24. Andrews, *Love, Marriage, and Divorce,* 38, 39, 40. See Lystra, *Searching the Heart.*

25. [Samuel Irenaeus Prime], "The 'Tribune' on Marriage," *New York Observer* 30 (November 11, 1852), 366. See also "A Letter to Mr. James," *Observer* 30 (November 25, 1852), 382; "Marriage: The Religious View" (December 9, 1852), 394; and "Marriage: The Religious View" (December 16, 1852), 402.

26. Andrews, *Love, Marriage, and Divorce,* 35, 46.

27. Stephen Pearl Andrews, Unpublished Autobiography, Stephen Pearl Andrews Papers, Wisconsin State Historical Society.

28. See William W. Freehling, *The Road to Disunion: Secessionists at Bay, 1776–1854* (New York, 1990), 372–82.

29. Stephen Pearl Andrews, Unpublished Autobiography, Wisconsin State Historical Society. For Andrews's biography, see also Madeleine B. Stern, *The Pantarch: A Biography of Stephen Pearl Andrews* (Austin, 1968); Wonderlich, *Modern Times.*

30. Andrews, *Love, Marriage, and Divorce,* 46, 48.

31. Andrews, *Love, Marriage, and Divorce,* 49.

32. [Anonymous], "Mr. James and Divorce," *New York Observer* 30 (December 30, 1852), 422.

33. Andrews, *Love, Marriage, and Divorce,* 53, 50, 51.

34. Andrews, *Love, Marriage, and Divorce,* 9, 23.

35. Henry James Sr., "Woman and the 'Woman's Movement,'" *Putnam's Monthly* 1 (March 1853), 279, 280–81.

36. *New-York Daily Tribune,* March 7, 1853.

37. Ibid., February 4, 1853. See also January, 15, March 5, 7, 1853.

38. For Greeley's mean-spirited assessment of Smith's dim view of marriage, see *New-York Daily Tribune,* February 22, 1853. For Smith's response, *New-York Daily Tribune,* March 5, 1853. Smith's expurgated biography contains several brief sketches of Greeley's character, but only generally mentions her exchange with Greeley and James on divorce. Elizabeth Oakes Smith, *Selections From the Autobiography of Elizabeth Oakes [Prince] Smith,* edited by Mary Alice Wyman (New York, 1980), 92–94, 152–53, 158.

39. See *Woman and Her Needs,* 49–92. William Leach's broader history of feminism and sexuality does not make clear the relationship of women's rights and the debate over marriage to the question of individualism. See Leach, *True Love and Perfect Union,* 10, 11, 134, see also 133–57, 263–346.

40. Basch, *Framing American Divorce,* 73–77.

41. On the new middle class family, child rearing, and the market, see Ryan, *Cradle of the Middle Class.* On the concept of separate spheres and its problems, see Amy Dru Stanley, "Home Life and the Morality of the Market," in *The Market Revolution in America,* ed. Melvin Stokes and Stephen Conway (Charlottesville, Va., 1996), 74–96.

42. Karl Marx and Friedrich Engels, *The Communist Manifesto* (New York, 1967), 83.

43. Alexis de Tocqueville, *Democracy in America,* vol. 2 (New York, 1994), 99, 192–203.

44. Basch, *In the Eyes of the Law,* 16–19, 27–29.

45. Basch, *In the Eyes of the Law,* 178–79.

46. Basch, *Framing American Divorce,* 3.

47. Commons, "Horace Greeley and the Working-Class Origins of the Republican Party," 471, 470.

5. Land Reform, Pragmatic Socialism, and the Rise of the Republican Party

1. Greeley to Schuyler Colfax, April 22, 1846, Horace Greeley Papers-New York Public Library; Greeley to Brockway, November 19, 1847, Horace Greeley Papers, Library of Congress; for Brockway's response, see Beman Brockway, *Fifty Years in Journalism: Embracing Recollections with an Autobiography* (Watertown, N.Y., 1891), 115.

2. See Jamie C. Bronstein, *Land Reform and Working-Class Experience in Britain and the United States, 1800–1862* (Stanford, 1999), a study that carefully reconstructs the delicate mixture of sympathy and suspicion between land reform and Associationism, as well as the radical, transatlantic, and working-class origins of the idea of land reform.

3. Foner, *Free Soil, Free Labor, Free Men,* 29.

4. On the relationship between Association and land reform, see Bronstein, *Land Reform,* 101–5.

5. Glickstein, *American Exceptionalism, American Anxiety,* 25.

6. Her encounter with genuine European aristocracy transformed her view of American antislavery: "After all, they had a high motive, something eternal in their

desire and life; and, if it was not the only thing worth thinking of it was really something worth living and dying for to free a great nation from such a terrible blot, such
a threatening plague." *New-York Daily Tribune,* January 1, 1848.

7. The land reform movement explained to Eastern workingmen why Western
lands mattered even though leading land reformers were all over the map on the
question of free soil. Some, such as George Henry Evans and Gerrit Smith, were
committed to antislavery, and some, such as John Campbell and Thomas Devyr,
argued that free blacks threatened white workers. Devyr hoped to make homesteads
a platform in the white-supremacist Democratic Party. See Bronstein, *Land Reform,*
17–18, 91–94, 87–111.

8. Quoted in Edward P. Cheyney, "The Antirent Movement and the Constitution of 1846," *History of the State of New York,* vol. 6, ed. Alexander C. Flick (New
York, 1934), 299.

9. In addition to what I cite below, see McCurdy, *Anti-Rent Era in New York Law
and Politics;* Reeve Huston, "Popular Movements and Party Rule: The New York
Anti-Rent Wars and the Jacksonian Political Order," in *Beyond the Founders: New
Approaches to the Political History of the Early Republic,* ed. Jeffrey L. Pasley, Andrew W.
Robertson, and David Waldstreicher (Chapel Hill, 2004). For a brief consideration of
the Anti-Rent movement's impact on state and national Whig politics, see Holt, *Rise
and Fall of the American Whig Party,* 240–43.

10. The *Express* argued later that "instead of crush[ing] the rebellion," which was
his "duty," Seward temporized and "it has ever since gained strength." Quoted in
New-York Daily Tribune, August 30, 1845.

11. Quoted in Henry Christman, *Tin Horns and Calico: A Decisive Episode in the
Emergence of Democracy* (New York, 1945), 37–8.

12. On Devyr, see Bronstein, *Land Reform,* 122–24; Thomas Ainge Devyr, *The
Odd Book of the Nineteenth Century* (New York, 1882; reprint, 1986).

13. *New-York Daily Tribune,* August 30, 1845. See also September 6, 1845.

14. Ibid., July 28, 1845.

15. See, for example, "The Pro and Con of Anti-Rent," in which Greeley argues
from the point of view of both sides in the conflict. Ibid., September 6, 1845.

16. For a reprint of the *Express*'s charges and the *Tribune*'s response, see ibid.,
August 4, 1845. See also September 2, 1845.

17. See Martin Bruegel, "Unrest: Manorial Society and the Market in the Hud-
son Valley, 1780–1850," *Journal of American History* 82 (March 1996): 1398. See also
Cheyney, "Anti-Rent," 308–13; McCurdy, *Anti-Rent Era;* see Morton J. Horowitz,
The Transformation of American Law (Cambridge, Mass., 1977), esp. xiii–xvii, 1–62.

18. Daniel Feller, *The Public Lands in Jacksonian Politics* (Madison, 1984); Helen Sara
Zahler, *Eastern Workingmen and National Land Policy, 1829–1862* (New York, 1941).

19. Jamie Bronstein estimates that the transatlantic movement mobilized some
130,000 adherents. See *Land Reform,* 18, 24–36.

20. See Wilentz, *Chants Democratic,* 164–67, 182–90, 335–43.

21. Bronstein, *Land Reform,* 37–43. On the debate over the nature of the right of
property, see Huston, *Calculating the Value of the Union.*

22. On the links between Anti-Rent and National Reform, see Bronstein, *Land
Reform,* esp. 166.

23. Wilentz, *Chants Democratic,* 219–54. See also Bronstein, *Land Reform and Working-Class Experience,* 119–22.

24. See Wilentz, *Chants Democratic,* 182–89; Eric Foner, *Tom Paine and Revolutionary America* (New York, 1976); Conkin, *Prophets of Prosperity,* 237–40; see also Ashworth, *"Agrarians" & Aristocrats,"* 92–99.

25. Zahler, *Eastern Workingmen,* 37, 43–44; *Courier and Enquirer,* September 16, 1845.

26. Zahler, *Eastern Workingmen,* 44; Bronstein, *Land Reform,* 218–19.

27. Coy F. Cross II, *Go West Young Man! Horace Greeley's Vision for America* (Albuquerque, 1995), 33–70.

28. *New-York Weekly Tribune,* August 4, 1845. Cited in Roy Marvin Robbins, "Horace Greeley: Land Reform and Unemployment, 1837–1862," *Agricultural History* 7 (1933): 23.

29. On labor and immigration, see *New-York Daily Tribune,* September 3, 5, 1845.

30. *New-York Weekly Tribune,* November 29, 1845, January 3, May 2, 1846. See also October 25, December 6, 1845.

31. Ibid., July 4, 1846; see also *New-York Daily Tribune,* April 24, 1846.

32. Bronstein, *Land Reform,* 73–77. Evans was a little more suspicious of the "the communities." He argued that the family was the most natural unit of association.

33. See Conkin, *Prophets of Prosperity;* Huston, *Securing the Fruits of Labor,* xvii, 153, 156–63, 170–82, and 250–51.

34. See Commons, "Working Class Origins of the Republican Party," 478–88; Robbins, "Horace Greeley," 18–41; Wilentz, *Chants Democratic,* 335–43.

35. See John Ashworth, *Slavery, Capitalism, and Politics in the Antebellum South,* vol. 1, *Commerce and Compromise, 1820–1850* (New York, 1995), 1–285.

36. Quoted in Zahler, *Eastern Workingmen,* 37.

37. The populist character of this culture in a later period is evoked in Mark Voss-Hubbard, *Beyond Party: Cultures of Antipartisanship in Northern Politics before the Civil War* (Baltimore, 2002). See Wilentz, *Rise of American Democracy),* 272–80.

38. Greeley to Weed, January 13, 1847, Horace Greeley Papers, New-York Historical Society.

39. See Howe, *Political Culture,* 351; Holt, *Rise and Fall,* 13, 14, 28–32.

40. See James C. N. Paul, *Rift in the Democracy* (Philadelphia, 1951), xi–xiv, 33–113; William R. Brock, *Parties and Political Conscience: American Dilemmas, 1840–1850* (Millwood, N.Y., 1979), 151–83; Kinley J. Brauer, *Cotton versus Conscience: Massachusetts Whig Politics and Southwestern Expansion, 1843–1848* (Lexington, Ky., 1967), 26.

41. John H. Schroeder, *Mr. Polk's War: American Opposition and Dissent, 1846–1848* (Madison, 1973); Brock, *Parties and Political Conscience,* 143–48; Edward L. Widmer, *Young America: The Flowering of Democracy in New York City* (New York, 1999), 26.

42. Sellers, *Market Revolution,* 423. See Reginald Horsman, *Race and Manifest Destiny: The Origins of American Racial Anglo-Saxonism* (Cambridge, Mass., 1981), 208–48.

43. Sellers, *Market Revolution,* 423; John L. O'Sullivan, "The Mexican Question," *Democratic Review* 16 (May 1845), 421–22, cited in Brock, *Parties and Political Conscience,* 144.

44. Walt Whitman, *the Gathering of the Forces,* vol. 1, (New York, 1920), 240, 242, 257, 259, 248, 249.

45. See Robert W. Johannsen, *To the Halls of Montezuma: The Mexican War in the American Imagination* (New York, 1985), 68–143.

46. Johannsen, *To the Halls of Montezuma*, 276.

47. Johannsen, *To the Halls of Montezuma*, 275–77; for opposition to the war, see esp. 270–301.

48. *New-York Daily Tribune*, May 12, 1846.

49. Ibid., May 23, August 17, October 18, 1846.

50. Among other accounts see Joseph A. Rayback, *Free Soil: the Election of 1848* (Lexington, 1970), 22–33; Frederick J. Blue, *The Free Soilers: Third Party Politics, 1848–1854* (Urbana, 1973), 20–23; Brock, *Parties and Political Conscience,* 180–83.

51. Schroeder, *Mr. Polk's War,* 48–49.

52. Whitman would soon lose his position as the editor of the *Brooklyn Eagle* because of his association with pro-Wilmot Democrats. See *Brooklyn Daily Eagle,* September 1, 1847; cited in Rayback, *Free Soil,* 60.

53. *Evening Post,* April 20, 1848; Rayback, *Free Soil,* 57–59.

54. *Courier,* August 11, 1847; cited in Rayback, *Free Soil,* 89–90.

55. *New-York Weekly Tribune,* March 18, January 29, 1848.

56. Ibid., June 17, 1848.

57. Van Deusen, *Horace Greeley,* 123.

58. *New-York Weekly Tribune,* June 17, 1848; see also Rayback, *Free Soil,* 39–44, 145–70. See also Greeley to Colfax, New York Public Library, September 15, 1848.

59. *Express,* February 3, 1848.

60. *New-York Weekly Tribune,* September 30, July 1, 1848.

61. *New-York Weekly Tribune,* October 7, 1848; Greeley to Giddings, June 20, 1848, Horace Greeley Papers, New-York Historical Society.

62. Cross, *Go West Young Man!,* 26.

63. *New-York Weekly Tribune,* August 31, 1850; November 18, 1854; January 7, 1860; see also Van Deusen, *Horace Greeley,* 130–33. The paper's centrality in the North, based on its circulation, is even more impressive given the fact that it was forcibly excluded from most of the South. The *Tribune* had, for example, more subscribers in the Sandwich Islands/Hawaii (117) than in North and South Carolina combined (28 and 17 respectively). Even border states, less bound to slave interests, excluded the paper. Delaware boasted only 90 subscribers, Maryland only 102, and Tennessee only 109. See *New-York Weekly Tribune,* April 14, 1855.

64. As late as September, Greeley was still ambivalent about his relationship to Whiggery and the Free Soil movement with which he sympathized: "I am going to vote for Taylor—at least, I think I am—and I am not clear that this is right. If I could make Van Buren President to-morrow I would. I don't like the man, but I *do* like the principles he now embodies—Free Soil and Land Reform." Quoted in O. J. Hollister, *Life of Schuyler Colfax* (New York, 1886), 53.

65. See Blue, *Free Soilers,* 152–231; Holt, *Rise and Fall,* 331–82.

66. Zahler, *Eastern Workingmen,* 88–92.

67. *New-York Weekly Tribune,* January 19, 1850; see also February 2, 23, 1850.

68. Thomas Devyr argued, on the other hand, "would it not be more fit and more fair that a man's success in life should... depend on himself alone? Under the system of Land Reform, for which I contend, every individual man could so 'organize' his own labor that it would produce him the rate of wages fixed by a power

that is alike liberal and just, and that knows thoroughly man's wants and capacities," *New-York Weekly Tribune,* August 17, 1850. Later, during the Kansas crisis, the *Tribune* urged a free-labor emigration according to the principles of Association; see *New-York Weekly Tribune,* April 11, 1857.

69. *New-York Weekly Tribune,* January 24, 1852.

70. Quoted in Zahler, *Eastern Workingmen,* 172.

71. *New-York Weekly Tribune,* July 31, 1852.

72. Bronstein, *Land Reform,* 231–32.

73. *New-York Weekly Tribune,* June 12, 1858. See also June 19, 1858.

74. Bronstein, *Land Reform,* 244, 242.

75. Today Greeley is a virtual company town where a massive meatpacking conglomerate, Con Agra, has transformed its mostly migrant workforce into a collection of disposable parts. See Eric Schlosser, *Fast Food Nation: The Dark Side of the All-American Meal* (New York, 2002). For the Homestead Act, see Richardson, *The Greatest Nation of the Earth,* 139–69.

76. Quoted in Bronstein, *Land Reform,* 236–37.

77. See *Courier and Enquirer,* September 16, 1846, quoted in Zahler, *Eastern Workingmen,* 44, 187; "Agrarianism," *Atlantic Monthly* 3 (1859), 393–97.

78. T. A. Devyr to Greeley, October 29, 1860, Horace Greeley Papers, New York Public Library, cited in Van Deusen, *Horace Greeley,* 81.

79. Historical portraits of the 1850s have varied greatly depending on subdiscipline. Historians of intellectual life and reform have long noted the increasing "consolidation" of American culture during the 1850s that accompanied the rise of capitalism. Historians of the Civil War, on the other hand, have traced the radicalization of American politics and the failure of the nation's political institutions to restrain these currents. For the conservative turn in American culture, see, for example, Higham, *From Boundlessness to Consolidation;* Levine, *Highbrow/Lowbrow.* For the "irrational" radicalization of American politics, see such "blundering generation" histories as Avery Craven, *The Repressible Conflict 1830–1861* (Baton Rouge, 1939); J. G. Randall, *Lincoln the President: Springfield to Gettysburg,* 2 vols. (New York, 1997).

80. *New-York Weekly Tribune,* July 13, 27, 1850.

81. See Howe, *Political Culture of the American Whigs,* 29–30, 84–85, 204–6. See also Glyndon G. Van Deusen, *William Henry Seward* (New York, 1967), 121–34; Van Deusen, *Thurlow Weed: Wizard of the Lobby* (Boston, 1947), 174–77. For the impact of the speech, see Leonard W. Levy, *The Law of the Commonwealth and Chief Justice Shaw* (Cambridge, Mass., 1957), 83–85; Kraditor, *Means and Ends in American Abolitionism,* esp. 3–38, 274–77; Elkins, *Slavery,* esp. 27–34.

82. See Holt, *Rise and Fall of the American Whig Party,* 489–515, esp. 489–93; Allan Nevins, *Ordeal of the Union: Fruits of Manifest Destiny, 1847–1852,* vol. 1 (New York, 1947), 298–302.

83. *New-York Weekly Tribune,* March 23, 1850.

84. I use the term antinomian here in the same spirit as Lewis Perry in *Radical Abolitionism: Anarchy and the Government of God in Antislavery Thought* (Knoxville, 1995), 35–37. For Perry on the concept of a "higher law," see 252–56.

85. See *New-York Weekly Tribune,* December 28, 1850; January 4, 11, May 10, 1851. For the 1850 election in New York State, see Holt, *Rise and Fall,* 583–96.

86. *New-York Weekly Tribune,* June 12, July 3, 1852. For protection, see *New-York Weekly Tribune,* March 13, 1852. See also *Why I am a Whig,* which was published in July 1852.

87. For the Scott candidacy and nomination, see Holt, *Rise and Fall,* 697–725.

88. *New-York Weekly Tribune,* "That Hunker platform," June 26, 1852.

89. *New-York Weekly Tribune,* February 12, 1853. See also April 23, May 7, 28, 1853.

90. Ibid., August 6, 1853. See also April 16, 1853. On the enlargement, see also Greeley to Colfax, March 17, April 4, December 26, 1850, Horace Greeley Papers, New York Public Library. The struggle over the paper's expansion, its price, and its radicalism, which alienated the city's conservative readers, continued throughout the decade. See also Greeley to W. E. Robinson, July 7, 1854, Greeley to Seward, April 15, 1855, Horace Greeley Papers, New York Public Library.

91. Seward Papers, Greeley to Seward, April 15, 1853; quoted in Van Deusen, *Horace Greeley,* 173–74.

92. See, for example, Henry Raymond to George Jones, March 11, 1846, Henry J. Raymond Papers, New York Public Library.

93. Quoted in Brown, *Raymond of the Times,* 98.

94. [Anonymous], *New York Family Journal,* March 10, 1855, 76; from a scrapbook in the Raymond Papers, New York Public Library.

95. Christopher Lasch, *The Revolt of the Elites and the Betrayal of Democracy* (New York, 1995), 161–75; Dan Schiller, *Objectivity and the News: The Public and the Rise of Commercial Journalism* (Philadelphia, 1981).

96. For Raymond and the rupture of the triumvirate, see Isely, *Horace Greeley,* 75–78; Van Deusen, *Horace Greeley,* 173–75; Brown, *Raymond of the Times,* 121–22; Greeley to Weed, August 10, 1853; Greeley to D. B. St. John, August 2, 13, 17, 1853; Greeley to Seward, February 6, 1853, Horace Greeley Papers, New York Public Library; Greeley to Scoville, April 25, 1853, Horace Greeley Papers, Library of Congress.

97. For the history of the *Times,* see Brown, *Raymond of the Times;* Meyer Berger, *The Story of the* New York Times, *1851–1951* (New York, 1951), a company history of the paper; and the less than reliable Augustus Maverick, *Henry J. Raymond and the New York Press for Thirty Years* (Hartford, Conn., 1870).

98. *New-York Weekly Tribune,* February 4, 1854.

99. Ibid., October 7; February 4, 25, March 18, 25, April 15, June 3, 1854.

100. Ibid., March 18, 1854. See also February 25, March 4, 1854.

101. Ibid., June 24, 1854. See also October 7, 1854.

102. For notable examples, see ibid., November 3, 1855; February 2, June 7, 1856. On the violent turn of American antislavery reform, see Ethan J. Kytle, "From Body Reform to Reforming the Body Politic: Transcendentalism and the Militant Antislavery Career of Thomas Wentworth Higginson," *American Nineteenth Century History* 8 (September 2007): 325–50.

103. *Herald,* April 28, 1860, quoted in Foner, *Free Soil,* 51–52.

104. The Dorr Rebellion was a small-scale civil war in Rhode Island in 1841–42. Rhode Island had the most restrictive suffrage requirements in the country and when efforts to bring the state into line with the rest of the country, which was making universal white-male suffrage the norm, failed, Thomas Dorr led an armed insurrection

against the state government. *New-York Weekly Tribune,* May 7, 14, 1842; August 9, 1845.

105. *New-York Weekly Tribune,* June 2, 1855. See also December 8, 15, 1855.

106. Ibid., April 26, 1856. See also April 18; May 2, 9; June 20; July 11, 18; August 8, 1857.

107. Ibid., December 27, 1856. See also January 10, 1857. Don E. Fehren-bacher, *The Dred Scott Case: Its Significance in American Law and Politics* (New York, 1978), 305.

108. *New-York Weekly Tribune,* March 7, 1857.

109. Ibid., April 25, 1857; see also March 21, 1857.

110. Ibid., March 14, 1857. For an overview of the responses to the decision, see Fehrenbacher, *Dred Scott Case,* 417–48.

111. *New-York Weekly Tribune,* October 22, 1859.

112. Ibid., November 5, 1859.

113. Ibid., December 3, 1859.

114. Ibid., November 10, 1860.

115. Ibid., November 17, 1860.

116. Ibid., December 15, 1860. For the *Tribune's* long-held suspicion of seces-sion's feasibility, see *New-York Daily Tribune,* February 21, August 8, 1850; October 17, 1851.

117. See David M. Potter, "Horace Greeley and Peaceable Secession," in his *The South and the Sectional Conflict* (Baton Rouge, 1968), 219–42; Thomas N. Bonner, "Horace Greeley and the Secession Movement, 1860–61," *Mississippi Valley Historical Review* 38 (December 1951): 425–44. See also Daniel W. Crofts, "Secession Win-ter: William Henry Seward and the Decision for War," *New York History* 65 (July 1984): 229–56.

118. The *Tribune* endorsed Helper's book, combining a laudatory full-page review with substantial extracts. His biographer calls Greeley a "key collaborator." David Brown, *Southern Outcast: Hinton Rowan Helper and* The Impending Crisis of the South (Baton Rouge, 2006), 125. See also Harvey Wish, ed., *Antebellum Writings of George Fitzhugh and Hinton Helper on Slavery* (New York, 1960), 22–39.

119. Quoted in Robert S. Harper, *Lincoln and the Press* (New York, 1951), 100.

120. Horace Bushnell, *Barbarism the First Danger* (New York, 1847), 251; quoted in Howe, *Political Culture of American Whigs,* 127.

121. On debate within the Republican Party between nationalism and states' rights, unionism and secession, political and extrapolitical agitation, and the enforce-ment of, and resistance to, law, see Foner, *Free Labor,* 133–43.

122. *New-York Weekly Tribune,* April 14, 1855.

123. Ibid., March 1, 1851. On civil disobedience, conscience, moral law, and the antebellum tension between the law as a neutral instrument and the law as the agent of political interest, see Robert M. Cover, *Justice Accused: Antislavery and the Judi-cial Process* (New Haven, 1975), esp. 131–58; Edward H. Madden, *Civil Disobedience and Moral Law in Nineteenth-Century American Philosophy* (Seattle, 1968). Seward was hardly a radical abolitionist, but his appeal to a "higher law" resonated with the long tradition of Protestant antinomianism and more particularly, the spirit of Garrisonian anarchism. See Perry, *Radical Abolitionism.*

6. The Civil War and the Dilemma of Free Labor

1. Junius Henri Browne, *The Great Metropolis: A Mirror of New York* (Hartford, 1869), 48, 49, 31, 32; see also Burrows and Wallace, *Gotham,* 917–28; Hale, *Horace Greeley,* 316.

2. Foner, *Free Soil, Free Labor, Free Men.*

3. Gabor S. Boritt, "Lincoln and the Economics of the American Dream," in *The Historian's Lincoln: Pseudohistory, Psychohistory, and History,* ed. Gabor S. Boritt (Urbana, 1988), 87–106; Richardson, *Greatest Nation of the Earth.*

4. Glickstein, *American Exceptionalism, American Anxiety.*

5. Foner, *Reconstruction;* Montgomery, *Beyond Equality.*

6. Quoted in David Roediger, "Ira Steward and the Anti-Slavery Origins of the American Eight-Hour Theory," *Labor History* 27 (1986): 421.

7. Glickstein, *American Exceptionalism,* 99.

8. It is not my intention here, however, to provide a detailed account of the *Tribune*'s coverage of the war itself. A few of the numerous accounts available of Civil War journalism are cited throughout this chapter.

9. Greeley, *Autobiography,* 137.

10. Schiller, *Objectivity and the News;* Louis M. Starr, *Bohemian Brigade: Civil War Newsmen in Action* (Madison, 1987), 104.

11. John Russell Young, *Men and Memories,* ed. May D. Russell Young (New York, 1901), 115; Starr, *Bohemian Brigade,* 18, see also 3–21, 89–90. Mark Wahlgren Summers, *The Press Gang: Newspapers and Politics, 1865–1872* (Chapel Hill, 1994), 5; Bernard A. Weisberger, *Reporters for the Union* (Boston, 1953), 42–73; Kluger, *The Paper,* 97. The classic account and critique of the rise of journalistic objectivity is Michael Schudson, *Discovering the News* (New York, 1978). In *The Press Gang,* Mark Wahlgren Summers documents the slow emergence of journalistic professionalism during Reconstruction, but also the way in which the era was plagued by, and benefited from, a heavily politicized press. See also Lasch, *Revolt of the Elites,* 161–75. In addition to what I cite above and below, important histories of Civil War journalism include Emmet Crozier, *Yankee Reporters, 1861–1865* (New York, 1956), and J. Cutler Andrews, *The North Reports the Civil War* (Pittsburgh, 1955).

12. Quoted in Starr, *Bohemian Brigade,* 24.

13. Harry W. Baehr Jr., *The New York* Tribune *since the Civil War* (New York, 1972), 34–35.

14. Browne, *Great Metropolis,* 214.

15. Hale, *Horace Greeley,* 299–323.

16. Weisberger, *Reporters for the Union,* 178.

17. Hale, *Horace Greeley,* 254; Weisberger, *Reporters for the Union,* 181–86.

18. Weisberger, *Reporters for the Union,* 178–79; Starr, *Bohemian Brigade,* 219–26.

19. Bernstein, *New York City Draft Riots,* 19–25.

20. Hale, *Horace Greeley,* 274. See Parton, *Life of Horace Greeley,* 478, 484, 486; Burrows and Wallace, *Gotham,* 887–99; Kluger, *The Paper,* 110; Hale, *Horace Greeley,* 271–74.

21. Hale, *Greeley,* 267–8; Kluger, *The Paper,* 109; David Herbert Donald, *Lincoln* (New York, 1995), 414, 521–23.

22. See David W. Blight, *Race and Reunion: The Civil War and American Memory* (Cambridge, Mass., 2001), 57–63.

23. Baehr, *New York* Tribune, 49–50.

24. *New-York Daily Tribune,* May 24, 1866.

25. Ibid., July 31, 1866.

26. Ibid., December 12, 1866.

27. Ibid., November 19, 1866.

28. Ibid., June 4, 1870.

29. Ibid., May 18, 1867.

30. Ibid., January 1, 1867.

31. Ibid., September 9, 1868.

32. Ibid., February 15, 1866. See also February 12, 1866.

33. Foner, *Reconstruction,* 247.

34. *New-York Daily Tribune,* February 12, 1866. See also February 13, 21, 23, March 2, 1866. On the Civil Rights bill, see March 1, 1866.

35. Ibid., February 1, 1869. Once again, he advised communal migration: see March 24, 1870. See also January 3, 1870.

36. Michael Perman, *Road to Redemption: Southern Politics, 1869–1879* (Chapel Hill, 1984), 88–107; C. Vann Woodward, *Reunion and Reaction: The Compromise of 1877 and the End of Reconstruction* (Garden City, N.Y., 1956); Thomas B. Alexander, "Persistent Whiggery in the Confederate South, 1860–1877," *Journal of Southern History* 27 (August 1961): 305–29.

37. *New-York Daily Tribune,* May 13, 17, 1867.

38. Ibid., May 17, 1867.

39. Two recent books that make this point forcefully are Michael A. Ross, *Justice of Shattered Dreams: Samuel Freeman Miller and the Supreme Court during the Civil War Era* (Baton Rouge, 2003), and Winger, *Lincoln, Religion.*

40. I capitalize Liberal to refer specifically to the group of laissez-faire reformers that emerged in the North during Reconstruction.

41. Michael Les Benedict argues that what bound Jeffersonian/Jacksonian and postwar advocates of laissez-faire together was a commitment to "equal rights" and opposition to "special privilege," but with one crucial distinction. The former worried about corruption from above, while the latter worried about corruption from below. See Michael Les Benedict, "Reform Republicans and the Retreat from Reconstruction," in *The Facts of Reconstruction: Essays in Honor of John Hope Franklin,* ed. Eric Anderson and Alfred A. Moss Jr. (Baton Rouge, 1991), 58–59.

42. *New-York Daily Tribune,* June 6, 1867.

43. Ibid., June 17, 1867.

44. Ibid., March 24, 1866. See also April 23, July 8, 1867; April 13, 1869.

45. Ibid., June 11, 1867.

46. Ibid., June 10, 1867.

47. Christopher Lasch makes this precise point in *Revolt of the Elites,* 7.

48. *New-York Daily Tribune,* January 15, 1870. See also May 3, 1867.

49. *New-York Weekly Tribune,* February 7, 1852. See also January 17, 1852.

50. Ibid., February 7, 1852. See also March 20, 1852.

51. Ibid., August 19, 1854. On December 6, 1856, the *Tribune* would argue that "clannishness, is not essentially a bad thing, but a good thing out-grown—something

which had its origin and justification in the perils and calamities of an age of insecurity, violence and strong-handed rapine." See also November 4, 1854.

52. Ibid., November 11, 1854. For the *Tribune's* swerving course on ethnic and cultural questions, see also June 24, 1854; April 8, 1854; April 14, 1855.

53. *New-York Daily Tribune,* June 23, 1870; for Chinese labor and the Knights of St. Crispin, see also July 9, 22, November 16, December 12, 29, 1870; January 2, April 24, 1871. For a postwar critique of convict labor that tied it to the evils of free trade and global competition with degraded or European "pauper" labor, see February 13, 1866. Glickstein, *American Exceptionalism, American Anxiety;* Messer-Kruse, *Yankee International,* 86–89, 116–25; Burrows and Wallace, *Gotham,* 989–91; Bernstein, *New York City Draft Riots,* 226–27.

54. *New-York Daily Tribune,* March 12, 1867.

55. James L. Huston, "A Political Response to Industrialism: The Republican Embrace of Protectionist Labor Doctrines," *Journal of American History* 70 (June 1983): 35–57; Horace Greeley, *Essays Designed to Elucidate the Science of Political Economy* (Boston, 1870); Jonathan Grossman, *William Sylvis, Pioneer of American Labor: A Study of the Labor Movement during the Era of the Civil War* (New York, 1973), 120.

56. Atkinson quoted in Benedict, "Reform Republicans," 58.

57. Benedict, "Reform Republicans," 66.

58. *New-York Daily Tribune,* July 3, 1867; April 17, September 2, 6, 1869; January 15, 1870.

59. The *New York Herald* proposed facetiously to send the forty thousand Communard prisoners, held by the French government, there to make the town into a penal colony: "We say to the Communists, 'come'.... Those of them who...like debating societies might go to Greeley, Colorado, where there is a colony of very mild Communistic ideas....In many ways they are exactly suited to the country; so we hope they will not wait till Greeley is President, but go west and buy land at once." Today Greeley is host to the very sort of industrial capitalism that would have horrified its namesake. *New-York Daily Tribune,* March 3, 6, 1871. See Schlosser, *Fast Food Nation.*

60. *New-York Daily Tribune,* June 24, 1867. For more on collective living, see June 3, 11, 1867.

61. Ibid., June 24, 1867.

62. Ibid., June 11, 1867.

63. Ibid., June 11, 18, 1867. For method, see also June 4, November 6, 1868.

64. Ibid., March 22, 1866.

65. Ibid., October 15, 1869. For a summary, see January 15, 1870.

66. Ibid., August 27, 1866.

67. Montgomery, *Beyond Equality,* 176–85, 230–60.

68. Bernstein, *New York City Draft Riot,* 89, 243–44.

69. See *New-York Daily Tribune,* August 7, 1848; May 27, 1850; April 6, 1866.

70. Ibid., August 25, 1866; January 10, 1872.

71. Ibid., August 17, 1850.

72. Ibid., April 6, 1866.

73. Ibid., May 16, May 26, June 6, 1866; April 5, 1867; Roediger, "Ira Steward," 411.

74. *New-York Daily Tribune,* April 6, 1866.

75. Kenneth Fones-Wolf, "Boston Eight Hour Men, New York Marxists, and the Emergence of the International Labor Union: Prelude to the AFL," *Historical Journal of Massachusetts* 9 (June 1982): 49–50.

76. Messer-Kruse, *Yankee International,* 220–23.

77. Messer-Kruse, *Yankee International,* 32, see also 31–34.

78. Quoted Montgomery, *Beyond Equality,* 267, see also 262–77.

79. Montgomery, *Beyond Equality,* 269.

80. *New-York Daily Tribune,* February 28, 1867.

81. Ibid. See also March 3, 15, 1867.

82. Ibid., March 6, 13, 14, 1867; Montgomery, *Beyond Equality,* 296–302.

83. Montgomery, *Beyond Equality,* 301–2; *New-York Daily Tribune,* April 5, 10, 1867.

84. *Harper's Weekly* 11 (May 25, 1867), 323, quoted in Montgomery, *Beyond Equality,* 303–4.

85. *New-York Daily Tribune,* October 7, 1869.

86. Montgomery, *Beyond Equality,* 302–34; *New-York Daily Tribune,* July 29, 1868.

87. Montgomery, *Beyond Equality,* 323, see also 311–23.

88. Messer-Kruse, *Yankee International,* 45–127.

89. *New-York Daily Tribune,* October 1, 1870.

90. Ibid., June, 17, July 6, 1871. *Boston Evening Transcript,* December 13, 1871, *Philadelphia Inquirer,* October 25, 1871, quoted in Richardson, *Death of Reconstruction* (Cambridge, Mass., 2001), 87. See also *New-York Daily Tribune,* December 15, 18, 1871.

91. Roger Magraw, *France 1815–1914: The Bourgeois Century* (New York, 1986), 187–205; Harry Hearder, *Europe in the Nineteenth Century, 1830–1880* (New York, 1988), 192–206.

92. Philip M. Katz, *From Appomattox to Montmartre: Americans and the Paris Commune* (Cambridge, Mass., 1998), 55–58.

93. Young, *Men and Memories,* 170.

94. Young, *Men and Memories,* 167, see also 165–207.

95. Charles Loring Brace, *The Dangerous Classes* (New York, 1872); Burrows and Wallace, *Gotham,* 1002–03; Messer-Kruse, *Yankee International,* 100–106; *Cincinnati Daily Gazette,* May 22, 1871, quoted in Richardson, *Death of Reconstruction,* 85; for Richardson generally on the influence of the Commune, see 85–89.

96. Bingham Duncan, *Whitelaw Reid: Journalist, Politician, Diplomat* (Athens, 1975), 55; Katz, *From Appomattox to Montmartre,* 19; Baehr, *New York* Tribune, 31. On the professional ideology of postbellum newspapers, see Summers, *Press Gang,* 4–6.

97. *New-York Daily Tribune,* February 9, April 15, September 6, 7, 13, 15, 1870; February 14, 1871; Katz, *From Appomattox to Montmartre,* 26–84.

98. *New-York Daily Tribune,* March 1, 11, 21, 27, 29, 30; April 10, 13, 14, 17, 22, 1871.

99. Bernstein, *New York City Draft Riots,* 195–236; James C. Mohr, "New York: The De-Politicization of Reform," in *Radical Republicans in the North: State Politics during Reconstruction,* ed. James C. Mohr (Baltimore, 1976), 73–75.

100. *New-York Daily Tribune,* May 23, June 9, 24, 28, 1871. Katz, *From Appomattox to Montmartre,* 44–117.

101. *New-York Daily Tribune,* June 28, 1871.

102. Katz, *From Appomattox to Montmartre,* 105–7; *New Orleans Daily Picayune,* April 26, 1871.

103. Bernstein, *New York City Draft Riots,* 219–22.

104. *Scribner's Monthly* 1 (1870), 106; *Harper's Weekly,* October 1, 1870, 626; quoted in Katz, *From Appomattox to Montmartre,* 94, see 85–117. On Republicans and the Commune, see Richardson, *Death of Reconstruction,* 85–97.

105. Burrows and Wallace, *Gotham,* 986–91, 1002–13; Montgomery, *Beyond Equality,* 296–326; Bernstein, *New York City Draft Riots,* 195–264; for the 1868 strike, see 209–15.

106. Montgomery, *Beyond Equality,* 325, see also 323–26.

107. Burrows and Wallace, *Gotham,* 986–91; *New-York Daily Tribune,* July 9, 1871.

108. *New-York Daily Tribune,* December 24, 1867; Bernstein, *New York City Draft Riots,* 237–39; Montgomery, *Beyond Equality,* 311–23, 328–29.

109. *New York Times,* May 21, 1872; Bernstein, *New York City Draft Riots,* 247.

110. Bernstein, *New York City Draft Riots,* 252.

111. *New-York Daily Tribune,* June 19, 1872; Montgomery, *Beyond Equality,* 326–27; Bernstein, *New York City Draft Riots,* 246–57. On the end of the strike, see *New-York Daily Tribune,* June 27, July 6, 1872. For an indispensable account of class formation and reformation in nineteenth-century New York, see Sven Beckert, *The Monied Metropolis: New York City and the Consolidation of the American Bourgeoisie, 1850–1896* (New York, 2001).

112. *New-York Daily Tribune,* August 23, 1871; for the paper's direct response to Butler, see August 26, 1871.

113. Ibid., September 17, 1870.

114. Ibid., August 28, 1868; June 19, 24, 27, July 6, 1872.

115. Ibid., March 31, 1866. See also April 12, 1866; April 1, June 26, August 28, 1868; March 30, 1869; May 11, 1871.

116. Ibid., March 28, May 3, June 6, 1867.

117. Ibid., April 1, 1868; see also June 8, 1872.

118. Ibid., March 30, 1869. See also June 11, 1867; December 4, 1868; June 19, 24, 1872.

119. Ibid., June 7, 8, 17, 19, May 28, 1872; Montgomery, *Beyond Equality,* 330, see also 328–34.

120. Montgomery, *Beyond Equality,* 247–48; John G. Sproat, *"The Best Men": Liberal Reformers in the Gilded Age* (New York, 1968), 211–14.

121. Bernstein, *New York City Draft Riots,* 62.

122. *New-York Daily Tribune,* August 1, 1868.

123. Bernstein, *New York City Draft Riots,* 241–43; Messer-Kruse, *Yankee International.*

7. Liberal Ambiguities

1. Eric Foner, *Reconstruction: America's Unfinished Revolution, 1863–1877* (New York, 1988), 508–9.

2. Quoted in Sproat, *"The Best Men,"* 82.

3. Foner, *Reconstruction,* 504, 505, 509.

4. See, for example, Horace White, *The Life of Lyman Trumbull* (Boston, 1913), 372–88.

5. Summers, *Press Gang,* 5.

6. Earle Dudley Ross, *The Liberal Republican Movement* (New York, 1919); Matthew T. Downey, "Horace Greeley and the Politicians: The Liberal Republican Convention in 1872," *Journal of American History* 53 (March 1967): 727–50; James M. McPherson, "Grant or Greeley? The Abolitionist Dilemma in the Election of 1872," *American Historical Review* 71 (October 1965): 43–61; Richard Hofstadter, *The Age of Reform* (New York, 1955); Ari Hoogenboom, *Outlawing the Spoils: A History of the Civil Service Reform Movement* (Urbana, Ill., 1961); Sprout, "The Best Men," 72–88; Foner, *Reconstruction,* 488–511; William Gillette, *Retreat from Reconstruction, 1869–1879* (Baton Rouge, 1979), 56–72; David M. Tucker, *Mugwumps: Public Moralists of the Gilded Age* (Columbia, Mo., 1998), 46–58; Blight, *Race and Reunion,* 122–30; Perman, *Road to Redemption,* 108–31; Michael Les Benedict, "Reform Republicans and the Retreat from Reconstruction," in *The Facts of Reconstruction: Essays in Honor of John Hope Franklin,* ed. Eric Anderson and Alfred A. Moss Jr. (Baton Rouge, 1991), 53–77.

7. John Mack Faragher, et al., *Out of Many: A History of the American People* (Upper Saddle River, N.J., 2005), 522–23. *Out of Many,* however, merely reflects the best recent scholarship, which rightly links the end of Reconstruction to the rise of a laissez-faire liberal ideology that discredited efforts by black Southerners and Northern workers to use government to advance their economic interests. See Foner, *Reconstruction;* Richardson, *Death of Reconstruction.*

8. For a summary of the rumors surrounding the Reid-Gould "partnership," see Kluger, *The Paper,* 131–36.

9. Royal Cortissoz, *The Life of Whitelaw Reid,* vol. 1 (New York, 1921), 137–39.

10. Summers, *Press Gang,* 13. On the paper's institutional history during its first three decades, see Donald A. Ritchie, *Press Gallery: Congress and the Washington Correspondents* (Cambridge, Mass., 1991), 35–56; Weisberger, *Reporters for the Union,* 51–62, 87–88, 175–78; Louis M. Starr, *Bohemian Brigade: Civil War Newsmen in Action* (New York, 1954), 66–73.

11. Starr, *Bohemian Brigade,* 98–134, 353–59; on Hill, 122–26; Kluger, *The Paper,* 107–8, 120.

12. Baehr, *New York* Tribune, ix, 22–40; Young, *Men and Memories,* 5.

13. Baehr, *New York* Tribune, 28–29; Kluger, *The Paper,* 120–23.

14. Young, *Men and Memories,* 113, 114.

15. Kluger, *The Paper,* 121–22; Young, *Men and Memories,* 164; Hans Louis Trefousse, *Ben Butler: The South Called Him Beast!* (New York, 1957), 211.

16. Whitelaw Reid, *After the War: A Tour of the Southern States, 1865–1866,* ed. C. Vann Woodward (New York, 1965), 580, 503–73, see also editor's introduction, ix–xxi; Duncan, *Whitelaw Reid,* 1–78; Baehr, *New York* Tribune, 67–86.

17. Duncan, *Whitelaw Reid,* 37–65; Baehr, *New York* Tribune, 67–86; Cortissoz, *Life of Whitelaw Reid,* vol. 1, 136–52.

18. *New-York Daily Tribune,* June 22, May 8, 1871; July 29, 1868.

19. Ibid., January 9, 1868. For other uses of the phrase, see January 9, 14, 31, July 13, 1868; December 14, 1869. John Reid, president of the Workingmen's Union,

also used the phrase: "We know that labor in a reasonable measure, is still necessary, and that 'root, hog, or die,' is still nature's mandate," April 6, 1866.

20. Ibid., November 12, 1866.

21. Ibid., February 23, April 23, June 17, 1866; September 17, 30, 1867.

22. Ibid., August 4, 1866.

23. For accounts of the Davis controversy, see ibid., May 13, 14, 15, 17, 20, 23, 28, 1867; Van Deusen, *Horace Greeley,* 352–55; *The Nation* 4 (May 23, 1867), 414; Foner, *Reconstruction,* 58–59; Roy F. Nichols, "United States vs. Jefferson Davis," *American Historical Review* 31 (January 1926): 266–84; William J. Cooper Jr., *Jefferson Davis, American* (New York, 2000), 535–67.

24. Richard Zuczek, *State of Rebellion: Reconstruction in South Carolina* (Columbia, S.C., 1996), 1–158.

25. Zuczek, *State of Rebellion,* 1–158.

26. Robert Franklin Durden, *James Shepherd Pike: Republicanism and the American Negro, 1850–1882* (Durham, N.C., 1957), vii–51. On Pike and the *Tribune's* Washington correspondents between 1841 and 1861, see Ritchie, *Press Gallery,* 35–56; Weisberger, *Reporters for the Union,* 51–62.

27. Durden, *James Shepherd Pike,* 159.

28. Durden, *James Shepherd Pike,* 160–219; Summers, *Press Gang,* 191–206.

29. See Richardson, *Death of Reconstruction,* 101–11.

30. Quoted in Durden, *James Shepherd Pike,* 31.

31. Reconstruction historiography was initially shaped by William Dunning and the many students he trained at Columbia who authored influential state histories in the early twentieth century. Dunning school historians argued that Radical Republican efforts to construct a biracial political order in the South were doomed from the beginning because the formerly enslaved were easily corrupted and unfit for self-government.

32. *New-York Daily Tribune,* March 5, 1872.

33. Ibid., May 31, 1871.

34. Durden, *James Shepherd Pike,* 186–88, 209.

35. Summers, *Press Gang,* 193, 191–234.

36. Durden, *James Shepherd Pike,* 186–88, 209.

37. James S. Pike, *The Prostrate State: South Carolina Under Negro Government,* intro. Henry Steele Commanger (New York, 1935), 11–12.

38. Quoted in Durden, *James Shepherd Pike,* 205.

39. Durden, *James Shepherd Pike,* 204–5.

40. Summers, *Press Gang,* 193–234.

41. *New-York Daily Tribune,* February 28, 1872; Van Deusen, *Horace Greeley,* 97; Durden, *James Shepherd Pike,* 190–200.

42. Horace Greeley, *Mr. Greeley's Letters From Texas and the Lower Mississippi* (New York, 1871), 53.

43. Greeley, *Mr. Greeley's Letters,* 37, 38, 39, 44, 45; Van Deusen, *Horace Greeley,* 382–84.

44. Greeley, *Mr. Greeley's Letters,* 48, 49. On the relationship between political violence and suffrage proscriptions, see also *New-York Daily Tribune,* January 3, 1868.

45. Greeley, *Mr. Greeley's Letters,* 51, 52. See *New-York Daily Tribune,* May 1, 1872.

46. *New-York Daily Tribune,* January 3, 1868.˙See Van Deusen, *Horace Greeley,* 366.

47. *New-York Daily Tribune,* June 21, 1870. Pro-Grant editorials continued into July 1871, see July 7, 1871.

48. Ibid., August 18, 1871. See also February 28, March 5, 27, 1872.

49. Ibid., November 27, December 5, 1871.

50. Ibid., February 5, March 14, 1872.

51. Foner, *Reconstruction,* 484.

52. *New-York Daily Tribune,* April 12, 1872. Cited in Durden, *James Shepherd Pike,* 189, and Richardson, *Death of Reconstruction,* 102.

53. *New-York Daily Tribune,* March 30, April 4, 10, 1872.

54. Ibid., April 13, May 4, 1872. On Adams, see September 13, 1872.

55. Ibid., March 16, April 4, 1872.

56. Sproat, *"Best Men,"* 173, see 172–82; *New-York Daily Tribune,* May 4, 1872. See *New-York Daily Tribune,* February 7, May 3, 1872.

57. *New-York Daily Tribune,* May 31, 1872.

58. Ibid., June 29, 1872. Sproat, *"Best Men,"* 81–82.

59. *New-York Daily Tribune,* May 22, 1872.

60. Ibid., May 17, 1872. Described in David Quigley, *Second Founding: New York City, Reconstruction, and the Making of American Democracy* (New York, 2004), 100–104.

61. *New-York Daily Tribune,* September 20, 1872.

62. Ibid., September 21, 23, 24, 25, 26, 28, 1872.

63. Ibid., May 17, 29.

64. Ibid., August 22, September 28, 1872.

65. Ibid., July 19, August 11, 12, October 7, 1872.

66. Quoted in Benedict, "Reform Republicans and the Retreat from Reconstruction," 60.

67. Van Deusen, *Horace Greeley,* 392–97; Burrows and Wallace, *Gotham,* 1008–12; Quigley, *Second Founding,* 99–121; James C. Mohr, "New York: The De-Politicization of Reform," in *Radical Republicans in the North: State Politics during Reconstruction,* ed. James C. Mohr (Baltimore, 1976), 67, 76, see 66–81; *The Nation* 4 (May 23, 1867), 416.

68. *New-York Daily Tribune,* June 30, 1871. See also December 19, 20, 1871; February 9, 16, 20, 1872.

69. Benedict, "Reform Republicans"; Richardson, *Death of Reconstruction;* Nancy Cohen, *The Reconstruction of American Liberalism* (Chapel Hill, N.C., 2002); Harp, *Positivist Republic;* Sklansky, *Soul's Economy;* Sidney Fine, *Laissez Faire and the General Welfare State: A Study of Conflict in American Thought, 1865–1901* (Ann Arbor, 1956).

70. *Nation* 1 (October 26, 1865), 517; 4 (March 21, 1867), 224–26; *Nation* 18 (April 16, 1874), 247–48; cited in Sproat, *"Best Men,"* 27, 39.

71. For a broad survey of the role of incentive and necessity within political-economic discourse during the mid-nineteenth century, see Glickstein, *American Exceptionalism, American Anxiety.*

72. Greeley, *Letters From Texas,* 46; Perman, *Road to Redemption,* 121, 122.

73. Sproat, *"Best Men,"* 81.

74. Cortissoz, *Life of Whitelaw Reid,* vol. 1, 199.

75. Mohr, "New York: The De-Politicization of Reform," 78.

76. Foner, *Reconstruction,* 567, 568, see 564–87.

77. George Fitzhugh, "Horace Greeley and His Lost Book," *Southern Literary Messenger* 31 (September 1860), 212, 213, 216; see Harvey Wish, *George Fitzhugh: Propagandist of the Old South* (Gloucester, Mass., 1962), 271–74.

78. Huston, *Calculating the Value of the Union;* Richardson, *Greatest Nation.*

79. Beyond the peculiar variables generated by the Civil War, assessing the character of mid-nineteenth-century party ideologies presents a number of basic theoretical obstacles. Not only do the parties' various constituencies, leadership, rhetoric, and legislation each tell a separate story but the parties were geographically diverse and changed over time. The Democratic Party was one thing in the 1830s and another in the 1850s; the party in New York City was quite different from its counterpart in Missouri and Georgia. Conflicts within parties were often as substantive and robust as those that erupted between competing parties. Throughout the 1840s, the *Tribune's* battles with the Democratic Party were almost secondary to its running feuds with more conservative elements of its own party.

80. Examples include Wilentz, *Rise of American Democracy;* Watson, *Liberty and Power;* Sellers, *Market Revolution;* Ashworth, *"Agrarians" & Aristocrats";* Schlesinger, *Age of Jackson.*

81. *New-York Weekly Tribune,* April 22, 1848.

82. Though the issue has not received the kind of general attention devoted to the second party system, the ideology of the Republican Party has also provoked rigorous historical debate. Major works include Charles A. Beard and Mary R. Beard, *The Rise of American Civilization,* vol. 2 (New York, 1927); Arthur C. Cole, *The Irrepressible Conflict* (New York, 1934); Avery Craven, *The Repressible Conflict, 1830–1861* (Baton Rouge, 1939); Martin B. Duberman, ed., *The Antislavery Vanguard* (Princeton, 1965); Dwight L. Dumond, *Antislavery, the Crusade for Freedom in America* (Ann Arbor, 1961); Louis Filler, *The Crusade against Slavery* (New York, 1960); Louis S. Gerteis, *Morality and Utility in American Antislavery Reform* (Chapel Hill, 1987); Alan M. Kraut, ed., *Crusaders and Compromisers: Essays on the Relationship of the Antislavery Struggle to the Antebellum Party System* (Westport, Conn., 1983); Richard Sewell, *Ballots for Freedom: Antislavery Politics in the United States, 1837–1860* (New York, 1976); John L. Thomas, *The Liberator, William Lloyd Garrison* (Boston, 1963); Ronald G. Walters, *The Antislavery Appeal: American Abolitionism after 1830* (Baltimore, 1978); William E. Gienapp, *The Origins of the Republican Party, 1852–1856* (New York, 1987); Michael F. Holt, *The Political Crisis of the 1850s* (New York, 1978). I have obviously focused on the Republican Party. Major studies of the post-1848 Democratic Party are Jean Harvey Baker, *Affairs of Party: The Political Culture of Northern Democrats in the Mid-Nineteenth Century* (Ithaca, 1983); Bruce Collins, "Ideology of Ante-Bellum Northern Democrats," *Journal of American Studies* 11 (April 1977): 103–21; see John Ashworth, "Free Labor, Wage Labor, and the Slave Power: Republicanism and the Republican Party in the 1850s," in *The Market Revolution in America,* ed. Melvyn Stokes and Stephen Conway (Charlottesville, 1996), 130; Joel H. Silbey, *A Respectable Minority: The Democratic Party in the Civil War Era, 1860–1868* (New York, 1977); Sibley, *The Partisan Imperative: The Dynamics of American Politics before the Civil War* (New York, 1985), 166–89.

83. To some scholars, this larger association with the transformation of the basis of the North's economy makes it a less than useful device to explain what

distinguished Civil War–era Republicans from their Democratic counterparts. See William E. Gienapp, "The Republican Party and the Slave Power," in *New Perspectives on Race and Slavery in America,* ed. Robert H. Abzug and Stephen E. Maizlish (Lexington, 1986), 51–78.

84. In *Free Soil, Free Labor, Free Men,* which married the materialism of Beard to the ideological breadth of the new cultural history, Eric Foner emphasized the centrality of the Republicans' free labor message because it explains the mystery that was at the heart of the antebellum Republican project: how was it that the vast majority of Northern voters became adamantly opposed to the expansion of slavery while remaining committed to white supremacy. Republicanism's contradictory impulses, Foner argues, can be understood, primarily, within the framework of a free-labor mentalité, which rejected slavery less out of moral or religious scruples—as was the case with the limited number of abolitionists in their midst—than to affirm the individualistic outlook of a bourgeois and "dynamic, expanding capitalist society" (11). When Foner first gave the notion of free labor ideology wide currency, he implied that it was somewhat synonymous with a bourgeois brand of liberalism associated with the emergence of capitalism and "capitalist virtues." Since the original 1970 publication *of Free Soil, Free Labor, Free Men,* Foner has reconsidered the overly "straightforward, unitary" nature of his original formulation, reflecting that it did not acknowledge the way in which "different Americans might have infused it with substantially different meanings." This reformulation is more in line with his later work. The central theme of his monumental history of Reconstruction was that competing conceptions of freedom, within the Republican Party and the North as a whole, were the major dilemma of the postwar period as the country grappled with the implications of emancipation and its meanings. See Eric Foner, *Reconstruction: America's Unfinished Revolution, 1863–1877* (New York, 1988), esp. 124–75, 460–511. The meaning of freedom was also the theme of Foner's *The Story of American Freedom* (New York, 1998), esp. 95–137. In more recent published essays, which also served as a new introduction to the 1995 edition of *Free Soil, Free Labor, Free Men,* Foner explicitly acknowledges the fluidity of free labor: "If nineteenth-century Americans shared a common language of politics, the very universality of that rhetoric camouflaged a host of divergent connotations and emphases. Concepts central to the era's political culture—independence, equality, citizenship, freedom—were subject to constant challenge and redefinition, their substance changing over time as different groups sought to redraw their boundaries and reshape their meanings." See Foner, "Free Labor and Nineteenth-Century Political Ideology," in *The Market Revolution in America,* ed. Melvyn Stokes and Stephen Conway (Charlottesville, 1996), 99, 100. Nonetheless, even in his later work Foner uses the free labor concept instinctually in a way that makes it synonymous with capitalist values and the bourgeois commitment to the ultimate justice of the market. For example, in *Reconstruction* he writes, "Despite the reality of increasing class conflict, most union leaders could not liberate themselves completely from the influence or free labor precepts (a situation all but inevitable given the broad hegemony of market values in the Age of Capital, and paralleled in the contemporaneous British labor movement)." See Foner, *Reconstruction,* 478.

85. See Jonathan Glickstein, *Concepts of Free Labor in Antebellum America* (New Haven, 1991); John C. Rodrigue, *Reconstruction in the Cane Fields: From Slavery to Free Labor in Louisiana Sugar Parishes, 1862–1880* (Baton Rouge, 2001).

86. See Ashworth, "Free Labor, Wage Labor, and the Slave Power," 130; Gienapp, *Origins of the Republican Party,* 353–57; Silbey, *Partisan Imperative,* 166–89.

87. Foner, *Reconstruction;* Montgomery, *Beyond Equality.*

88. Quoted in Gienapp, *Origins of the Republican Party,* 381.

89. These are detailed at length in Richardson's *Greatest Nation of the Earth.*

90. Cohen, *Reconstruction of American Liberalism,* 4. See also Sklansky, *Soul's Economy.*

91. Dorothy Ross, "Liberalism," in *Encyclopedia of American Political History: Studies of the Principal Movements and Ideas,* vol. 2, ed. Jack P. Greene (New York: Charles Scribner's Sons, 1984), 756.

BIBLIOGRAPHY

Primary Sources
Manuscript Collections

Andrews, Stephen Pearl, Papers. Wisconsin State Historical Society.

Bennett, James Gordon, Papers. New York Public Library.

Brown, James Wright, Collection. New-York Historical Society.

Bryant-Godwin Papers. New York Public Library.

Curtis, George William, Papers. New York Public Library.

Dana, Charles Anderson, Personal Miscellaneous Manuscripts. New York Public Library.

Dwight, John, Brook Farm Collection. Boston Public Library.

Fisher, James T. Massachusetts Historical Society.

Greeley, Horace, Collection. Library of Congress, Manuscripts Division.

Greeley, Horace, Collection. New Castle Historical Society.

Greeley, Horace, Letters. Wisconsin State Historical Society.

Greeley, Horace, Papers. New-York Historical Society.

Greeley, Horace, Papers. New York Public Library.

Griswold, Rufus Wilmot, Manuscript Collection. Boston Public Library.

Jones, George, Papers. New York Public Library.

Lincoln, Abraham, Autograph Collection. New-York Historical Society.

Madigan, Thomas F., Collection. New York Public Library.

Parker, Theodore, Papers. Massachusetts Historical Society.

Parton Family Papers. Houghton Library.

Preston-Dodge Family Papers. Massachusetts Historical Society.

Raymond, Henry J., Miscellaneous Manuscripts. New-York Historical Society.

Raymond, Henry J., Papers. New York Public Library.

Ripley, George, Papers. Massachusetts Historical Society.

Schouler, James, Autograph Collection. Massachusetts Historical Society.

Schouler, William, Papers. Massachusetts Historical Society.

Weed, Thurlow, Papers. New-York Historical Society.

Webb Family Papers. New York Public Library.

Books and Articles

Andrews, Stephen Pearl, ed. *Love, Marriage, and Divorce, and the Sovereignty of the Individual: A Discussion by Henry James, Horace Greeley, and Stephen Pearl Andrews.* New York: Stringer & Townsend, 1853. Reprint, New York: Source Book Press, 1972.

[Anonymous]. "Agrarianism." *Atlantic Monthly* 3 (April 1859): 393–97.

Blanc, Louis. *History of Ten Years.* 2 vols. Translated by Walter K. Kelly. Philadelphia: Lea & Blanchard, 1848.

Börnstein, Heinrich. *Fünfundsiebzig Jahre in der Alten und Neuen Welt: Memoiren eines Unbedeutenden.* 2 vols. Edited with an English introduction by Patricia A. Herminghouse. New York: P. Lang, 1986.

——. *Memoirs of a Nobody: The Missouri Years of an Austrian Radical, 1840–1866.* Translated and edited by Steven Rowan. St. Louis: Missouri Historical Society, 1997.

Bowen, Francis. "The War of the Races in Hungary." *North American Review* 70 (January 1850): 78–136.

Brisbane, Albert. *Association; or, A Concise Exposition of the Practical Part of Fourier's Social Science.* New York: Greeley & McElrath, 1843.

——. *Social Destiny of Man; or, Association and Reorganization of Industry.* Philadelphia: C. F. Stollmeyer, 1840.

Brisbane, Redelia. *Albert Brisbane: A Mental Biography; with a Character Study by His Wife Redelia Brisbane.* Boston: Arena, 1893.

Brockway, Beman. *Fifty Years in Journalism: Embracing Recollections with an Autobiography.* Watertown, N.Y.: Daily Times Printing and Publishing House, 1891.

Browne, Junius Henri. *The Great Metropolis: A Mirror of New York.* Hartford: American Publishing Co., 1869.

Brownson, Orestes. "The Laboring Classes." *Boston Quarterly Review* (1840): 358–95.

Channing, William Ellery. *Works.* 6 vols. Boston: George C. Channing, 1849.

Child, L. Maria. *Letters From New York: Second Series.* New York: C. S. Francis, 1845.

Cleveland, Cecilia. *The Story of a Summer; or, Journal Leaves from Chappaqua.* New York: Carleton & Co., 1874.

Codman, John Thomas. *Brook Farm: Historic and Personal Memoirs.* Boston: Arena, 1894.

Curtis, George W. *Early Letters to John S. Dwight, Brook Farm and Concord.* Edited by G. W. Cooke. New York: Harper, 1898.

Dana, Charles. *Proudhon and his "Bank of the People."* New York: B. R. Tucker, 1896.

——. *Recollections of the Civil War: With the Leaders at Washington and in the Field in the Sixties.* 1898. Reprint, Lincoln: University of Nebraska Press, 1996.

——. "Proudhon and His Bank of the People." Republished in *Proudhon's Solution of the Social Problem.* Edited by Henry Cohen. New York: Vanguard, 1927.

Depew, Chauncey M. *My Memories of Eighty Years.* New York: Scribner's Sons, 1924.

Duffy, John J., ed. *Coleridge's American Disciples: The Selected Correspondence of James Marsh.* Amherst: University of Massachusetts Press, 1973.

Dwight, Marianne. *Letters from Brook Farm, 1844–1847.* Edited by Amy L. Reed. Poughkeepsie, N.Y.: Vassar College, 1928.

Emerson, Ralph Waldo. *The Collected Works of Ralph Waldo Emerson.* 5 vols. to date. Cambridge: Harvard University Press, 1971–.

——. *The Correspondence of Emerson and Carlyle.* Edited by Joseph Slater. New York: Columbia University Press, 1964.

——. *The Early Lectures of Ralph Waldo Emerson*. Edited by Stephen E. Whicher, Robert E. Spiller, and Wallace E. Williams. 3 vols. Cambridge: Harvard University Press, 1959–72.

——. *The Journals and Miscellaneous Notebooks of Ralph Waldo Emerson*. Edited by William Gilman et al. 16 vols. Cambridge: Harvard University Press, 1960–82.

——. *The Letters of Ralph Waldo Emerson*. Edited by Ralph L. Rusk and Eleanor Tilton. 8 vols. to date. New York: Columbia University Press, 1939–.

——. *Selections from Ralph Waldo Emerson: An Organic Anthology*. Edited by Stephen Whicher. Boston: Houghton, Mifflin, 1957.

Emerson, Ralph Waldo, W. H. Channing, and J. F. Clarke, eds. *Memoirs of Margaret Fuller Ossoli*. 2 vols. Boston: Phillips, Sampson, and Co., 1851.

Fitzhugh, George. *Cannibals All! or, Slaves Without Masters*. Cambridge: Belknap Press of Harvard University Press, 1960.

——. "Horace Greeley and His Lost Book." *Southern Literary Messenger* 31 (September 1860): 212–20.

——. "Slavery and Freedom." *Southern Quarterly Review* 1 (April 1856): 62–95.

——. *Sociology For the South; or, The Failure of Free Society*. New York: B. Franklin, 1965.

Fitzhugh, George and Hinton Helper. *Antebellum Writings of George Fitzhugh and Hinton Helper on Slavery*. Edited by Harvey Wish. New York: Capricorn Books, 1960.

Foster, George. *New York by Gas-Light and Other Urban Sketches*. Edited with an introduction by Stuart M. Blumin. Berkeley: California University Press, 1990.

Fuller, Margaret. *The Letters of Margaret Fuller*. Edited by Robert Hudspeth. 5 vols. to date. Ithaca: Cornell University Press, 1983–.

——. *"These Sad But Glorious Days": Dispatches from Europe, 1846–1850*. Edited by Larry J. Reynolds and Susan Belasco Smith. New Haven: Yale University Press, 1991.

Godkin, Edwin Lawrence. *Life and Letters of Edwin Lawrence Godkin*. Edited by Rollo Ogden. 2 vols. New York: Macmillan, 1907.

Godwin, Parke. *Democracy, Constructive and Pacific*. New York: J. Winchester, 1844.

——. *A Popular View of the Doctrines of Charles Fourier*. New York: J. S. Redfield, 1844.

Greeley, Horace. *The American Conflict: A History of the Great Rebellion in the United States of America, 1860–64; Its Causes, Incidents, and Results; Intended to Exhibit Especially Its Moral and Political Phases, With the Drift and Progress of American Opinion Respecting Human Slavery From 1776 to the Close of the War For the Union*. 2 vols. Hartford: O. D. Case, 1864–66.

——. *The Autobiography of Horace Greeley: Or, Recollections of a Busy Life*. New York: E. B. Treat, 1872.

——. *Essays Designed to Elucidate the Science of Political Economy: While Serving to Explain and Defend the Policy of Protection to Home Industry as a System of National Cooperation For the Elevation of Labor*. Boston: Fields, Osgood, 1870.

——. *Glances at Europe: In a Series of Letters From Great Britain, France, Italy, Switzerland, Etc., During the Summer of 1851*. New York: Dewitt & Davenport, 1851.

——. *Hints Toward Reforms, in Lectures, Addresses and Other Writings*. New York: Harper, 1850.

——. *A History of the Struggle for Slavery Extension or Restriction in the United States From the Declaration of Independence to the Present Day.* New York: Dix, Edwards, & Co., 1856.

——. *Mr. Greeley's Letters from Texas and the Lower Mississippi.* New York: Tribune Office, 1871.

——. *An Overland Journey From New York to San Francisco in the Summer of 1859.* New York: C. M. Saxton, Barker, 1860.

——. *What I Know of Farming.* New York: Arno Press, 1975.

Greeley, Horace, and Robert Dale Owen. *Divorce: Being a Correspondence Between Horace Greeley and Robert Dale Owen.* New York: Source Book Press, 1972.

Greeley, Horace, and H. J. Raymond. *Association Discussed; or, The Socialism of the Tribune Examined.* New York: Harper, 1847.

Griswold, Rufus Wilmot. *Passages From the Correspondence and Other Papers of Rufus W. Griswold.* Cambridge, Mass.: W. M. Griswold, 1898.

Helper, Hinton R. *The Impending Crisis of the South: How to Meet It.* Edited by George Frederickson. Cambridge: Belknap Press of Harvard University Press, 1968.

Kirby, Georgiana Bruce. *Years of Experience: An Autobiographical Narrative.* New York: Putnam, 1887.

Lazarus, Marx Edgeworth. *Love vs. Marriage: Part I.* New York: Fowlers & Wells, 1852.

Marx, Karl, and Friedrich Engels. *The American Journalism of Marx and Engels: A Selection from the* New York Daily Tribune. Edited by Henry Christman with an introduction by Charles Blitzer. New York: American Library, 1966.

Miller, Perry, ed. *The Transcendentalists: An Anthology.* Cambridge: Harvard University Press, 1950.

Parton, James. *Life of Horace Greeley: From His Birth to the Present Time.* Boston: James R. Osgood, 1872.

Pike, James S. *First Blows of the Civil War: Ten Years of Preliminary Conflict in the United States.* New York: American News Co., 1879.

——. *The Prostrate State: South Carolina Under Negro Government.* Introduction by Henry Steele Commager. New York: Loring and Mussey, 1935.

Proudhon, Pierre Joseph. *Selected Writings.* Translated by Elizabeth Fraser and edited by Stewart Edwards. Garden City, N.Y.: Anchor, 1969.

——. *What is Property?* Edited and translated by Donald R. Kelly and Bonnie G. Smith. New York: Cambridge University Press, 1994.

Reid, Whitelaw. *After the War: A Tour of the Southern States, 1865–1866.* Edited by C. Vann Woodward. New York: Harper & Row, 1965.

Sams, Henry W., ed. *Autobiography of Brook Farm.* Englewood Cliffs, N.J.: Prentice-Hall, 1958.

Smith, E. Oakes. *Selections From the Autobiography of Elizabeth Oakes [Prince] Smith.* Edited by Mary Alice Wyman. New York: Ayer Co., 1980.

——. *Woman and Her Needs.* New York: Fowler & Wells, 1851. Reprint, New York: Arno Press, 1974.

Stanton, Henry B. *Random Recollections.* Johnstown, N.Y.: University of North Carolina & Leaning Printers, 1885.

Warren, Josiah. *Equitable Commerce: A New Development of Principles as Substitutes for Laws and Governments, for the Harmonious Adjustment and Regulation of the Pecuniary,*

Intellectual, and Moral Intercourse of Mankind Proposed as Elements of New Society. New York: Fowler & Wells, 1852. Reprint, New York: Burt Franklin, 1967.

Whitman, Walt. *The Gathering of the Forces.* Vol. 1. New York: G. P. Putnam's Sons, 1920.

Secondary Sources

Allen, Gay Wilson. *Waldo Emerson: A Biography.* New York: Viking, 1981.

Allen, Margaret V. "The Political and Social Criticism of Margaret Fuller." *South Atlantic Quarterly* 72 (Autumn 1973): 560–73.

Allen, Robert C. *Horrible Prettiness: Burlesque and American Culture.* Chapel Hill: University of North Carolina Press, 1991.

Anderson, Benedict. *Imagined Communities: Reflections on the Spread of Nationalism.* New York: Verso, 1991.

Anderson, Eric, and Alfred A. Moss Jr., eds. *The Facts of Reconstruction: Essays in Honor of John Hope Franklin.* Baton Rouge: Louisiana State University Press, 1991.

Andrews, J. Cutler. *The North Reports the Civil War.* Pittsburgh: University of Pittsburgh Press, 1955.

Arieli, Yehoshua. *Individualism and Nationalism in American Ideology.* Cambridge: Harvard University Press, 1964.

Ashworth, John. *"Agrarians" & "Aristocrats": Party Ideology in the United States, 1837–1846.* London: Royal Historical Society, 1983.

Baehr, Harry W., Jr. *The New York* Tribune *since the Civil War.* New York: Octagon Books, 1972.

Baker, Jean Harvey. *Affairs of Party: The Political Culture of Northern Democrats in the Mid-Nineteenth Century.* Ithaca: Cornell University Press, 1983.

Baker, Thomas N. *Sentiment and Celebrity: Nathaniel Parker Willis and the Trials of Literary Fame.* New York: Oxford University Press, 1999.

Banning, Lance. *The Jeffersonian Persuasion: Evolution of a Party Ideology.* Ithaca: Cornell University Press, 1978.

Barney, William L. *The Passage of the Republic: An Interdisciplinary History of Nineteenth-Century America.* Lexington, Mass.: D. C. Heath, 1987.

Barth, Gunther. *City People: The Rise of Modern City Culture in Nineteenth-Century America.* New York: Oxford University Press, 1980.

Basch, Norma. *In the Eyes of the Law: Women, Marriage, and Property in Nineteenth-Century New York.* Ithaca: Cornel University Press, 1982.

———. *Framing American Divorce: From the Revolutionary Generation to the Victorians.* Berkeley: University of California Press, 1999.

Bassett, T. D. Seymour. "The Secular Utopian Socialists." In *Socialism and American Life,* edited by Donald Drew Egbert and Stow Persons. Vol. 1. Princeton: Princeton University Press, 1952.

Baym, Nina. *Novels, Readers, and Reviewers: Responses to Fiction in Antebellum America.* Ithaca: Cornell University Press, 1984.

Bean, Judith Mattson, and Joel Myerson, eds. *Margaret Fuller, Critic: Writings from the* New-York Tribune, *1844–1846.* New York: Columbia University Press, 2000.

Beecher, Jonathan. *Charles Fourier: The Visionary and His World.* Berkeley: University of California Press, 1986.

———. *Victor Considerant and the Rise and Fall of French Romantic Socialism.* Berkeley: University of California Press, 2001.

Bender, Thomas. *New York Intellect: A History of Intellectual Life in New York City from 1750 to the Beginnings of Our Own Time.* Baltimore: Johns Hopkins University Press, 1987.

———, ed. *The Antislavery Debate: Capitalism and Abolitionism as a Problem in Historical Interpretation.* Berkeley: University of California Press, 1992.

Benedict, Michael Les. "Reform Republicans and the Retreat from Reconstruction." In *The Facts of Reconstruction: Essays in Honor of John Hope Franklin,* edited by Eric Anderson and Alfred A. Moss Jr. Baton Rouge: Louisiana State University Press, 1991.

Benson, Lee. *The Concept of Jacksonian Democracy: New York as a Test Case.* Princeton: Princeton University Press, 1961.

Bercovitch, Sacvan. *The American Jeremiad.* Madison: University of Wisconsin Press, 1978.

———. *The Rites of Assent: Transformations in the Symbolic Construction of America.* New York: Routledge, 1993.

Berger, Meyer. *The Story of the* New York Times, *1851–1951.* New York: Simon and Schuster, 1951.

Bernstein, Iver. *The New York City Draft Riots: Their Significance for American Society and Politics in the Age of the Civil War.* New York: Oxford University Press, 1990.

Bestor, Arthur. "Albert Brisbane—Propagandist for Socialism in the 1840s." *New York History* 28 (April 1947): 128–58.

———. *Backwoods Utopias: The Sectarian Origins and the Owenite Phase of Communitarian Socialism in America, 1663–1829.* 2nd ed. Philadelphia: University of Pennsylvania Press, 1970.

Blackmar, Elizabeth. *Manhattan for Rent, 1785–1850.* Ithaca: Cornell University Press, 1989.

Blake, Casey Nelson. *Beloved Community: The Cultural Criticism of Randolph Bourne, Van Wyck Brooks, Waldo Frank, and Lewis Mumford.* Chapel Hill: University of North Carolina Press, 1990.

Blanchard, Paula. *Margaret Fuller: From Transcendentalism to Revolution.* New York: Delacorte Press, 1978.

Blight, David W. *Race and Reunion: The Civil War and American Memory.* Cambridge: Harvard University Press, 2001.

Blue, Frederick J. *The Free Soilers: Third Party Politics, 1848–1854.* Urbana: University of Illinois Press, 1973.

Bode, Carl. *The American Lyceum: The Town Meeting of the Mind.* Carbondale: Southern Illinois Press, 1956.

Booraem, Hendrik V. *The Formation of the Republican Party in New York: Politics and Conscience in the Antebellum North.* New York: New York University Press, 1983.

Borden, Morten. "Some Notes on Horace Greeley, Charles Dana, and Karl Marx." *Journalism Quarterly* 34 (Fall 1957): 457–65.

———, ed. "Five Letters of Charles A. Dana to Karl Marx." *Journalism Quarterly* 36 (Summer 1959): 314–16.

Boritt, Gabor S., ed. *The Historian's Lincoln: Pseudohistory, Psychohistory, and History.* Urbana: University of Illinois Press, 1988.

Boyer, Paul S. *Urban Masses and Moral Order in America, 1820–1920.* Cambridge: Harvard University Press, 1978.

Brauer, Kinley J. *Cotton versus Conscience: Massachusetts Whig Politics and Southwestern Expansion, 1843–1848.* Lexington: University of Kentucky Press, 1967.

Brock, William R. *Parties and Political Conscience: American Dilemmas, 1840–1850.* Millwood, N.Y.: KTO Press, 1979.

Bromell, Nicholas K. *By the Sweat of the Brow: Literature and Labor in Antebellum America.* Chicago: University of Chicago Press, 1993.

Bronstein, Jamie C. *Land Reform and Working-Class Experience in Britain and the United States, 1800–1862.* Stanford: Stanford University Press, 1999.

Brown, David. *Southern Outcast: Hinton Rowan Helper and* The Impending Crisis of the South. Baton Rouge: Louisiana State University Press, 2006.

Brown, Francis. *Raymond of the Times.* New York: W. W. Norton, 1951.

Bruegel, Martin. "Unrest: Manorial Society and the Market in the Hudson Valley, 1780–1850." *Journal of American History* 82 (March 1996): 1393–1424.

Buckley, Peter. "To the Opera House: Culture and Society in New York City, 1820–1860." PhD diss., State University of New York at Stony Brook, 1984.

Burrows, Edwin G., and Mike Wallace. *Gotham: A History of New York City to 1898.* New York: Oxford University Press, 1999.

Capper, Charles. *Margaret Fuller: An American Romantic Life; The Private Years.* New York: Oxford University Press, 1992.

——. "Margaret Fuller as Cultural Reformer: The Conversations in Boston." *American Quarterly* 39 (Winter 1987): 509–28.

Capper, Charles, and Conrad Edick Wright, eds. *Transient and Permanent: The Transcendentalist Movement and Its Contexts.* Boston: Massachusetts Historical Society, 1999.

Cayton, Mary Kupiec. *Emerson's Emergence: Self and Society in the Transformation of New England, 1800–1845.* Chapel Hill: University of North Carolina Press, 1989.

——. "The Making of an American Prophet: Emerson, His Audiences, and the Rise of the Culture Industry in Nineteenth-Century America." *American Historical Review* 92 (June 1987): 597–620.

Charvat, William. *The Profession of Authorship in America: The Papers of William Charvat.* Edited by Matthew J. Bruccoli. Columbus: Ohio State University Press, 1968.

Chevigny, Bell Gale. "To the Edges of Ideology: Margaret Fuller's Centrifugal Evolution." *American Quarterly* 38 (Summer 1986): 173–201.

——. *The Woman and the Myth: Margaret Fuller's Life and Writings.* Boston: Northeastern University Press, 1994.

Christman, Henry. *Tin Horns and Calico: A Decisive Episode in the Emergence of Democracy.* New York: Henry Holt, 1945.

Cmiel, Kenneth. *Democratic Eloquence: The Fight over Popular Speech in Nineteenth-Century America.* Berkeley: University of California Press, 1990.

Cohen, Nancy. *The Reconstruction of American Liberalism, 1865–1914.* Chapel Hill: University of North Carolina Press, 2002.

Commons, John R. "Horace Greeley and the Working-Class Origins of the Republican Party." *Political Science Quarterly* 24 (1909): 468–88.

Commons, John R., et al. *History of Labour in the United States.* Vol. 1. New York: Macmillan, 1921.

Conkin, Paul K. *Prophets of Prosperity: America's First Political Economists.* Bloomington: Indiana University Press, 1980.

Cooney, Terry A. *The Rise of the New York Intellectuals: The* Partisan Review *and Its Circle, 1934–1945.* Madison: University of Wisconsin Press, 1986.

Cooper, William J., Jr. *Jefferson Davis, American.* New York: Alfred A. Knopf, 2000.

Cortissoz, Royal. *The Life of Whitelaw Reid.* 2 vols. New York: Charles Scribner's Sons, 1921.

Cover, Robert M. *Justice Accused: Antislavery and the Judicial Process.* New Haven: Yale University Press, 1975.

Crofts, Daniel W. "Secession Winter: William Henry Seward and the Decision for War." *New York History* 65 (July 1984): 229–56.

Cross, Coy F. *Go West Young Man! Horace Greeley's Vision for America.* Albuquerque: University of New Mexico Press, 1995.

Cross, Whitney R. *The Burned-Over District: The Social and Intellectual History of Enthusiastic Religion in Western New York, 1800–1850.* Ithaca: Cornell University Press, 1950.

Crouthamel, James L. *Bennett's* New York Herald *and the Rise of the Popular Press.* Syracuse: Syracuse University Press, 1989.

———. *James Watson Webb: A Biography.* Middletown, Conn.: Wesleyan University Press, 1969.

Crowe, Charles. *George Ripley, Transcendentalist and Utopian Socialist.* Athens: University of Georgia Press, 1967.

Crozier, Emmet. *Yankee Reporters, 1861–1865.* New York: Oxford University Press, 1956.

Curtis, Eugene N. "American Opinion of the French Nineteenth-Century Revolutions." *American Historical Review* 29 (January 1924): 249–70.

Darnton, Robert. "The Great Book Massacre." *New York Review of Books* 47 (April 26, 2001): 16–19.

Davis, David Brion. *The Problem of Slavery in the Age of Revolution, 1770–1823.* Ithaca: Cornell University Press, 1975.

———. *Slavery and Human Progress.* New York: Oxford University Press, 1984.

Degler, Carl. *Out of Our Past: The Forces That Shaped Modern America.* New York: Harper, 1959.

Denholm, Tony. "Louis Auguste Blanqui: The Hamlet of Revolutionary Socialism." In *Intellectuals and Revolution: Socialism and the Experience of 1848,* edited by Eugene Kamenka and F. B. Smith. London: Edward Arnold, 1979.

Denning, Michael, *Mechanic Accents: Dime Novels and Working-Class Culture in America.* London: Verso, 1987.

Dewey, John. *Liberalism and Social Action.* New York: Prometheus Books, 2000.

Ditzion, Sidney. *Marriage, Morals, and Sex in America: A History of Ideas.* New York: Octagon Books, 1969.

Dobert, Eitel W. "The Radicals." *The Forty-Eighters: Political Refugees of the German Revolution of 1848.* New York: Columbia University Press, 1950.

Donald, David Herbert. *Lincoln.* New York: Simon and Schuster, 1995.

Dorfman, Joseph. *The Economic Mind in American Civilization.* Vol. 2. New York: Augustus M. Kelley, 1966.

Douglas, Ann. *The Feminization of American Culture.* New York: Anchor Books, 1977.

Dudden, Faye. *Women in the American Theater: Actresses and Audiences, 1790–1870.* New Haven: Yale University Press, 1994.

Duncan, Bingham. *Whitelaw Reid: Journalist, Politician, Diplomat.* Athens: University of Georgia Press, 1975.

Durden, Robert Franklin. *James Shepherd Pike: Republicanism and the American Negro, 1850–1882.* Durham: Duke University Press, 1957.

Elkins, Stanley M. *Slavery: A Problem in American Institutional and Intellectual Life.* Chicago: University of Chicago Press, 1959.

Elkins, Stanley, and Eric McKitrick. *Age of Federalism: The Early American Republic, 1788–1800.* New York: Oxford University Press, 1993.

Emerson, Ellen Tucker. *The Life of Lidian Jackson Emerson.* Edited by Delores Bird Carpenter. Boston: Twayne, 1980.

Emery, Edwin, and Henry Ladd Smith. *The Press and America.* Englewood Cliffs, N.J.: Prentice-Hall, 1954.

Engerman, Stanley L., and Robert E. Gallman. "The Emergence of a Market Economy before 1860." In *A Companion to 19th Century America,* edited by William L. Barney. Malden, Mass.: Blackwell, 2001.

Faust, Drew Gilpin. *A Sacred Circle: The Dilemma of the Intellectual in the Old South.* Baltimore: Johns Hopkins University Press, 1977.

Fehrenbacher, Don E. *The Dred Scott Case: Its Significance in American Law and Politics.* New York: Oxford University Press, 1978.

Feller, Daniel. *The Public Lands in Jacksonian Politics.* Madison: University of Wisconsin Press, 1984.

Fellman, Michael. *The Unbounded Frame: Freedom and Community in Nineteenth-Century American Utopianism.* Westport, Conn.: Greenwood Press, 1973.

Field, Peter S. *The Crisis of the Standing Order: Clerical Intellectuals and Cultural Authority in Massachusetts, 1780–1833.* Amherst: University of Massachusetts Press, 1998.

———. *Ralph Waldo Emerson: The Making of a Democratic Intellectual.* Lanham, Md.: Rowan and Littlefield, 2002.

Fine, Sidney. *Laissez-Faire and the General Welfare State: A Study of Conflict in American Thought, 1865–1901.* Ann Arbor: University of Michigan Press, 1956.

Fink, Leon. *Progressive Intellectuals and the Dilemmas of Democratic Commitment.* Cambridge: Harvard University Press, 1997.

———. *Workingmen's Democracy: The Knights of Labor and American Politics.* Urbana: University of Illinois Press, 1983.

Fink, Leon, Stephen T. Leonard, and Donald M. Reid, eds. *Intellectuals and Public Life: Between Radicalism and Reform.* Ithaca: Cornell University Press, 1996.

Fink, Steven. *Prophet in the Marketplace: Thoreau's Development as a Professional Writer.* Princeton: Princeton University Press, 1992.

Foner, Eric. "Abolitionism and the Labor Movement in Antebellum America." In *Antislavery, Religion, and Reform: Essays in Memory of Roger Anstey,* edited by Christine Bolt and Seymour Drescher. Hamden, Conn.: Archon Books, 1980.

——. *Free Soil, Free Labor, Free Men: The Ideology of the Republican Party before the Civil War.* New York: Oxford University Press, 1970.

——. *Politics and Ideology in the Age of the Civil War.* New York: Oxford University Press, 1980.

——. *Reconstruction: America's Unfinished Revolution, 1863–1877.* New York: Harper and Row, 1988.

——. *The Story of American Freedom.* New York: W. W. Norton, 1998.

Francis, Richard. *Transcendental Utopias: Individual and Community at Brook Farm, Fruitlands, and Walden.* Ithaca: Cornell University Press, 1997.

Frederickson, George M. *The Black Image in the White Mind: The Debate on Afro-American Character and Destiny, 1817–1914.* New York: Harper and Row, 1971.

——. *The Inner Civil War: Northern Intellectuals and the Crisis of the Union.* New York: Harper, 1965.

Freehling, William W. *The Road to Disunion: Secessionists at Bay, 1776–1854.* New York: Oxford University Press, 1990.

Friedman, Lawrence. *Inventors of the Promised Land.* New York: Knopf, 1975.

Frothingham, Octavius Brooks. *George Ripley.* Boston: Houghton Mifflin, 1882.

Gemme, Paola. *Domesticating Foreign Struggles: The Italian Risorgimento and Antebellum American Identity.* Athens: University of Georgia Press, 2005.

Genovese, Eugene D. *The Slaveholders's Dilemma: Freedom and Progress in Southern Conservative Thought, 1820–1860.* Columbia: University of South Carolina Press, 1992.

——. *The World the Slaveholders Made: Two Essays in Interpretation.* New York: Pantheon, 1969. Reprint, Middletown, Conn.: Wesleyan University Press, 1988.

Gerteis, Louis S. *Morality and Utility in American Antislavery Reform.* Chapel Hill: University of North Carolina Press, 1987.

Gettleman, Marvin E. *The Dorr Rebellion: A Study in American Radicalism, 1833–1849.* New York: Random House, 1973.

Gienapp, William E. *The Origins of the Republican Party, 1852–1856.* New York: Oxford University Press, 1987.

Gilfoyle, Timothy. *City of Eros: New York City, Prostitution, and the Commercialization of Sex, 1790–1920.* New York: W. W. Norton, 1992.

Gilje, Paul A. "The Rise of Capitalism in the Early Republic." *Journal of the Early Republic* 16 (1996): 159–82.

Gillette, William. *Retreat from Reconstruction, 1869–1879.* Baton Rouge: Louisiana State University Press, 1979.

Gilmore, Michael T. *American Romanticism and the Marketplace.* Chicago: University of Chicago Press, 1985.

Glickstein, Jonathan A. *American Exceptionalism, American Anxiety: Wages, Competition, and Degraded Labor in the Antebellum United States.* Charlottesville: University of Virginia Press, 2002.

——. *Concepts of Free Labor in Antebellum America.* New Haven: Yale University Press, 1991.

——. "'Poverty Is Not Slavery': American Abolitionists and the Competitive Labor Market." In *Antislavery Reconsidered: New Perspectives on the Abolitionists,* ed. Lewis Perry and Michael Fellman. Baton Rouge: Louisiana State University Press, 1979.

Goldin, Gurston. "Business Sentiment and the Mexican War with Particular Emphasis on the New York Businessman." *New York History* 33 (1952): 54–70.

Golemba, Henry. *George Ripley.* Boston: Twayne, 1977.

Gorn, Elliot, *The Manly Art: Bare-Knuckle Prize Fighting in America.* Ithaca: Cornell University Press, 1986.

Gougeon, Len. *Virtue's Hero: Emerson, Antislavery, and Reform.* Athens: University of Georgia Press, 1990.

Grossberg, Michael. *Governing the Hearth: Law and the Family in Nineteenth-Century America.* Chapel Hill: University of North Carolina Press, 1985.

Gross, Robert A. "Printing, Politics, and the People." *Proceedings of the American Antiquarian Society* 99 (October 1989): 375–97.

Grossman, Jonathan. *William Sylvis, Pioneer of American Labor: A Study of the Labor Movement during the Era of the Civil War.* New York: Octagon Books, 1973.

Guarneri, Carl J. *The Utopian Alternative: Fourierism in Nineteenth-Century America.* Ithaca: Cornell University Press, 1991.

——. "Brook Farm, Fourierism, and the Nationalist Dilemma in American Utopianism." In *Transient and Permanent: The Transcendentalist Movement and Its Contexts,* ed. Charles Capper and Conrad Edick Wright. Boston: Massachusetts Historical Society, 1999.

Habegger, Alfred. *The Father: A Life of Henry James, Sr.* New York: Farrar, Straus and Giroux, 1994.

Habermas, Jürgen. *The Structural Transformation of the Public Sphere: An Inquiry into a Category of Bourgeois Society.* Translated by Thomas Burger. Cambridge: MIT Press, 1991.

Habich, Robert D. *Transcendentalism and the Western Messenger: A History of the Magazine and Its Contributors.* Rutherford, N.J.: Fairleigh Dickinson University Press, 1985.

Hale, William Harlan. *Horace Greeley: Voice of the People.* New York: Harper, 1950.

——. "When Karl Marx Worked for Horace Greeley." *American Heritage* 8 (April 1957): 20–25.

Halttunen, Karen. *Confidence Men and Painted Women: A Study of Middle-Class Culture in America, 1830–1870.* New Haven: Yale University Press, 1982.

Harp, Gillis J. *Positivist Republic: Auguste Comte and the Reconstruction of American Liberalism, 1865–1920.* University Park: Pennsylvania State University, 1995.

Harper, Robert S. *Lincoln and the Press.* New York: McGraw-Hill, 1951.

Hartz, Louis. *The Liberal Tradition in America: An Interpretation of American Political Thought since the Revolution.* New York: Harcourt, Brace, 1955.

Haskell, Thomas L. *The Emergence of Professional Social Science: The American Social Science Association and the Nineteenth-Century Crisis of Authority.* Urbana: University of Illinois Press, 1977.

Hatch, Nathan O. *The Democratization of American Christianity.* New Haven: Yale University Press, 1989.

Hearder, Harry. *Europe in the Nineteenth Century, 1830–1880.* New York: Longman, 1988.

Henkin, David M. *City Reading: Written Words and Public Spaces in Antebellum New York.* New York: Columbia University Press, 1998.

Higham, John. *From Boundlessness to Consolidation: The Transformation of American Culture, 1848–1860.* Ann Arbor, Mich.: William L. Clements Library, 1969.

Higginson, Thomas Wentworth. *Margaret Fuller Ossoli*. Boston: Houghton, Mifflin, 1884.

Hobsbawm, E. J. *The Age of Revolution: Europe, 1789–1848*. London: Abacus, 1977.

Hollinger, David A. "Historians and the Discourse of Intellectuals." In *New Directions in American Intellectual History*, edited by John Higham and Paul K. Conkin. Baltimore: Johns Hopkins University Press, 1979.

Hollister, O. J. *Life of Schuyler Colfax*. New York: Funk and Wagnalls, 1886.

Holt, Michael F. *The Political Crisis of the 1850s*. New York: W. W. Norton, 1978.

——. *The Rise and Fall of the American Whig Party: Jacksonian Politics and the Onset of the Civil War*. New York: Oxford University Press, 1999.

Horowitz, Morton J. *The Transformation of American Law*. Cambridge: Harvard University Press, 1977.

Horsman, Reginald. *Race and Manifest Destiny: The Origins of American Racial Anglo-Saxonism*. Cambridge: Harvard University Press, 1981.

Howe, Daniel Walker. *Making the American Self: Jonathan Edwards to Abraham Lincoln*. Cambridge: Harvard University Press, 1997.

——. *The Political Culture of the American Whigs*. Chicago: University of Chicago Press, 1979.

——. *The Unitarian Conscience: Harvard Moral Philosophy, 1805–1861*. Cambridge: Harvard University Press, 1970.

——. *What Hath God Wrought: The Transformation of America, 1815–1848*. New York: Oxford University Press, 2007.

Huston, James L. *Calculating the Value of the Union: Slavery, Property Rights, and the Economic Origins of the Civil War*. Chapel Hill: University of North Carolina Press, 2003.

——. *Securing the Fruits of Labor: The American Concept of Wealth Distribution, 1765–1900*. Baton Rouge: Louisiana State University Press, 1998.

Hutchison, William R. *The Transcendental Ministers: Church Reform in the New England Renaissance*. New Haven: Yale University Press, 1959.

Ingersoll, Lurton Dunham. *The Life of Horace Greeley: Founder of the* New York Tribune, *With Extended Notices of Many of His Contemporary Statesmen and Journalists*. Chicago: Union Publishing Co., 1873.

Isley, Jeter Allen. *Horace Greeley and the Republican Party, 1853–1861: A Study of the* New York Tribune. Princeton: Princeton University Press, 1947.

Izenberg, Gerald N. *Impossible Individuality: Romanticism, Revolution, and the Origins of Modern Selfhood, 1787–1802*. Princeton: Princeton University Press, 1992.

Jenkins, William Sumner. *Pro-Slavery Thought in the Old South*. Chapel Hill: University of North Carolina Press, 1935.

Johannsen, Robert W. *To the Halls of Montezuma: The Mexican War in the American Imagination*. New York: Oxford University Press, 1985.

Karcher, Carolyn L. *The First Woman in the Republic: A Cultural Biography of Lydia Maria Child*. Durham, N.C.: Duke University Press, 1994.

Kasson, John F. *Amusing the Million: Coney Island at the Turn of the Century*. New York: Hill and Wang, 1978.

——. *Rudeness and Civility: Manners in Nineteenth-Century Urban America*. New York: Hill and Wang, 1990.

Katz, Philip M. *From Appomattox to Montmartre: Americans and the Paris Commune.* Cambridge: Harvard University Press, 1998.

Kaufman, Allen. *Capitalism, Slavery, and Republican Values: Antebellum Political Economists, 1819–1848.* Austin: University of Texas Press, 1982.

Kloppenberg, James T. *Uncertain Victory: Social Democracy and Progressivism in European and American Thought, 1870–1920.* New York: Oxford University Press, 1986.

———. *The Virtues of Liberalism.* New York: Oxford University Press, 1998.

Kluger, Richard. *The Paper: The Life and Death of the* New York Herald-Tribune. New York: Knopf, 1986.

Kohl, Lawrence Frederick. *The Politics of Individualism: Parties and the American Character in the Jacksonian Era.* New York: Oxford University Press, 1989.

Kopacz, Paula. "Feminist at the *Tribune:* Margaret Fuller as Professional Writer." *Studies in the American Renaissance* (1991): 119–39.

Kraditor, Aileen S. *Means and Ends in American Abolitionism: Garrison and His Critics on Strategy and Tactics, 1834–1850.* New York: Pantheon Books, 1967.

Kraut, Alan M, ed. *Crusaders and Compromisers: Essays on the Relationship of the Antislavery Struggle to the Antebellum Party System.* Westport, Conn.: Greenwood Press, 1983.

Lasch, Christopher. *The Revolt of the Elites and the Betrayal of Democracy.* New York: W. W. Norton, 1995.

Leach, William. *True Love and Perfect Union: The Feminist Reform of Sex and Society.* Middletown, Conn.: Wesleyan University Press, 1989.

Leverenz, David. *Manhood and the American Renaissance.* Ithaca: Cornell University Press, 1989.

Levine, Bruce. *The Migration of Ideology and the Contested Meaning of Freedom: German Americans in the Mid-Nineteenth Century.* Washington, D.C.: German Historical Institute, 1992.

———. *The Spirit of 1848: German Immigrants, Labor Conflict, and the Coming of the Civil War.* Urbana: University of Illinois Press, 1992.

Levine, Lawrence F. *Highbrow/Lowbrow: The Emergence of Cultural Hierarchy in America.* Cambridge: Harvard University Press, 1988.

Lobove, Roy. "The New York Association for Improving the Condition of the Poor: The Formative Years." *New-York Historical Society Quarterly* 43 (July 1959): 307–27.

Lustig, R. Jeffery. *Corporate Liberalism: The Origins of Modern American Political Theory, 1890–1920.* Berkeley: University of California Press, 1982.

Lystra, Karen. *Searching the Heart: Women, Men, and Romantic Love in Nineteenth-Century America.* New York: Oxford University Press, 1989.

Macpherson, C. B. *The Political Theory of Possessive Individualism: Hobbes to Locke.* New York: Clarendon Press, 1964.

Magraw, Roger. *France 1815–1914: The Bourgeois Century.* New York: Oxford University Press, 1986.

———. *A History of the French Working Class.* 2 vols. Cambridge: Harvard University Press, 1992.

Madden, Edward H. *Civil Disobedience and Moral Law in Nineteenth-Century American Philosophy.* Seattle: University of Washington Press, 1968.

Mandel, Bernard. *Labor, Free and Slave: Workingmen and the Anti-Slavery Movement in the United States.* New York: Associated Authors, 1955.

Manuel, Frank E. *The Prophets of Paris: Turgot, Condorcet, Saint-Simon, Fourier, and Comte.* New York: Harper and Row, 1962.

Maverick, Augustus. *Henry J. Raymond and the New York Press for Thirty Years: Progress of American Journalism From 1840–1870.* Hartford, Conn.: A. S. Hale, 1870.

McCormick, Richard P. *The Second American Party System: Party Formation in the Jacksonian Era.* Chapel Hill: University of North Carolina Press, 1966.

McCoy, Drew R. *The Elusive Republic: Political Economy in Jeffersonian America.* New York: W. W. Norton, 1980.

McCurdy, Charles W. *The Anti-Rent Era in New York Law and Politics, 1839–1865.* Chapel Hill: University of North Carolina Press, 2001.

McInerney, Daniel J. *The Fortunate Heirs of Freedom: Abolition and Republican Thought.* Lincoln: University of Nebraska Press, 1994.

McLellan, David. *Karl Marx: A Biography.* London: Papermac, 1995.

McPherson, James M. *Battle Cry of Freedom: The Civil War Era.* New York: Oxford University Press, 1988.

Mead, David. *Yankee Eloquence in the Middle West: The Ohio Lyceum, 1850–1870.* East Lansing: Michigan State University Press, 1951.

Merk, Frederick. "Dissent in the Mexican War." In *Dissent in Three American Wars,* edited by Samuel Eliot Morison, Frederick Merk, and Frank Freidel. Cambridge: Harvard University Press, 1970.

Messer-Kruse, Timothy. *The Yankee International: Marxism and the American Reform Tradition, 1848–1876.* Chapel Hill: University of North Carolina Press, 1998.

Mitchell, Edward P. *Memoirs of an Editor: Fifty Years of American Journalism.* New York: Scribner's Sons, 1924.

Mize, Sandra Yocum. "Defending Roman Loyalties and Republican Values: The 1848 Italian Revolution in American Catholic Apologetics." *Church History* 60 (December 1991): 480–92.

Mohr, James C, ed. *Radical Republicans in the North: State Politics during Reconstruction.* Baltimore: Johns Hopkins University Press, 1976.

Montgomery, David. *Beyond Equality: Labor and the Radical Republicans, 1862–1872.* New York: Knopf, 1967.

Mott, Frank Luther. *American Journalism, a History: 1690–1960.* New York: Macmillan, 1962.

Myerson, Joel. *The New England Transcendentalists and the Dial; A History of the Magazine and Its Contributors.* Rutherford, N.J.: Fairleigh Dickinson University Press, 1980.

Neill, Charles Patrick. "Daniel Raymond: An Early Chapter in the History of Economic Thought." *Johns Hopkins Studies in Historical and Political Science,* series 15, no. 6. Baltimore: Johns Hopkins University Press, 1897.

Nevins, Allan. *The Evening Post: A Century of Journalism.* New York: Boni and Liveright, 1922.

——. *Ordeal of the Union: Fruits of Manifest Destiny, 1847–1852.* New York: Charles Scribner's Sons, 1947.

Nichols, Roy F. "United States vs. Jefferson Davis." *American Historical Review* 31 (January 1926): 266–84.

Nissenbaum, Stephen. *Sex, Diet, and Debility in Jacksonian America: Sylvester Graham and Health Reform.* Westport, Conn.: Greenwood Press, 1980.

Novak, William J. *The People's Welfare: Law and Regulation in Nineteenth-Century America.* Chapel Hill: University of North Carolina Press, 1996.

O'Brien, Frank M. *The Story of the* Sun. New York: Greenwood Press, 1928.

Ostrander, Gilman M. *Republic of Letters: The American Intellectual Community, 1776–1865.* Madison: University of Wisconsin Press, 1999.

Pasley, Jeffrey L. *"The Tyranny of Printers": Newspaper Politics in the Early American Republic.* Charlottesville: University of Virginia Press, 2001.

Paul, James C. N. *Rift in the Democracy.* Philadelphia: University of Pennsylvania Press, 1951.

Penta, Constance. "Fuller's Folly: The Eccentric World of Margaret Fuller and the Greeleys." MA thesis, Columbia University, 1960.

Perman, Michael. *The Road to Redemption: Southern Politics, 1869–1879.* Chapel Hill: University of North Carolina Press, 1984.

Perry, Lewis. *Radical Abolitionism: Anarchy and the Government of God in Antislavery Thought.* Knoxville: University of Tennessee Press, 1995.

Pessen, Edward. *Most Uncommon Jacksonians: The Radical Leaders of the Early Labor Movement.* Albany: State University of New York Press, 1967.

Pocock, J. G. A. *The Machiavellian Moment: Florentine Political Thought and the Atlantic Republican Tradition.* Princeton: Princeton University Press, 1975.

Pred, Allan R. *Urban Growth and the Circulation of Information: The United States System of Cities, 1790–1840.* Cambridge: Harvard University Press, 1973.

Quigley, David. *Second Founding: New York City, Reconstruction, and the Making of American Democracy.* New York: Hill and Wang, 2004.

Raddatz, Fritz J. *Karl Marx: A Political Biography.* Translated by Richard Barry. Boston: Little, Brown, 1978.

Rayback, Joseph A. *Free Soil: The Election of 1848.* Lexington: University Press of Kentucky, 1970.

Reynolds, David. *Beneath the American Renaissance: The Subversive Imagination in the Age of Emerson and Melville.* New York: Knopf, 1988.

Reynolds, Larry J. *European Revolutions and the American Literary Renaissance.* New Haven: Yale University Press, 1988.

——. "From *Dial* Essay to New York Book: The Making of *Woman in the Nineteenth Century.*" In *Periodical Literature in Nineteenth-Century America,* edited by Kenneth M. Price and Susan Belasco Smith. Charlottesville: University of Virginia Press, 1995.

Rhodes, James Ford. "Newspapers as Historical Sources." *Atlantic Monthly* 103 (May 1909): 650–57.

Richards, Leonard L. *Antislavery Reconsidered: New Perspectives on the Abolitionists.* Baton Rouge: Louisiana State University Press, 1979.

——. *Gentlemen of Property and Standing: Anti-Abolition Mobs in Jacksonian America.* New York: Oxford University Press, 1970.

Richardson, Heather Cox. *The Death of Reconstruction: Race, Labor, and Politics in the Post–Civil War North, 1865–1901.* Cambridge: Harvard University Press, 2001.

——. *The Greatest Nation of the Earth: Republican Economic Policies during the Civil War.* Cambridge: Harvard University Press, 1997.

Richardson, Robert D., Jr. *Emerson: The Mind on Fire.* Berkeley: University of California Press, 1995.

Ritchie, Donald A. *Press Gallery: Congress and the Washington Correspondents.* Cambridge: Harvard University Press, 1991.

Robbins, Roy Marvin. "Horace Greeley: Land Reform and Unemployment, 1837–1862." *Agricultural History* 7 (1933): 18–41.

Roberts, Timothy M. "The American Response to the European Revolutions of 1848." PhD diss., Oxford University, 1998.

——. "Margaret Fuller's Rome and the Problem of Provincial American Democracy." *Patterns of Prejudice* 40 (March 2006): 45–60.

Robinson, David. *Apostle of Culture: Emerson as Preacher and Lecturer.* Philadelphia: University of Pennsylvania Press, 1982.

——. "Margaret Fuller and the Transcendental Ethos: Woman in the Nineteenth Century." *Publications of the Modern Language Association* 97 (January 1982): 83–98.

Rodgers, Daniel T. "Republicanism: The Career of a Concept." *Journal of American History* 79 (1992): 11–38.

Rodrigue, John C. *Reconstruction in the Cane Fields: From Slavery to Free Labor in Louisiana Sugar Parishes, 1862–1880.* Baton Rouge: Louisiana State University Press, 2001.

Rohrs, Richard C. "American Critics of the French Revolution of 1848." *Journal of the Early Republic* 14 (Fall 1994): 339–77.

Rose, Anne C. *Transcendentalism as a Social Movement, 1830–1850.* New Haven: Yale University Press, 1981.

Rosebault, Charles J. *When Dana Was the* Sun. New York: R. M. McBride, 1931.

Rosenberg, Carroll Smith. *Religion and the Rise of the American City: The New York City Mission Movement, 1812–1870.* Ithaca: Cornell University Press, 1971.

Ross, Dorothy. *The Origins of American Social Science.* New York: Cambridge University Press, 1991.

Ross, Michael A. *Justice of Shattered Dreams: Samuel Freeman Miller and the Supreme Court during the Civil War Era.* Baton Rouge: Louisiana State University Press, 2003.

Rourke, Constance M. *Trumpets of Jubilee: Henry Ward Beecher, Harriet Beecher Stowe, Lyman Beecher, Horace Greeley, and P. T. Barnum.* New York: Harcourt, Brace, 1927.

Rubin, Joan Shelley. *The Making of Middlebrow Culture.* Chapel Hill: University of North Carolina Press, 1992.

Rusk, Ralph L. *The Life of Ralph Waldo Emerson.* New York: Scribner's, 1949.

Rutland, Robert. *The Newsmongers: Journalism in the Life of the Nation.* New York: Dial Press, 1973.

Ryan, Barbara. "Emerson's 'Domestic and Social Experiments': Service, Slavery, and the Unhired Man." *American Literature* 66 (September 1994): 458–508.

Ryan, Mary P. *Cradle of the Middle Class: The Family in Oneida County, New York, 1790–1865.* New York: Cambridge University Press, 1981.

Sacks, Kenneth S. *Understanding Emerson: The "American Scholar" and His Struggle for Self-Reliance.* Princeton: Princeton University Press, 2003.

Sanders, Elizabeth. *Roots of Reform: Farmers, Workers, and the American State, 1877–1917.* Chicago: University of Chicago Press, 1999.

Sanford, Charles L. *The Quest for Paradise: Europe and the American Moral Imagination.* Urbana: University of Illinois Press, 1961.

Schiller, Dan. *Objectivity and the News: The Public and the Rise of Commercial Journalism.* Philadelphia: University of Pennsylvania Press, 1981.

Schlesinger, Arthur M., Jr. *The Age of Jackson.* Boston: Little, Brown and Co., 1945.

Schlosser, Eric. *Fast Food Nation: The Dark Side of the All-American Meal.* New York: Harper Collins, 2002.

Schneirov, Richard. *Labor and Urban Politics: Class Conflict and the Origins of Modern Liberalism in Chicago, 1864–1897.* Urbana: University of Illinois Press, 1998.

Schroeder, John H. *Mr. Polk's War: American Opposition and Dissent, 1846–1848.* Madison: University of Wisconsin Press, 1973.

Schudson, Michael. *Discovering the News.* New York: Basic Books, 1978.

Schulze, Suzanne. *Horace Greeley: A Bio-Bibliography.* New York: Greenwood Press, 1992.

Scott, Donald. "The Popular Lecture and the Creation of a Public in Mid-Nineteenth-Century America." *Journal of American History* 66 (March 1980): 791–809.

——. "Print and the Public Lecture System." In *Printing and Society in Early America,* edited by William L. Joyce, David D. Hall, Richard D. Brown, and John Hench. Worcester, Mass.: American Antiquarian Society, 1983.

Seitz, Don C. *Horace Greeley: Founder of the* New York Tribune. Indianapolis: Bobbs-Merrill, 1926.

Sellers, Charles. *The Market Revolution: Jacksonian America, 1815–1846.* New York: Oxford University Press, 1991.

Sewell, William H. *Work and Revolution: Language and Labor from the Old Regime to 1848.* New York: Cambridge University Press, 1980.

Shalhope, Robert E. "Individualism in the Early Republic." In *American Chameleon: Individualism in Trans-National Context,* edited by Richard O. Curry and Lawrence B. Goodheart. Kent, Ohio: Kent State University Press, 1991.

——. *John Taylor of Caroline: Pastoral Republican.* Columbia: University of South Carolina Press, 1980.

——. "Toward a Republican Synthesis: The Emergence of an Understanding of Republicanism in American Historiography," *William and Mary Quarterly* 29 (1972): 49–80.

Silbey, Joel H. *The Partisan Imperative: The Dynamics of American Politics before the Civil War.* New York: Oxford University Press, 1985.

——. *A Respectable Minority: The Democratic Party in the Civil War Era, 1860–1868.* New York: W. W. Norton, 1977.

Sklansky, Jeffrey. *The Soul's Economy: Market Society and Selfhood in American Thought, 1820–1920.* Chapel Hill: University of North Carolina Press, 2002.

Sklar, Martin J. *The Corporate Reconstruction of American Capitalism, 1890–1916.* New York: Cambridge University Press, 1988.

Smith, Henry Nash. "Emerson's Problem of Vocation: A Note on the 'American Scholar.'" *New England Quarterly* 12 (March 1939): 52–67.

Sokolow, Jayme A. *Eros and Modernization: Sylvester Graham, Health Reform, and the Origins of Victorian Sexuality in America.* Cranbury, N.J.: Associated University Presses, 1983.

Sotheran, Charles. *Horace Greeley and Other Pioneers of American Socialism*. New York: Mitchell Kennerley, 1915.

Spann, Edward K. *Brotherly Tomorrows: Movements for a Cooperative Society in America, 1820–1920*. New York: Columbia University Press, 1988.

——. *Ideals and Politics: New York Intellectuals and Liberal Democracy, 1820–1880*. Albany: State University of New York Press, 1972.

——. *The New Metropolis: New York City, 1840–1857*. New York: Columbia University Press, 1981.

Sperber, Jonathan. *The European Revolutions, 1848–1851*. New York: Cambridge University Press, 1994.

Sproat, John G. *"The Best Men": Liberal Reformers in the Gilded Age*. New York: Oxford University Press, 1968.

Spurlock, John C. *Free Love: Marriage and Middle-Class Radicalism in America, 1825–1860*. New York: New York University Press, 1988.

Staloff, Darren Marcus. *The Making of an American Thinking Class: Intellectuals and Intelligentsia in Puritan Massachusetts*. New York: Oxford University Press, 1998.

Stansell, Christine, *City of Women: Sex and Class in New York*. Urbana: University of Illinois Press, 1987.

Starr, Louis M. *The Bohemian Brigade: Civil War Newsmen in Action*. New York: Knopf, 1954.

Steele, Janet. *The Sun Shines for All: Journalism and Ideology in the Life of Charles A. Dana*. Syracuse: Syracuse University Press, 1993.

Stern, Madeleine B. *Heads and Headlines: The Phrenological Fowlers*. Norman: University of Oklahoma Press, 1971.

——. *The Life of Margaret Fuller*. New York: E. P. Dutton, 1942.

——. *The Pantarch: A Biography of Stephen Pearl Andrews*. Austin: University of Texas Press, 1968.

Stoddard, Henry Luther. *Horace Greeley: Printer, Editor, Crusader*. New York: G. P. Putnam's Sons, 1946.

Stoehr, Taylor. *Free Love in America: A Documentary History*. New York: AMS Press, 1979.

——. *Nay-Saying in Concord: Emerson, Alcott, and Thoreau*. Hamden, Conn.: Archon Books, 1979.

Stokes, Melvin, and Stephen Conway, eds. *The Market Revolution in America*. Charlottesville: University of Virginia Press, 1996.

Stone, Candace. *Dana and the Sun*. New York: Dodd, Mead, 1938.

Stott, Richard B. *Workers in the Metropolis: Class, Ethnicity, and Youth in Antebellum New York City*. Ithaca: Cornell University Press, 1990.

Summers, Mark Wahlgren. *The Press Gang: Newspapers and Politics, 1865–1872*. Chapel Hill: University of North Carolina Press, 1994.

Teichgraeber, Richard F. *Sublime Thoughts/Penny Wisdom: Situating Emerson and Thoreau in the American Market*. Baltimore: Johns Hopkins University Press, 1995.

Tomsich, John. *A Genteel Endeavor: American Culture and Politics in the Gilded Age*. Stanford: Stanford University Press, 1971.

Trefousse, Hans L. *Ben Butler: The South Called Him Beast!* New York: Twayne, 1957.

——. *The Radical Republicans: Lincoln's Vanguard for Racial Justice*. New York: Knopf, 1969.

Tuchinsky, Adam-Max. "'The Bourgeoisie Will Fall and Fall Forever': The *New-York Tribune*, the 1848 French Revolution, and the Evolution of Social Democratic Discourse in the United States." *Journal of American History* 92 (September 2005): 470–97.

———. "'Her Cause against Herself': Margaret Fuller, Emersonian Democracy, and the Nineteenth-Century Public Intellectual." *American Nineteenth Century History* 5 (Spring 2004): 66–99.

Tucker, David M. *Mugwumps: Public Moralists of the Gilded Age.* Columbia: University of Missouri Press, 1998.

Tuveson, Ernest Lee. *Redeemer Nation: The Idea of America's Millennial Role.* Chicago: University of Chicago Press, 1968.

Van Deusen, Glyndon G. *Horace Greeley: Nineteenth-Century Crusader.* Philadelphia: University of Pennsylvania Press, 1953.

———. *Thurlow Weed: Wizard of the Lobby.* Boston: Little, Brown and Co., 1947.

———. *William Henry Seward.* New York: Oxford University Press, 1967.

Vincent, K. Steven. *Pierre-Joseph Proudhon and the Rise of French Republican Socialism.* New York: Oxford University Press, 1984.

Voss-Hubbard, Mark. *Beyond Party: Cultures of Antipartisanship in Northern Politics before the Civil War.* Baltimore: Johns Hopkins University Press, 2002.

Walters, Ronald G. *The Antislavery Appeal: American Abolitionism after 1830.* Baltimore: Johns Hopkins University Press, 1978.

Walzer, Michael. *The Company of Critics: Social Criticism and Political Commitment in the Twentieth Century.* New York: Basic Books, 1988.

———. *Interpretation and Social Criticism.* Cambridge: Harvard University Press, 1987.

Ware, Norman F. *The Industrial Worker, 1840–1860: The Reaction of American Industrial Society to the Advance of the Industrial Revolution.* Boston: Houghton Mifflin, 1924.

Watson, Harry L. *Liberty and Power: The Politics of Jacksonian America.* New York: Hill and Wang, 1990.

Weisberger, Bernard A. *Reporters for the Union.* Boston: Little, Brown, and Co., 1953.

Wennersten, John R. "Parke Godwin, Utopian Socialism, and the Politics of Antislavery." *New-York Historical Society Quarterly* 60 (July–October 1976): 107–27.

———. "A Reformer's Odyssey: The Public Career of Park Godwin of the New York *Evening Post, 1837–1870*." PhD diss., University of Maryland, 1970.

White, Horace. *The Life of Lyman Trumbull.* Boston: Houghton Mifflin, 1913.

Widmer, Edward L. *Young America: The Flowering of Democracy in New York City.* New York: Oxford University Press, 1999.

Wiebe, Robert. *The Opening of American Society: From the Adoption of the Constitution to the Eve of Disunion.* New York: Knopf, 1984.

Wilentz, Sean. *Chants Democratic: New York City and the Rise of the American Working Class.* New York: Oxford University Press, 1984.

———. *The Rise of American Democracy: Jefferson to Lincoln.* New York: W. W. Norton, 2005.

———. "Society, Politics, and the Market Revolution." In *The New American History*, edited by Eric Foner. Philadelphia: Temple University Press, 1990.

Williams, Raymond. *Culture and Society, 1780–1950.* New York: Columbia University Press, 1983.

Williams, Robert C. *Horace Greeley: Champion of Freedom.* New York: New York University Press, 2006.

Wilson, James H. *Life of Charles Dana.* New York: Harper, 1907.

Wilson, R. Jackson. *In Quest of Community: Social Philosophy in the United States, 1860–1920.* New York: John Wiley and Sons, 1968.

Winger, Stewart. *Lincoln, Religion, and Romantic Cultural Politics.* De Kalb: Northern Illinois Press, 2003.

Wish, Harvey. *George Fitzhugh: Propagandist of the Old South.* Gloucester, Mass.: Peter Smith, 1962.

Wittke, Carl. *Refugees of Revolution: The German Forty-Eighters in America.* Philadelphia: University of Pennsylvania Press, 1952.

Wonderlich, Roger. *Low Living and High Thinking at Modern Times, New York.* Syracuse: Syracuse University Press, 1992.

Wood, Gordon S. *The Creation of the American Republic, 1776–1787.* New York: W. W. Norton, 1969.

Woodward, C. Vann. *Reunion and Reaction: The Compromise of 1877 and the End of Reconstruction.* Garden City, N.Y.: Doubleday, 1956.

Young, John Russell. *Men and Memories.* Edited by May D. Russell Young. New York: F. Tennyson Neely, 1901.

Zabriskie, Francis Nicoll. *Horace Greeley: The Editor.* New York: Funk and Wagnalls, 1890.

Zahler, Helene Sara. *Eastern Workingmen and National Land Policy, 1829–1862.* New York: Columbia University Press, 1941.

Zboray, Ronald J. *A Fictive People: Antebellum Economic Development and the American Reading Public.* New York: Oxford University Press, 1993.

Zuczek, Richard. *State of Rebellion: Reconstruction in South Carolina.* Columbia: University of South Carolina Press, 1996.

Zwarg, Christina. *Feminist Conversations: Fuller, Emerson, and the Play of Reading.* Ithaca: Cornell University Press, 1995.

Index

Page numbers in *italics* indicate photographs and illustrations.